AZTEC & MAYA
LIFE IN AN ANCIENT CIVILIZATION

AZTEC & MAYA

LIFE IN AN ANCIENT CIVILIZATION

THE EVERYDAY WORLD OF THE AZTECS, MAYA AND OTHER NATIVE CIVILIZATIONS OF
CENTRAL AMERICA AND MEXICO, WITH OVER 500 PHOTOGRAPHS AND FINE ART IMAGES

CHARLES PHILLIPS • CONSULTANT: **DR DAVID M JONES**

HERMES
HOUSE

CONTENTS

INTRODUCTION   6

Discovering the Past   10
Wonders in the Jungle   12
Painstaking Excavations   14
Translating an Ancient Writing   16

PART ONE:
THE MESOAMERICAN WORLD   18
Timeline of Mesoamerica   20

CHAPTER ONE
Land of Danger and Reward   22
Highland and Lowland   24
Sacred Heights   26
Life-giving Waters   28
Towering Trees, Rocky Sands   30
Life in the Wild   32
Fruits of the Earth   34
Creating a Sacred World   36

CHAPTER TWO
From Village to Metropolis   38
The Beginnings of Settled Life   40
Urban Ceremonial Centres   42
The Rise of the Great Cities   44
The Glory of Teotihuacán   46
Power Changes Hands   48
The Collapse of Social Order   50
The Triumph of the Toltecs   52
Land Raiders   54
The México Forge an Empire   56

CHAPTER THREE
Infinite Riches   58
First Traders   60
A City of Merchants   62
Trading Over Great Distances   64
By Canoe and Paddle   66
Traders, Spies, Protectors   68
Markets Large and Small   70
The Great Market at Tlatelolco   72
A Network of Tribute   74
The Sacred Way   76

CHAPTER FOUR
The World of Work   78
Raising Crops on Land and Water   80
Garden Experts   82
Fresh from the Wild   84
Skilled in Ancient Crafts   86
Masters of the Painted Word   88
A Soldier's Life   90
In the State's Service   92
Noble Servants of the Gods   94

CHAPTER FIVE
Everyday Life   96
Life in the Home   98
The Matchmaker's Art   100
A Child is Born   102
The First Years   104
The Gift of the Maize God   106
Clothes and Hairstyles   108
Beating the Odds   110
The Beat of the Drum   112
Lyrics at the Feast   114

CHAPTER SIX
Sacred Culture   116
The Game of the Gods   118
Cycles of Time   120
Holy World, Sacred Sky   122
The Healing Arts   124
Sacred Theatre   126
The Round of Festivals   128
The Cult of Violence   130
Reverence for Ancestors   132
Where the Ancestors Go   134

PART TWO:
ART AND ARCHITECTURE 136

CHAPTER SEVEN
Palaces, Temples and Sacred Centres 138
From Huts to Temples 140
Building Styles 142
A Love of Decoration 144
Hidden Meanings in Sacred Buildings 146
The Impact of Colour and Sound 148
Arenas for a Sacred Contest 150
Palatial Style of Maya Rulers 152
The Aztec Pattern of Elegance 154
The Magnificence of Moctezuma 156

CHAPTER EIGHT
Building the Cities 158
Sacred Towns: San Lorenzo and La Venta 160
City of the Zapotecs: Monte Albán 162
Capital of the Ball Game: El Tajín 163
The Place of the Gods: Teotihuacán 164
Towering Monuments: Tikal 166
Pacal's Glory: Palenque 168
City of the Jaguar Kings: Yaxchilán 170
The Elegant City: Copán 172
Pride of the Toltecs: Tollán 174
Twin Styles: Chichén Itzá 175
Hill Forts: Cacaxtla, Xochicalco
  and Teotenango 176
Tarascan Stronghold: Tzintzuntzan 178
City of Priests: Mitla 179
Centre of the World: Tenochtitlán 180

CHAPTER NINE
Potters and Weavers 182
Millennia of Pottery 184
Figures of Clay 186
Models from the Western Isle 188
Many-coloured Scenes of Court Life 190
Pottery for Banquets and Temples 192
Tenochtitlán's Life-size Ceramic Figures 194
Basketwork, Mats and Furniture 195
Richly Decorated Robes 196
A Gathering of Feathers 198

CHAPTER TEN
The Carver's Art 200
The King's Head: Olmec Carving 202
From Three to Two Dimensions: The
  First Stelae 204
Set In Stone: The Power of Maya Kings 206
The Work of Maya Stonemasons 208
Intricate Carving in Stucco 210
Men and Gods in Stone: Aztec Carving 212
Carving in Wood 214

CHAPTER ELEVEN
Precious Work 216
An Imported Craft 218
Golden Ornaments 220
Work of the Goldsmiths 222
Bells and Repoussé Discs 224
Faces of Gods and Kings 226
Shell and Precious Stone Decoration 228
Chipped and Carved Stones 230

CHAPTER TWELVE
Images, Symbols and Words 232
The Dating of Events 234
Reference Books for Priests 236
Record of a Vanishing Culture 238
Glyphs and Images 240
Sacred Symbols 242
Scenes of Religious Life 244
The Bonampak Murals 246
Wall Paintings and Murals 248
Symbolism and Naturalism 250

Index 252
Acknowledgements 256

INTRODUCTION

On Good Friday, 21 April 1519, an expedition of 600-odd adventurers from the Spanish colony of Cuba dropped anchor off the beaches of San Juan de Ulúa, on the Gulf coast of Mexico, close to where the port of Veracruz would later be established. Under the command of Hernán Cortés, the men came ashore with their horses and exchanged gifts with the Totonac inhabitants of the region. About 300km (200 miles) inland, in the capital of the Aztec empire, the *tlatoani* (ruler) Moctezuma II received reports of the fair-skinned sailors, of the ships – which the trader-spies who were his informants saw as mountains floating on the sea – and of the Spanish cavalry or 'man-beasts'.

The landing in 1519 was not the first meeting between Europeans and the peoples of what became modern Mexico and Guatemala. There had been a number of brief encounters, including one in 1502

Below: Chacmools *received offerings of human hearts. This* chacmool *stood before the temple to Tláloc in Tenochtitlán.*

between Christopher Columbus and traders from the lands of the Aztecs' Maya neighbours. Yet this momentous day in 1519, which was the first step in an invasion that would bring the Aztec empire to its knees, inaugurated the first prolonged contact between two very different and essentially alien cultures: the European and the Mesoamerican.

MANY CIVILIZATIONS

Human activity in the region of Mexico and neighbouring Guatemala dates back 20,000 years or more, to the time when the first hunter-gatherers settled in the area. In the period between that time and the height of the Aztec empire, in the 14th–16th centuries AD, a number of civilizations rose and fell in the locality.

Historians apply the name 'Mesoamerica' both to these civilizations and to the area in which they arose. This ran southwards from the desert regions of north-central Mexico, then eastwards to include the Isthmus of Tehuantepec, the Yucatán peninsula, Guatemala, Honduras, western Nicaragua and north-western

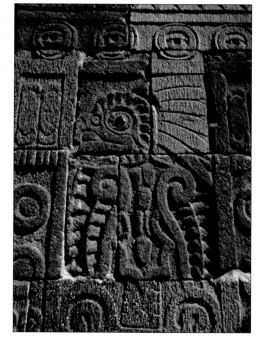

Above: A carving of an enigmatic quetzal-butterfly adorns the elegant Quetzalpapálotl Palace in Teotihuacán.

Costa Rica. Among these civilizations were the Olmecs, carvers of magnificent stone monuments and creators of a vast trading network in the 2nd millennium BC; the Zapotecs, builders of a mountaintop settlement at Monte Albán in Oaxaca, who may have been the first people in the region to develop written communication *c.*500BC; and the builders of the mysterious monumental city of Teotihuacán in highland Mexico *c.*100BC–*c.*AD500, who excelled in trade, the manufacture of enigmatic masks and the painting of evocative murals.

Others included the Maya, who in the period *c.*AD250–900 raised magnificent temples and palaces in the jungles of Guatemala and in parts of eastern Mexico, and who continued to thrive until the Spanish Conquest; the militaristic Toltecs, who built their capital Tollán north-west of Teotihuacán *c.*AD950 and developed bloodthirsty religious rites involving human sacrifice; the Mixtecs, who succeeded the Zapotecs in Oaxaca and

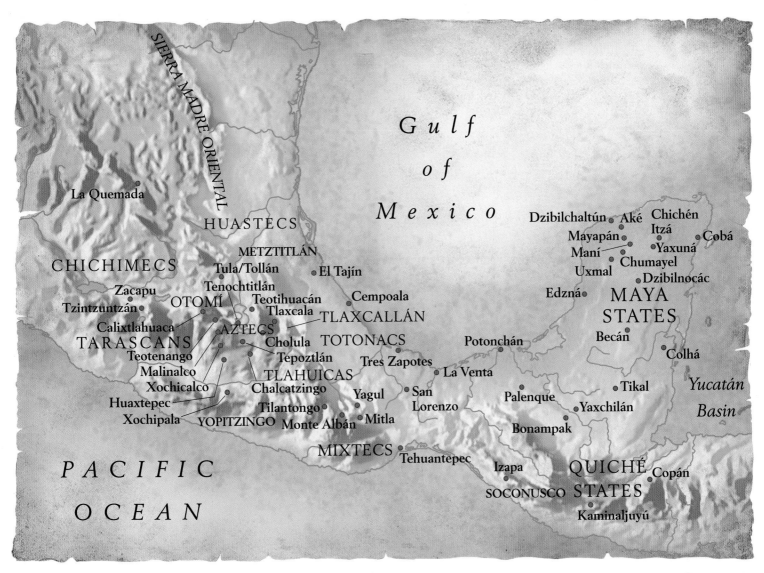

Above: Mesoamerican cultural sites ranged over the years from San Lorenzo to Tenochtitlán and over miles from Tikal to La Quemada.

who excelled in metalworking and hand-painted screenfold books; the Tarascans of Michoacán in western Mexico, highly skilled metalworkers who forged an empire after 1200; and the México, or Aztecs, who in the years after founding their capital of Tenochtitlán in 1325 built a vast empire encompassing 150,000sq km (58,000sq miles).

ALIEN CULTURES

Both the Mesoamericans and the Spanish invaders found plenty to marvel at and to disapprove of in the behaviour of their opponents. For example, it would appear that the Mesoamericans were shocked by the poor hygiene of the Spaniards. The conquistadors' accounts of the invasion tell of many occasions on which the locals doused them with incense. The invaders took this as a mark of respect, but historians suspect that the nobles of Tenochtitlán, who kept themselves very

clean, were attempting to keep the stench of the unwashed soldiers at bay. On the other hand, the Spanish conquistadors were both attracted and repelled by what they found in Tenochtitlán when, after marching inland, allying with locals in Tlaxcala and defeating the lords of Cholula, they entered the Aztec capital on 7 November 1519.

The conquistadors were captivated by the beauty of the vast city laid out on islands in Lake Texcoco, by the elegance of the palaces and gardens inhabited by the ruler and nobility and by the astonishing range of goods for sale in the city's vast

Right: Aztec pilgrims took this greenstone mask from Teotihuacán and offered it in the Templo Mayor, Tenochtitlán.

market. However, they were equally shocked by the temples and ceremonial areas laid out to celebrate rites of human sacrifice, by the sight of priests with blood-matted hair and smoke-blackened skin, by images of Aztec gods and by blood-spattered reclining stone figures known as *chacmools* into which the still-warm hearts of sacrificial victims were placed.

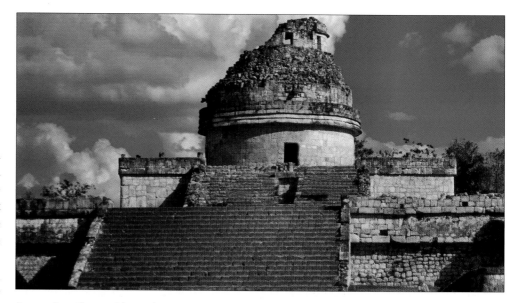

CULTURE CLASH

The Spanish did encounter certain elements familiar from their own European culture. As in Europe, the warriors' achievements were lauded and military might enforced political power, networks of trade and tribute were vibrant and a strong sense of the sacred informed all parts of life. However, other elements of Mesoamerican civilization were bafflingly strange or broke European taboos. For example, while the conquistadors were certainly not unfamiliar with torture and slaughter, nor squeamish about the sight of blood or even the display of prisoners' remains, they were unprepared for the Aztecs' ritual celebration of slaughter, in which human hearts were torn out as a key element of public religious ritual. They were shocked by the vast numbers of victims sacrificed and by the gods and goddesses honoured. They were horrified to learn that certain Aztec religious rites included cannibalism. Nobles and priests shared the flesh of victims who had earlier been sacrificed on the steps before the temple and whose hearts were displayed on the *chacmool*.

This cannibalistic rite was informed by the Aztecs' understanding that a sacrificial victim impersonated and finally became the god to whom he was sacrificed. The elite members of Aztec society admitted to the feast were thus able to share in the divine essence. Aztec worshippers frequently understood several distinct performers of and elements in ritual to share the identity of a god or goddess. This included priests and victims dressed in honour of deities as well as natural elements used in dedication or worship. At the blessing of a new aqueduct carrying water into Tenochtitlán during the reign of the Aztec *tlatoani* (ruler) Ahuítzotl (1486–1502), priests, dressed in the jade skirt associated with the water goddess Chalchiúhtlicue, offered incense and precious turquoise (a stone linked to the goddess) as the aqueduct was opened and the waters ran for the first time. The goddess, the priests

dressed as the goddess, the turquoise and the water itself were all understood to be one in a concept typical of Mesoamericans but different to Western thought.

CYCLES OF TIME

Another key element of Mesoamerican culture that was immediately alien to the Europeans was the idea that the gods made time move in cycles. The Aztecs believed that the current world was the fifth in a succession of creations and that, within the current world age, events were destined to be repeated in a way which followed large, cyclical patterns.

Mesoamericans had a very deep respect for the past. In both Aztec and Maya lands, worshippers made respectful journeys to the great cities built by their ancestors such as Teotihuacán and Tollán for the Aztecs and Tikal and Chichén Itzá for the Maya. Indeed, the desire to recreate in the present the glories of the past was one of the driving forces behind the Aztec empire. The Aztecs wanted to honour the achievements of the Toltec founders of Tollán. They were also keen to celebrate the sacred city of Teotihuacán, which they viewed as the birthplace of the gods. Here, according to Aztec religious narrative, on the very ground and before the very buildings still visible today, the gods had gathered in the primordial past to create the sun and moon and set them in motion in the sky through offering their own divine blood.

Aztec builders and stonemasons made reverent use of architectural and sculptural styles from these ancient cities in creating the sacred precinct of Tenochtitlán. Aztec

Above: In observatories such as the Caracol at Chichén Itzá, the patterns of the night sky were interpreted.

pilgrims took masks and other sacred items from graves in Teotihuacán and Tollán to reuse them in their own temple offerings in Tenochtitlán. Aztec priests and worshippers enthusiastically practised the rituals of human sacrifice which (although they had ancient beginnings in the Mesoamerican past) had been decisively escalated by the honoured Toltecs.

Below: Maya sculptors reached great heights of artistic expression. This head represents King Pacal of Palenque in middle age.

At Chichén Itzá in northern Yucatán, a group of Maya, also influenced by the Toltecs, similarly used *chacmools*, arranged the skulls of victims on skull racks and held vast public rites of human sacrifice.

DUALITY AND CHANGE

The Mesoamericans' understanding that time moved in cycles governed by the gods was balanced by an acute awareness of patterns of change and structures of duality. The Aztecs and the Maya understood the universe to be structured according to a divinely ordained duality: life and death, day and night, light and darkness, wet and dry, the celestial realm and the underworld realm all balanced one another. They also tended to succeed one another. Day was followed by night, the rainy season alternated with the dry season, life was followed by death – and then by new life. A king's death was the prelude to his voyage to the underworld, land of the dead, and followed by his ascent to the celestial realm. However, the gods could break this sacred pattern of alternation at any time.

Each night, the sun took the form of a jaguar and had to fight its way through the underworld during the hours of darkness before it could be reborn in the eastern sky. A day might come on which the gods withdrew their favour and the sun did not rise.

Within the complex patterns of years created by Mesoamericans' use of twin 260-day and 365-day calendars, the period of 52 solar years had great sacred significance. It measured the time that elapsed before a day in the 260-day calendar would coincide with a day in the 365-day calendar. The end of a 52-year cycle was also viewed as a time of particular danger, when the gods might be particularly inclined to break the patterns of succession and bring the world to an end. Priests ensured that the sacred calendars of ritual were observed with particular care at such times of risk.

FATE AND FATALISM

Across Mesoamerica, astronomer-priests made observations of the cycles of planets and movements of stars, while shaman-priests interpreted the ritual calendars and performed rites of divination using psychotrophic substances.

Those who relied on the statements of these experts believed that the diviners had the power to identify sacred influences on human activity in the

Left: Sacred symbols in nature. This Maya vase from the Sula valley, Honduras, shows a divine monkey-spider and a bird-man.

Above: Serpent imagery abounds in this Mixtec representation of water goddess Chalchiúhtlicue. The snake was associated with water, fertility and the earth.

patterns of the sky and in the cycles of time. Some historians argue that beliefs in divination, the power of omens and the inevitability of time's repeating patterns made Mesoamericans more fatalistic than they would otherwise have been when faced with a challenge.

The so-called 'Maya collapse' – when in the 9th and 10th centuries AD a series of powerful cities across Guatemala stopped erecting dated monuments to the glory of their kings and fell into rapid decline – had many causes, principally environmental degradation, but was possibly also encouraged by a fatalistic belief among some Maya that the decline could be predicted from the patterns of time, that, by the gods' choice, these events mirrored others many centuries earlier and so were not worth resisting.

Equally, there were many practical causes for the defeat of the mighty Aztec empire by a small band of Spanish invaders fighting in alliance with local peoples, but historical accounts reveal that Aztec leaders were aware that the omens were bad and appeared to prophesy their downfall. Some in Tenochtitlán thought Cortés was destined for victory, and some Aztecs even believed that Cortés was the Mesoamerican god Quetzalcóatl making a long-promised return to claim his rightful inheritance in Tenochtitlán.

DISCOVERING THE PAST

Mesoamericans themselves were Central America's first archaeologists. The Aztecs and Maya had a deep reverence for their own shared past and the achievements of their forebears, and investigated the evocative ruins of once majestic cities such as Tollán, Teotihuacán and Tikal.

Both Maya and Aztecs engaged with the ruined cities as religious centres rather than as historical sites. They came to satisfy a religious and cultural yearning to touch and be touched by the past. They saw nothing wrong in entering monuments and tombs to gather funerary masks and golden grave offerings for their own religious use, or in adding offerings of their own to a temple cache.

The Aztecs carried artefacts back from Teotihuacán and Tula to Tenochtitlán for use as temple offerings in the great Templo Mayor, where later generations of archaeologists would discover them. In Maya lands, pilgrims from Chichén Itzá may have travelled to the ruins of Tikal to perform religious ceremonies; in later times both Uxmal and Chichén Itzá were pilgrimage sites. The Aztecs also carried out sacrifices and sacred rites at the city of Teotihuacán.

The Spanish invaders of the early 16th century treated the great architectural achievements of Mesoamerica with scant respect. They set out to destroy the temples and religious statuary of the Aztecs, which they believed to be touched by evil. They erected the capital of their colony, New Spain, atop the rubble and shattered remnants of the Aztecs' great metropolis of Tenochtitlán.

Left: This view of the archway at Labná is by English artist Frederick Catherwood who, with American author John L. Stephens, was a pioneer of Maya exploration in the 1830s–40s. It is taken from their 1841 book on Maya ruins.

WONDERS IN THE JUNGLE

The first organized archaeological investigation of Mesoamerican ruins took place in the 17th century. A Mexican Jesuit priest called Carlos de Siguenza y Gongora (1645–1700) led a dig at Teotihuacán which mainly focused on the Pyramid of the Moon, as part of a lifelong attempt to research and write a history of ancient Mexico.

The 18th century saw the modern rediscovery of important Mesoamerican relics and sites, notably of Maya cities that had been abandoned and overgrown by tropical jungle. Palenque, in the densely forested foothills of the Chiapas mountains and overlooking the coastal plain that stretches 128km (80 miles) to the Gulf of Mexico, was rediscovered in 1746 by Padre Antonio Solis.

The first excavation of the Palenque site, which began in May 1786, was carried out by Spanish artillery captain Don Antonio del Río, who had orders from King Carlos III of Spain to search for gold and other valuables. Del Río left with a stucco head, the carved leg of a throne and other pieces of decorative carving, which he sent to Spain by way of Guatemala. Many years later, the captain's report of his excavations was published in English in London in 1822 with copies of del Río's sketches reproduced as lithographs by Johann-Friedrich Maximilien von Waldeck. The book generated interest in further investigation of Maya cities. It was followed by the publication in Paris in 1834 of *Antiquités Mexcaines*, the account of an 1805–6 visit to Palenque by Frenchman Guillaume Dupaix in the company of Mexican artist Luciano Castañeda. Waldeck himself visited the site in 1821 and published his own meticulously rendered images in 1865.

GODDESS IN THE EARTH
An important discovery had occurred at the site of the former Aztec capital Tenochtitlán in 1790. Workmen laying paving stones discovered a 2.5 metre (8ft)-tall stone statue of the Aztec earth

Above: Désiré Charnay, first to conduct archaeological excavations at Tula, made this engraving of Palenque in 1887.

goddess Coatlícue, together with a 3.6 metre (almost 12ft) diameter carved stone monument that commemorated the five suns or world ages of Aztec belief (later known as the Sun Stone). The finds were the first evidence of the wealth of archaeological remains that lay directly beneath the surface of Mexico City. The Sun Stone was placed on display on one of the towers of the city's Metropolitan Cathedral, while the statue of Coatlícue was given to the Royal and Pontifical University of Mexico.

THE TREASURES OF THE JUNGLE
In the 19th century, many of the great abandoned cities of the Maya civilization were rediscovered among dense jungle foliage and explored. An important catalyst for the surge of interest in central American ruins was the publication in 1841 of the two-volume *Incidents of Travel in Central America, Chiapas and Yucatán* by American traveller John Lloyd Stephens (1805–52). This work was based on an 1839–40 voyage to Honduras, Guatemala and Mexico, which was undertaken by Stephens in the

Left: This romanticized view of the Temple of the Cross, at Palenque, was made by Johann-Friedrich Maximilien von Waldeck.

company of English architect and artist Frederick Catherwood (1799–1854). Stephens and Catherwood visited the magnificent site of Copán, which Stephens was able to buy for $50, discovered Quiriguá and also examined Palenque and Uxmal. On a second voyage in 1841–2, the two men explored sites including Chichén Itzá, Cozumel, Tulum, Dzilam, Izamal and Ake. They published another two-volume survey, *Incidents of Travel in Yucatán*, in 1843. Sites they publicized include Copán, Palenque, Chichén Itzá, Tulum, Uxmal and Quiriguá.

TOWERS AMONG THE TREES

The remains of the great Classic Period Maya city of Tikal, in the northern part of the Petén region of Guatemala, were also rediscovered in the mid-19th century. They were first noticed by a local gum-sapper named Ambrosio Tut, who saw the roofcombs of the city's soaring pyramid temples while working at the top of a sapodilla tree.

Tut reported the finding to Modesto Méndez, Governor-Magistrate of the Petén region, and a six-day exploratory expedition was despatched by the Guatemalan government under Méndez and Tut in 1848. Méndez's report, with fanciful images by artist Eusebio Lara, was published that year in the Guatemalan newspaper *La Gaceta* and in 1853 in the magazine of the Berlin Academy of Sciences.

Significant later 19th-century expeditions to the site included that of the Swiss botanist Gustave Bernoulli, who removed carved sapodilla-wood lintels from Temples I and IV and carried them off to the Museum für Völkerkunde in Basel. They also included that of the English archaeologist-explorer Sir Alfred Percival Maudslay (1850–1931), who visited in 1881 and 1882. Using recently invented camera equipment, Sir Alfred took the earliest photographs of the city of Tikal's magnificent monuments.

Above: This Catherwood engraving, from the 1841 Incidents of Travel in Central America, Chiapas and Yucatán, *is of the partly overgrown Castillo in Chichén Itzá.*

Other cities were being rediscovered in the jungle. In 1882, Sir Alfred led an official Guatemalan government expedition to a major but little known settlement on the Usumacinta river. Then known as Macanche, the riverbank city was later renamed Yaxchilán.

With official approval, Sir Alfred removed the superbly carved lintels from Yaxchilán to prevent their loss to less scrupulous visitors. In the same year, the French explorer and archaeologist Désiré Charnay visited and photographed the site. At Copán, George Gordon of Harvard University's Peabody Museum led a three-year investigation in 1891–4.

In the 1880s, Désiré Charnay also conducted the first archaeological dig at the site identified as the capital of the Toltecs, near the modern town of Tula in Hidalgo State, Mexico. In 1873, Antonio García Cubas, a member of the Mexican Society of Geography and History, had published a written description of the site. Charnay went on to excavate two houses and the structure known as the Adoratorio, in the middle of the main square. Later archaeologists were less than impressed by his unsubtle methods. These

included the use of dynamite for clearance. Charnay did, however, also take some of the earliest photographs of ancient Mesoamerican ruins. He also experimented with papier-mâché to make impressions of ancient hieroglyphs.

Below: Beneath ground level in modern Mexico City archaeologists uncover Aztec remains. This is part of the Templo Mayor.

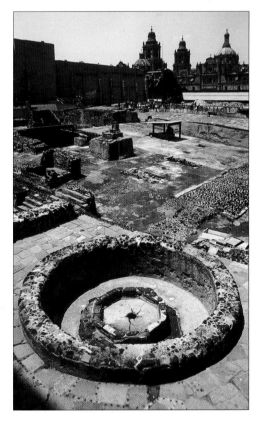

PAINSTAKING EXCAVATIONS

Throughout the 20th century, extensive and painstaking archaeological programmes gradually uncovered more and more evidence of how Mesoamericans lived, fought and worshipped.

CARNEGIE EXCAVATIONS

A pioneering archaeological project at Chichén Itzá in north-central Yucatán was led by Sylvanus Morley of the Carnegie Institution, Washington DC, for 20 years from 1924. The project excavated and restored many buildings, in the process discovering beneath them several almost intact constructions. These provided important evidence of the typical Mesoamerican building practice in which new structures were erected on top of their predecessors on sites already sanctified by ritual use. The work led to the scholarly division of Chichén Itzá's buildings into two groups. Those in the local 'Puuc style' from the end of the Classic Period and those exhibiting a Toltec-Mexican influence in the first years of the Postclassic Period.

The Carnegie Institution also conducted archaeological investigation at Uaxactún, 40km (25 miles) north of Tikal, in the years 1926–37. From the calendrical carvings, ceramic remains and buildings at Uaxactún, the Carnegie scholars plotted a chronology of cultural development for the region in the Classic Period that is still widely used by archaeologists today.

NEW MAP OF AN ANCIENT CITY

At Tikal, the combined efforts of Teobert Maler, Alfred Tozzer and R.E. Merwin led to the publication by Tozzer and Merwin of the first map of the site in 1911. Sylvanus Morley made a detailed study of Tikal's monuments and inscriptions on four visits in 1914, 1921, 1922 and 1928, while in 1926, Edwin Shook of the Carnegie Institution found a previously undiscovered group of buildings (now known as Group H) and two *sacbeob* or sacred causeways (now named in honour

of Maudslay and Maler). Shook became the first field director of a major 14-year survey, the Tikal Project, which was conducted by the University Museum of Pennsylvania University 1956–70.

Major programmes were also carried out at Tula. In the 1930s, the work of ethnologist Wigberto Jimenez Moreno established that the site excavated by the Frenchman Désiré Charnay in the 19th

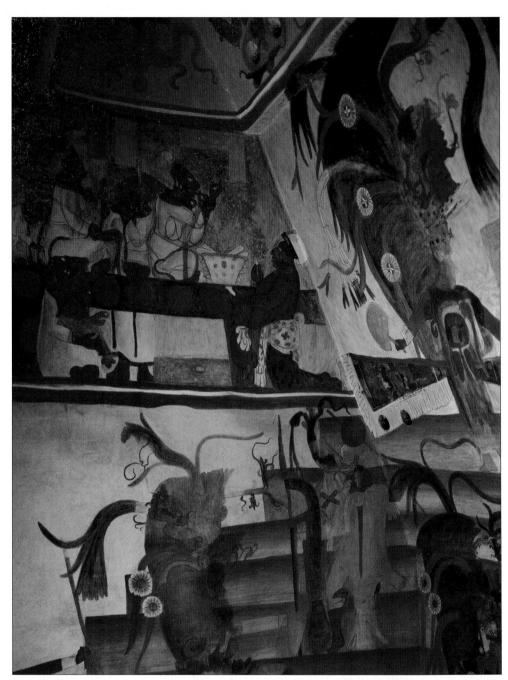

Above: A corner of one of the painted rooms at Bonampak depicts the members of the royal court enjoying a lavish feast.

century was the Toltecs' celebrated city, known also as Tollán. Subsequently, Jorge Acosta of the Mexican National Institute of Anthropology and History (INAH) led a 20-year archaeological programme at Tula in 1940–60, during which his teams investigated and partly restored one of the site's ball courts (now known as Ball Court 1), Temples B and C, the Coatepantli and the Palacio de Quetzalcóatl. Based on pottery remains, Acosta also worked out a chronology of events and occupying groups for the site. His work was extended through joint excavations by the University of Missouri Colombia (UMC) under Richard Diehl and an INAH team under Eduardo Matos Moctezuma in 1966–76.

The second INAH team conducted a major survey of the surrounding land and restored a second ball court. Together with that of the UMC, their work established that Tula was a large and lively city, at its peak and that, for a period, it was Mesoamerica's prime power.

PAINTED WALLS
About 30km (18 miles) to the south of Yaxchilán, in the densely forested valley of the Río Lacanha in Chiapas state, a Maya site previously known only to locals was revealed to the wider world in 1946. American photographer Giles Healey was on a field trip looking for picturesque ruins when his guides led him to a small settlement they called Bonampak ('Painted Walls'). Healey found a three-roomed building containing vivid, brightly coloured images of court life in a Maya

Above: The ball court at Palenque lies to the north-east of the imposing Palace and the celebrated Temple of Inscriptions.

city during the 8th century AD. His report and pictures naturally provoked wide interest and the Carnegie Institute organized an archaeological programme at the site, which also contains an acropolis, a large plaza and a number of stelae. As at some other major Maya sites such as Palenque, there are buildings still unexcavated in the surrounding forest.

PALENQUE'S STEPPED PYRAMID
At Palenque, Sylvanus Morley, Oliver LaFarge, Franz Blom and Edward Seler all carried out work in the early part of the 20th century. In 1952, Mexican architect Alberto Ruz Lhuillier discovered the magnificent royal tomb of King Pacal, Palenque's ruler in the 7th–8th

centuries AD, in a crypt beneath the Temple of Inscriptions. Historians had believed that Maya stepped pyramids were used only as temple platforms; that is, to lift their temples above other buildings; Lhuiller's find was the first indication that the pyramids were in some places built primarily as royal funerary monuments.

TENOCHTITLÁN
In the centre of what was once Tenochtitlán, a major excavation of the Aztecs' great temple, the Templo Mayor, began in 1978. The programme was inspired by a chance find, when an electrical company worker digging in central Mexico City uncovered part of a clearly remarkable sculpture. The team of archaeologists who took over to clear away debris uncovered a vast monolith, 3.25m (10ft) in diameter, representing the dismembered form of the goddess Coyolxauhqui who, in Aztec creation narrative, was cut up by her brother Huitzilopochtli in the first moments of his life.

Excavation revealed that the Aztecs built the Templo Mayor in layers, each new construction enclosing an earlier structure. Archaeologists uncovered the successive constructions back to c.1390, showing the twin shrines to rain god Tláloc and Lord Huitzilopochtli.

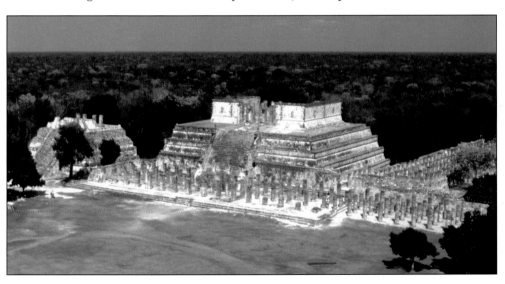

Left: The Group of the Thousand Columns is one of the imposing structures in Chichén Itzá reflecting later, Toltec, influence.

TRANSLATING AN ANCIENT WRITING

The first modern visitors to Maya sites such as Yaxchilán or Copán were enthralled by tall stelae elegantly carved with inscriptions in artistically arranged picture glyphs. Historians were also deeply intrigued by the writing in four surviving Maya codices and by a list of glyphs presented as the 'Maya alphabet' by Bishop Diego de Landa in his 16th-century work, *Relacion de las Cosas de Yucatán*. Historians were frustrated that they could not read this ancient writing and so glean invaluable information about the Maya way of life.

DECIPHERING THE PAST

In the years up to the 1950s, linguists made slow but steady progress in interpreting Maya writing. Figures such as Léon de Rosny, Ernst Förstemann, Sylvanus Morley and J. Eric Thompson catalogued the glyphs and successfully identified some. Förstemann and Rosny, for example, translated the glyphs for 'north', 'south', 'east', 'west', 'zero' and 'twenty'. However, the entire world of Maya scholarship laboured under two misconceptions. The scholars wrongly believed that the inscriptions on Maya stelae contained religious and astronomical information, but no historical facts. Historians were also mistaken in their belief that the glyphs were logographic. The pictures represented whole words or ideas and did not stand for spoken sounds.

The first misconception was removed by the work of Heinrich Berlin and Tatiana Proskouriakoff in the 1950s. Berlin, a German-Mexican scholar, first identified an emblem glyph specific to each of several Maya sites and suggested that it recorded the place name or the name of the ruling dynasty. Proskouriakoff, a Russian-American expert on Maya art, then showed that carved inscriptions on stelae at Piedras Negras celebrated the birth, accession to the throne and other life events of a series of rulers of that city. In her work on Piedras Negras and then Yaxchilán, she identified glyphs for 'was born', 'acceded to throne', 'captor', 'captured' and 'died'.

Above: Stela 6 from Piedras Negras shows the king seated cross-legged in a recess with glyphs dating the monument to AD687.

The second misconception was laid to rest, also in the 1950s, by the Soviet linguist Yuri V. Knorosov, who demonstrated that, alongside their function as logograms, the glyphs had a 'phonetic' element; they represented spoken sounds. Working with the de Landa 'alphabet', Knorosov saw that many of the elements of the list were not letters but syllables combining a consonant and a vowel. There were no signs for a single consonant. When writing a word with the pattern consonant-vowel-consonant, he argued, a Maya scribe would use two of the combined signs, consonant-vowel plus consonant-vowel. The vowel in the second sign would match that in the first, but would be read as silent. For example, to write the word *cutz* ('turkey'), a scribe

emblem-glyph affixes

a bat
(Copán)

a cacao tree with
pod (Quiriguá)

'cleft sky'
(Yaxchilán)

a bundle
(Tikal)

'Quincunx'
(Piedras Negras)

a bone
(Palenque)

a skull
(Palenque)

Cauac
(Seibal)

crossed sky
bands (Naranjo)

bundle
(Petexbatun)

Left: 'Emblem glyphs' specific to particular cities were identified by Heinrich Berlin in 1958. The symbols identifying the cities were written with a pair of affixes (appended signs) meaning 'holy king of'.

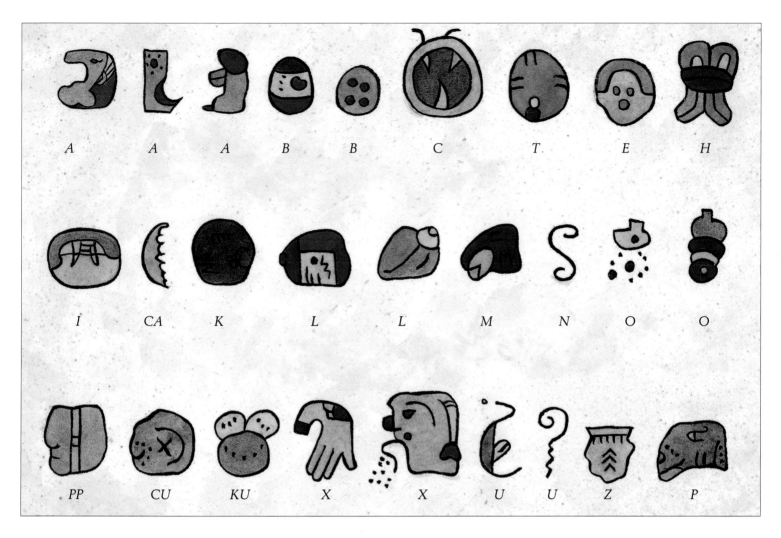

A	A	A	B	B	C	T	E	H

I	CA	K	L	L	M	N	O	O

PP	CU	KU	X	X	U	U	Z	P

Above: Bishop Diego de Landa's 'alphabet' of Maya writing was dismissed by scholars until linguist Yuri Knorosov showed that it was a list of syllables rather than an 'abc'.

would write the signs *cu* and *tzu*. The two *U*s would agree, and the word would be read 'cutz' (with the last u silent.) The idea that the vowels would agree was dubbed 'synharmony' by Knorosov.

Knorosov's theory provoked outrage among many Maya scholars, but has proved to be largely correct. As Knorosov argued, Maya script contains both logographs and phonetic elements. The latest thinking is that the script, which was in use for more than 1,500 years, was originally mainly logosyllabic (pictures stood for syllables or words), but over time increasingly included more phonetic elements. However, further progress in deciphering Maya script has partially undermined Knorosov's idea of synharmony. When words were spelled phonetically, they often did not have the matching vowels that his theory suggested they should.

Left: In a detail from Piedras Negras Stela 40, an individual performs a sacred rite of scattering in honour of an ancestor.

REINTERPRETATIONS

Historians have continued to make breakthroughs in interpreting glyphs, often with important implications for our understanding of the Maya. In 1979, Peter Matthews showed that an ear spool found at Altun Ha in Belize was labelled *u tup* ('his ear spool') with the name of the owner. Several other writers have since shown that the practice Matthews termed 'name tagging' was used by the Maya on bowls, plates and carved bones.

David Stuart and Stephen Houston have identified a glyph used to describe the spirit familiar or companion that Mesoamericans believed accompanied each of us. The discovery has led to the reinterpetation of many scenes on Maya pots or stelae, where figures once thought to be gods or rulers can now be positively identified as spirit familiars.

Linguistic work has also revealed that the Maya referred to stelae as 'stone trees' and to the objects historians generally label 'altars' as 'stone thrones'.

PART ONE

THE MESOAMERICAN WORLD

In a time before time, Huitzilopochtli, tribal god of the México/Aztecs, sprang from his mother fully armed to defend her against his jealous siblings on the sacred heights of Mount Coatepetl. In the mature years of the fifth sun or world age of the Aztecs, in the ceremonial precinct of the imperial capital Tenochtitlán, the great mass of the Templo Mayor was celebrated as a recreation of the mountain where the tribal god was born and was called Coatepetl or Coatepec. Both Aztec and Maya architects intended their temple-platforms to represent sacred mountains as part of a wider desire to honour and recreate in their cities and social organization the holy patterns of the natural world.

Mesoamericans saw divine meaning threaded through all natural phenomena. Theirs was a sacred universe, whose rules were established in the 'holy time' of religious narrative. They performed sacrificial ritual in obedience to demands established in this holy time, as a way of honouring the creative sacrifice of the gods.

This survey of the Mesoamerican world begins with a look at its terrains and wildlife, then examines the spread of human settlement across Middle America. It then proceeds to describe the vibrant trade that fuelled much of this expansion and to investigate Mesoamerican patterns of daily life and work, before concluding with a description of the ways in which Mesoamericans celebrated the sacred patterns of their universe in religious life and culture.

Maya warriors attack a village in Yucatán. As among the Aztecs, successful warriors were rewarded with social prestige and preferential treatment in the afterlife.

TIMELINE OF MESOAMERICA

PRECLASSIC PERIOD TO AD250

Above: Olmec stone heads may have been used in rites honouring royal ancestors.

3114BC The start date of the Maya Long Count dating system is equivalent to 13 August 3114BC.

2300BC Artist at Tlapacoya makes the oldest surviving ceramic figurine.

1400BC Oldest known ball court constructed at Paso de la Amada, Chiapas.

c.1400BC Potters in highland Mexico, fashion many ceramic figurines, probably for use as grave offerings.

1250–900BC Olmecs lay out pyramids and courts in their holy town of San Lorenzo.

1200BC Coapexco becomes a centre for the growing trade in obsidian.

1100BC Olmec influence seen in rock carvings at the trading centre of Chalcatzingo.

800–500BC Olmec stone heads set up in La Venta. Maya settlers build the pyramid Mound 30a at Izapa.

500BC The Zapotec city of Monte Albán is established in Oaxaca.

300BC Zapotec builders construct the main plaza of Monte Albán.

250BC Building of the North Acropolis begins at Tikal.

c.200BC Carvings of war prisoners added to Building L at Monte Albán.

200BC–AD300 Building J, an astronomical observatory and military conquest monument built at Monte Albán.

150BC–AD150 Vast El Tigre monument built in the Maya city of El Mirador.

100BC–AD150 Teotihuacán established as a sacred city and a major population centre. The Pyramid of the Sun is built and the Street of the Dead laid out.

31BC Stela C at Trez Zapotes, on the Mexican Gulf Coast, is carved with a date in the Maya Long Count equivalent to 3 September 31BC.

AD36 Stela 1 at El Baúl, Guatemala, is carved with a standing figure and the date AD36.

AD100 A ball court is built at Monte Albán.

AD156 Stela 1 at La Mojarra in Veracruz is carved with a standing figure and the dates AD143 and AD156.

c.AD200 The *talud-tablero* architectural feature is used on the Temple of the Feathered Serpent in Teotihuacán's Citadel area.

c.AD250 Artists decorate Teotihuacán temples with wall paintings.

C.AD250–900 CLASSIC PERIOD

Above: Tikal was a major city by AD300 and at its zenith in the 8th century AD.

AD300 The Zapotecs of Monte Albán establish the nearby settlement of Mitla, which contains many tombs. They call it Lyobaa ('Site of Burials').

AD400 Teotihuacáno influence is seen at the Maya site of Kaminaljuyú, where buildings begin to use the *talud-tablero* architectural feature.

AD426 The first ritual buildings are erected at Copán in the reign of King Yax Kuk Mo' (r. AD426–37).

AD647 King Pacal (r. AD615–83) begins a major building programme at the city of Palenque, with the construction of the Olvidado temple ('Unnoticed Shrine') to the west of the main plaza.

AD650 Potters at Remojadas and other sites in Veracruz produce ceramic figures for use in religious ritual.

AD692 At Palenque the temples of the Cross Group are dedicated.

c.AD700 El Tajín, in Veracruz, contains 12 ball courts and the remarkable Pyramid of the Niches, which contains 365 openings, one for each day of the solar year.

C.AD250–900 CLASSIC PERIOD

AD726 In Yaxchilán Lord Shield Jaguar (*r.* AD681–742) dedicates Temple 23 (Queen's House) to his wife, Lady Xoc.

AD734 Tikal's King Ah Cacau (*r.* AD682–734) buried beneath Temple I, which he built as his funerary monument.

AD738 King 18-Rabbit (*r.* AD695–78) completes building work on the Great Ball Court at Copán.

AD749 Copán's King Smoke Shell (*r.* AD749–763) completes the Hieroglyphic Stairway.

*c.*AD750 Builders erect Tikal's Temple VI (Temple of the Inscriptions) and the city's tallest building, Temple IV – 70m (230ft) tall.

*c.*AD750 Artists at Cacaxtla paint a series of magnificent murals.

AD775 At Copán, King Yax Pac (*r.* AD763–820) dedicates the monument known as Altar Q, which bears portraits of all 16 kings of the dynasty founded by Yax Kuk Mo'.

*c.*AD800 Tula/Tollán is laid out, like Teotihuacán, on a grid pattern.

*c.*AD900 Builders at Chichén Itzá erect the Caracol, perhaps as a temple to the wind god, but more likely as an astronomical observatory.

*c.*AD900 The Pyramid of the Feathered Serpent is built at Xochicalco.

POSTCLASSIC AND MODERN PERIODS AD900–2005

AD909 Monument 101 at Toniná is last carving with date in the Maya Long Count.

*c.*1230 The *Grolier Codex*, a calendar of the cycles of the planet Venus, is written.

*c.*1325 The México/Aztecs build the Templo Mayor in Tenochtitlán.

*c.*1345 The *Dresden Codex* is made.

*c.*1390 A larger pyramid-temple is constructed over the original Templo Mayor.

1431 The México/Aztecs build a third and much larger version of the Templo Mayor on the same site in Tenochtitlán.

1450–1500 A series of fine murals are painted in the Maya city of Tulum.

*c.*1450 The *Paris Codex* is compiled, perhaps in the Maya city of Mayapán.

1469 México/Aztec artisans carve a stone image of Coyolxauhqui to place at the foot of a staircase on the western face of the Templo Mayor pyramid.

22 Aug 1700 Death of Carlos de Siguenza y Gongora, Jesuit priest, pioneering historian and the first to lead archaeological investigations at Teotihuacán.

1746 Ruins of Palenque discovered.

May 1786 First archaeological investigations at Palenque.

1840 John Lloyd Stephens finds Quiriguá.

1848 First expedition to explore Tikal.

1853 Report on Tikal by Modesto Méndez published by Berlin Academy of Science.

Above: The first archaeological investigations at Palenque were in 1786.

1882 Sir Alfred Maudslay leads an official exploration of Yaxchilán.

1924–44 The Carnegie Institution (Washington DC) carries out an archaeological programme at Chichén Itzá.

1940–60 Acosta leads dig at Tula/Tollán.

1946 Giles Healey discovers Bonampak.

1971 Ancient sacred cave found beneath Pyramid of the Sun, Teotihuacán.

1978 Electrical worker discovers vast carving of Coyolxauhqui in Mexico City.

1997 'Codex' murals found at Mayapán.

1998 Archaeologists discover the oldest known Mesoamerican ball court at Paso de la Amada, Chiapas, *c.*1400BC.

2002 Guatemalan Maya jade artefacts found in an elite ceremonial burial at Teotihuacán's Pyramid of the Moon.

2003 Finds at San Andrés suggest the Olmec used a logographic writing system.

CHAPTER ONE

LAND OF DANGER AND REWARD

The Aztecs and Maya made their home in an unstable and unpredictable physical environment. They feared the sudden shiftings of the 'earth monster' when earthquakes struck. They dreaded the onset of drought, the tightening of the dry earth that squeezes life out of the withering crops. They were wary of the beasts of jungle and plain, not least the majestic jaguar; in coastal regions they fled the onslaught of hurricanes and violent storms.

They saw the gods and goddesses everywhere. Partly because the world could turn on them suddenly and destructively, they became convinced of the need to honour the gods. The Aztecs, following long-established Mesoamerican practice, believed that the cycle of the sun's morning birth following death at evening might suddenly stop if blood sacrifices to the gods were not maintained. Equally, Mesoamericans celebrated the gods for the glory of divine energy and the pattern of sacred meaning they saw in all things.

Life in Mesoamerica, lived in the presence of death and catastrophe, was keenly experienced. Mesoamericans entered an intense relationship with their land, a region of rich contrasts – from the mountains of highland Mexico to the plains of the Pacific and Gulf Coasts, from desert and semi-arid landscapes to river valleys, lake shores and the dense jungles of lowland Guatemala.

Left: Aztecs and Maya feared the anger of the region's many volcanoes. The oval crater of Popocatépetl has near-vertical sides. Poisonous volcanic gases erupt from vents in the walls.

HIGHLAND AND LOWLAND

Mesoamerica's first settlers in the second millennium BC could choose between living at sea level along estuaries rich in marine life, in well-watered lowland tropical forests teeming with animals or on dry, elevated plateaux surrounded by rocky uplands well provided with minerals and other resources. Their choice of altitude would largely have determined the climate they would have experienced.

ALTITUDE VARIATIONS

From sea level up to altitudes of about 900m (3,000ft), in lands dubbed *tierra caliente* ('hot territory'), average temperatures were high, with little seasonal variation. In these low-lying tropical regions today, the temperature variation between summer and winter months is generally as little as 5°C and winter is marked by the coming of the rains. In Veracruz, the region on the Gulf of Mexico where the Olmec civilization emerged in the second millennium BC,

Below: Pine forests occupy elevated tierra fria *('cold territory') beneath the peak of Nevado de Toluca, 4,577m (15,016ft) high.*

the average year-round daily temperature is 25°C (77°F). Average temperatures of 24–28°C (75–82°F) hold in the Yucatán peninsula, which was home to many northern Maya settlements.

At altitudes of 900–1,800m (3,000–6,000ft), in *tierra templada* ('temperate territory'), average temperatures are about 5°C lower. The mountaintop Zapotec city of Monte Albán sat at an altitude of 1,600m (5,200ft); average temperatures in the region today are around 18°C (64°F). At 1,800–3,400m (6,000–11,000ft) or *tierra fria* ('cold territory') an average temperature is 5°C or lower, with much greater seasonal variation than at higher altitude. Mexico City, which arose on the ruins of Aztec Tenochtitlán, lies at 2,300m (7,500ft) and has an average daily temperature of 15°C (59°F). Temperatures there can rise to 26°C (78°F) in the hottest month (May) and may fall to a low of 12°C (54°F) in the coldest month (January).

With experience, Mesoamericans discovered that the deep-coloured highland soils of the Valley of Mexico or the Valley of Oaxaca were extremely

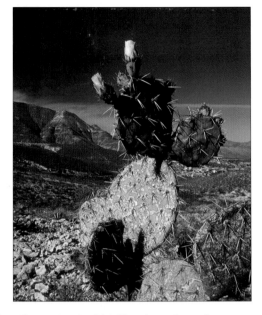

Above: Parched highlands such as this sweep of desert north of Chihuahua, Mexico, are typically rich in minerals.

mineral-rich and could be farmed intensively and on steep slopes. By comparison the earth in such lowland areas as El Petén in Guatemala often needed to be left fallow for prolonged periods to safeguard its fertility. Here farmers developed slash-and-burn agriculture, in which land was cleared with fire then used for perhaps three seasons before being left for as many as ten to recover its richness.

RAINFALL VARIATION

In parts of Mesoamerica drought was a persistent threat. Today, the Valley of Mexico receives as little as 600mm (23in) of rain in a year. However, other regions receive such abundant precipitation that they can support the vibrant growth of tropical rainforests. The Gulf coastal plain as far east as Tabasco, adjoining the Chiapas highlands, in whose foothills the great Maya city of Palenque arose, generally receives an annual average of 2,000mm (78in) of rain. To the southeast, in the jungle region of El Petén, average rainfall is around 1,350mm (53in) each year.

Above: Swamplands on the Mexican Gulf Coast made a resource-rich home for the earliest Mesoamerican settlers.

DROUGHTS OF 1450s

In the first years of rule by the Aztec *tlatoani* Moctezuma I (1440–69), a series of terrible calamities befell the peoples of the Valley of Mexico. In 1446 their harvests were lost to a plague of locusts, then in 1449 the island city of Tenochtitlán was flooded. Frosts and drought struck the crops for four consecutive years in 1450–4.

Chronicle accounts suggest that at the close of the 16th century – 150 years afterwards – people still told breathless tales of the privations of these times, when the weak and starving went hopelessly in search of food and watched with despairing eyes the circling shadows of vultures on the bone-dry ground. Sacrifices were urgently offered to the gods and finally, in 1455, the goggle-eyed rain god Tláloc returned with drenching rains. The people rejoiced in a bumper harvest of maize.

Across Mesoamerica the rainy season generally occurs between June and October. Rainfall can be very strong at the height of the season. Mexico City typically receives almost one third of its annual rainfall of 160mm (6in) in July alone, while Tabasco may be hit by 300mm (11in) in its wettest month (September). In El Petén the rainy season runs from June to December.

FLOODS AND HURRICANES

The Mesoamerican region was also vulnerable to storms, hurricanes and flooding. The Aztecs in their island city of Tenochtitlán were subject to periodic flooding, when the waters of Lake Texcoco rose with the spring rains. The east coast of Mexico adjoining the Gulf of Mexico and the eastern edge of the Yucatán peninsula frequently lay in the path of hurricanes. The Aztec god Tezcatlipoca had special power over hurricane winds, as did the Palenque god Tahil (Obsidian Mirror) and the Quiché Maya sky god Huracán.

The land was young: the great peaks of Citlaltépetl and Popocatépetl were recent outcrops in geological terms, having been driven upwards in the late Tertiary period (as little as 1.6 million years ago).

Mesoamericans must have felt deep respect for the untameable power of nature. They lived in one of the most dynamic areas of the Earth for volcanic and seismic activity and were familiar with the shudderings of the earth monster and the periodic explosions of the volcanoes that spotted the landscape.

Below: Tezcatlipoca, Lord of the Hurricane, was feared for his capricious nature. The Aztecs called him called Yáotl ('Adversary').

SACRED HEIGHTS

The Aztec territories in the Valley of Mexico are surrounded by mountains. The Aztecs and their forebears watched rain clouds gather around the great peaks before being blown by sweet winds to water the maize crops. Their priests taught that the rain god Tláloc stored his life-giving waters on the mountainsides and sent his assistants, the *tlaloques*, to gather the water and pass it to the lord of winds, Éhecatl-Quetzalcóatl. The great peak of Popocatépetl, part of the transverse volcanic axis that cuts across the southern part of the Mesa Central plateau, was sacred to Tláloc.

MOUNTAIN PERSONAE

Popocatépetl, whose name means 'Smoking Mountain' in the Aztecs' Nahuatl language, lies 72km (45 miles) to the south-east of the centre of Mexico City, in full view of the spot where the people of Tenochtitlán once raised their great temple pyramid to the glory of

Below: Popocatépetl is still an active volcano, belching smoke and gas as recently as 2000.

Tláloc and their patron deity Huitzilopochtli. Permanently snow-capped, it climbs to 5,465m (18,000ft), its height second only to Citlaltépetl (or Orizaba) in Mesoamerica. Offerings were made to Popocatépetl in Aztec times and shrines to Tláloc were built on its slopes. Popocatépetl remains active. The smoking peak erupted in 1947 and in 1994 it emitted a vast cloud of ash and gas that scientists feared was the prelude to another major eruption. It belched smoke and gas in 2000, but the volcano has since remained quiet.

The great mountain's twin, Ixtaccíhuatl ('White Lady' in Nahuatl), has three snow capped peaks that are said to resemble the head, feet and chest of a reclining woman. An Aztec folk tale cast Ixtaccíhuatl as a princess mourning the loss of her lover, who had been dispatched by her jealous father to a war in Oaxaca. The volcano is dormant.

The steep cone of Citlaltépetl ('Star Mountain'), Mexico's highest mountain, rises to 5,700m (18,700ft) about 80km (120 miles) to the east of Tenochtitlán

Above: A snow-covered plateau lies beneath one of the three peaks of Ixtaccíhuatl. Now dormant, the volcano last erupted in 1868.

and 40km (60 miles) from the Gulf of Mexico. The snowcapped peak of this volcano is also known as Pico de Orizaba. It held a significant place in Aztec religious narrative, for it was in the crater of Citlaltépetl that the revered prince-god Quetzalcóatl was said to have died after his retreat from the Toltec city of Tollán. He then reappeared in human form and departed into the Gulf of Mexico on a raft of snakes. An Aztec garrison named Ahuilzapán ('Pleasant Waters') lay at the foot of Citlaltépetl, on the site of the modern settlement of Orizaba. The volcano was active in Aztec times, but it has been dormant since 1687.

Another peak sacred to the Aztecs was Nevado de Toluca, Mexico's fourth-highest mountain, which rises to 4,577m (15,016ft) above the valley that bears its name to the west of Tenochtitlán. Nevado de Toluca was known as Xinantecatl in Nahuatl. Natural lakes in its dormant crater were used for religious rites and sacrificial offerings in Aztec times.

In the south western Valley of Mexico rose the Xitle volcano, whose eruption in *c.*50BC devastated the developing ceremonial centre of Cuicuilco, at that time the arch-rival of Teotihuacán. Mesoamerican history in the Valley of

Mexico might have taken a very different course had this catastrophe not occurred, and ceremonial centres might have been flanked by round stepped pyramid-platforms like the one built at Cuicuilco rather than the square or rectangular platforms developed at Teotihuacán and elsewhere. The builders of Teotihuacán laid out their city to align with another very important Mexican peak, Cerro Gordo ('Fat Mountain'), which formed a

northern backdrop for the Pyramid of the Moon and the Street of the Dead. Cerro Gordo was itself the site of a temple and small ceremonial plaza.

MAYA MOUNTAINS

Large numbers of Maya lived far from mountains, in the jungled lowlands of El Petén or in the low-lying scrub of northern Yucatán. However, they shared the reverence of their Mesoamerican cousins for the sacred heights: the towering stone temples of cities such as Tikal were recreations in stone of the mountains that they believed were home to their ancestors after death. Sacred buildings such as those in Group E at Uaxactún were adorned with stucco masks signifying that they were holy mountains.

In the southern Maya territories of eastern Mexico and the southern highlands, which run from the border of the Chiapas region across Guatemala and into north-eastern Honduras, lay the mountains of the Sierra Madre de Chiapas. Of the Chiapas peaks, the volcano Tacana ('Fire House') rises to 4,050m (13,290ft).

The mountains of the southern highlands are mostly young and active volcanoes. The highest is the twin-peaked Tajumulco, which rises to 4,220m

Above: Four tectonic plates – Pacific, Cocos, Caribbean and North American – clash in Mesoamerica, pushing up great mountain chains and causing frequent earthquakes.

(13,845ft) and is dormant. In central Guatemala the extinct San Pedro volcano and the still active 3,535m (11,600ft) Atitlán volcano rise majestically above the waters of Lago Atitlán. The 3,158m (10,358ft) Toliman and the 3,763m (12,340ft) Fuego volcanoes, which are also in Guatemala, have been active as recently as 2002 and 2004 respectively.

Below: Beneath the Atitlán volcano in Guatemala, the waters of Lago Atitlán fill a large crater formed by volcanic subsidence.

LIFE-GIVING WATERS

The lakes of the Valley of Mexico were formed in prehistoric times when the sacred heights of Popocatépetl, Ixtaccíhuatl and other peaks of the transverse volcanic axis rose, damming the south-easterly drainage of the region's waters. Lake Texcoco, site of the Aztecs' island capital, was one of five expanses of water. It lay between lakes Zumpango and Xaltocán to the north and Xochimilco and Chalco to the south.

Lake Texcoco was the lowest of these in altitude. In the rainy summer season the other lakes would rise beyond their normal extent and flow into Lake Texcoco, creating one single expanse of water that the Aztecs dubbed Moon Lake. In the dry season, however, the two northern lakes, which lay 3.5–6m (11–19ft) higher in altitude than Lake Texcoco, would effectively disappear. The southern lakes of Xochimilco and Chalco,

Below: Mesoamerican rivers, notably the long Usumacinta in Yucatán/Guatemala, were major facilitators of trade.

3m (10ft) higher than Lake Texcoco, were fed by freshwater springs and remained, although they were separated from the central lake.

Scholars believe that farming using *chinampa*, or artificial islands, was pioneered in the Classic Period *c.*AD800 by the people of a settlement named Xico by Lake Chalco. By the time of the Aztec empire, Lake Chalco and Lake Xochimilco were the setting for great expanses of *chinampa* fields.

FROM HIGHLANDS TO SEA

To the west of the Valley of Mexico, the Lerma river rises in the region of Nevado de Toluca and flows north-westward to create Lake Chapala. From here, the Santiago river flows south down across the Sierra Madre Occidental into the Pacific Ocean. To the south of the Valley of Mexico the major river is the Balsas, which runs west into the Pacific Ocean and gives its name to the low-lying region known as the Balsas Depression. A second waterway, the Papaloapan, flows

Above: The Sacred Cenote *at Chichén Itzá is around 30m (100ft) across. There is a drop of 22m (70ft) from the rim.*

at a stately pace eastward into the Gulf of Mexico. Archaeologists believe that it was in fertile lands near the Balsas that early Mesoamerican farmers succeeded in domesticating maize from the wild grass known as *teosinte*.

To the east, beyond the low-lying Isthmus of Tehuantepec, the major rivers are the Usumacinta and the Grijalva, which together drain the waters of the Chiapas highlands. The Grijalva forms from headstreams that arise in the Sierra de Soconusco in Mexico and the Sierra Madre of Guatemala. It flows in a north-westerly direction through the state of Chiapas. The Usumacinta, formed in the Chiapas highlands by the combination of the Pasión and Chixoy rivers of Guatemala, flows north-westward towards the region of Tabasco and the Bay of Campeche. One of its three branches combines with the Grijalva before flowing into the Bay of Campeche near the modern town of Frontera, while a second, now called the San Pedro y San Pablo, feeds into the bay near the settlement of San Pedro. A third, now known as the Palizada, flows into the Términos Lagoon in the state of Campeche. The Usumacinta was an important 1,000km (600 mile) trading route.

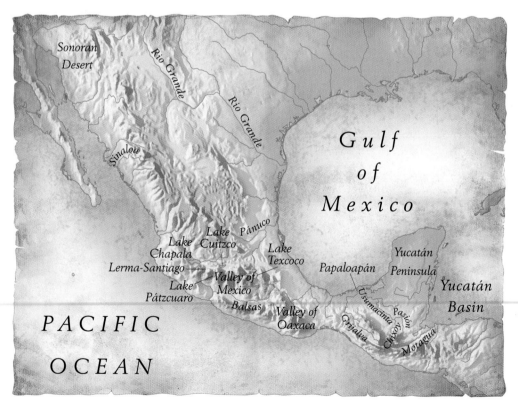

Sonoran Desert

Río Grande

Río Grande

Sinaloa

Gulf of Mexico

Pánuco

Lake Cuitzco

Lake Chapala

Lerma-Santiago

Lake Texcoco

Papaloapán

Yucatán Peninsula

Lake Pátzcuaro

Valley of Mexico

Valley of Oaxaca

Balsas

Usumacinta

Pasión

Chixoy

Grijalva

Motagua

Yucatán Basin

PACIFIC

OCEAN

WATERWAYS AND SETTLEMENT

Several important Maya settlements grew up close to these waterways. The ceremonial centre known as Altar de Sacrificios was founded at the very point where the Pasión and Chixoy rivers join to form the Usumacinta. A carved stela of AD455 shows the site was occupied in the early-to-mid Classic Period, while later evidence shows that it reached a peak of prosperity after AD600 for around two centuries. Farther west, Bonampak was built on the banks of the small Lacanja river. Around 80km (50 miles) down the Usumacinta from Altar de Sacrificios, Yaxchilán was founded on a terrace overlooking the river after AD300. A further 50km (30 miles) downstream, the Maya city of Piedras Negras was built on a hill in a bend of the Usumacinta. Still farther north-west, Palenque was built on the Otulum River, a small tributary of the Usumacinta, and overlooking the Usumacinta floodplain that runs down to the Bay of Campeche.

In the south-eastern Maya region the river Motagua rises in the central Guatemalan highlands in the region occupied by the Quiché Maya and runs for 400km (250 miles) eastwards to empty into the Gulf of Honduras. It was a major route for trade moving from highland Guatemala to the Caribbean. The Maya city of Quiriguá was established

Left: The Aztecs held the waters of lakes, rivers and sea sacred to Chalchiúhtlicue. This image is from the Codex Vaticanus.

close to the river by the 5th century AD. Copán drew much of its wealth from trade in obsidian and other natural resources on this river before it lost control of the trade to Quiriguá in AD738.

UNDERGROUND WATERS

On the Yucatán peninsula of Mexico, towards the northern edge of the Maya realm, there are no significant rivers. Rainfall drains away underground through porous limestone rock and there are very few surface streams. In places, this rock collapses to expose underground stores

Above: This engraving of the Bolonchen cenote is from Incidents of Travel in Central America, Chiapas and Yucatán *(1841).*

of water in natural wells named *cenotes* – from the Yucatec term *dz'onot*. *Cenotes* can be very large, measuring up to 60m (200ft) across and 30m (100ft) deep. There are around 6,000 *cenotes* in north-eastern Yucatán.

Cenotes were important sources of water for the Maya. They were also used for religious sacrifice and were understood to be entrances to the underworld. Of the two *cenotes* at Chichén Itzá, one was reserved for religious offerings and one was used for water supply. *Cenotes* were sacred to the rain god Chac.

TOWERING TREES, ROCKY SANDS

Many Maya made their living among dense jungle forests, tracking game or the rare quetzal bird, cutting back and burning the dense growth to fashion fields to grow crops and raising great stone temples that rivalled the height of the towering jungle trees. The wide variety of terrains, altitudes and climates encompassed by the Maya territories produced a range of distinct forests.

In the Alta Verapaz of Guatemala, at the northern edge of the southern Maya highlands, stand the highland rainforests, home of the rare and sacred quetzal, whose brightly coloured tail feathers were a valued item of trade among the Maya and other Mesoamericans. These humid

Below: The partly ruined Nohuch Mul pyramid rises 24m (80ft) to imitate a natural mountain at the Maya city of Cobá.

greenlands, sometimes called cloud forests, are dense with tropical growth of evergreens, lichens and mosses, delicate wild orchids, bromeliads and astonishing ferns that reach a height of 15m (50ft). Here professional hunters would track the quetzal in order to capture it alive, pluck its wondrous tail feathers and then set it free once more. In the wild the bird would grow new feathers after moulting.

STOREYED FOREST LIFE
In the lower altitude and denser rainforests of the southern Maya lowlands, different types of plant life thrive at distinct levels above ground. At the topmost level, perhaps 70m (230ft) above ground, towering mahogany and ceiba, a form of cottonwood, predominate. At a lower level, up to 50m (165ft) above ground, Spanish cedar, sapodilla, bari and

Above: The Lacandón rainforest in Chiapas, an ancient Maya homeland, is today under threat from farmers and loggers.

American fig trees grow densely. A third level, at up to 25m (80ft) in height, is vibrant with palms, avocado trees, rubber trees, breadnut trees and others. Vines, bromeliads and lianas climb their trunks. Beneath, at ground level, in dense shade, young trees and ferns are found.

TREE OF LIFE
The majestic ceiba, or silk-cotton tree, was sacred to the Maya and identified by them as the cosmic tree or tree of life. They believed that it linked the levels of the universe, sinking its roots through the earth to the lowest of the nine levels of the underworld and sending its towering branches to the topmost of the 13 levels of heaven. In some versions of their cosmology, the Maya told that five great trees supported the heavens, one in each of the four points of the compass and a fifth, the green ceiba, in the centre.

The vines that hang far down from the great ceiba's branches may have symbolized a spirit voyage from the ground level of earthly reality to the heights of heaven in the tree's great umbrella-shaped canopy. There, far above the forest floor, both epiphytes (aerial plants) and many species of animal make their home;

Above: Dry lands. Hunters cross a stretch of desert in a detail from the Mapa Tlotzin, *a genealogy of the governors of Texcoco.*

10m (30ft), palms, allspice and other species predominate. The growth of ferns and young trees at ground level is less vibrant here than further south. Here and there the forest gives way to seasonal swamps and grasslands. Tikal, Uaxactún, El Mirador and Calakmul all arose to glory in the central lowlands.

A PLACE OF NO CULTURE
At the other extreme of Mesoamerican terrains lay arid or semi-arid regions such as the wide plateau where the Toltec capital of Tollán was founded in highland Mexico and regions in Guatemala such as the Motagua Valley in the Maya highlands. In such areas the cult of the rain god was prominent and knowledge of irrigation techniques was key to agricultural success. Desert lay to the north in the northern part of the Mexican plateau, a region characterized by the Aztecs and their fellow inhabitants of the Valley of Mexico as a place of no culture, the place from which they had escaped in moving south. In the *Historia Tolteca Chichimeca*, an image of the seven caves from which the tribes were said to have emerged depicts several types of cacti, indicating that the primal landscape of origin in the first days was a sunblasted desert.

Below: At Labná in Yucatán, trees crowd close to the palace arch. To either side are stone representations of Maya village huts.

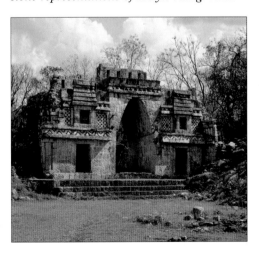

birds nest, mammals move about along the great branches, even frogs raise their young in the pools that form on branches and in tree trunks.

The ceiba blooms in the evening, producing tiny flowers very reminiscent of the ear flares worn by kings in Maya carving and ceramic images. Some authorities suggest that the king dressed himself as the silk-cotton tree, to signify that he was blessed like the holy ceiba and that he anchored the kingdom in sacred order. The carving on the lid of the sarcophagus in which King Pacal of Palenque was interred shows the king descending into the spirit realm of the underworld along the length of the cosmic tree. The Maya carved great canoes from the vast trunk of their sacred tree.

SEASONAL RAINFOREST
Farther north, in the region known as the central lowlands, the jungle is described as 'seasonal rainforest' because each year extended dry periods interrupt the supply of rainwater. The upper canopy of American fig, ceiba and mahogany is lower and often less complete, but still climbs to 50m (165ft) above ground. Beneath, a thick growth of fig, sapodilla and other trees form a very dense canopy, while lower still, at a height of around

LIFE IN THE WILD

The lands of the Aztecs and Maya were teeming with animal life. Mesoamericans so revered these creatures for their energy and marvellous abilities that they cast many of them in religious and creation narratives and even saw some, such as the jaguar and eagle, as principal physical forms of great gods.

KING JAGUAR

Throughout the region, the jaguar was king. The largest member of the *felidae* family of cats, the jaguar (*Felis onca*) can thrive in scrubland and desert as well as in its preferred habitat of dense forests and swamps. It can climb with ease and track prey along branches tens of metres above ground, but is also happy to leap into water and is a strong swimmer. The male, which is significantly larger than the female, can grow to 2.7m (9ft) in length and weigh up to 160kg (350lbs.) The jaguar hunts alone. It prefers to stalk

Below: Bird sacred to Huitzilopochtli. This detail of a stone carving on the Platform of the Jaguars and Eagles at Chichén Itzá depicts an eagle eating a human heart.

peccaries (pig-like mammals) and the capybara (a large rodent), but will also kill and eat deer, sloths, monkeys, anteaters, alligators, birds, turtles and even fish. The jaguar does not usually attack humans, unless cornered, when it is a savage opponent.

The jaguar played an important role in Mesoamerican religious life from early times. In the second millennium BC, Olmec craftsmen were carving intriguing jaguar-faced figures resembling human babies. The jaguar was associated with the ancient practice of shamanism (spirit travel) and was adopted by shamans as one of their animal forms.

Because of its fearsome capacity to hunt in darkness, it was an animal aspect of Tezcatlipoca, the Aztec lord of night and of dark fate, while elsewhere in Mesoamerica it was associated with the god of the underworld and with the realm of darkness. When the sun visited the underworld by night, it took the form of the jaguar. Like the lion in Europe, the jaguar became a symbol of royalty and bravery in Mesoamerica: Maya kings wore its pelt and were named after the jaguar, while in the Aztec army the two elite groups of fighters were called eagle and jaguar warriors.

The Aztecs called the jaguar *océlotl*. The smaller cat now known as the ocelot was known to the Aztecs as the *tlacaoocélotl* (literally, 'little jaguar'; *Felis pardalis*).

HUNTING ANIMALS AND BIRDS

When Mesoamericans went hunting they most commonly killed rabbits and white-tailed deer. Rabbits, perhaps because of their skittering speed of movement and rapid rate of reproduction, were associated by the Aztecs with drunkenness and with the alcoholic drink *pulque*. Maya and Aztec people also killed and ate ducks, geese, swans and other birds. The Hero Twins of Mayan mythology were celebrated for their skill in hunting birds using blowpipes.

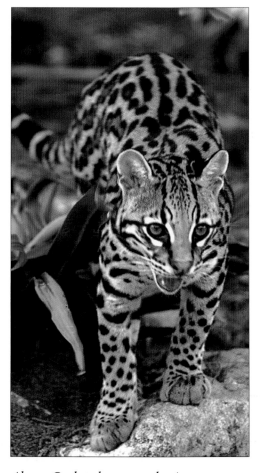

Above: Ocelots, known to the Aztecs as 'little jaguars', were common in the fertile lowlands of Mesoamerica along with opossums and tapirs.

Mesoamericans also hunted the rare quetzal bird, which was tracked and captured for its magnificent tail plumes, but never killed. The quetzal is found in the highland cloud forests that run from Chiapas to western Panama. Just 35cm (14in) long, it has tail feathers of up to 1m (3ft 3in) in length. These plumes change colour in the light, a shimmer of gold, emerald green and blue that sets off the bird's bright red breast.

Only the male bird possesses the iridescent tail feathers that are so highly prized: as with the peacock and peahen, the female bird is much plainer in appearance. The quetzal was an animal form of the great Plumed Serpent

Quetzalcóatl and the feathers of the sacred bird were, like the jaguar pelt, symbolic of kingly authority.

Probably the most revered of birds was the eagle. An animal form taken by the Aztecs' tribal god Huitzilopochtli, it was central to Aztec origin narrative: the México/Aztecs founded their city of Tenochtitlán at the place where they saw an eagle destroying a snake upon a cactus, in fulfilment of a prophecy of Huitzilopochtli. The harpy eagle was found in the jungles of Maya lands while the golden eagle was known in central Mexico.

Other notable birds included parrots, macaws and toucans, falcons, owls, hawks and other birds of prey and, in estuaries and along coastlines, herons, giant storks and egrets. In the *Popol Vuh* of the Quiché Maya, the scarlet macaw, a vividly coloured species of parrot, attempted to set himself up as the pre-eminent god and to take the place of the sun, but he was outwitted by the Hero Twins. The hummingbird was another bird associated with Huitzilopochtli by the Aztecs.

BATS
The bat was also widely found. In the jungle bats nested beneath the vast roots of the ceiba that was viewed as the tree of life and understood to link the earth with the underworld and the heavens. Partly for this reason, and partly because of their natural associations with darkness, bats were linked to the underworld. The Zapotecs of Monte Albán associated the bat god with maize and fertility.

SNAKES AND MONKEYS
The snake was a complex and central religious symbol, associated with Tláloc and the rain, with the fertility of the earth, with the sun and heavens, with sacrificial blood and with religious and visionary experience. Mesoamericans also revered turtles and crocodiles: they sometimes said that the earth took the form of a

crocodile or was resting on the back of a giant turtle. The Maya also identified the constellation Orion as a celestial turtle.

Monkeys were common in the lowlands. Species included howlers, spider monkeys and marmosets. Howlers, stocky, bearded monkeys up to 70cm (28in) long, live mainly in the upper branches of trees and would rarely have been seen. However, they would certainly have been heard: they take their name from the extremely resonant howl that they emit at dawn and dusk and during storms. The howler's cry can be heard more than 5km (as much as 3 miles) away. Marmosets are small, long-tailed monkeys that move quickly along branches, while spider monkeys are much larger with pot bellies. They forage in small groups among the very highest jungle branches. They rarely descend to the ground, but can be seen leaping from one tree to another. The Quiché Maya creators of the *Popul Vuh* narrative, which imagines a series of failed creations before the current one, told that monkeys were the descendants of a failed race of wooden people fashioned in early days by the creators.

Above: The jaguar is the largest New World cat. Like the lion in Europe, it became a symbol of royalty and bravery in Mexico.

Below: The intricate decoration in the Nunnery Quadrangle, Uxmal, contains twin images of the sacred rattlesnake.

FRUITS OF THE EARTH

The first humans in Mesoamerica were hunter-gatherers who survived on a diet of seeds and plants supplemented both by mammoths and mastodons and by smaller game, birds and fish. They lived in this way for many millennia before beginning to domesticate plants such as avocados, squash, beans and chilli peppers and turning to a settled, agricultural way of life.

PEOPLE OF MAIZE

The plant that would become their descendants' staple food – maize – was probably first domesticated from a wild cereal grass called *teosinte*. Archaeological evidence from the Tehuacán Valley in the Puebla region to the south-east of the Valley of Mexico suggests that, in the wild, the grass produced cobs that were no more than 2.5cm (1in) long: at this size, they could be an addition to a diet but not a staple food. In domesticating the plant, the first Mesoamerican farmers

Below: Images of the revered maize plant were carved on the sides of this basalt block used as an altar by the Aztecs.

succeeded in enlarging the cobs. In the wild, beans and squash grew alongside *teosinte* and other grasses, climbing up the grass stalks in the protection of the shade provided by the leaves. The first farmers, who had already domesticated varieties of squash and beans, might have copied this method of planting.

Archaeologists report that the first cereal domesticated in Mesoamerica was not *teosinte* but another, related to modern grain millet (*Setaria geniculata*). *Teosinte* itself was probably first domesticated in the lands adjoining the Balsas river of western Mexico some centuries before 5000BC. From archaeological remains we know that its use spread slowly eastwards, reaching the Tehuacán Valley by *c.*5000BC, Oaxaca by *c.*4000BC and Veracruz by *c.*2250BC. Its first cultivators perfected the making of stone mortars and used them to grind the maize ears.

Mesoamericans saw themselves as people reliant on, dedicated to and even made of maize. The word used by the Aztecs for the maize dough from which

Above: Xilonen, the Aztec goddess of young maize cobs, was worshipped in the form of a virginal adolescent girl.

they made tortillas is *toneuhcayotl* ('our flesh'). In some versions of both Maya and Aztec creation narratives, the first people were fashioned from a soft maize dough. In the *Popol Vuh*, the creators Huracán and Gucumatz gave ears of maize to a grandmother goddess Xmucané who ground them to flour, made a paste by mixing it with water and then moulded the first people.

According to Maya folk tradition, the first Mesoamericans were led to identify *teosinte* as a food source when they saw its grains in the dung of a wild cat. The *Popol Vuh* also recorded this debt to animals: Huracán and Gucumatz were led to the discovery of maize by four corn-eating creatures – a coyote, a fox, a parrot and a crow – who had tasted the maize

Above: In a detail from one of the murals in Building A at Cacaxtla, a bird swoops to seize a cocoa pod from a sturdy cacao tree.

THE SEARCH FOR FOOD

Mesoamerican creation narratives proposed that before the current world age began there were a number of previous creations. The Aztec account of the five suns or world ages revealed that in each of the five creations the earth's inhabitants found a more satisfactory staple food than eaten by their predecessors.

In the era of the first sun, which was governed by Black Tezcatlipoca, the world was inhabited by a race of giants who lived on acorns. The second sun, whose presiding god was Quetzalcóatl, saw the emergence of a race of primitive humans who lived on the seeds of the mesquite tree.

After the third age, which was ruled by Tláloc, in which people lived on plants that grew on water, such as the water lily, people returned to a diet of wild seeds in the fourth age of Chalchiúhtlicue. It was only in the fifth and current age, an age subject to the sun god Tonatiuh, that the peoples of Mesoamerica learned how to plant and harvest maize.

and found it good. In Aztec religious narratives, the god Quetzalcóatl – in some accounts, also a culture hero who taught people how to sow and harvest crops – discovered maize deep in the heart of a mountain, where it had been hidden by ants. He was unable to split the mountain to bring the maize to humans, but the god Nanahuatzin – who at the beginning of the current world age rose in the sky to become the sun – broke the peak apart with a thunderbolt.

FIELD AGRICULTURE

Mesoamericans developed different methods of field agriculture in the varied parts of their region. In arid and semi-arid areas fields were laid out where they could be watered by diverted springs and rivers, while in the region of Lake Texcoco farmers developed the technique of building *chinampa*, artificial islands, to reclaim land from the lake. In the dense jungles of the lowlands, fields were cut and the soil enriched by burning vegetation, while in the highlands further south, terraces were carved from the steep slopes.

By 1300BC, the four foods that would become the staple plants of the Mesoamerican civilization were well established in the fields of the pioneer farmers. Together they provided a balanced diet: carbohydrates from maize, protein from beans and squash, oils and fats from avocado. They could be supplemented with meat from rabbits, deer, ducks and geese and with fish.

Below: Cocoa beans are found within cocoa pods, the fruit of the cacao tree. The pods grow on the tree trunk and branches.

CREATING A SACRED WORLD

The oldest religion in Mesoamerica was the cult of the earth's fertility. At the very beginnings of settled life in central America, settlers were fashioning clay female figurines, believed to be representations of an archaic fertility goddess.

MOTHER AND MONSTER
From prehistoric times, Mesoamericans revered the earth as a mother with the capacity to gestate the seeds of domesticated plants and bring forth food. The ancient 260-day ritual calendar celebrated a sacred timespan that was possibly derived from both the lapse between planting and harvest in the Mesoamerican agricultural cycle and the time from conception to

Below: The duality of life and death is represented in a man/skeleton figure made by an Olmec craftsman c.500BC.

birth in a human pregnancy. The earth was a mother, but also a monster. In Aztec religious narrative, the earth monster Tlatecuhtli spread terror in the first days of the current era, when there was nothing but water. She was tamed by the gods Quetzalcóatl and Tezcatlipoca who tore her in two, making the sky from one half and the earth from the other.

OPPOSITES IN BALANCE
Mesoamericans believed the universe to be patterned by duality. Tlatecuhtli consumed the sun god each dusk, consigning him to the underworld for the hours of darkness, but the earth mother then gave birth to the sun once more in the redness of dawn. The earth goddess gave life in the form of crops but also demanded life in the form of sacrificial blood. Mesoamericans saw opposites held in balance. Darkness balancing light, death opposing life, dampness countering dryness, weakness balancing strength.

Duality also structured the divine sphere and was the hidden power of creation. The primal Aztec god Ometeotl ('Lord of Duality') took twin male and female forms, as Tonacatecuhtli ('Lord of our Sustenance') and Tonacacíhuatl ('Lady of our Sustenance') joined in a creative embrace. In Quiché Maya creation narrative, the earth was made when two gods, the sky god Huracán and the sea god Gucumatz came together in discussion. The gods had both benign and threatening aspects: the Maya rain god Chac or the Aztec rain deity Tláloc could deliver drought or lifegiving waters, destructive storms as well as the light moisture falling gently on crops.

The gods also had both spirit forms and physical forms, and most had animal aspects: Mesoamericans viewed the many powerful creatures of their landscape with deep reverence. In one version of the Aztec religious narrative

describing the creation of the sun and moon, the assembled gods who gave of their own blood to set the sun in motion afterwards became the animals of the plains, hills and jungles. The earth was opposed by the heavens, and also balanced the underworld.

In the Mesoamerican vision, the flat earth was both the lowest of the thirteen levels of heaven and the topmost of the nine levels of the underworld. The earth also gave access to the spirit realms of the underworld – the land was marked with sacred caverns that opened the way. The earth was also associated with snakes. According to the Maya, those in a state of religious ecstasy might be delivered

Below: The eagle, symbol of the god Huitzilopochtli and of warrior might, is celebrated on an Aztec wooden drum.

Above: Zoomorph P at Quiriguá shows a young ruler in the jaws of a monster, representing the entry to the underworld.

into the presence of ancestors or the gods by following the coils of a great snake known as the Vision Serpent.

SACRED PATTERNS

For Mesoamericans, the universe was structured according to sacred patterning. One of the forms of this patterning was that of the cyclical movement of time. Mesoamericans believed that everything happened in regular, periodic timespans. For this reason they structured their lives and religious ceremonies around the 260-, 365- and 584-day cycles of the moon, the sun and the planet Venus. Both the Maya and the Aztecs saw the current world as one of a series of creations, subject to periodic destruction and renewal.

In the Aztec view, the present age was the fifth sun or era, and this fivefold pattern was seen also in that of the five directions on the flat earth – north, south, east, west and the centre. In the centre was the great cosmic ceiba tree, and – for the Aztecs – the Templo Mayor of Tenochtitlán. The earth itself was also the centre point of creation, for Mesoamericans believed the earth to be surrounded by water. This gave sacred

meaning to the island setting of the Aztecs' imperial capital of Tenochtitlán. The physical characteristics of Mesoamerica informed the range of associations that clustered around the directions of north and south.

To the north of the Valley of Mexico lay desert lands, inhospitable regions from which many nomads, including the México/Aztecs, had escaped. The Aztecs saw the north as a place of dryness and death. It was the direction of the lord of deception and fate, Tezcatlipoca, and was linked to his colour, black – the hue of death. It was associated with xerophyte plants such as the Joshua tree that are adapted to desert climates. In the opposite direction, the south was said by the Aztecs to be the land of dampness, and of their tribal lord Huitzilopochtli, master of the arts of war through which they gathered sacrificial victims. In some versions, the south was the land of the rain god Tláloc, and like his heaven Tlálocan, a place of ease and lifegiving waters.

North and south appear to have been pre-eminent among the four directions. From at least Olmec times in the second millennium BC, many Mesoamerican sites were laid out on a roughly north–south plan. The same pattern was applied in Maya cities such as Tikal and Copán. For the Maya, north was the direction of the

celestial realm, home of the gods, and south the way to the underworld. East and west were associated with the daily path of the sun.

Above the earth was the sacred sky, home of the sun god to whom the Aztecs, the people of the sun, dedicated themselves. By night, the movements of the stars followed paths established by the gods in religious and creation narrative. For example, the Great Bear constellation was identified with Tezcatlipoca and its dipping into the sea re-enacted the moment during his struggle with the earth monster at which he lost a foot. The cycle of the planet Venus eternally celebrated the achievements of the Aztec god Quetzalcóatl or the Maya Hero Twins in confronting the lords of the underworld.

In the sacred arenas of their cities, Mesoamericans created idealized versions of their world. Stone pyramids stood for mountains, wide plazas for lakes. Carved stone stelae – known to the Maya as stone trees – honoured the great trunks of the forest. Many scholars believe that the ball court was like a sacred cavern.

Below: This tiny Olmec female figurine was one of many Preclassic Period figures thought to have been used in fertility cults.

CHAPTER TWO

FROM VILLAGE TO METROPOLIS

In the great northern Yucatán city of Chichén Itzá, probably in the 9th–10th century or a little later, labourers raised the Temple of the Warriors, a four-level pyramid with a wide central stairway leading to a *chacmool* sacrificial figure and beyond it a square *cella* or temple. This awe-inspiring sacred building appears to be a copy of or tribute to the main pyramid-temple at Tollán in highland Mexico, the capital of the revered Toltecs. At one time scholars thought that Toltecs conquered Chichén Itzá, but most now agree that Toltec architectural features are present in the Yucatán city as a result of the peaceful spread of Toltec influence.

The debate over Chichén Itzá is typical of the many difficulties in tracing patterns of influence through Mesoamerican history. In attempting to make sense of the spread of settlements, we will rely on the conventional division of the region's history introduced elsewhere in this book, into the Preclassic Period (20,000BC–AD250), the Classic Period (*c.*AD250–AD900) and the Postclassic Period (AD900 –1521). This tripartite division is certainly useful but the labels must not be applied too rigidly, for the divisions can fall at different chronological points in different areas of Mesoamerica: for example, in Belize and arguably northern Yucatán, historians agree that the Classic Period continues past AD900 until as late as 1200.

Left: The Great Plaza was the heart of the mountain-top settlement of Monte Albán, one of Mesoamerica's first cities.

THE BEGINNINGS OF SETTLED LIFE
7000–2000BC

In Mesoamerica, hunter-gatherer bands of humans first began to domesticate wild plants *c*.7000BC. Over 5,000 years they gradually became more successful at growing crops, little by little abandoning their nomadic pattern of existence and establishing permanent settlements, which were supported mainly by farming. Archaeological evidence suggests that the first settlements were established in two areas of Mesoamerica – in highland Mexico and along the coasts of the Gulf of Mexico, the Gulf of Tehuantepec and the Caribbean. Archaeologists suspect that in other areas, such as the central Maya region, people may have been following the same long, slow path from nomadic life to settled farming at the same time but the evidence has not been found in these places.

BEFORE FARMING

The evidence from highland Mexico shows that before humans first experimented with domesticating plants they were living as nomads in small bands of up to eight, hunting, trapping and gathering. They hunted species of antelope and horse that are now extinct, as well as rabbits, rats, birds, gophers and turtles. They used knives and sharpened points of chipped flint. They sometimes

Right: Mesoamerica's first hunter-gatherers trapped birds and other prey. This Totonac stone axe-shaped head is from after AD900.

drove mammoths and other large creatures into marshy land, where they killed them with sharpened flints. Archaeological finds show that two mammoths were killed in this way at the edge of Lake Texcoco in the Valley of Mexico some time around 7700BC.

THE FIRST CROPS

Over the following two millennia, *c*.7000–5000BC, the nomads of highland Mexico began to domesticate avocados, chillis and squash. They also ate the black seeds of a weed called amaranth, which were probably gathered in the wild, and chewed a wild cereal grass named *teosinte* that would become the staple food of Mesoamerica in the form of maize.

In this period, humans were living in the Tehuacán Valley in the south-eastern part of modern Puebla province, at an altitude of around 1,400m (4,600ft). They made milling stones as well as mortars and pestles and began to experiment with

weaving and woodworking. Groups settled in seasonal camps, but in spring left on nomadic trips. They killed cottontail rabbits and deer for meat. They buried skulls in baskets – perhaps as a rite of human sacrifice.

People were also living in the Infiernillo complex of caves in a desert environment in the south-western part of modern Tamaulipas province. They made fire-sticks, traps, rods and darts from wood and pioneered the making of mats and bags from yucca and agave plants. They ate wild runner beans, agave and prickly pear cactus and domesticated the bottle gourd and the chilli pepper.

At the same time, people in the Balsas region of western Mexico succeeded in domesticating *teosinte*. Another group made their living in caves near Mitla in Oaxaca. Like their cousins elsewhere, they hunted cottontail rabbits and deer, made flint tools and weapons and experimented with domesticating squash.

In 5000–3400BC, the inhabitants of the Tehuacán Valley began to establish semi-permanent camps that they inhabited for parts of the year, probably splitting into smaller nomadic groups only in the dry season. They succeeded in domesticating more plants, including *teosinte*, as well as

Left: From early days, Mesoamericans made alcoholic drinks from the maguey agave plant, which grew in Oaxaca.

the common bean, the crookneck squash and the bottle gourd. They cultivated sapotes, plum or apple-sized fruits with a sweet flavour. At another site in Oaxaca, Gheo-Shih, people were living in a semi-permanent site through summer and autumn, hunting but also raising maize.

From 3400 to 2000BC, the people of the Tehuacán Valley built larger settlements on river terraces they probably occupied all year round. They domesticated new plants, including the pumpkin, and began to keep and eat dogs. They made bowls from stone and long blades of obsidian. They trapped small animals such as foxes, turtles and birds rather than larger creatures such as puma or deer. However, as before, some members set off in nomadic hunting groups during the dry season and left evidence of their passing in highland caves.

A LAKESIDE HOME

In the more fertile setting of Lake Chalco in the Valley of Mexico, people began to live in permanent settlements much earlier, perhaps c.5500BC. At Zohapilco, near the volcano of Tlapacoya to the east of Lake Chalco, settlers had a wide choice of foods: molluscs, turtles and fish from the lake; water lentils and other plants from the marshy shoreline; wild fruits and

deer, rabbits, dogs, coyotes and rodents from the forested hills. The soil was rich and they grew amaranth and early domesticated forms of *teosinte*. Each winter they could also hunt or trap any of a large number of migratory birds such as Canada geese, teals, pintails and mallards. They made tools from locally available andesite and obsidian. However, this attractive setting had its drawback in the form of the nearby volcanoes. Some time before 3000BC, major eruptions devastated the area and people were not able to resettle the lakeside for about 500 years.

COASTAL SETTLEMENTS

At the eastern edge of Mesoamerica, on the Caribbean coast of Belize, groups of people were living in permanent settlements by 4200BC, eating shellfish, fish, turtles, seabirds and reptiles. On the Pacific coast, south of the Sierra Madre del Sur, groups lived at sites near Acapulco in Guerrero and Matanchén in Nayarit. The remains suggest that they lived there at least semi-permanently from as early as 3000BC, eating shrimps, clams and fish. In Veracruz on the coast of the Gulf of Mexico, people lived at Santa Luisa on the Tecolutla river

Above: The countryside of Oaxaca was the setting for an early Mesoamerican cave settlement near Mitla in 7000–5000BC.

in the years 3500–2000BC, by hunting, fishing and gathering wild foods. They left no evidence that they had even begun to experiment with farming. Farther east, beyond the Isthmus of Tehuantepec, the ancestors of the Maya were making a living on the Pacific coasts of Guatemala by c.2000BC. People were also settled very early in north-western Yucatán, in the region of the later settlement of Dzibilchaltún, about 20km (12 miles) inland from the coast.

Below: Copper axe heads like these were not made in Mesoamerica before the 9th–10th centuries AD.

URBAN CEREMONIAL CENTRES
c.2500–300BC

In slightly over 2000 years from *c.*2500 to *c.*300BC, Mesoamericans laid the foundations of a great civilization. Larger settlements increasingly reliant on farming rather than hunting, gathering and fishing developed. More efficient ways of irrigating and using land meant farmers were able to produce surpluses of food.

Populations rose rapidly and people began to specialize in small industries and crafts, such as producing pottery, tools or items valued for their use in religious ritual. Social divisions emerged and, in some areas, elite groups took control. Public buildings such as temples were raised and large ceremonial centres laid out.

There was busy interaction between population centres, as people shared or swapped products, raw materials, plants and ideas. This enabled the development of a unified Mesoamerican culture and was a precursor of the long-range trade that was later one of the key defining features of Mesoamerica. Stonemasons began to use basic hieroglyphic signs. The first great Mesoamerican culture, that of the Olmec people, emerged about 1500BC in southern Veracruz and grew to a peak between 1100–600BC.

Below: At Izapa on the Pacific coastal plain of south-east Mexico, Maya settlers built a pyramid (Mound 30a) in 800–500BC.

Above: The image of the ruler in a monster's mouth representing the entrance to the spirit world was established by the time of the Olmec.

A major Olmec centre was established at San Lorenzo, at a spot advantageously situated where the Coatzacoalcos and Chiquito rivers meet and close both to lowland forests and resource-rich highlands, overlooking the fertile flood-plain. San Lorenzo was at the height of its power and influence in the years 1150–900BC. Its people established exchange or trading links with sites in Oaxaca, Guerrero and highland Mexico, and Olmec influence spread far and wide.

Between 900 and 700BC, the era of San Lorenzo came to an end: the Olmec monuments were attacked, defaced and buried. However, the centre was not abandoned until 400BC. A second major Olmec centre at La Venta, in Tabasco, was constructed from 1150BC onwards and reached its peak in the years 800–500BC. It grew up in a region where villagers had been living and raising maize since *c.*2250BC, supplementing their diet with crocodiles, toads and aquatic birds. The Olmec centre at La Venta was a large ceremonial site containing several

platforms and pyramids generally oriented north–south, but set at 8 degrees west of true north – as at San Lorenzo. It also contained carved colossal heads, whose individuality suggests that they might be portrayals of rulers, and other monuments. The main Olmec sites were probably independent of each other. There was certainly no Olmec empire and there is no real evidence of military conquest – although Altar 4 at La Venta and Monument 14 at San Lorenzo bear carvings of one figure leading another by a rope, suggesting a captor and his captive and indicating there were inter-city rivalries.

OAXACAN HIGHLANDS

In the area of the modern Mexican state of Oaxaca, San José Mogote became an important centre. From a few simple public buildings *c.*1350BC, the settlement grew to cover 20ha (50 acres) by 1000BC,

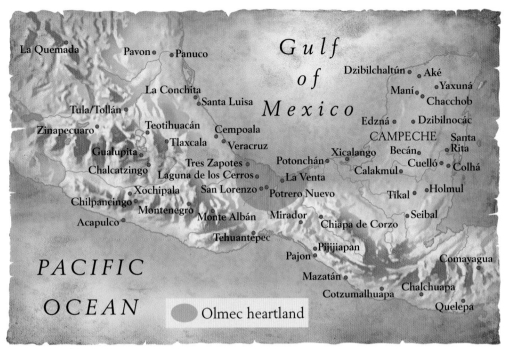

with splendid stone temples and platforms. Its creators were independent of, but influenced by, the Olmec. San José's public buildings, like those at San Lorenzo, were oriented 8 degrees west of north. Craftsmen lived in quarters according to their speciality – for example, tool manufacturers, jade workers and basket-makers lived in separate areas.

Around 500BC the great Zapotec city of Monte Albán was established nearby in a hilltop position dominating the three valleys of Zaachila to the south, Etla to the north and Tlacolula to the east. The hilltop, 400m (1,300ft) above the floor of the valleys, was a strategic position that would have been easily defended in conflict, but there is no archaeological evidence that the city was ever attacked. This inspires historians to argue that the hilltop may simply have been chosen by competing Zapotec valley groups as a neutral setting for a central ceremonial and administrative settlement.

ABOVE THE VALLEY OF MEXICO

The village of Coapexco, perched at an altitude of 2,600m (8,500ft) on the side of Mount Ixtaccíhuatl, appears to have been a centre for trade in the highly prized volcanic glass obsidian c.1200BC, or it was perhaps the home to manufacturers of obsidian blades – archaeologists have found obsidian from distant and exotic sources at the site. Below in the Valley of Mexico villages established at Tlatilco on the western edge of Lake Texcoco and at Tlapacoya on the shore of Lake Chalco left remarkable stores of skilfully hand-modelled ceramic figures dating from c.1100BC. They represent mothers with babies, ball players, dwarfs, musicians, shamans, acrobats, hunchbacks and musicians. Some were found in household waste, but others were placed in graves: as many as 60 were interred in a single grave at Tlatilco.

A ceremonial centre was constructed at Cuicuilco to the west of Lake Xochimilco in the Valley of Mexico c.400BC. Labourers raised a pyramid in four stages, from a circular base, finally facing it in stone and building two staircases climbing 27m (90ft) to a platform that held twin shrines. This is the earliest

Left: This stone pillar is one of the few pieces of Olmec monumental art to represent a woman. It was found in 1925.

Above: Olmec centres existed at Tres Zapotes, Río Chiquito, Portero Nuevo and Laguna de Los Cerros as well as at La Venta and San Lorenzo. Olmec influence spread as far as Chalcatzingo and Guatemala.

known pyramid-platform supporting two shrines. This feature would be adopted by many Mesoamerican peoples including the Aztecs, whose Great Pyramid in Tenochtitlán bore twin shrines to Tláloc and Huitzilopochtli. Cuicuilco rose to become a major population centre covering 400ha (1,000 acres) and home to 20,000 people. Just 1km (0.6 miles) to the east lay a collection of 11 sacred mounds at Peña Pobre.

CENTRAL AND SOUTHERN MAYA

The site of Nakbé in the lowlands of Guatemala was one of the pioneer centres of Maya civilization and was well established by 600BC. Public buildings included temples dedicated to the gods rather than individual rulers.

In southern Maya lands by c. 1800BC, people along the Pacific coast of Guatemala were living in permanent villages of 400–1,000 inhabitants, a size that suggests that a chieftain or leader was in control of the village. He might have established pre-eminence by giving gifts. The people of these settlements began to specialize in making salt, in fishing and in pottery.

THE RISE OF THE GREAT CITIES
300BC–AD250

The 500-odd years from 300BC to AD250 saw the emergence of great cities ruled by a king or members of a powerful elite. In the central highlands of Mexico, the most important was Teotihuacán, in the north-east part of the Valley of Mexico. In Oaxaca, Monte Albán was dominant. In the central Maya region, several significant centres emerged, including El Mirador and Tikal, where large stucco masks carved on temples and pyramids celebrated powerful royal dynasties.

A vibrant trade and exchange network arose and the elite groups clearly possessed great wealth. This is evident from the richness of palaces and other upper-class residences, the construction of lavish tombs and the laying out of wealthy grave offerings. The people of Teotihuacán prospered by trade rather than war, but the other major cities were built with the spoils of conquest. The Zapotecs of Monte Albán made a number of conquests and forced several communities to pay tribute. The cities of the central Maya region waged bitter war. Many centres – including Tikal, Monte Albán, Calakmul and Edzna – erected defensive walls and dug moats. Carved images of the period depict prisoners of war and sacrificial victims.

Above: The Zapotecs of Monte Albán had laid out their ball court on the north-eastern corner of the Great Plaza by AD100.

THE HOLY CITY

At the start of the period, Teotihuacán in the north-east part of the Valley of Mexico began to emerge as a centre to rival Cuicuilco in the southern part of the valley. Villages had existed in the Teotihuacán region since *c*.900BC.

The area was an ancient religious centre because of its network of caves and tunnels. (Mesoamericans viewed caverns as sacred places providing access to the underworld.) By *c*.300BC, Teotihuacán was growing, with evidence of obsidian workshops and other craft centres.

Both Cuicuilco and Teotihuacán drew people from throughout the Valley of Mexico; the two centres may have been rivals and perhaps even foes, as fortified and hilltop sites developed around the lakes of the Valley of Mexico in this period. However, an eruption of the Xitle volcano near Cuicuilco *c*.50 BC decided the matter. The area around Cuicuilco was devastated and the city abandoned in favour of Teotihuacán. The latter expanded rapidly: by AD150, it covered 20km (12 miles) and was home to around 80,000 people. Elsewhere in the Valley of Mexico settlers established villages for the first time on the eastern edge of Lake Texcoco. They could not farm these lands, so must have made their living from the waters of the lake.

OAXACA

In Oaxaca, Monte Albán established itself as the capital of the whole region, powerful in trade. Population rose from around 7,000 in 300BC to as many as 17,000 inhabitants one hundred years later, living in three distinct communities. As the centre of Monte Albán grew in importance and wealth, so did the area's previously pre-eminent community, San José Mogote, gradually become abandoned.

Like the Olmec before, the ruling elite in Monte Albán was able to command a vast labour force. Around the city's western and northern edge, 3km (2 miles) of defensive walls up to 4m (13ft) high were erected in a massive building project.

Left: This pyramid (E-VII) at Uaxactún is part of the Group E sacred complex aligned to solar and astronomical events.

Another Oaxaca people, the Mixtecs, built hilltop centres at Yucuita and Monte Negro at the two ends of the Nochixtlán Valley in this era. Both featured ceremonial buildings laid out on an L plan, rather than around a plaza. Both sites were at their apogee *c*. 200BC.

SOUTHERN AND CENTRAL MAYA
In contrast to the far-reaching centralized powers of Teotihuacán and Monte Albán, in Maya territories several small, competing kingdoms developed.

In the southern Maya region, Kaminaljuyú was established in the Valley of Guatemala. In the years 400BC–AD100 its people laid out a large ritual centre, with several temple-pyramids – some containing burials – on either side of a long rectangular plaza or ceremonial way. Surviving statues depict rulers with divine characteristics – some wear a bird mask. These, together with lavish elite burials, suggest that the Kaminaljuyú nobility ruled with absolute authority. Izapa – on the Pacific coastal plain below the Sierra Madre de Chiapas – underwent a great expansion: more than 250 stone stelae, altars and carved boulders were added in 300–50BC. The style of carving on these

stelae, which reveals some Olmec influence, would become highly influential, spreading as far to the east as the settlements of Belize and as far to the west as Tres Zapotes and Veracruz. Other expanding sites in the Pacific coastal region included Abaj Takalik, El Baúl, Monte Alto and Santa Leticia.

In the central Maya region, El Mirador was the largest city of this era, built *c*.150BC–AD150. It was at the hub of a system of causeways that linked it to several other cities, including Nakbé. Its central area was 2km (1⅕ miles) across and contained the vast El Tigre monument, which consists of a central pyramid with two smaller adjoining structures, all erected on a single base – and has a surface area six times larger than that of Temple IV, the largest building at nearby Tikal. Some historians believe that, alongside the settlement at Calakmul in the Campeche region of Mexico, El Mirador governed a state encompassing 10,000km (6,200 miles); monuments at Calakmul and El Mirador celebrated the same ancestral gods.

Tikal grew from a village in 300BC to a major dynastic city by AD300. Its oldest ceremonial structure, the North

Above: The Pyramid of the Moon, which is 46m (151ft) high, was built in Teotihuacán in the 1st century AD.

Acropolis, was begun *c*.250BC. The Mundo Perdido ('Lost World') complex was rebuilt many times up to AD300. A stela celebrating King Jaguar Paw I (*r*. AD278–317) erected in AD292 is the oldest known stela marked with a date in the Maya Long Count in the lowlands.

At Uaxactún, four temples were laid out according to precise astronomical alignment, in a pattern copied in many other cities, known to archaeologists as Group E. In this arrangement, three temples on the eastern side of a court were aligned so that at solstices and equinoxes the sun would rise above one of them when viewed from a fourth building erected to the west. Using these sightings, priests could keep precise track of time by pinpointing the year's shortest and longest days.

Río Azul in north-east Guatemala was established on the banks of the river Azul. Two temple platforms were built there in this era. In Belize, pyramids and plazas were laid out to celebrate the power of the king of Cerros beginning in 50BC.

THE GLORY OF TEOTIHUACÁN
AD300–500

Teotihuacán continued to expand in size and influence. Thousands of apartment buildings were constructed in the years AD300–500. They were built in compounds, each with room for 60–100 people, probably grouped by kin relationship or craft specialization. Elite dwellings alongside the Street of the Dead were built for higher social groups. The city reached its peak *c.*AD500, with a population of 125,000–200,000. This made it the sixth largest city in the world at the time.

GROWING SPHERE OF INFLUENCE
Some members of this vast population were incomers from other parts of Mesoamerica. One area in the north-eastern part of the city was dubbed the Merchants' Barrio by archaeologists because a large amount of pottery from other Mesoamerican regions was found there. Historians now believe that people from the Gulf coast and the central Maya region made their home there in the years AD300–500. Farther west, another part of the city was home to Zapotec incomers from the Oaxaca region.

Teotihuacán was a major religious centre, built on an ancient sacred site. More than 1,000 shrines and temples lined the Street of the Dead. A large number of full-time priests and temple staff must have resided in the city. Nevertheless, two-thirds of the population were farmers, primarily raising crops of amaranth, maize and squash. Some 9,700 hectares were irrigated, stretching to a distance of around 15km (9 miles) from the city centre. Many artisans and traders lived and worked in the city and its influence – so significant and far-reaching that one could almost speak of an empire – was spread by trade and exchange rather than by war or threat of military force.

The Maya city of Kaminaljuyú in the Guatemala Valley was drawn into Teotihuacán's sphere of influence through trade, probably in obsidian from the

Left: Clay figurines, such as this warrior, were used in religious rites in Teotihuacano homes.

Guatemalan site of El Chayal. In this period, Kaminaljuyú's ceremonial centre was remodelled in the *talud-tablero* (sloping apron/vertical panel) architectural style of Teotihuacán. There might even have been intermarriage between the elites of the two cities. Teotihuacán traders also established a centre at Matacapan in Veracruz in AD400–500.

Monte Albán also continued to thrive, and its population grew. Farmers began to specialize, promoting the growth of a market in agricultural goods. The Zapotecs established a sacred site at Mitla in the Oaxaca region after *c.*AD300. Its name comes from its Aztec Nahuatl name *Mictlan* ('Realm of the Dead').

CENTRAL MAYA REGION
In the central Maya region, the population reached a maximum of about a million by *c.*AD300, after 600 years of steady growth since 300BC. Tikal rose to a pre-eminent position, eclipsing the power of El Mirador.

Many buildings in the North Acropolis were built over earlier constructions between AD250 and AD550. The area was a necropolis celebrating the city's ruling dynasty: eight funerary temples were laid out in a symmetrical pattern on a vast platform of 80m (260ft) by 100m (320ft). Like the structures at Kaminaljuyú, Tikal's buildings show evidence of the influence of Teotihuacano *talud-tablero* architectural style.

A ruler named Yax Moch Xoc was afterwards celebrated at Tikal as the founder of this dynasty. He laid the foundations of Tikal's greatness by establishing the city as an independent ruling centre either through political acumen or military might. His early successors included Moon Zero Bird (whose accession *c.*AD320 and might are celebrated on the jadeite celt known to scholars as the Leyden plaque) and the great king Stormy Sky, whose mortuary shrine was built in Tikal's North Acropolis.

Lowland rivals Tikal and Uaxactún were drawn into increasingly fierce competition that culminated in AD378 when Tikal took control of its rival. A member of the Tikal dynastic elite named Smoking Frog – perhaps the brother of King Great Jaguar Paw – was either installed on the throne at Uaxactún or led a successful war against the city and seized power there. Two carved monuments at each site commemorate the event: bodies found in a tomb at Uaxactún near one of these monuments may be those of the Uaxactún king's family, buried there while the defeated king himself was taken to Tikal for ceremonial slaughter. In the reign of Smoking Frog's successor, Curl Nose, Tikal appears also to have conquered Río Azul c.AD385: altars at Río Azul commemorate the execution of eight local rulers, and Tikal kings are commemorated elsewhere at the site.

Tikal maintained close links to southern Mayan centres, notably Kaminaljuyú. The tomb of the Tikal king Curl Nose, who died c.AD425, contains offerings that prove links with elite burals at Kaminaljuyú. Some scholars have suggested that Curl Nose was a native of Kaminaljuyú who married into the ruling Tikal dynasty. By this route, the influence of Teotihuacán, which was strong at Kaminaljuyú, might have reached Tikal and can be seen in the style of carvings during the reigns of Curl Nose and his son and successor Stormy Sky.

Above: Monte Albán temples use a version of the talud-tablero *(sloping apron/vertical panel) design developed in Teotihuacán.*

Alternatively, there might have been direct trading contacts between Teotihuacán and Tikal. In Stormy Sky's reign, Tikal's power spread further still, to reach Yaxchilán, Quiriguá and even Copán in modern Honduras. A Tikal emblem was carved on a lintel at Yaxchilán c.AD504 and a style associated with Tikal appeared in the carving of monuments at both Copán and Quiriguá during this period.

SOUTHERN MAYA REGION

In the south-east Maya lowlands, Copán in western Honduras became a major centre in the 5th century AD. People had lived in villages in this fertile valley setting since c.1000BC, but the settlement began to expand significantly from c.AD250 onwards. The great dynasty of Copán was founded by Yax Kuk Mo' in AD426. In his reign, the first ritual and administrative buildings were erected at Copán.

Left: Tikal's North Acropolis is one of the city's oldest parts. The towering Temple I (right) was built in the 8th century AD.

POWER CHANGES HANDS
AD500–700

Teotihuacán continued to thrive until c.AD550–650, when its vibrant trading network began to fail in the face of competition from the east. In the period up to c.AD750, the city maintained a prosperous appearance, despite the fact that decline had set in. The palace of Quetzalpapálotl in the south-west of the Plaza of the Moon, was built after AD500 and the magnificent murals in the Techinantitla apartment building were painted c.AD650–750.

Monte Albán expanded greatly in the years AD500–750, covering 6.5km (4 miles) and supporting a population of as many as 24,000.

There were friendly relations between the Zapotec capital and Teotihuacán. Not only were Zapotecs resident in Teotihuacán but, according to carvings on stelae at the South Platform of the Main Plaza at Monte Albán, Teotihuacáno diplomats paid a state visit to the Oaxacan capital.

Below: The Palace of Quetzalpapálotl is an example of the high-status residential and public buildings that continued to be erected in Teotihuacán, despite the city's continuing decline.

Above: This figurine, found in Palenque, represents one of the members of the city's elite group of astronomer-priests.

CENTRAL MAYA REGION

Population of the Maya lowlands in AD500 was an estimated one million, but by c.AD600, numbers of people began to climb very significantly, reaching a peak c.AD800 of 2.6–3.4 million.

In the first part of this period Tikal continued to thrive. Its success throughout this early-to-mid Classic Period was derived partly from its position: the site was rich in the highly prized natural resource of flint (needed for making chipped stone tools), and lay close to two seasonal swamps or lakes that could be used for intensive farming. The swamps, situated to east and west, helped to make the site easily defensible in times of conflict. Close to rivers that connected it ultimately both to the Gulf and to the Caribbean, Tikal was ideally situated for trade and commerce.

The city appears to have had a vibrant society, with potential for upward movement through military or trading success and this probably helped to inspire its rise and expansion. Tikal was also a major religious centre and place of pilgrimage. It was, finally, one of the pioneers of dynastic kingship in the Maya world. When places such as Calakmul, Yaxchilán, Caracol and Copán were rising to prominence, Tikal was revered as a divinely inspired forerunner.

However, from c.AD530, Tikal's position was eclipsed by rivals for a period and its wealth declined severely for about 150 years. Following an attack on Caracol in AD556, in the reign of the Tikal king Double Bird, Tikal was defeated by its rival. A carved ball game marker at Caracol, which archaeologists used to believe was an altar and therefore labelled Altar 21, celebrates the victory of King Lord Water over Tikal in AD562. This probably led to the sacrifice of Double Bird. Tikal entered a period in which its royal burials were far less rich and no significant stelae were erected. The city might well have been diverting much of

Above: Caracol was a major Maya city in Belize. Its core contained 128 plaza groups; the site covered 50sq km (19sq miles).

its wealth to Caracol, which expanded greatly, and Tikal's rulers may have been forbidden by Caracol to erect any stelae.

Refugees from Tikal travelled southwards to the rainforested Petexbatun region close to a major tributary of the Usumacinta river named the Pasión river, where they founded twin capitals at Dos Pilas and Aguateca. The first ruler, Flint Sky, was in power in Dos Pilas in AD647. His emblem glyph was almost identical to that of the Tikal dynasty. Meanwhile, Calakmul in the south-eastern Campeche region of Mexico rose to prominence in the years after AD600 and was an ally of Caracol in wars in the Maya lowlands. With Calakmul's backing, Caracol defeated Naranjo in AD631. Calakmul also entered into alliance with Dos Pilas.

Dos Pilas went on to challenge the formerly mighty Tikal and fought several campaigns, culminating in the defeat of the Tikal ruler Shield Skull by Flint Sky of Dos Pilas in AD679. Flint Sky celebrated his victories in a hieroglyphic stairway at Dos Pilas. However, Tikal's pride was to be reborn. In AD695, King

Ah Cacau of Tikal captured and sacrificed Jaguar Paw-Jaguar of Calakmul. Meanwhile, in the south-western Maya lowlands, Palenque established itself as a major power and the dominant force in the region in the early 7th century AD. Inscriptions at the site provide a long dynastic list, going back as far as the probable founder, Balam Kuk, who came to the throne in AD431 and even further beyond to an assuredly mythical figure named Kin Chan, who was said to have come to the throne in 967BC. However, the city's great success coincided with the long and stable reign of King Pacal, whose splendid tomb would be laid beneath the Temple of Inscriptions in his city. Pacal came to the throne in AD615 and the earliest surviving use of the Palenque emblem glyph is dated to his reign.

SOUTHERN MAYA REGION
Kaminaljuyú thrived greatly by trade in obsidian, but began to decline after AD550, perhaps because the waning of Teotihuacán affected trade. The settlements of the Guatemala Valley became markedly less prosperous and were abandoned altogether by c.AD800, as their inhabitants retreated to more easily fortified and defended hilltop positions.

Copán greatly expanded its sphere of influence, particularly in the long reigns of Butz' Chan (AD578–628) and Smoke Jaguar (AD628–95). In this time of great dynastic strength and stability, Copán took control of Quiriguá in AD653 and of much of the valley of the Motagua river, and thus of the trade in jade and obsidian that travelled down that corridor from the highlands to the Caribbean sea.

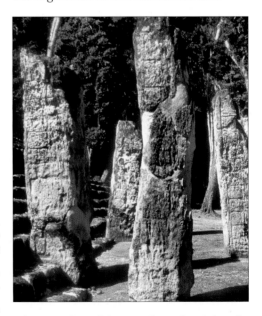

Above: Stelae celebrate rulers of Calakmul in south-eastern Campeche. Calakmul was at least as large as its famed rival Tikal.

49

THE COLLAPSE OF SOCIAL ORDER
AD700–900

In the years after AD700, Teotihuacán continued its slow collapse in prestige and power as the city's merchants endured the decay of the trade network that had once connected them to Veracruz, Tikal, the Guatemala Valley and beyond. After a fire c.AD750, the centre was abandoned, but about 40,000 people continued to live in outlying parts of the city. Monte Albán declined at the same time, beginning c.AD750, as the people of the Oaxaca valleys turned to local centres such as Lambityeco and Jalieza rather than the regional capital for the focus of their ritual life and work. Monte Albán's hilltop was abandoned and its population declined to about 4,000 by AD900.

The collapse of the centuries-old social order embodied by large centres such as Teotihuacán created a period of flux and of military conflict between small kingdoms. Peoples competed for trade and pre-eminence: many groups were on the move in the 7th, 8th and 9th centuries, leading to shifts in balance of

Below: Xochicalco and El Tajín were among the centres that rose to prominence with the decline of Teotihuacán and Monte Albán.

power and the emergence of new settlements. A Maya group named the Olmeca-Xicalanga travelled westwards from southern Veracruz and Tabasco to establish their capital in the fortress of Cacaxtla, on a hilltop dominating the Tlaxcala Valley, some time after AD650. The city, renowned for its murals, was at its peak until AD900. Settlements were established at Azcopatzalco, Cerro Portesuelo, Xico and Cerro de la Estrella in the Valley of Mexico.

To the south of the Valley of Mexico the fortified city of Xochicalco, in the western part of the Morelos region, won itself a regional state reaching west into the Balsas Depression, north into the Ajusco Mountains and south-west into the region known as Mixteca Baja. Xochicalco, although occupied in the previous centuries, was at its height in the years c.AD700–900.

In the tropical rainforest of northern Veracruz, El Tajín became an important centre. The site had been settled as early as c.AD100 and had thrived by contact with Teotihuacán: as Teotihuacáno influence waned, El Tajín began to assert its authority over its region. The same

Above: Carved columns on the roof of the Temple of the Warriors, Chichén Itzá, once supported the roof. The Castillo is beyond.

process – of increasing independence following the decline of Teotihuacán – applied to Cholula (in modern Puebla) and other city-states.

THE RISE OF THE ITZÁ
Other Maya groups known as the Chontal-speaking Maya, the Putún and the Itzá spread out from a base in the region of Chontalapa, in northern coastal Tabasco and south-western Campeche, at the western edge of the Yucatán peninsula. They were warrior-merchants, seeking political control and wealth through trade. Some established themselves at Palenque in the 7th to 9th centuries, others moved inland along the Usumacinta river to Yaxchilán, Altar de Sacrificios and Seibal. Putún Maya may have travelled into the southern Maya region along the upper reaches of the Usumacinta in the northern highlands.

The Itzá moved up the western coast of the Yucatán peninsula, then went inland towards the cities of Uxmal and Chichén Itzá. Most historians believe that the Itzá were established in Chichén Itzá by AD850. Inscriptions on important buildings at Chichén Itzá raised in the years AD869–81 praise an early Itzá leader named Kakupacal, who claimed to be related to the dynasty of Palenque.

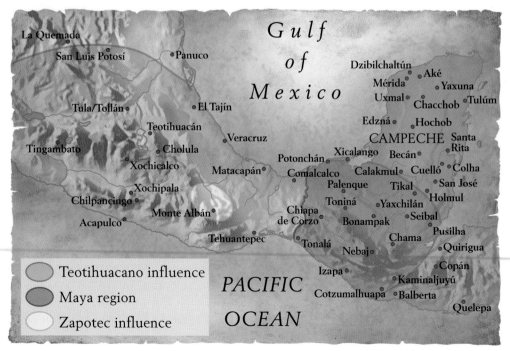

La Quemada
San Luis Potosí • • Panuco

Gulf of Mexico

Dzibilchaltún •
Mérida • • Aké
Uxmal • • Yaxuna
• Chacchob • Tulúm
Edzná • • Hochob

Tula/Tollán • • El Tajín
Teotihuacán •
Veracruz •
Tingambato • • Cholula
• Xochicalco
Matacapán •
Xochipala •
Chilpancingo •
Acapulco • Monte Albán •
Tehuantepec •

CAMPECHE Santa Rita
Xicalango • Becán •
Potonchán • Calakmul • Cuelló • Colha
Comalcalco • Palenque Tikal • San José
Toniná • • Holmul
Chiapa • Yaxchilán
de Corzo • Bonampak • Seibal
Tonalá • Chama Pusilha •
Nebaj • • Quirigua
Izapa • • Copán
Kaminaljuyú •
Cotzumalhuapá • Balberta
• Quelepa

Legend:
Teotihuacano influence
Maya region
Zapotec influence

PACIFIC OCEAN

CENTRAL MAYA REGION

In the Petexbatun region, Dos Pilas built a short-lived empire through warfare and diplomacy. After the death of the city's founder, Flint Sky, his son – known to historians as Shield God K – took power in AD698 and entered an alliance with Naranjo. His successor, who is known only as Ruler 3, defeated Seibal in AD735, made a marriage alliance with Cancuén and was also allied to the great power of Caracol. His successor, Ruler 4, extended the empire to cover *c.*4,000km (2,500 miles), but in AD761 he was captured and beheaded by a rival lord at Tamarindito. The power at the centre was gone and the area plunged into bitter conflict. Dos Pilas was largely abandoned after the AD761 war.

Palenque was at war with the city of Toniná in the Ocosingo Valley in the early 8th century. King Kan Xul II of Palenque was captured and beheaded by the ruler of Toniná in AD711.

In the Maya lowlands, Tikal enjoyed a great renaissance after more than 150 years in which it had erected no stelae and apparently suffered a severe decline in wealth. King Ah Cacau restored the city's military and political standing abroad by defeating the rival city of Calakmul and embarked on major building projects at home, including the erection of Temples I and II.

THE MAYA COLLAPSE

In the late 8th and 9th centuries the city-states of the Maya lowlands one by one stopped erecting stelae celebrating their divine kings. The cities fell into decline before being finally abandoned altogether. Historians believe that the decline was caused by a chain of events kick-started by overpopulation in the region, which led to ever more intensive farming and the degradation of the environment, matched by a fiercer form of warfare that focused less on raiding for prestige and more on territorial expansion. The result

was population decline – numbers in the southern lowlands fell by one-third in the century after AD830. Several sites – including Piedras Negras, Quiriguá, Naranjo and Calakmul – erected their last stela in AD810. The last carved stela was raised at Caracol in AD859 and at Tikal in AD869.

At Tikal, as at Dos Pilas and many other formerly magnificent centres, the cities were invaded by squatters who eked out a living in thatched homes on the great ceremonial plazas: they were not afraid to move monuments and even break into the tombs of once great kings in search of riches. However, this collapse

Above: A Cacaxtla mural figure showing a man transformed into a jaguar, c.*AD900.*

did not take effect farther east in coastal or riverside settlements in Belize, where Rita Caracol, Lamanai and other sites continued to thrive after AD900.

Quiriguá in the Motagua Valley had been subject to Copán since AD653, but rose to challenge its overlord. In AD738 Cauac Sky of Quiriguá beheaded King 18 Rabbit of Copán. In this way, Quiriguá gained control of the lucrative trade in obsidian, jade and other items passing from the Guatemalan highlands along the Motagua valley.

THE TRIUMPH OF THE TOLTECS
AD900–1200

The city of Tollán (modern Tula) in the state of Hidalgo took over from Teotihuacán as the pre-eminent centre of highland Mexico c.AD950. It stood on a ridge overlooking a tributary of the Pánuco river named the Tula, near to the northern limit of Mesoamerica. It ruled for more than 200 years.

HOME OF THE TOLTECS
The Aztecs and early chroniclers wove a web of religious narrative around the origins of this city, home to the Toltecs so revered by the México of Tenochtitlán and also to the great feathered serpent god, Quetzalcóatl. According to this narrative, Quetzalcóatl or Ce Acatl Topiltzin was the son of a leader of the Chichimec people, who left his home at

Below: Towering carved warriors facing west atop the Temple of Tlahuizcalpantecuhtli at Tollán (Tula) proclaim Toltec might.

Above: Each of the temple-top figures at Tollán (Tula) wears warrior garb: a butterfly breastplate and feathered headdress.

Culhuacán in the Valley of Mexico to assume leadership of the Toltec community of Tollán. Here he presided over a wondrous age of artistic expression and scientific achievement, but a Toltec named Huastec – in conjunction with Tezcatlipoca, god of darkness and fate – brought disgrace upon Ce Acatl Topiltzin, who departed from the city. Different versions recount that he either cast himself on a sacrificial pyre and rose into the heavens as the planet Venus or that he sailed away to the east on a raft of snakes, promising to return.

Historians do not know for sure who the Toltec founders of Tollán were. The evidence suggests that they were warlike incomers from the north.

The city they built covered 13sq km (8sq miles) and was home to a population of up to 60,000 people. It was a centre for craftspeople working obsidian, making pots, stoneware and tools from chert. The ritual centre – consisting of two plazas, two pyramids, meeting halls and two ball courts – was oriented precisely 18 degrees east of true north.

From Tollán the Toltecs exerted control over – and probably received tribute from – a sizeable area, incorporating the northern part of the Valley of Mexico, the region of modern Hidalgo state as far east as Tulancingo, plus the Toluca Valley, areas of the Bajío and territories around the Lerma River. The empire's days of glory were numbered, however, and the city was overrun and burned c.1150–1200.

In the period of Tollán's pre-eminence, the settlement of Cholula in the Puebla region of Mexico was also thriving. The town's wealth and prestige were such that its pyramid was rebuilt to a height of 55m (180ft). Historians are uncertain whether Cholula was a rival or an ally of Tollán.

CHICHÉN ITZÁ
Another legend concerning the Toltecs suggests that a group from Tollán led by Quetzalcóatl travelled to the Gulf Coast in the 10th century and then under the

Above: The six tiers and crowning temple of the Pyramid of the Niches, El Tajín, were built over a similar earlier version of the building.

leadership of Kukulcán (the Maya form of Quetzalcóatl) made their way to northern Yucatán, where they settled in Chichén Itzá. Many elements of Toltec/Mexican style in architecture and religious iconography appeared at Chichén Itzá; these were most likely spread through trade.

Chichén Itzá was by now the heart of a growing tributary empire. The Tutil Xiu, an Itzá elite and ruling dynasty, grew wealthy by trading in salt from the Yucatán salt beds, in obsidian, which they imported from Mexico, in ceramics and in basalt. They developed port facilities on Ilsa Cerritos, an island just off the northern coast of Yucatán. They ruled through a group of nobles rather than through a single, divinely blessed king. However, the Itzá apparently made many enemies, for native chronicles contain many slighting references to these successful incomers. Around 1100, the city of Mayapán was founded around 100km (80 miles) to the west of Chichén Itzá and quickly became its principal rival.

A NICHE IN VERACRUZ

El Tajín continued to thrive in northern Veracruz. Its six-tier Pyramid of the Niches is an elaborate variation on Teotihuacáno *talud-tablero* architectural style. The site also contains no fewer than 12 ball courts: the city may have been a centre for playing the game and could have hosted regional competitions. There is even the possibility that many centuries before El Tajín's independent glory, the ball game could have been developed in this part of Mesoamerica.

SOUTHERN MAYA LANDS

In the period of Chichén Itzá's glory, northern raiders appear to have brought terror to Southern Maya regions, where many settlements on valley floors were abandoned as people moved to easily defensible hilltop settings, and built ditches, walls and other fortifications. These incomers came either from northern Yucatán or from the Gulf Coast region of Chontalapa. They brought their architectural style and warrior imagery along with them.

A settlement at Chuitinamit-Atitlan on Lake Atitlan has a carving of a feathered serpent mouth opening to release human heads that is reminiscent of imagery at Chichén Itzá. Another at Chalchitan, on the Uscaminta tributary the Chixoy, contains a platform that may be a Chichén Itzá-style skull rack or *tzompantli*, on which skulls were displayed.

LAND RAIDERS
1200–1325

Tollán was sacked by raiders in c.1150–1200. The city's violent demise was followed by 150 years of turmoil in the central highlands of Mexico, as warring groups of nomads known collectively as Chichimecs ('Sons of the Dog') spread through the Valley of Mexico and beyond, scrambling for control of the strategic settlements and well-watered agricultural land. All claimed descent from the Toltecs and a link to the glory that had been Tollán.

RICH PICKINGS

One powerful Chichimec leader, Xólotl, founded the settlement of Tenayuca, to the west of Lake Texcoco, then later transferred his capital across the water to establish Texcoco. Another group, which claimed to have the closest links to the Toltecs, settled at Culhuacán, south of the lake. The Tepanecs settled at Azcapotzalco, which had been founded towards the end of Teotihuacán's era of

Below: The fortress-town of Tulum, above the Caribbean Sea, was protected by cliffs and an 800m (half-mile) wall.

Above: Five circular platforms supported temples and might have housed elite burials in the Tarascan capital, Tzintzuntzan.

glory c.AD800–900. Lands all around Lake Texcoco were settled by Chichimecs and descendants of survivors from the fall of Teotihuacán and Tollán: towards the northern end were Tenayuca and Azcapotzalco; to the east lay Huextola and Coatlichan; to the south was Chalco, Cuitláhauc, Xochimilco, Xico, Mixquic

and Amecameca as well as Culhuacán. A tribe calling themselves the México, who were destined to establish the Aztec empire, came into the region after all the best land had been taken, probably towards the end of the 13th century.

THE FIRST AZTECS

Historians cannot easily supply an accurate account of the early years of the tribe, for the México/Aztecs later embellished their history in an attempt to justify their standing and to emphasize their links to the Toltecs of yore. It appears that they came into the region under the leadership of Tenoch, and settled near Chapultepec to the west of Lake Texcoco. When they were attacked by the Tepanecs of Azcapotzalco and the people of Culhuacán, the México cast themselves upon the mercy of Culhuacán. They settled nearby at a place named Tizapán and proved themselves capable agriculturists, adapting swiftly to the lakeside setting. They married into local families

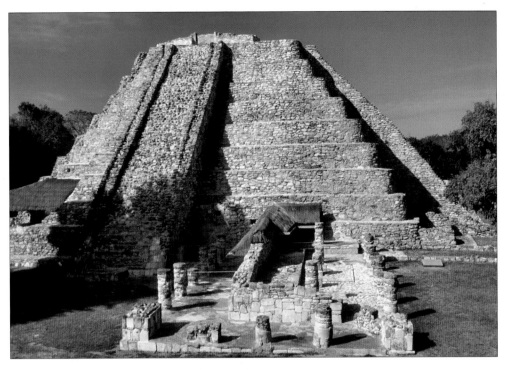

and began to call themselves the México-Culhua. They fought alongside the Culhua against Xochimilco and also served the Tepanecs of Azcapotzalco. Then, after a dramatic dispute with the leaders of Culhuacán – in one account after they sacrificed the daughter of a leading Culhua lord – they moved on to the south and established their own city, named Tenochtitlán in Tenoch's honour, on an island in Lake Texcoco. This probably occurred in 1325. Tenoch was the first leader of Tenochtitlán, and was celebrated as *tlatoani* ('He who Speaks'), the title given to the ruler of the city, until the collapse of the Aztec empire in 1521.

POWER STRUGGLE IN YUCATÁN

The Tutul Xiu rulers of Chichén Itzá were driven from power in the 13th century by the Cocoms, a rival group of Itzá from Mayapán. According to the chronicles, the Cocoms hired a mercenary named Hunac Ceel from Tabasco who, by trickery and military force, forced the

Below: This haunting shell carving was made by a craftsman from Mayapán, rising power and controller of coastal trade.

Tutul Xiu from power and seized control of the city. The chronicles set these events *c.*1221 or 1283. There is archaeological evidence that Chichén Itzá was sacked in the early 13th century, but there are also signs that it was gradually abandoned. The Tutul Xiu might have been unable to maintain the elite that gathered around them and the city may also have suffered from drought and starvation.

Whether gradually or at a stroke, Mayapán became the major city of the area and took control of the lucrative coastal trade. It founded a league of city-states in northern Yucatán – itself, Chichén Itzá and Uxmal – that built a tributary empire. In the new capital at Mayapán, the Cocom built a smaller-scale version of the magnificent Temple of Kukulcán at Chichén Itzá. Mayapán was a city of around 15,000 people at its height. As a way of maintaining central authority, the Cocom rulers brought in the heads of tributary-paying states to reside in the capital city, as the Aztecs would later do.

On the east coast of Yucatán the fortified clifftop settlement at Tulum was established *c.*1200, probably by the rulers of Mayapán, as a coastal trading centre. At Tulum, and nearby Xelhá and Tancah, on the Isla de Cozumel, and farther south on the east coast of Yucatán, several settlements grew prosperous under the rule of the Mayapán alliance.

Above: Mayapán's principal sacred building is the nine-tiered Temple of the Feathered Serpent, now called Kukulcán's Castle.

Some of the survivors of the fall of Chichén Itzá headed south into the rain forests of El Petén and founded a new capital called Tayasal on Lake Petén Itzá in north-western Guatemala. There they would thrive until 1697, when they were finally conquered by the Spanish.

HIGHLAND KINGDOMS

In southern Maya lands, another wave of 'Mexicanized' Putún Maya warriors established kingdoms in the highlands. They arrived from the Gulf Coast lowlands *c.*1200 and set up mountain-top fortresses from which they brutally subjugated the local people. By *c.*1350, one group, the Quiché, had established rule over the central highlands. They established their capital, Ismachi, on a narrow piece of land between two ravines.

THE TARASCANS AND TZINTZUNTZAN

At Lake Patzcuaro in Michoacán four communities were established by *c.*1200: Tzintzuntzan, Ihuatzio, Pátzcuaro and the island settlement of Pacanda. The king of Tzintzuntzan, Tariácuri, took control of the four local powers and set out to forge an empire. This Tarascan kingdom became an arch rival of the México/Aztecs.

THE MÉXICA FORGE AN EMPIRE
1325–1517

On Lake Texcoco, the México/Aztecs founded a second settlement, named Tlatelolco, on a nearby island in 1358. They won acclaim as mercenaries, fighting for Tezozómoc, the Tepanec leader of Azcapotzalco, in wars against Texcoco and Culhuacán, as he built up a great empire.

The México/Aztecs expanded their territorial holdings by gaining *chinampa* agricultural fields in the region of Lake Xochimilco, to the south of Lake Texcoco. However, they came increasingly to resent their subject position and the Tepanecs warily watched their neighbours straining at the leash.

Below: The Selden Codex, *probably written in the Nochixtlán valley, Oaxaca, contains Mixtec genealogies covering* AD794–1556.

In 1428, following the death of Tezozómoc, the México/Aztecs rose up in alliance with Texcoco and Tlacopán to defeat the might of Azcapotzalco. The victorious members of this Triple Alliance divided the Tepanec empire three ways. Tenochtitlán took land to the north and south of Lake Texcoco. Land to the east went to Texcoco and territories in the western part of the Valley of Mexico went to Tlacopán. The Triple Alliance held sway over the Valley of Mexico and beyond until the arrival of the Spanish in the early 16th century. It was the basis of the Aztec empire.

The Aztec *tlatoani* Moctezuma I (*r.* 1440–69) led a great campaign of expansion, extending territorial holdings as far as the Gulf Coast. His successor and

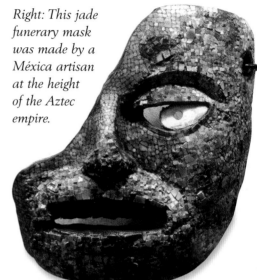

Right: This jade funerary mask was made by a México artisan at the height of the Aztec empire.

grandson Axayácatl (*r.* 1469–81) led campaigns towards the west but was defeated by the Tarascans of Tzintzuntzan, and towards the east where he established control in central parts of Veracruz. He also took control of neighbouring Tlatelolco for Tenochtitlán in 1473. After Axayácatl was succeeded briefly by his undistinguished brother, Tízoc (*r.* 1481–6), a third of Moctezuma's grandsons, Ahuítzotl (*r.* 1486–1502), took power. He gained control over the basin of the Balsas river and coastal lands in Guerrero, as well as much of the Isthmus of Tehauntepec. After several attempts, the Aztecs conquered the sacred site of Mitla, in the Oaxaca region in 1494, and forced the Mixtec residents to pay tribute to Tenochtitlán. Under Moctezuma II in 1519, Aztec imperial holdings covered 150,000sq km (58,000sq miles).

POWER SHIFT IN YUCATÁN
Mayapán was sacked and burned *c.*1450. The nobles of the Tutul Xiu dynasty ousted at Chichén Itzá in the early 13th century had been living in exile among the ruins of Uxmal, a site sacred to them. One of their number, Ah Xupán, led a rebellion against Mayapán's ruling Cocom elite, slaughtering all of the city's rulers bar one, who was on a trading mission.

Above: A coatepantli ('serpent wall') encloses three sides of the Aztec pyramid at Tenayuca, near modern Tlalnepantla in Mexico City.

Most of the larger cities of northern Yucatán entered a decline following the fall of Mayapán. Survivors established new cities: one noble family, the Chels, founded Tecoh; the one surviving Cocom ruler made a new start at Tibolon, close to Sotuta. And the Tutul Xiu, glorying in revenge, founded a new settlement at Mani.

In this period, Chichén Itzá and Uxmal were pilgrimage sites, often visited as shrines. Times were hard in northern Yucatán. A hurricane struck in 1464 and the people were severely reduced by a plague in 1480. This was followed by an epidemic of smallpox in 1514.

In the wake of Mayapán's collapse, a settlement was founded at Santa Rita Corozal on the eastern coast at Chetumal Bay. Known as Chetumal, the city was the capital of a state of the same name. Chetumal/Santa Rita Corozal and other settlements in coastal regions of eastern Yucatán continued to thrive until the arrival of the Spanish in the 16th century.

At Tulum and Santa Rita Corozal, delicately rendered murals were painted in the second half of the 15th century in the Mixteca-Puebla style familiar from centres in Puebla and Oaxaca, such as Mitla. A wealthy elite in eastern Yucatán was rich enough to be able to pay for renowned artists from Mexico to produce these splendid wall paintings.

SOUTHERN MAYA LANDS

The Quiché abandoned their capital of Ismachi and founded another, Gumarcaaj or Utatlan, in the early 1400s. They subjugated other peoples and established a Quiché realm, but in 1470 one of these peoples, the Cakchiquels, rebelled and created a rival state. They set up their own capital at Iximche. The two groups fought fiercely. The Cakchiquels held the ascendancy when the Spanish arrived in the region. Other highland city-states included one established by the Pokomam, with a capital at Mixco Viejo; one built by the Mam, with a stronghold at Zaculeu; and the territory of the Tzutuhil at Atitlan, on Lake Atitlan. All these peoples claimed to be descended from the Toltecs.

WESTERN MEXICO

In Michoacán, the small empire of the Tarascans, based at Tzintzuntzan on Lake Pátzcuaro, was strong. They succeeded in holding the Aztecs at bay. Neither the efforts of Moctezuma I nor the expansionist campaigns of Itzcóatl succeeded in bringing the Tarascans into the Aztec empire. The Tarascan army maintained tight control over a small area in the basin of Lake Pátzcuaro within the boundaries of the modern state of Michoacán.

Below: The Mixtecs, Zapotecs, Totonacs and Huastecs were within the Aztec empire, but the Tarascans held imperial forces at bay.

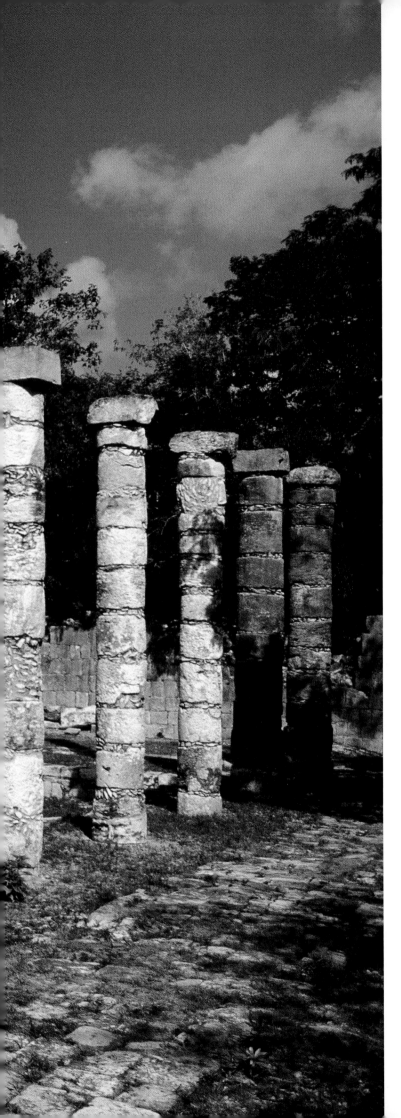

CHAPTER THREE

INFINITE RICHES

All principal Aztec towns in the Valley of Mexico contained a bustling marketplace, located close to the main temple. Merchants were required by law to take their goods to this commercial centre and were forbidden to attempt to sell elsewhere – buyers and sellers risked incurring the wrath of the market god if they did business away from the official place of commerce. On a busy day, 60,000 people might be crammed in the Aztec empire's marketplace in Tlatelolco, Tenochtitlán's twin settlement in Lake Texcoco – making it the largest market in the world at the time. The Aztecs relied on trade – and on goods from an extensive network of tribute-paying areas within the empire – to provide them with foodstuffs, military equipment and other necessaries and with the rare and exotic goods used in their colourful religious ceremonies.

Long-distance trade was a key element of Mesoamerican life, with beginnings in the Olmec civilization of the 2nd millennium BC. Throughout the region's history, trade links between far-flung communities provided conduits along which religious practices, political ideas and artistic styles could pass. Trade was an alternative to warfare as a means of spreading dynastic and political influence, so much so that it is often difficult to establish whether architectural features or religious imagery from the city of Teotihuacán, for example, reached Guatemalan sites such as Kaminaljuyú and Tikal through conquest or trade.

Left: These columns, carved in the Toltec style, stand in the area of Chichén Itzá believed to have been the marketplace.

FIRST TRADERS

Trade flourished in Mesoamerica from early times because of the region's great geographic diversity across relatively short distances. The wide variety of terrain, soil and climate – from tropical jungle to river valley, coastal estuary to highland lake – meant that materials could be found and items manufactured in one setting that were much in demand in a nearby region. Trade networks were established by at least the 2nd millennium BC; they might have grown from a pattern of exchange and gift-giving between elite groups at different sites.

FIRST SETTLEMENTS

The first large Mesoamerican settlements arose in the Gulf Coast lowlands because the productive coastal land allowed its Olmec settlers to produce agricultural surpluses. Elite groups emerged with the power and resources to construct ceremonial and ritual centres. They were also well situated to import raw materials from highland areas inland. At San Lorenzo, on a plateau raised around 50m (164ft) above the surrounding land, settlers built a ritual centre after c.1250BC.

Below: Trade promoted political contact. This Olmec carving from La Venta is thought to be of a visiting ambassador.

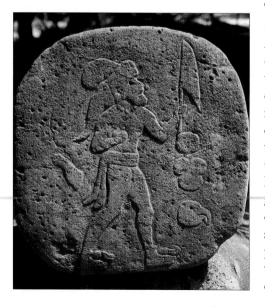

Using earth and coloured clay, labourers erected platform mounds around rectangular courts arranged on a north–south axis, but oriented 8 degrees west of true north. They arranged colossal carved stone heads and altars or thrones in the ritual centre.

The basalt for these sculptures was imported from the Tuxtla mountains 70km (40 miles) away; the blocks were carved at the mountains and then floated on rafts by sea and up the Coatzacoalco river to San Lorenzo. Historians believe that the heads were images of Olmec rulers and the large 'altars' were their thrones. A remarkable buried basalt drain was 170m (550ft) long and with three branches, connected to fountains and ponds, which might have been used either functionally or in religious ceremony.

TRADING NETWORKS

The Olmec established centres – such as Chalcatzingo in the valley of the Amatzinac and Teopantecuanitlán rivers close to the Amacuzac river – to trade with and exploit the resources of less developed local cultures. Olmec trading networks extended over very long distances – there is evidence of contact with the valley of the Motagua river in Guatemala and as far as Chalchuapa in El Salvador. The networks distributed goods manufactured in the large Olmec centres in return for minerals and rare stones. In this period the Olmec were probably importing obsidian from or through the village of Coapexco. This clung to the side of the Ixtaccíhuatl

Left: Demand for elite goods propelled the growth of trade. This mask of c.AD200 is made of precious jade.

volcano at a height of 2,600m (8,500ft) and seems to have been a centre for trading in or manufacturing blades of obsidian. Archaeologists have found Olmec pots, grinding tools, ritual figurines and stamps at the site, but they cannot be sure whether these finds are evidence of Olmec trade with local people or of communities of Olmec living in Coapexco.

At Tlatilco on the western shore of Lake Texcoco, people buried their dead with Olmec pots and clay figurines. Here and elsewhere in Oaxaca and Puebla large numbers of Olmec 'dolls' – small hollow clay figures with chubby, outspread legs and baby faces – were collected. Las Bocas in Puebla has yielded a number of these baby figurines and it must have had significant contact with Olmec traders.

TRADING CENTRES

In the Morelos region, Chalcatzingo grew wealthy as a trading centre. The village lies in the valley of the River Amatzinac at the foot of a cliff and would have been well situated as a centre for three trade routes: one heading north to the Valley of Mexico, one going south towards Guerrero and a third running south-east to the Olmec region of the Gulf Coast and the Zapotec sites of Oaxaca. From the Amatzinac valley came cotton, hematite, lime and kaolin; from the region of the Valley of Mexico traders arrived carrying salt and obsidian; while from

Above: Zapotec artists painted this mural in Tomb 105, one of the best-preserved tombs in Monte Albán, c.AD200.

Guerrero merchants came bearing loads of hematite, jadeite and magnetite. Before 1100BC, Chalcatzingo was equipped with a stone-paved public area and two stone-covered platforms about 2m (7ft) in height. Olmec-style monuments were carved in the period 1100–700BC. One, called El Rey by archaeologists, depicts a king or ruler seated in the mouth of a monster that experts identify as the entrance to the underworld; above him are carved rain clouds and three descending raindrops identified as a symbol of authority. This image presents the king as the link between the underworld and the heavens of the rain clouds, like the cosmic tree or world axis. In his person he ensured fertility (rain) and order.

In 700–500BC, Chalcatzingo rose to its highest point of prestige. Many monuments were carved in the style of the Olmec centre at La Venta, which was also then at its peak. The elite rulers of Chalcatzingo, who may have been merchants themselves,

established trading contact with La Venta and elsewhere on the Gulf Coast, with Monte Albán and other Oaxacan sites and with Izapa, far away on the Pacific coastal plain of south-east Mexico.

Another major trading centre of the Olmec era lay in the Guerrero region at Teopantecuanitlán. The site was linked to Chalcatzingo by the Cuautla and Amacuzac rivers, and itself provided

access to the great Balsas river, which could carry loads all the way to the Pacific Ocean. Trading in precious stones, tin, copper and highly prized jade from Guerrero, Teopantecuanitlán became a major centre by 600BC. A pyramid and two ball courts were built and finds of marine shells there suggest that the town was linked to marine trading networks.

In Oaxaca, San José Mogote and other developing villages were trading with San Lorenzo from c.1150BC onwards. Two main lineages or family groups grew prominent, both associated with Olmec motifs. One was linked to the image of the jaguar-faced human or were-jaguar, thought by scholars to represent the earth, while the second was connected to a fire-serpent image thought to be the sign for lightning.

San José Mogote became a great craft centre, with craftsmen housed in one of the four quarters of the settlement according to their speciality.

Left: Spring god Xipe Totec, represented in this Zapotec brazier, may have derived from an Olmec deity known as God VI.

A CITY OF MERCHANTS

The great city of Teotihuacán was a beacon for merchants. It was a major centre for Mesoamerican trade in obsidian, the volcanic glass. This was in demand because craftsmen could fashion it into mirrors, dart-tips for weapons and cutting edges used both in everyday activities and in sacred ritual for letting blood and dispatching sacrificial victims.

Teotihuacán grew up on an ancient site of pilgrimage, and could support a rising population because its position on the San Juan Teotihuacán river made irrigation of farm fields easy. It thrived because it was close to sources of obsidian and because it lay on a major trade route running from the Valley of Mexico to the Gulf Coast.

OBSIDIAN AND OTHER GOODS
In the city's workshops, workers manufactured stone masks, ceremonial tripod vessels, obsidian blades, household furnishings, clay figurines, stone and basalt tools, stonework in shell, serpentine and jade, domestic pots and ornaments of slate. Merchants sold a range of manufactured goods to the large population or organized their export far and wide. Teotihuacáno interests also controlled a

Below: Teotihuacán was renowned from ancient times as a sacred site as well as a major trade centre.

Right: Quetzalcóatl's head adorns the staircase of the Temple of Quetzalcóatl at Teotihuacán.

major obsidian-processing site at Tepeapulco, to the north-east of the city. Obsidian forms when igneous volcanic flow cools rapidly and is only found in highland areas with active volcanoes. The glass appears black, but when some varieties are fashioned into flakes or a transparent edge, the colours grey and green are visible. Minerals in the molten matrix can also produce green obsidian, and because this form was much rarer in Mesoamerica than black-grey obsidian it was consequently much more highly valued. Near Teotihuacán, there was only one source of green obsidian, Cerro de las Navajas at Puchuca, in modern Hidalgo state, but there were at least 15 sources of black and grey obsidian.

By performing trace-element analysis, geochemists have established the source of the obsidian worked in or around Teotihuacán. In workshops at Tepeapulco, workers manufactured items from obsidian which were delivered by footpath from sources at Cerro de las Navajas, at Tulancingo, Paredón and Barrance de los Estetes. From here blades, darts, sacrificial knives and other artefacts were transported to Tulancingo in the Metztitlán Valley and from there to sites such as El Tajín.

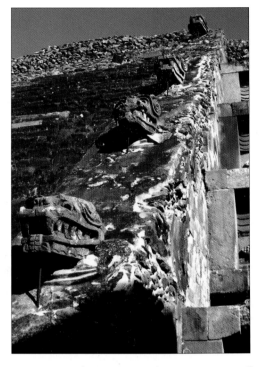

Tepeapulco was the centre of Teotihuacán's obsidian industry, but there were also obsidian craftsmen within the city. One group near the Great Compound, for example, specialized in working high-status green obsidian.

Teotihuacán also controlled trade in and distribution of fine-paste pottery bowls and effigy jars known to archaeologists as thin orange pottery. As many as eight settlements in the region of Tepexi, in Puebla state, specialized in the manufacture of these pots, which were distributed far and wide via Teotihuacán.

Teotihuacán's marketplace was probably situated in the Great Compound, on the opposite side of the Street of the Dead from the Ciudadela or Citadel in the centre of the city. Here merchants from near and far dealt in locally manufactured and imported goods, as well as raw materials such as marine shells, rubber, luxury feathers, cotton, magnetite, hematite and chert.

Groups of foreign merchants made their homes in this great metropolis. One part of the city has been dubbed the Merchants' Barrio by archaeologists, who found large amounts of pottery there from Veracruz and from Maya lands in northern Belize and the Yucatán peninsula. Another quarter was home to merchants from Oaxaca, who built tombs modelled exactly on those in their ancestral home of Monte Albán.

THE TRADE ROUTE

A major trade route, dubbed the Teotihuacán corridor by historians, connected the city to markets and sources of raw materials to the east and south. It left the city via its East Avenue and headed to Calpulalpán, in Tlaxcala, then south-east to Huamantla. Two branches left Huamantla, one heading east to Veracruz and the second turning south by way of Teotihuacán. On the route, passes and gateways allowed officials to regulate the movement of raw materials into Teotihuacán and manufactured artefacts on the way out of the city.

Farther afield, Teotihuacán set up a trading centre in Matacapán, situated in fertile land in southern Veracruz between the volcano of San Martin Tuxtla and the waters of Lake Catemaco. It was close to the coast and to rivers leading inland,and might well have controlled trade by sea for Teotihuacáno merchants. Matacapán, a source of kaolin, became a major production centre for fine paste pottery. Artisans also made elite products of the kind made in the 'mother city' of Teotihuacán. They lived in an apartment compound of the sort built in Teotihuacán. Farther south, Teotihuacán had prolonged trading and diplomatic links with Monte Albán in Oaxaca. Carvings at Monte Albán, including four stelae erected around the Main Plaza's South Platform, depict figures that scholars interpret as a record of peaceful visits by high-ranking Teotihuacános.

Teotihuacán had trading contacts as far afield as Kaminaljuyú in the Guatemala Valley and Tikal in the central Maya region. Archaeological evidence suggests

Right: This evocative Teotihuacano mask has survived intact with its mould.

that traders from Teotihuacán may have become well established in an enclave at Kaminaljuyú. Some scholars have suggested that Teotihuacán used force against Kaminaljuyú, which sat on a trade route for valuable cacao beans and was situated close to a major source of obsidian. Perhaps the Teotihuacános attempted to gain a monopoly over mining and distribution of obsidian. A central area of Kaminaljuyú was reconstructed in Teotihuacáno architectural style.

Settlements to the west of Kaminaljuyú on the Pacific coastal plain probably also had close links with Teotihuacán in the cacao trade and may have been home to Teotihuacáno merchants. One settlement produced Teotihuacán-style ceramic ritual vessels. There was probably also direct trading contract between Teotihuacán and Tikal. After Tikal's victory over Uaxactún in AD378, the Maya of Tikal adopted the style of warrior-costume associated with Teotihuacán, and began to plan battle campaigns according to the cycle of Venus, following the Teotihuacáno tradition.

In other directions, Teotihuacán dominated the Valley of Mexico to the south-west, while to north and west the city's interests were confined to sourcing raw materials. Far to the north-west, the city established a settlement at Alta Vista, in the modern state of Zacatecas, to exploit its sources of jadeite, turquoise and precious green stones, flint, chert, hematite and malachite. The raw materials were taken back by porters to be worked in the city's workshops.

TRADING OVER GREAT DISTANCES

The pattern of long-distance trading established by the Olmecs and Teotihuacános continued into the era of the Aztecs. Throughout this vast time span, trade and exchange networks were also vibrant over small distances within the many regions of Mesoamerica. Short-range trade tended to be in foodstuffs and other everyday commodities such as clothing and household pottery, while long-range trade was in rare commodities highly prized for their use in religious ritual or as status symbols by members of the elite. Quetzal feathers – used in priestly and royal costumes – jaguar skins and sacred greenstones used for divine effigies and masks all commanded a high value at market.

MAYA CONNECTIONS

The Maya, who were in the path between the markets and raw materials of Central America and Mexican sites such as San Lorenzo, Teotihuacán, El Tajín or Tenochtitlán, played a crucial role in long-distance trade connections. Maya lands were also sources of prized commodities. Quetzal feathers, jadeite, serpentine, pyrite and obsidian were exported from the southern Maya highlands. Jaguar skins and teeth, valued for use in royal ceremonial, were exported from the lowlands of the central Maya region, together with parrot and macaw feathers. From coastal areas of the southern Maya region came sharks' teeth, coral, shells and sting-ray spines used for bloodletting in rites of autosacrifice, as well as cacao. Salt was traded from the coasts of Yucatán.

Below: Tarascan artisans made these lip ornaments from gold, obsidian and turquoise before 1500.

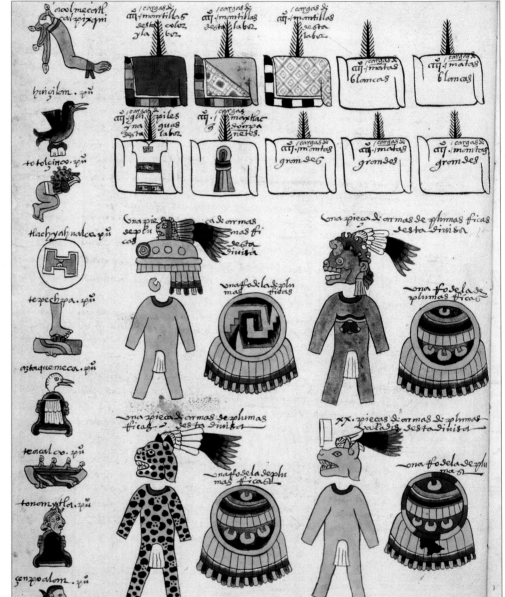

Above: Many goods travelled long distances on the Aztec tribute network. This codex page lists tribute from 16 imperial towns.

Merchants were trading over long distances from the central Maya region by at least 300BC. There were three principal routes through Maya lands. The northern way ran along the coast of Yucatán, the central route followed tracks and waterways through the lowlands of El Petén and the southern route came down the coastal plain adjoining the Pacific Ocean. Some traders followed the Usumacinta, Pasíon, Chixoy and other rivers southwards into the southern Maya highlands, and they were able to make their way through to the Motagua Valley and its path to the Gulf of Honduras. Within Maya territories, trade routes linked the northern parts of Yucatán with their salt industry and with the southern regions that were the important source of obsidian and quetzal feathers.

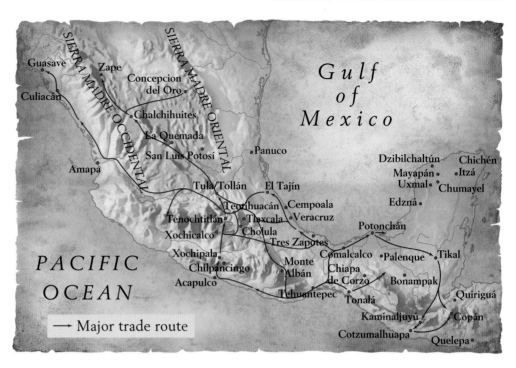

Goods were laboriously transported by porters. Mesoamericans certainly knew how to make wheels, for they left wheeled toys in tombs, but they did not make wheeled vehicles for transport. In part this was because they lacked large traction animals but, in addition, many parts of Mesoamerica were unsuited to wheeled transport and more easily traversed on foot or by boat. A porter secured a load around his head or chest using rope and often travelled in convoy with several colleagues. In Aztec times the maximum load permitted was about 22kg (50lb) per person. Goods were also packed in great canoes and taken to sea or along rivers.

NORTHERN TRADE
In the north of Mexico, La Quemada (in modern Zacatecas state) lay in a good position for north–south trade, including turquoise from what is now the US state of New Mexico, and throve throughout the Classic Period until c.AD850. It is part of the Chalchihuite culture, whose remains provide early evidence of religious and military iconography (skull racks, *chacmools* and symbols of the god of the north, darkness and fate, Tezcatlipoca), which would become very important in Aztec times. In the far north, Casas Grandes, in modern Chihuahua state, was a major centre from c.1050, part of an important trading network linking Mesoamerica to sites in the south-west USA. Marine trade across the Caribbean also linked the islands and the south-east USA.

AZTEC TRADE ROUTES
In Aztec times, merchants doubtless operated from Tenochtitlán to the north, in the modern states of Zacatecas and Durango, and to the north-west in Querataro and Hidalgo, but historians know more about trade towards the

Right: Chachihuite settlements in northern Mexico combined fortified trading sites with farming villages and religious centres.

south. Routes from Tenochtitlán led down to Tuxtepec, where they divided, with one path leading into Oaxaca and on into the Isthmus of Tehuantepec and Soconusco, and one leading to the coast of the Gulf of Mexico and the towns of Coatzacoalco and, inland a little way, Cimatan.

From Cimatan traders could follow the River Grijalva into the Chiapas Highlands, where amber was to be found, or travel east into the region of Chontalapa, where there were no fewer than 25 Aztec trading posts with warehouses to store goods.

Beyond, on the Gulf coast, the port of Xicalango at the western edge of the Laguna de Terminos was almost certainly an Aztec trading centre, although it was peopled by Chontal-speaking Maya. From Xicalango, merchants could follow tracks

Above: Wherever possible, traders chose to follow low-lying routes through river valleys or along coastal plains.

and waterways down to the forests of El Petén in the central Maya region and beyond to trading posts on the coast of the Caribbean Sea.

From Tenochtitlán, merchants exported luxury goods manufactured in the imperial capital from raw materials brought in by trade or as tribute from subject regions of the empire, as well as obsidian, bells and ornaments of copper, combs and herbs. Slaves were also exported to areas needing cheap labour such as cacao plantations on the coasts of the Gulf, the Pacific and the Caribbean. They imported cacao, gold, animal skins, precious stones and brightly coloured feathers.

BY CANOE AND PADDLE

In the 10th century, the powerful merchants of Chichén Itzá built a trading post on Isla Cerritos, a small island just off the coast of northern Yucatán and about 90km (55 miles) from their capital city. They built or improved existing piers and docks, together with a 330m (1,000ft) sea wall to guarantee calm waters for unloading from large seagoing canoes. These vessels, recently developed, transformed seagoing trade. At 15m (50ft) long and 2m (6ft 6in) wide, they were far bigger than earlier canoes and able to voyage into far rougher waters.

SEA TRADE

Through Isla Cerritos, Chichén Itzá imported basalt from Belize, gold jewellery from Central America, pottery from Guatemala and obsidian from sites in Mexico. Itzá sea traders travelled as far as the ports of Naco and Nito in Honduras.

Coastal settlements were probably operated in this way as trading posts for powerful inland cities or states throughout Mesoamerican history. For example, Cerros, on a peninsula of coastal Belize

Below: Caribbean waves wash the shore by the trading centre of Cozumel. Goats were traded by canoe along the coast and among offshore islands.

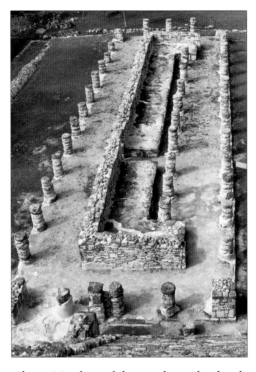

Above: Members of the merchant elite lived in the Palace of the Kings, a sumptuous residence in the trading city of Mayapán.

that projects into Chetumal Bay, was transformed from a small village into a significant settlement with large pyramids, public buildings and platforms in the period 50BC–AD100, probably at the behest of an inland centre seeking an outlet into the Caribbean Sea. The style

and appearance of the stucco deity-masks on these buildings suggest links to nearby Lamanai or, farther afield, to Tikal. Archaeological evidence has led historians to suggest that Cerros operated in tandem with Komchen, far away in northern Yucatán, as a trading partner, probably in the movement of salt from the northern region. Jade and obsidian from the southern Maya region were also traded at Cerros.

Mesoamericans carried on sea trade from earliest times. The peoples of western Mexico were in contact along the Pacific coast with tribes in Ecuador as early as 1500BC – as suggested by the appearance of Ecuadorian-style chamber tombs. In the Olmec centre at Teopantecuanitlán, in the Guerrero region, a workshop produced elite items using marine shells from distant points on the Pacific Coast.

TRADING POSTS

Many sites along the coasts of the Yucatán peninsula and Belize thrived through seagoing trade for many centuries. Jaina Island, the settlement off the west coast of the peninsula celebrated for its cemetery and the clay figures left in its graves, was a thriving trading and fishing port for at least 700 years. Tancah, a fortified town on the eastern coast of northern Yucatán,

Above: The elite of Yucatán combined warfare with trade. This is a mural in the Temple of the Warriors in Chichén Itzá.

appears to have been a centre for trade in the *Strombus gigas*, a type of conch shell used in religious ritual from at least the time of Teotihuacán, where the shells are depicted in murals. Tancah was a trading post from the last centuries BC onwards, handling obsidian, jade, pyrite, granite and slate vessels exported from the Maya cities of the Puuc region inland. The neighbouring coastal settlement of Xelha was a port for the inland city of Cobá from at least the 10th century. A *sacbé* or raised causeway left the main square of Xelha and ran inland to Cobá.

CONTROL OF SEA TRADE

Around 6km (3½ miles) south along the coast lay Tulum, which was founded on the cliff top overlooking the Caribbean Sea in 1200 at a time when maritime commerce was a source of great wealth and prestige for the merchants of the northern Yucatán peninsula.

A cliff-top beacon guided sailors through a gap in the reef that runs parallel to the shore and on to a safe landing on the beach beneath the town. At this time, the cities of the League of

Mayapán – Mayapán, Uxmal and a Chichén Itzá much reduced from its former independent glory – had control of seagoing trade, and probably built Tulum.

The League's merchant elite also maintained an offshore trading centre on the Isle of Cozumel, a little further north opposite the mainland settlement of Xcaret. On Cozumel, large platforms right across the island were used as seasonal stores for products such as honey, cacao and salt. The island traded all year in obsidian and building stone. The western part of Cozumel was the site of one of the region's most important religious shrines, to the Maya Moon Goddess Ix Chel.

Below: Lying in the sacred east, Tulum – together with Xelhá and Tancah – was a religious as well as a trading site. This structure is a clifftop temple to the wind god.

TRADERS, SPIES, PROTECTORS

Long-range trade in the Aztec empire was handled by professional merchants called *pochteca*. Working both on their own behalf and as emissaries of rulers and members of the nobility, they specialized in importing luxurious materials such as animal skins, rare feathers, precious shells and stones used in religious ritual. The Aztec word *pochteca* is derived from their name for the *Bombax ceiba*, the great tropical tree that was viewed by the ancient Mesoamericans as the tree of life that linked the terrestrial realm to heaven and to the underworld. The tree of life was an image for the king or rule, and the association of *pochteca* with the tree suggests that merchants were viewed – like kings – as protectors or guarantors of stability and fertility.

MERCHANT WARDS
Pochteca were an elite hereditary group, whose members lived together as a *capultin* kin body in a part of the city reserved for them. Such was the size of Tenochtitlán and the number of *pochteca* serving the empire that there were six wards for merchants in the capital: Amachtlan, Atlauhco, Itztotolco, Pochtlán, Tepetitlán and Tzonmolco.

Ten other towns in the Valley of Mexico were renowned for their communities of professional merchants. These were: Azcapotzalco, Chalco, Coatlinchán, Cuauhtitlán, Huexotla, Huitzilopochco, Otumba, Mixcoac, Texcoco and Xochimilco.

There was a strict hierarchy among *pochteca*. The *pochtecatlatoque* were the most senior merchants, handpicked by the *tlatoani* and his advisers to organize

Left: This exquisite jade ear ornament, carved delicately with Maya glyphs, was found by archaeologists at Pomona, Belize.

trading expeditions and to supervize the activities of younger traders. They were proven merchants with wide experience of travel, usually drawn from the 'aristocracy' of trading families. The *pochtecatlatoque* stayed in Tenochtitlán and followed the progress of an expedition through reports sent back by the travelling merchants; both overseer and trader took a share in the profits. Perhaps most prestigious of all the responsibilities of the *pochtecatlatoque* was to ensure that the capital's markets were orderly and honest places. They sat in judgement on dishonest *pochteca* and customers in special merchants' courts and no other authority could interfere with or challenge their judgements. A trader found guilty of cheating or selling stolen goods or a person caught trying to steal would be sentenced to death.

SLAVE TRADERS
Second in the hierarchy of *pochteca* were traders in slaves. They were called *tlaltlani* ('washers of slaves'), a reference to the ritual bathing that slaves underwent before they were taken to be sacrificed. Bernardino de Sahagún recounts in his *General History of the Things of New Spain* that *tlaltlani* were the wealthiest of all merchants. By tradition they were particularly devout and were treated with the greatest respect as providers of sacrificial victims.

Beneath them were the travelling *pochteca*, the veterans of long-range expeditions who brought luxury produce back to Tenochtitlán's eager markets. They were sometimes called *oztomeca* ('front-line merchants'). Those among the *oztomeca* who worked only for the *tlatoani* were called *tencunenenque* ('king's voyagers'); they often worked as collectors of tribute from subject states within the empire.

Pochteca held a special position of privilege. Unlike their fellows, they were not required to perform personal services for the *tlatoani*. Instead they provided elite goods as tribute. In 1500, as a reward for the role played by *pochteca* in the military conquest of Soconusco, the *tlatoani* Ahuítzotl (*r.* 1486–1502) made a proclamation praising long-range merchants and granting them the right to wear loincloths and capes that were normally reserved for the nobility on special occasions.

SPIES BEHIND ENEMY LINES

One group of merchants, the *naualoztomeca* ('traders in disguise'), performed a vital function for the *tlatoani*, his military advisers and the army commanders. Wherever they went, ostensibly travelling as merchants, they were working as spies, looking for signs of potential unrest and listening for mutterings of discontent against the Aztec rulers. When the military elite in Tenochtitlán was planning a military campaign, it would send *naualoztomeca* into the region to seek useful preliminary information.

In the early Aztec era, traveller-spies went through the empire disguised as locals in order to learn what they could from gossip in the marketplace. However, later the travellers began to take the guise of merchants. It was a dangerous occupation; if caught, a spy was likely to be slain and perhaps cooked. Upon landing in Mexico, Hernán Cortés made first contact with a group of *naualoztomeca*. It was these trader-spies who carried the first news of strange bearded beings in 'flying' ships back to the court of Moctezuma II in Tenochtitlán.

NOBLE MAYA TRADERS

The Aztecs' Maya contemporaries did not have professional merchants comparable to the *pochteca*. Among the Maya, long-distance trade was carried out by rulers and members of the nobility. At Chichén Itzá and Mayapán, the rulers appear to have been merchants. One account of the fall of Mayapán recounts that all the city's rulers were slaughtered in an attack, save one who was away from the city on his travels, seeking trade.

In both Maya and Aztec lands, short-distance trading was performed either by small-scale entrepreneurs, peddlers who bought and sold as they travelled hither and

Right: Danger on the road. A detail from the Codex Mendoza *shows Aztec trader-spies being attacked by lawless locals.*

thither, or by the producers and manufacturers of the goods – the farmers, weavers, toolmakers and potters. From ancient times, across Mesoamerica, long-distance trade was the preserve of a wealthy ruling elite. Trade was the lifeblood of development: because they brought wealth to the community, and because they traded in

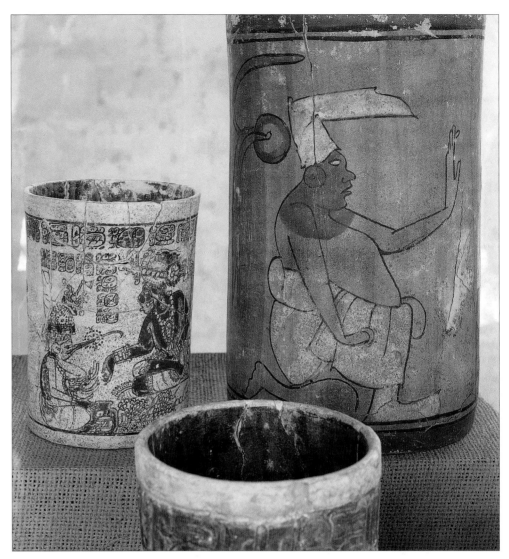

Above: The largest of these vases from Tikal shows a fat Maya merchant who was clearly wealthy enough to indulge himself.

elite goods such as feathers, jaguar skins and sacrificial knives that were needed for religious ceremony, traders began to enjoy religious prestige.

MARKETS LARGE AND SMALL

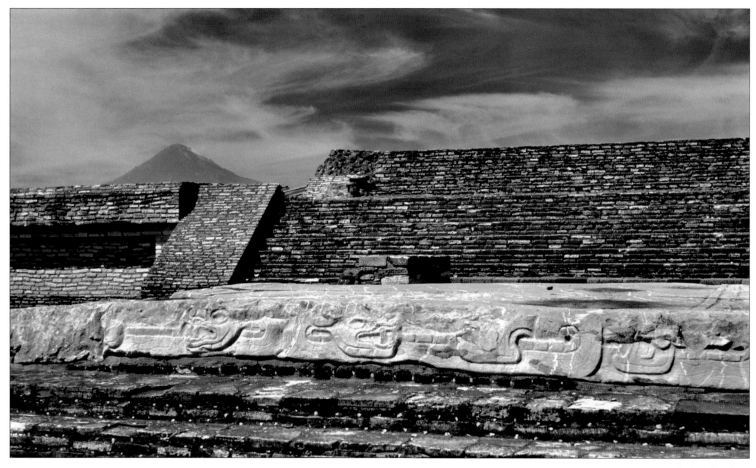

The Aztec capital contained several outdoor markets of various sizes. (The outdoor marketplace was called *tian-quiztli* in Nahuatl.) In addition to the justly celebrated marketplace in Tlatelolco, there was another substantial market in Tenochtitlán proper, alongside the ceremonial precinct. There were also many smaller places of sale scattered throughout the city in its various wards.

WHO SOLD WHAT, WHEN

The sale of elite goods that had been transported from distant parts of the empire was probably restricted to the Tlatelolco and the main Tenochtitlán market. Sales in the different wards were probably of local agricultural produce brought in from *chinampa* fields or of craft products made at workshops in the vicinity. Transactions at these markets were not purely economic, but were bound into the fabric of life and

Above: The walls, steps and frieze carving are part of the vast Pyramid of Quetzalcóatl in Cholula, a town sacred to that god.

Right: These steps and walls are another part of the pyramid remains at Cholula, a major trading as well as a religious centre.

intimately connected with entertainment, socializing, politics and religion. Markets were places where people made friends, swapped news and gossip, perhaps hatched plots and formed alliances, places through which people made their way to the temple.

It is possible that market days were scheduled to coincide with important days in the ritual calendar. Pilgrims would have travelled to a town to make offerings at its shrine and then gone on to the marketplace. Merchants would have taken part in the pilgrimage.

RELIGION AND COMMERCE

Above: The Descending God, Tulum.

Many Mesoamerican trading settlements were also important religious centres. In the highlands of Mexico, Cholula's marketplace was thronged with people while the city's great Temple of Quetzalcóatl was a major draw for pilgrims.

Several trading sites on the eastern seaboard of the Yucatán peninsula were believed to have sacred power because of their position towards the direction of the moon's rising and the reappearance of Venus. The Isle of Cozumel, an important trading port for the League of Mayapán, contained a shrine to moon goddess Ix Chel on its eastward-facing shore; the goddess was believed to speak through an oracle there. On the mainland, the fortified trading centre at Tancah was the site of a *cenote* or large natural well with a holy cave lying on an east–west axis and painted with murals delineating the fearful power of the sea. At nearby Tulum, the Temple of the Descending God was adorned with a carving of a creature diving towards earth; the curious image, only found at Tulum and Cobá, is thought to be associated with the cult of the planet Venus in the form of Xux Ek, the Maya 'wasp star' god.

It is likely that the holy day was enjoyed as a holiday, with entertainments and perhaps a ball game tournament.

Some markets specialized in local produce. Cholula, for example, won a wide reputation for the excellence of its chillies, while Coyoacán was known for the wood grown near the town. Fine gourds, cloth and ceramics were the speciality of Texcoco market. The best places to go for slaves were Azcapotzalco and Itzocán, and the best dog market was at Acolman. In the Mixtec area, the market at Miahuatlán was widely renowned, not least for its sale of exquisite local gold work. Smaller markets were usually held each day or sometimes on a rota with other nearby centres.

MAYA MARKETS

Many Maya towns and cities also held centralized markets in open squares. There is little archaeological evidence of marketplaces, however. Commercial activity usually took place in the open, with perhaps a few pole-and-thatch buildings to provide shade or to keep the rain off, that have since decayed. There is evidence that Classic Period Tikal had a permanent central marketplace. Archaeologists believe that the commercial zone was probably an enclosed area of the city's East Plaza, containing buildings with many doorways. We know that in the post-Classic Period, Iximche in the southern Maya region had a market plaza with overseers to settle arguments, ensure that regulations were observed and levy taxes. As at Tlatelolco, Maya markets were efficiently organized, with different types of goods laid out in separate areas.

Markets contained areas for visiting and foreign merchants, but rival controlling interests sometimes came into opposition. For example, Aztec *pochteca* trading in elite goods were not welcome in areas where Maya nobles ran long-distance trade. Where necessary, representatives of the two sides met in neutral areas.

Below: At Tollán, the remains of the Palacio Quemado lie to the west of the raised temple platform sacred to Quetzalcóatl.

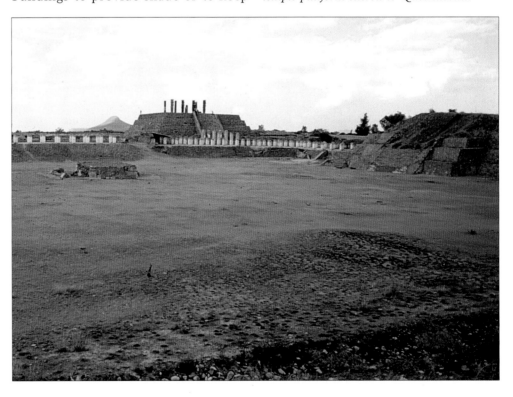

THE GREAT MARKET AT TLATELOLCO

The greatest marketplace of the Aztec empire was at Tlatelolco, the island city that adjoined the imperial capital of Tenochtitlán. Even on a quiet day, 25,000 people would throng the Tlatelolco marketplace, according to the conquistador Anónimo, while every five days a special market attracted more than double that number. Hernán Cortés declared that he saw around 60,000 people in the market. His colleague Bernal Díaz reported that even in the course of two days a curious person would not be able to see the vast range of produce sold there.

The market square at Tlatelolco was surrounded by a covered arcade. In its centre stood a raised platform from which officials made public pronouncements and where thieves and dishonest merchants were shamed and put to death by stoning. The traders' stalls were arranged in a grid pattern around the central platform. At one corner of the market square was the court of the *pochtecatlatoque*, the most senior merchants whose responsibility was to levy sales taxes, to maintain order in the marketplace and also to sit in judgement on those who broke the law.

Above: This illustration, from the Florentine Codex, *is of Aztecs storing amaranth.*

The goods were laid out in areas according to type. The *pochtecatlatoque* organized the market, ensuring products were sold in the right area and at the right price. Every raw material and product imaginable, the produce of a great empire, was available in the Tlatelolco market.

ANCIENT CORNUCOPIA
A canal ran down one side of the marketplace, and a stream of heavily laden porters carried goods from canoes to market stalls. In one area were farmers and merchants selling fresh

Left: These jewellery pieces are typical of the artefacts the elite could buy at Tlatelolco.

produce: beans, vegetables, herbs and fruits. In another were turkeys, deer, ducks, rabbits, dogs and hares. Elsewhere, a customer could find fish and all kinds of marine life; in another place, tortillas, honey cakes and other cooked foods were on offer, including, according to the conquistador Bernal Díaz, cakes with the flavour of cheese made by fisherwomen using a weed that grows in Lake Texcoco.

In another part of the market, shoppers could browse among a vast range of pots, plates, water jars and bowls before moving on to look for bark paper and inks, then to seek out reeds filled with tobacco. A person could buy sandals, coloured robes and lengths of plain cloth. Another could buy timber or pine torches. Those seeking elite items would find them in plentiful supply: feathers of many colours, including the magnificent quetzal tail feathers of up to 1m (more than 3ft) in length; the skins of jaguars, lions and deer; magnificent gold masks and jewellery fashioned by the best Mixtec goldsmiths; delicately finished mosaic masks; elegant sacrificial knives; statues, and other stone carvings; turquoise, jade and other precious stones. A warrior could find all kinds of military equipment, including padded cotton armour, leather shields, the sharpest *atlatl* darts of obsidian and splendid ceremonial cloaks and shields decorated with feathers and mosaic.

Slaves were also for sale. Merchants fitted them with collars and bound them to a long pole to prevent them running away. Any slaves who did escape could gain their freedom if they managed to reach the palace of the *tlatoani* without being caught. Only the merchant who owned them could give chase. Some merchants bought slaves to offer as sacrifices, particularly for the festival of Panquetzalíztli ('Lifting of the Banners'), which was held after the harvest each year. Others purchased strong male slaves to transport and sell to cacao plantations or as canoe oarsmen in coastal regions. Some female slaves were sold as prostitutes. The going rate for a slave was 25 cotton cloaks, rising to 35 cloaks for one who was skilled in dancing.

All goods were counted out or sold by measuring their size, never by weight. Customers usually bartered with merchants, although some products, such as cacao beans, cotton mantles, pieces of tin, copper axe-blades, transparent quills full of gold dust and the feathers of tropical birds, were used as forms of currency.

PUNISHMENTS AND PROCESSIONS

Cheats sometimes got away with making counterfeit cacao beans from amaranth dough and wax. When the *pochtecatlatoque* found a merchant guilty of trying to cheat his customers they sentenced him to be put to death on the platform in the centre of the square. The merchant's goods were confiscated and his dishonest measures smashed. A person caught stealing from a stall or storehouse would be similarly sentenced to death.

The marketplace was a vibrant place where people gathered to chat, street performers entertained the crowds and drummers set bystanders dancing. Religious processions passed through the market from the ceremonial precinct of Tlatelolco nearby. Priests waving smoking censers, their bodies painted black and long hair matted with sacrificial blood, made an unnerving spectacle. Sometimes they were at the head of a procession of victims bound for sacrifice in the temple.

Below: Today office buildings crowd close to excavated ruins of Tlatelolco platforms in the heart of the Mexican capital.

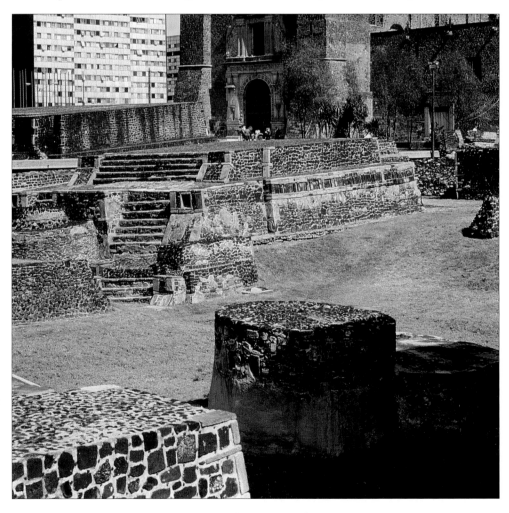

A NETWORK OF TRIBUTE

Large quantities of produce entered Tenochtitlán in the form of tribute payments from provinces within the Aztec empire. The activities of tribute collectors complemented those of *pochteca* merchants in providing sumptuous goods to please the nobles of the imperial capital and to supply the materials used in the city's magnificent religious ceremonies.

A TRIBUTARY EMPIRE

Some *pochteca* worked as itinerant tribute collectors, but generally collectors were appointed to reside in a conquered territory to ensure payments were made. The Triple Alliance of Tenochtitlán, Texcoco and Tlacopán built its tributary empire through military might: its armies pursued battle to the point at which a conquered state or city agreed to pay tribute, when the conquerors imposed a schedule of amounts and timings. The rulers of the defeated state remained in power, and the collector made sure that they honoured the tribute agreement, under threat of further military action.

Tribute payments maintained the infrastructure and daily operations of the empire. Some provinces were required to send labourers for construction projects, others tools and building materials, some

Below: The Zapotecs of Monte Albán celebrated their conquest-led tribute network in carvings on the arrow-shaped Building J.

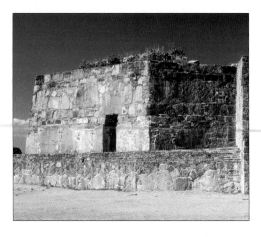

sent soldiers, others military equipment such as shields and padded cotton war jerkins. Many areas sent maize, beans and other basic foodstuffs, while others provided firewood for the braziers of the nobility. Certain states were contracted to send local products such as obsidian or cacao, fine metalwork or ceramics, jaguar skins or colourful feathers. One of the most highly prized Aztec tributary provinces was the resource-rich region of Soconusco, defeated after four years' conflict by Ahuítzotl in 1486; it provided tribute of jaguar skins and jewellery.

RECORDS OF PAYMENT

Details of the tribute network operated by Texcoco are found in the 16th-century document the *Mapa Quinatzin*. They show how meticulously tribute operations were planned. There were eight tributary regions, each with its own tribute collector required, among other responsibilities, to furnish the administrative buildings, city temples and royal palaces in Texcoco with foodstuffs and wood for braziers. In particular, two groups of 13 tributary towns were arranged in a rota to provide firewood for the *tlatoani*'s main palace throughout the year. The *Codex Mendoza* (*c.*1541) contains a lengthy tribute list detailing the responsibilities throughout the year of various tributary towns and states. Cuauhnahuac is listed as one of 16 towns contracted to dispatch a consignment of cotton skirts, loincloths and robes to Tenochtitlán twice a year, supplemented by an annual delivery of shields and war equipment. With so many tribute payers required to provide materials according to a regular schedule, there must have been a steady stream of porters and canoes bringing deliveries from far and wide, which would have required detailed administrative control.

Before the Triple Alliance, other cultures – including the Zapotecs of Monte Albán and the Toltecs of Tollán – established tributary empires. At Monte

Above: Portable wealth. This pendant earring of solid gold was one of the pieces found in Monte Albán Tomb 7 in 1932.

Right: A page from the Codex Mendoza *shows the tribute collected by Aztec civil servants from the province of Tochtepec.*

Albán, the curious arrow-shaped structure known to archaeologists as Building J, erected between *c.*200BC and AD300 in the Main Plaza, bears about 50 carvings that appear to represent areas conquered or required to pay tribute to the Zapotecs. Some carvings specify the kind of tribute that must be paid.

They included Cuicatlán, a mountain settlement on the border between Oaxaca and the Téhuacan Valley, and Tututepec on the coast of the Pacific Ocean. At Cuicatlán the Zapotecs acted with great ruthlessness: they destroyed entire villages, moved other settlements, established military strongholds and terrified surviving locals by building skull racks in their villages to display the heads of their conquered menfolk.

In many areas they did not need to use military force, however. In return for supplying elite goods from Monte Albán to the leading figures of a village, the Zapotecs exacted an agreement that they would receive tribute of agricultural produce. Many centuries later, the warriors of Xochicalco, in the western part of Morelos, established a tributary empire in the period AD700–900, as evidenced by glyphs of tribute-paying towns carved on the upper part of the Pyramid of the Feathered Serpent there.

The Putún Maya traders who ruled Chichén Itzá and later Mayapán both built tribute networks. At Mayapán, cotton, copal, cacao, honey and turkeys were among the forms of tribute received. In the southern Maya realm the warlike Quiché Maya also exacted tribute payments from those they conquered. However, the Quiché did not allow local leaders to remain in place, as the Aztecs did; instead, triumphant warlords had their enemies executed and took the dead men's wives into their own families.

THE GIVING OF GIFTS

From earliest times goods moved across Mesoamerica in the form of gifts between elite groups in different areas. Such gift-giving was a mark of mutual respect between rulers and a way of sharing resources between regions rich in different source materials – for instance, a highland group might make a gift of obsidian cutting blades in return for surplus maize or cacao grown by another group in the coastal lowlands. The gift of sumptuous and prestigious materials was also a statement of power on behalf of the giver, an attempt to demonstrate status. Moctezuma II attempted to prove his divine grandeur and magnificence by making splendid gifts of gold, silver and magnificent featherwork to Hernán Cortés and the conquistadors in 1519.

THE SACRED WAY

The Maya built raised causeways known as *sacbeob* (singular: *sacbé*) between settlements. These paved roads eased communications and passage for merchants while giving solid form to political alliances among cities.

GREAT CAUSEWAY

The greatest of these roads was built *c.*AD800 in Yucatán, and ran for 100km (60 miles) from the Castillo pyramid at Cobá to Yaxuná. Cobá lay at the intersection of some 43 roads. It was also connected, for example, to its seaport at Xelhá. Some scholars believe that the rulers of Cobá embarked on this remarkable feat of engineering in an attempt to consolidate their power at a time when the aggressive Putún Maya incomers at Chichén Itzá were making unwelcome intrusions into the region. The attempt may have succeeded: the Itzá attacked and defeated Yaxuná in *c.*AD850, but there is no evidence they overcame Cobá. Its people maintained their independence, although the city's trading success was limited, its ambitious building programmes were curtailed and various outer parts of the settlement were gradually abandoned.

Several *sacbeob* were constructed in northern Yucatán. Typically they were elevated 2.5m (8ft) above the surround-

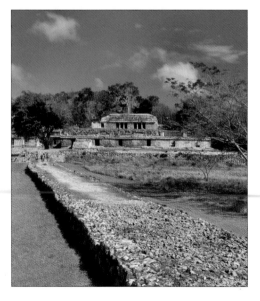

Left: A sacbé *connects a small group of buildings to the two-storey palace at Labná. The palace is similar to that at Sayil.*

Above: Several causeways were in use at the fortified trading centre at La Quemada in Zacatecas state, Mexico.

ing land, were around 4.5m (15ft) wide and covered with lime cement. Labourers used a 5-ton roller to finish the surface; this would have needed 15 workers to push it. The roads did not curve: they ran perfectly straight, then made a sudden turn to change direction if necessary. One – 4m (13ft) wide – ran for 18km (11 miles) between Uxmal and Kabah. At Kabah it passed through a remarkable stone corbelled arch with a span of 5m (16ft) and led to the central civic area. Another ran for 18km from the settlement at Ucí. It was a remarkable 8m (26ft) wide.

The Maya built *sacbeob* from the time they erected their first monumental buildings in the lowlands. The earliest known system links El Mirador to Nakbé, 13km (8 miles) away, Tintal and other nearby sites. These roads were built in the Late Preclassic Period (*c.*400BC–AD250). The *sacbeob* between cities were expanded versions of the sacred ways that the Maya built to link areas within their cities. At El Mirador, causeways connected different parts of the city centre. A series of *sacbeob* ran from the Great Plaza in the centre of Tikal. One led north, to the buildings labelled Pyramid Group 3D-2 and Group H by archaeologists. Another went directly west to Temple IV and a third ran south-east to the Temple of Inscriptions. At Chichén Itzá a stone *sacbé* 6m (20ft) wide and 300m (985ft) long connected the Temple of the Feathered Serpent to the Sacred cenote.

SACRED SYMBOLISM

The causeways in cities such as Tikal were integrated into the sacred symbolism of the site layout. The arcane meaning of the layout was that the north was the realm of supernaturals, glorious deceased ancestors who had risen to the heavens, while the south was the region of the Underworld. A ball court was often built between north and south to represent an entrance to the Underworld. Buildings to the east and west suggested the east–west passage of the sun and the rule of the king, whose symbol was the sun.

Causeways were used to link different symbolic areas and to emphasize the unity of the design. At Tikal, for example, the sacred north position was filled both by the North Acropolis, which contained many tombs of ancestors, and further out by the Pyramid Group 3D-2. South was the South Acropolis, west was Temple IV and east was the Temple of the Inscriptions. The three causeways completed the design. A ball court in the East Plaza was an additional way into the Underworld between north and south.

In many cities, for example Yaxhá and Caracol, causeways were built to lead out from the centre to outer settlements. At Caracol there were no fewer than seven causeways providing access from the centre to living areas and plazas, with one running for 8km (5 miles) to the allied smaller settlement at Cahal Pichik. At Seibal the three main groups of buildings were laid out on a cluster of hilltops and connected to one another by causeways. A few *sacbeob* were built in other parts

Below: Archaeologists have dated this well-preserved roadway at Cantona in Puebla state to AD700–950.

of Mesoamerica. At Xochicalco, paved causeways like *sacbeob* were the connecting link between different parts of the ancient city. In northern Mexico the trading settlement of La Quemada, in southern Zacatecas state, also used causeways to link different parts of the settlement.

AZTEC ROADS

There is little archaeological evidence of Aztec roads. Whereas in Maya lands labourers built paved *sacbeob*, in southern and central highland Mesoamerica there was generally no need to build formal roads between settlements. However, scholars know that a network of routes carried trade within the Aztec empire.

Above: The carving on the façade of the Governor's Palace at Uxmal is reproduced in Catherwood's 1841 drawing. From Uxmal a sacbé *ran directly to Kabah, where it passed beneath an archway.*

There are references in post-Conquest accounts to roads, roadside gods, rest houses and teams of couriers and there was certainly a road inland from Veracruz to Tenochtitlán, for Cortés followed it in 1519. Aztec *pochteca* followed well-trodden paths with their long caravans of human porters, heavily laden with goods, or had their loads transferred to canoes for transport by river and in coastal waters. Aztec garrisons were established at vulnerable points on the trade routes.

CHAPTER FOUR

THE WORLD OF WORK

Opportunities for Mesoamericans were limited by birth. We know this from Spanish records about the Aztecs, their contemporaries and the Maya in the 16th century. Also, because the archaeological record of preceding Mesoamerican cultures is similar to that of the Aztec and Maya and indicates that there was continuous development, we can project the nature of Aztec society back into pre-Aztec times. The top military, legal, administrative and priestly positions were open only to members of the hereditary nobility; among the middle class of skilled artisans and merchants, most were probably glad to follow their family profession, since it could provide sufficient wealth to secure a good level of comfort. Most people had their living from the land, the men working as fishermen, hunters and farmers.

In terms of food and basics, common people could be self-sufficient. They grew most, if not all, of the food they ate. They often had sufficient skills to produce pots, clothing, basketwork and tools for their own use. Some might produce a surplus of cloth or tools that could be bartered for luxury items – a turkey, some meat or extra vegetables, decorated clothing and so on – at market. They were also connected to the wider world of religious life, ceremonial centres and military campaigns through their responsibilities to pay taxes or tribute to their rulers and to serve in the army or as labourers in construction projects when required.

Left: A codex scene depicts the harvesting of cacao. Farming was the principal livelihood of most Mesoamericans.

RAISING CROPS ON LAND AND WATER

At Tenochtitlán farmers relied on *chinampa* fields in Lake Texcoco. The first *chinampas* were constructed along the shore or around islands, but by the reign of Moctezuma I, water control techniques made it possible to reclaim fields from the lake.

CREATING CHINAMPAS

A farmer building a *chinampa* plot would ideally use a shallow or swampy part of the lake. First he would mark out a rectangular area around 30m (100ft) long and 2.5m (8ft) across with four corner posts, then build fences around the area with wattles, vegetation and mud. He or a member of his kin group could make another *chinampa* directly alongside the first, with a canal running between the two, and proceeding in this way the farmers of Tenochtitlán could create large areas of *chinampas* on a grid pattern. In some areas the *chinampas* were laid out in pairs between canals, with a foot-path running between the two *chinampa* 'fields'. Some *chinampas* were very much

Above: One of several scenes of agricultural life in the Florentine Codex *of c. 1570 depicts Aztec farmers harvesting maize.*

bigger than the plot of 75sq m described, and could be as large as 850sq m (9,000sq ft); plots such as this supported as many as 15 farmers.

Farmers would plant willows at the edges of their plots. Their roots grew down into the lakebed and strengthened the walls. The trees required regular pruning to prevent them casting shade on the crops. The 'fields' within the fences were built up with layers of fertile sediment dredged from the lakebed. Farmers turned the earth with a hand-held implement and planted seeds in holes made with a planting stick or *coa*. In the dry season, farmers lifted water in a container from the canal onto the *chinampa* alongside. To fertilize the earth they used human excrement, which was carried by canoe from the city along the network of canals. Springs from the Ajusco mountains fed into lakes Chalco and Xochimilco, where great expanses of *chinampa* fields lay. The Aztecs needed to control the supply of water to prevent flooding in the wet season or drought in the dry period. They created a system of dams, canals and sluices – channels with end-gates that could be lifted or dropped to control the flow of water.

The main crops grown by the Aztecs were maize, beans, squashes, tomatoes and chillies. Farmers in Chalco and Tlaxcala grew large amounts of maize, and these areas became associated with the staple crop in Aztec times. Elsewhere other *chinampa* farmers in the Valley of Mexico grew vegetables and flowers.

BURNING FIELDS

In other parts of Mesoamerica, farmers used a range of agricultural methods, according to local conditions. In highland areas, which usually had mineral-rich soil, they cut terraces from the steep hillsides

Left: Chinampa *fields at Xochimilco, constructed by Aztecs in the 15th century, are still in use by Mexicans today.*

Above: The method of building up a chinampa *field using stakes and mud is seen in this painting based on a 16th-century manuscript.*

and built aqueducts to irrigate the fields from mountain streams. In the tropical lowlands of the central Maya region, where soils were poorer, farmers practised 'slash-and-burn', first cutting down the dense jungle growth with stone axes, then leaving the plants to dry before burning them to enrich the soil and recover its fertility. They could use a field so made for perhaps three years, but then had to leave it fallow for as long as eight years to allow the soil to become enriched with minerals once more. Many farmers using this method then moved on to clear another area.

Where possible, lowland and other Maya agriculturalists also cut terraced fields, which helped to prevent water draining from the soil. They also made raised fields in swampy ground. The farmers cut channels in the wet ground and piled up the cleared earth, creating raised fields intersected with waterways for irrigation. Maya farmers were growing food on raised fields beside the Hondo river in Belize as early as 1100BC. The method was also used in the Quintana Roo area of Yucatán and alongside the Candelaria river in Campeche. In Belize, humidity and high rainfall allowed farmers to grow highly valued crops of cacao, as well as cotton. At Pulltrouser Swamp in Belize, locals grew cacao, cotton, amaranth and maize on their raised-field agricultural land.

In the Maya lowlands, farmers planted maize, squash and beans together. The squash vines helped to prevent soil erosion, while the beans climbed the tall stalks of the corn. As in Tenochtitlán's *chinampa* fields, farmers turned earth using hand-held implements, then used a planting stick to make holes and dropped five or six seeds into each hole.

People kept kitchen gardens close to their houses: here they planted vegetables and the breadnut tree, which yields a fruit high in vegetable protein that can be stored without decaying for as long as 18 months. They may have grown fields of ramon, sapodilla, avocado and cacao.

FEEDING AN EXPANDING CITY

By the mid-1400s Tenochtitlán's population had grown to upwards of 150,000 – five times larger than its lakeside near-neighbour Texcoco, which had some 20–30,000 inhabitants. The Aztec capital, which did not have its own zone of *chinampa* fields, had a pressing need for more agricultural land. The *tlatoani* or ruler Itzcóatl seized control of the *chinampa* zone in the southern lakes, Chalco and Xochimilco. In the reign of Moctezuma I, sizeable new areas of *chinampa* were created in the lakebed. Imperial conquests also helped, by bringing substantial quantities of staple and luxury foods in the form of tribute payments from conquered regions.

GARDEN EXPERTS

In Aztec Tenochtitlán there was a hierarchy among agriculturalists. The men who worked the fields had a wide variety of skills and knowledge: they took responsibility for turning the soil, weeding, levelling land, measuring out fields, planting, watering by hand and using irrigation systems, harvesting and storing produce. However, there was also a group of experts in horticulture, widely respected for their knowledge in seeding and transplanting. These men were valued for their skills by members of the nobility and the political and priestly hierarchies. Combining their knowledge with information from the sacred *tonalamatl* calendar books, the garden experts decided the most propitious and the most practical times for sowing crops and harvesting them.

PLEASURE GARDENS

Garden experts were also much in demand for planning and maintaining the gardens of the empire. Many of the villas of Tenochtitlán had splendid pleasure gardens. Moctezuma II kept three: at his palace in Tenochtitlán, at Chapultepec and at Ixtapalapa. When the conquistador Bernal Díaz visited Moctezuma's garden at Ixtapalapa, he was astonished by the variety of trees, fruits and flowers and their captivating aromas. He declared there was probably no land on earth to match the one that contained such a garden. Hernán Cortés also visited the garden and described it in a 1520 letter to Carlos V of Spain as containing many trees, flowers and places for bathing, with an orchard and areas of aromatic herbs and a wide walkway around a central pool containing fish and visited by waterfowl.

At Texcotzingo, Netzahualcóyotl of Texcoco followed an established Aztec tradition in keeping a botanical garden. The most splendid of these botanical gardens was that founded in 1467 by Moctezuma I of Tenochtitlán in a warm, fertile spot at Huaxtepec, beneath Mount Popocatépetl in the modern Mexican state of Morelos.

When the Aztecs discovered an ancient garden created by their forerunners at Huaxtepec, Moctezuma appointed an official named Pinotetl to upgrade and revamp the already elaborate irrigation works, which included springs, reservoirs and fountains. Then the *tlatoani* ordered the transport from Cuetlaxtlán in Veracruz of cacao trees, vanilla orchid plants and other rare species and for herbs, cypresses and other plants from far-flung parts of the Aztec empire. The plants were carefully dug up, wrapped in cloth and sent to Huaxtepec along with experts in their cultivation.

Religious ceremonies were held to bless the plants and the enterprise. The specialist gardeners from far and wide joined in an eight-day fast before taking part in a bloodletting ceremony in which they pierced their earlobes and sprinkled the blood over the plants. Priests made offerings of incense and sacrificed a large number of quail in order to bless the earth with the birds' blood. These ceremonies must have won the gods' approval for

Left: Tribute sent to Tenochtitlán by Cihuatlan, on the coast, included cacao beans and rare seashells used in ritual.

Above: This 16th-century manuscript juxtaposes drawings showing the medicinal uses of various plants used by Mesoamericans with a picture of an Aztec god.

the plants took to their new home and grew fast and strong. When finished, Moctezuma's gardens – 11km (7 miles) in circumference – contained more than 2,000 species of herbs, shrubs and trees. It also contained an aviary and a zoo.

HEALING HERBS

In the botanical gardens at Huaxtepec and Texcotzingo, the garden experts grew a wide range of medicinal herbs. The use of healing herbs was an ancient Mesoamerican art. Most people knew enough to treat themselves and grew herbs among the vegetables on their garden plots. Some of the herbs grown in the botanical gardens were used in doctors' experiments. Members of the nobility paid for the experiments, in return for medical treatment when

needed. Ordinary citizens were able to volunteer as guinea pigs, receiving free experimental treatment on condition that they return to report the results to the doctors and planting experts.

THE MAYA AND CACAO

Foremost among elite crops grown by the Maya was cacao. To flourish, cacao needs a thick layer of good soil and humidity in all seasons. One of the prime exports from Maya lands to Mexico, it was grown in plantations, primarily in Soconusco (the Pacific coastal region of Guatemala and Chiapas), in the valley of the River Motagua and at sites in Belize.

The Maya merchant god Ek Chuah – known as god M by some scholars – was lord of cacao and the owners of plantations made offerings to him in the 15th month, Muan. According to the account given by

Right: This Maya chocolate pot was made c. AD300–900. It was used to pour the chocolate drink to generate a pleasing froth.

Diego de Landa of Maya religious festivals in 16th-century Yucatán, the plantation owners found a dog with cacao-coloured dots on his coat to kill and, amid the burning of incense also offered sacrifices of blue bird feathers and blue-coloured iguanas. To conclude the rite, each plantation owner was given a cacao pod to hold.

FRESH FROM THE WILD

Throughout their history Mesoamericans supplemented their diet with meat and fish. In the earliest days, hunting-gathering groups were self-sufficient, but as village life developed, people increasingly had specialized occupations and markets sprang up at which villagers could barter and exchange foods and other necessities. Skilled hunters doubtless brought their meat to market. Fishermen or traders carried dried fish from coastal, riverside or lakeside areas to inland settlements.

MAYA HUNTERS

Among the Maya, hunters used snares and traps to catch deer for their meat. They also hunted rabbits, pig-like mammals called peccaries and rodents – including squirrels, porcupines, agouti and paca. They were skilled with the blowpipe, sending tiny clay pellets at velocity to kill monkeys, macaws, raccoons and other animals in their habitat in the branches. In coastal, lakeside and riverside areas Maya fishermen thrived, using dugout canoes, nets and lines with bone fishhooks. All around the coasts of Maya lands and inland on freshwater lakes and rivers, fish and shellfish were an important part of the diet.

The Maya also domesticated and raised some animals. They kept dogs as guards and hunting companions and may also have fattened some for food. They also kept turkeys, doves – and perhaps

Above: Mesoamericans knew the coyote for its cunning and ability as a night hunter. This statue was made c.1250–1450.

the Muscovy duck – to eat. According to some authorities, the Maya raised herds of domesticated deer in large fenced areas for food. Describing the Maya of Yucatán in the 16th century, Bishop Diego de Landa reported that the women made a habit of breastfeeding young deer, who became entirely tame. In areas such

as the lands beside the Candelaria river in Campeche, the Maya might also have 'farmed' fish and molluscs in the waterways between their raised fields and in artificial ponds. They might have introduced freshwater fish into these enclosed areas of water and caught the excess produced by breeding.

De Landa also reported that Maya hunters in Yucatán believed that success in tracking, catching and killing animals was in the gift of the hunting gods Acanum and Suhui Dzipitabai. He reported that in the second and third month of the year, Uo and Zip, hunters partook in ceremonies honouring the gods. In waterside areas they were joined by fishermen praising the fishing deities Ah Kak Nexoy, Ah Pua, Ah Cit and Dzamal Cum. They prayed for success in the field. In the eleventh month, Zac, hunters celebrated another festival in honour of Acanum and Suhui Dzipitabai, this time seeking forgiveness for the blood they had spilled in the hunt. To the Maya, shedding blood was always a wicked act, for which a man or woman must seek forgiveness. Sacrificial offerings of one's own or a victim's blood were excepted.

IN HIGHLAND MEXICO

In Aztec times, the inhabitants of Tenochtitlán and other cities around the lakes of the Valley of Mexico had easy access to fish, shellfish and aquatic birds. Boys often hunted for birds with nets on the end of long poles while their fathers fished with canoes and nets on the waters of the lake. The men were also skilled in catching frogs and iguanas, a kind of lizard, for food. They collected *axolotl* newts, which were abundant in the lakes and were highly prized as a food and medicine. Many people kept small, hairless dogs as companions and pets – and as a

Left: In a scene from the Florentine Codex, *an Aztec seated on a reed mat eyes the turkey and dogs he keeps for meat.*

Above: A detail from a Maya mural depicts scenes of village life including fishing, hunting and digging the house garden.

source of food. Otherwise, animal meat was available at market, from local hunters, from traders and as part of the regular and substantial deliveries of tribute from around the empire. Diego Durán's account of the myriad kinds of tribute delivered to Tenochtitlán listed deer, rabbits, quails, weasels, moles, snakes and rats as well as larger animals including jaguars and ocelots.

From ancient times, the Aztecs' forerunners and ancestors in Mexico had hunted in small bands by tracking and trapping. They used chipped flint and obsidian weapons such as spears and *atlatl* darts to kill mammoths and other large game, but also trapped and hunted many other small creatures including turtles, birds, rabbits and gophers. The Aztec god of hunting, Mixcóatl, probably originated in these archaic times as a hurricane or storm god. His name means 'Cloud Serpent' and he was associated with lightning, thunder and tempests – his followers saw lightning bolts as the hunter god's darts. He appeared as a deer or rabbit or as a hunter carrying a bundle of arrows. He was also identified as the father of the Feathered Serpent god Quetzalcóatl. In the account of the Toltecs' southward migration from the northern deserts, Mixcóatl was their leader and his son was Topiltzin-Quetzalcóatl the revered ruler of Tollán. In another narrative, Mixcóatl took the form of a deer to chase the fertility and earth goddess Cihuacóatl ('Female Serpent'), and – catching her at last – fathered the Feathered Serpent god.

In the Aztec era, Mixcóatl and fellow hunting god Camaxtli were honoured in Tenochtitlán in the festival of Tóxcatl ('Drought'), when impersonators of these gods and of the dark lord of fate Tezcatlipoca were put to death, and in that of Quecholli ('Treasured Feather'), when hunting contests were held and prisoners of war dressed as deer were sacrificed. The Aztecs also made offerings to Opochtli ('Left-handed'), the god of bird-catchers and fishermen, praising him as the inventor of the nets used for catching birds and the harpoon with which eagle-eyed fishermen speared fish in the waters.

Right: This ceramic vessel in the form of a duck is decorated with jade and shells. It was made in Teotihuacán c.AD500.

SKILLED IN ANCIENT CRAFTS

The skilled craftsmen and women of the Aztec empire were a discrete class who could claim social status partway between the common folk and the *pipiltin* nobility. Workers such as basketmakers, potters and weavers were the inheritors of ancient Mesoamerican tradition and passed their skills down the generations.

AZTEC ARTISANS

From the time of San José Mogote *c*.1350BC, craftworkers traditionally occupied their own quarters of a settlement. In the Aztec era, most lived in the large cities of the Valley of Mexico, although there were concentrations of artisans in other parts of the Aztec domain.

Below: The intricate patterns of relief brickwork at sites such as Mitla might have been inspired by designs on woven robes.

Right: Scholars believe that traditional weaving in Mexico today follows patterns established in ancient times.

The *amanteca* or feather-workers were based in their own quarter in Tlatelolco, where they elected officials from their number to govern craft business and worshipped their own patron deity in a local temple. The *amanteca* made clothing, dancing costumes, bracelets, banners, magnificent headdresses and ceremonial military items such as shields. Theirs was painstaking work. When they were making feather-decorated clothes, they tied the feathers' stems one at a time into the fabric when weaving. When they were making a banner or a shield, they sewed the feathers individually on to a backing, usually made of paper attached to reeds and covered in leather. They used a

mixture of feathers from local birds and brightly coloured plumage brought by traders from the tropical rainforests of the Maya lowlands. Friar Bernardino de Sahagún describes their craft, adding that the use of tropical feathers was a recent innovation among the Aztecs.

ROBES, BASKETS AND POTS

Weavers made cloth of plant fibres from maguey agave or henequen for the clothes of the common people and spun cotton cloth for the nobility. Women performed the spinning and weaving of the cloth. Cotton was imported into highland Mexico from lowland areas of Mesoamerica. The fineness of the material was the sole difference between the clothes of rich and poor: weavers produced the same range of clothes – loincloths, capes, skirts and large cloaks called *huipiles* – for both nobles and commoners. These often bore embroidered, woven, painted or dyed decorations to signal social class or region of origin.

Like their forebears for thousands of years, Aztec basketmakers made use of the reeds that grew thickly around the lakes of the Valley of Mexico. They also used the leaves of maguey agave, palmleaf and several cacti in their work. They made a wide range of baskets, from compact, tightly woven containers for small valuables to large lidded chests for use as clothes baskets. They also made containers for grain and foodstuffs. The reed craftsmen also made mats and simple stools. Mats

TOOLS AND TOOLMAKERS

For many thousands of years, artisans, soldiers and farmers used tools of obsidian, flint and wood developed in the earliest days of Mesoamerica. Only in the last few centuries of the region's history did its people – notably the Tarascans – begin to make and use metal weapons.

Among the oldest known tools in Mexico is a collection of obsidian scrapers, knives and weapon points, together with some flint blades, made in the region of Lake Texcoco *c*.7700BC. Prehistoric hunter-gatherers also made cutting tools from the volcanic rock andesite. The first farmers developed the use of a sharpened wooden planting stick. With some improvements, these basic tools remained in use across the millennia. Elite soldiers in the Aztec army were still using weapon points of obsidian in their wooden *atlatl* dart-throwers some 9,000 years later. Generations of Mesoamericans made their livelihood from mining and trading in obsidian, or fashioning it into tools, weapons and other items in workshops.

Metal weapons and tools were not made in Mesoamerica until after *c*.AD800. The necessary skills were passed along trade routes from South America, probably by sea to western Mexico and overland to the Maya regions of Guatemala, Belize and Mexico. However, it is striking that in western Mexico comparatively few metal tools or weapons were made. Most production was of bells, pins, figurines and jewellery for the elite. The quality of stone and shell tools must have been high enough to prevent their being superseded. In addition to copper, gold and silver were also worked.

were in particularly high demand both for common houses and royal residences, since the Aztecs rarely used furniture.

Potters made a variety of ceramic wares for home cooking and storage, for decorative use by the wealthy and nobility and for ritual use in temples. Without the use of the potter's wheel, they made all their containers and figurines by hand moulding. One favoured method was to build up coils of clay then use a scraping tool to thin out the walls of the pot. Both Aztec and Maya potters produced work of great delicacy and expressiveness.

MAYA CRAFTS

In Maya lands, as in Aztec cities, it was common for craft specialists to live grouped together in a residential area. The craft was probably handed down through the generations, so a craft living unit might also have been a family group. As among the Aztecs, weaving was performed by women. As a spindle they used a thin stick weighted at one end with a ceramic disc. Resting the heavy end on a gourd on the ground, the spinner twirled the spindle to spin the cotton thread. Her companion worked a simple loom on her lap to produce a cloth around 1m (3ft)

Above: This richly coloured painted bowl, probably made for a Maya nobleman or prince, has been dated to c.AD600–900.

wide. The goddess of weaving, Ix Chebal Yax, gave her blessing to this method and was shown using this type of loom in an image in the *Madrid Codex*. The weavers produced different types of cloth and traditional designs in different areas.

Maya basketmakers created containers of intricate and varied weave. None has survived to be examined by archaeologists, but a representation of a basket on Lintel 24 at Yaxchilán shows a complex pattern and indicates the quality of Maya basketwork.

Feather-workers produced a magnificent range of headdress decorations, capes, ceremonial shields and weapons, fans and fringed cloth. They also decorated wicker frames that dancers wore on their backs and protective canopies for royal thrones. In some areas, for instance among the Quiché Maya, birds were bred in captivity for their plumage. Hunters and trackers brought back the feathers of the macaw, the quetzal and other birds from tropical forests. The quetzal was sacred, its feathers symbolic of royal authority.

MASTERS OF THE PAINTED WORD

Scribes were talented, highly educated individuals who combined the skills of painter and writer. In the Aztec empire they were trained in the elite *calmecac* schools at which the children of the nobility and a few precociously talented commoners learned the use of the sacred calendar, the timing of religious festivals, temple rituals, history, astronomy, arithmetic, oratory and the art of *tlacuilloli* or how to 'write-paint'. They were known as *tlacuiloque* or painter-writers. The script they used, which combined pictures that stood for ideas, words and numbers with others that represented a sound from spoken language, was closely derived from ancient Mesoamerican writing systems developed by the Olmec and Zapotecs. It was read in the Aztec tongue Nahuatl, but would have been largely comprehensible to the Maya and to other peoples. This made it highly suitable for keeping records of trade and tribute among the many ethnic and linguistic groups of the empire.

WRITTEN FORMS

The Aztec literate elite produced many different types of book, and scribes probably specialized in one kind. In addition to manuscripts on the ritual calendar and astronomy used for telling fortunes and predicting the future, Aztec scribes made maps, genealogies, histories or annals, law books, tribute lists and documents on dreams. They made ritual

Above: The Maya logograph for 'book', pronounced hun, *represents leaves of bark paper pressed between jaguar-skin covers.*

books or *tonalamatls* and annals or *xiuhamatls* in the form of screenfolds, often from pieces of deerskin stuck together with glue and covered on both sides with white lime. Scribes fashioned some screenfold books from *amatl* paper, produced from the bark of the wild fig tree. They also used *amatl* paper to make long pull-out scrolls or *tiras* and also, one piece at a time, for legal and administrative documents. They painted genealogies and maps on *lienzos*, large pieces of cotton.

KEEPER OF THE BOOKS

Among the Maya of the Classic Period, scribes were treated with great respect as men of genius. Here too, scribes were both writers and artists. Yucatec-speaking Maya called a scribe *ah ts'ib* ('He who Performs Writing and Painting'). From post-conquest accounts, we know that the Maya, like the Aztecs, wrote and kept a wide range of books, including maps, genealogies, medical treatises, books on healing plants, documents about the animals of the wild, as well as priestly

Left: Frederick Catherwood's 19th-century drawing is of a head of Itzamná, inventor of writing, carved in a wall at Izamal, Yucatán.

Left: Aztec scribes wrote the Codex Borbonicus *around the time of the Spanish* Conquest *to delineate divine influences.*

In representations of high-ranking groups on vases, in murals and in relief carvings, Michael Coe has identified that a batch of sticks worn in the headdress was intended to represent scribal pens and was a sign that the individual either held the position of a scribe or, while occupying another court position, was proud of his ability to read and write. Even kings were depicted with the scribal pens in their headdress.

It is indicative of the high regard for individual scribe-artists and their work among the Maya that the scribes who decorated and wrote on the beautiful ceramic products of the Classic Period signed their names on the pots as they finished them. A city-state's chief scribe appears to have lived in the utmost splendour. At Copán, a magnificent building known to archaeologists as the House of the Bacabs has been identified as the home of Max Chanal, chief scribe in the reign of King Yax Pac (AD763–820).

textbooks on the ritual calendar and the movements of the stars. Unfortunately these books were almost all destroyed in the frenzy of book-burning unleashed by Spanish administrators and churchmen who considered them to be idolatrous.

The scholar Nikolai Grube showed that the highest-ranking Maya scribes were also known as *ah k'u'hun* or *ah k'un* ('Keeper of the Sacred Books') and suggested that they were in charge of the king's library. Fellow Maya expert Michael Coe then demonstrated that the *ah k'un* was a key senior administrator who served as master of ceremonies for state and religious ritual, a marriage negotiator and as the writer of royal genealogies and keeper of tribute lists.

In the Classic Period, Maya scribes were educated in scribal schools close to the palace in the centre of Maya cities. The schools were open to the elite, to the offspring of rulers and the upper nobility. Eldest sons would probably have been destined for military training and power, but younger sons, and probably also sons by less senior wives or concubines, would have entered the schools, happy to take the first steps in the prestigious life of the scribe. Women could also be scribes among the Maya and the schools must have taken princesses and the daughters of the nobility.

LITERARY ELITE

Scribes' work was performed by the elite for the elite. In Classic Period Maya cities, an estimated one-quarter of the population could read and write. A larger number, perhaps, could read inscriptions on stelae without being able to write and many more again could admire the artistic achievement of the *ah ts'ib* while having the meaning of the words explained. Among the elite, it was a matter of great pride to be literate.

Right: This figure of a seated Maya scribe was displayed in one of the houses of the elite quarter of Las Sepulturas in Copán.

A SOLDIER'S LIFE

The attractions of a soldier's life were many. In Aztec society members of the army were respected as paragons of courage and fortitude. They were understood to be fulfilling Tenochtitlán's sacred destiny as an imperial power and to be following divine orders to bring prisoners home for sacrifice. When they died, their souls would travel to the east and be made honourable companions of the great sun Tonatiuh himself. Moreover, the military offered one of the few avenues by which a commoner could climb through the ranks of Aztec society. Success in battle, particularly the capture of many prisoners, won a war hero many coveted privileges, such as the right to wear more elaborate clothes, to partake of the alcoholic drink *pulque* in public or even to join the elite military cadres of the jaguar- and eagle-warriors. These top-ranking figures wore magnificent battle costume to go to war and to take part in ceremonial dances and sacred rituals.

A successful warrior won acclaim and seniority within his own *capultin* or clan. Because he had brought glory on the

Below: The soldiers shown in this mural may be mythical figures representing the forces of night taking on the armies of day.

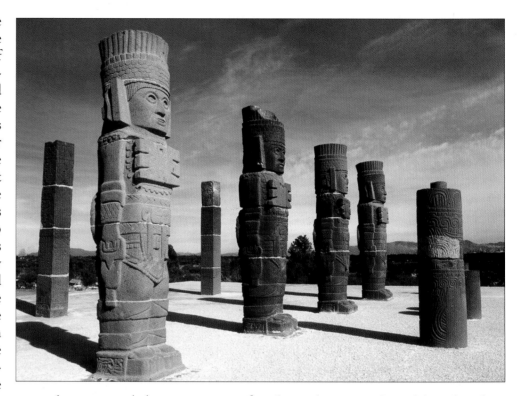

Above: The Atzecs inherited from the Toltecs the ideal of warriors as embodiments of manly vigour and defenders of divine order.

group, he was awarded extra portions of land, or a larger share of any imperial tribute accorded them. He might be named *tecuhtli* ('Grandfather') and in meetings of the clan council his views were respected.

AZTEC RANK AND FILE

Most soldiers were conscripts called up for a campaign by the military establishment in units of around 400 from each *capultin*, or units in a tribute payment of fighting men supplied to the army of the Triple Alliance by one of the empire's subject cities. They would have had a good military training as part of their education in the *telpochcalli* school attached to the local temple. Many also took part in ceremonial military activities as part of religious festivals. Where possible, inexperienced men fought behind veteran warriors. Sometimes novice fighters wore no protective armour, as the wearing of quilted cotton body armour was often restricted to warriors who had achieved glory by killing or capturing many victims. Clan group members wore tribal symbols.

INJURED IN BATTLE

Most Aztec battles were over swiftly, with prisoners of war often far outnumbering battlefield casualties and fatalities. Nevertheless, Mesoamerican armies contained skilled doctors, who accompanied soldiers on campaign equipped with herbs and other natural materials and a wealth of traditional medical knowledge. Army surgeons used obsidian knives to make surgical cuts and human hair to sew up wounds. They even made plaster from tree sap and feathers to set broken bones.

When a soldier was injured by a sharp obsidian *atlatl* dart, the doctor would first clean the wound with whatever sterile liquid was available – if necessary, by using his own urine. Afterwards he looked in his medical bag for a little of the herb he called *coapatli* (a wild form of the common dayflower) to stop the soldier's bleeding. The sap of the maguey agave, which when fermented made the favoured drink *pulque*, was an effective dressing. The doctor gave a herbal painkiller to soldiers who were in terrible pain.

ESCAPING ONE'S ORIGINS

Among the Maya, those who won status as warriors rose from the mass of farmer-commoners to a position halfway up the social pyramid, on a level with artisans and administrators. As among the Aztecs, successful warriors were rewarded with social prestige. Any killed in battle would receive preferential treatment in the after-life, for they were earmarked – along with sacrificial victims, priests, rulers, those who died giving birth and those who hung themselves – for a heavenly place of rest, while the unhappy majority of humankind went down to the dark place of trials, Xibalba. Maya rank and file

Below: Wielding spears, Maya warriors sweep resistance aside as they capture a village in Yucatán.

Above: A detail from the Mixtec Codex Zouche-Nuttall *depicts warrior leaders crossing a river in order to take an island.*

soldiers fought in cotton jerkins or simple loincloths and cloaks, while nobles and elite warriors wore feather-bedecked helmets and jade jewellery. The king went to battle magnificently attired in a jaguar tunic, a symbol of royalty and of ferocious martial strength. He must have been more of a figurehead than a combatant

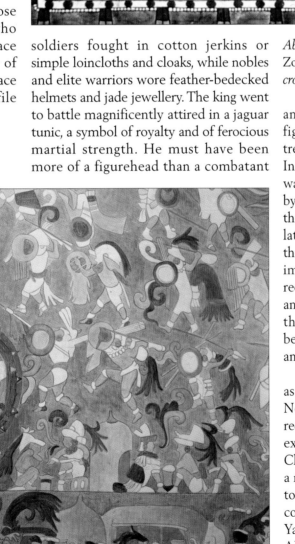

and was protected by a group of elite fighters. The capture of a king was a tremendous coup and ended any battle. In Aztec and Maya realms, the warrior was an ideal, a role occupied or assumed by the ruler. The images of kings carved on the stelae erected in Maya cities from the late Preclassic Period onwards presented the king as warrior and priestly sacrificer, imbued with divine power. The king received this power from his predecessor and passed it on to his successor. He was the link – like the great ceiba tree – between the terrestrial plane of daily life and the heavenly realm of the ancestors.

Martial vigour and achievement was seen as proof of the king's stature and status. Newly elected Aztec *tlatoanis* were required to conduct a war as part of their extended coronation rites; the king of a Classic Period Maya city often undertook a military raid in order to obtain victims to be sacrificed as part of the king's own coronation ceremony. Shield Jaguar II of Yaxchilán took a notable local lord, Ah Ahau, captive in a raid of AD680 that scholars believe was a prelude to Shield Jaguar II's coronation the following year.

IN THE STATE'S SERVICE

The administration of the Aztec empire and its largely self-governing constituent units was a major task and provided employment for large numbers or people. All the most important and senior positions were filled by members of the *pipiltin* nobility. Nobles served as advisers to the ruler, as ambassadors, as governors of allied provinces, as judges, as collectors of tax and tribute, as leading members of the military hierarchy and as bureaucrats. Others joined the priesthood, where they had opportunities to pursue intellectual interests in, say, astronomy, mathematics or writing. All these men were graduates of elite *calmecac* priestly schools.

Commoners – whose living came from farming, fishing, hunting, soldiering, artisan work or mercantile activity – could rise to positions of authority within the *capultin* or tribal clans to which they

Below: A painted Maya pot of c.AD600–900, from the Motagua valley, shows a dignitary carrying shield and spear.

belonged. One was elected *calpullec*, who oversaw economic matters, such as grants of land, within the clan; another was the *teochcautin*, the keeper of laws. At times of conflict, the *teochcautin* led the clan's conscripts to war.

THE KING'S MEN

Similarly, in Maya culture commoner-farmers, fishermen and soldiers could not rise to the most senior administrative and economic positions. In the Maya cities of the Classic Period, the top military staff, administrators and traders were all members of the upper nobility. The top military chief, *sahal*, was generally one of the king's closest relatives.

In Postclassic Yucatán, as described by Bishop Diego de Landa, the ruler of a regional state, called the *halach uinic*, appointed those who governed the towns

Above: Clay figurines from Jaina Island show the elaborate headdresses, jewellery and other adornments of the Maya elite.

and villages of the region from the highest levels of royalty and the nobility, including his own nephews, cousins and brothers. Each of these men, who were called *batabs*, ruled through a council of two or three and decisions on regional matters had to be approved unanimously by all councillors.

The *batab* was the local judge and military leader. He ensured that his town or region was ready with its economic tribute when required by the *halach uinic*. The *batab* had two or three deputies called *ah kulelob* to perform his bidding. He worked closely with a military specialist called a *nacom*, a noble who served in this highly prestigious and coveted position for three years. During this period, he was required to live a celibate and sober life, with no contact of any kind with women. Even those who waited upon him and served his food were required to be men.

Another group of senior administrators were the *ah holpopob* who ran the council meeting house and were well informed on matters of foreign interaction. Day-to-day matters such as village disputes or petty crimes were the province of the *tupiles* or local law officers.

COPÁN'S GOVERNORS

Archaeologists working at Copán have uncovered details of civil administrators in the reign of King Yax Pac (AD763–820). Leading nobles, who lived in the region of Copán called Las Sepulturas by historians, were members of Copán's ruling council and each headed a prestigious blood lineage. Their houses have been excavated and contain splendid carved benches that suggest that these men had significant independent authority and wealth.

One of these was the king's chief scribe, Max Chanal, whose house contains several portraits of him holding his tools. A delicately carved bench dedicated in AD781 celebrates his own rank, his proud descent and the might of his king.

Yax Pac's brothers, Yahua Chan and Yax K'amlay, were also important figures in the administration. Scholars believe that the king's authority was failing and that he attempted to bolster it by giving more power to his brothers and to leading nobles. However, the attempt was doomed to failure. After his death, the dynasty and Copán itself suffered the effects of a decline that had already begun some years earlier.

THE QUICHÉ ARISTOCRACY

Among the Quiché Maya of highland Guatemala, once again, commoners were excluded from the highest levels of government and administration. The nobility or *ahauab* were descendants of the Quiché founders, who were probably originally Putún Maya merchants from the Gulf Coast lowlands of Mexico. The *ahauab* provided rulers, military leaders, priests and administrators.

Members of the middle class could find work as land managers, soldiers, traders and bureaucrats. The *ahauab* were organized into groups depending on descent from a common father. Members of particular kin groups specialized in serving as priests, warriors or administrators. The leaders of these kin groups governed their relatives and served as advisers to the Quiché ruler.

At the Quiché capital Utatlan in the 15th century, three lineages were pre-eminent and identified with gods: the Ahau Quiché were followers of the sky god, the Nihaib were dependents of the moon goddess and the Cawek were devotees of the sun god. Their elite members filled the top administrative posts of army captain, judge and other positions identified as 'speaker' and 'receiving officer', a kind of ambassador and master of ceremonies who received important visitors. Above them all was the ahpop ('Ruler or Mat Lord'). He was high priest, army leader and chairman of the ruling council.

Above: A jade chest piece from Nebaj, Guatemala, c.AD300–900, depicts a seated nobleman.

Below: A limestone carving from Palenque shows King Pacal, seated on a regal jaguar-head stool, receiving a headdress – and so divine authority to rule – from his mother Zac Kuk. Archaeologists found the relief inside House E of the Palenque palace.

NOBLE SERVANTS OF THE GODS

In Maya lands, entering the priesthood was not generally an option for the sons of farmers, artisans or merchants: the most important priestly positions – like the top administrative and legal opportunities – were hereditary and passed down the generations by members of the nobility. Bishop Diego de Landa reported that in the 16th century the leading Maya priests trained their own sons or the younger boys of important lords, while the high priest was succeeded by his son or nearest blood relative.

SERVANTS OF THE SUN

De Landa wrote that the high priest was called *ahuacan* ('Lord Snake') and was kept in fine style by gifts and contributions from secular rulers. He was the final authority on arcane priestly matters concerning astronomy, divination, writing and record keeping, interpreting holy books, the setting of festivals and the ritual to be followed. He led sacrifices and ritual worship only on very important occasions and also oversaw the training and appointment of more junior priests.

The word for priest was *ah kin* ('Servant of the Sun'). One was appointed to discover and interpret the prophecies associated with each of the 13 *katuns* – periods of 7,200 days – that recurred in a cycle as part of the Maya Long Count. Other leading Maya priests at the time of Bishop de Landa were the *chilanes* ('Declaimers'), who functioned as oracles, passing on to eager listeners the decrees and warnings of the gods. These men were shaman-diviners, who reported on the reality they discovered during spirit voyages or in the course of religious visions inspired by mind-altering drugs.

Another priest was the *nacom*, who was entrusted with the crucial sacrificial task of slicing open the victim's chest and removing the heart. This skilled executioner's position was held by a man for his lifetime. His four helpers, who held down the writhing body of the victim on the sacrificial stone, were named *chacs* in honour of the rain god. They also had the task of lighting a new sacred fire at the beginning of each year.

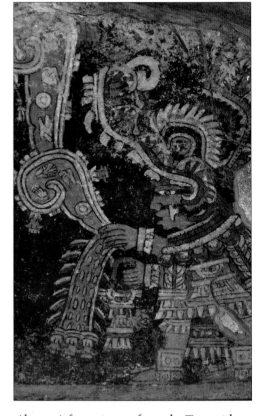

Above: A fresco image from the Tepantitla apartment building in Teotihuacán depicts a priest making obeisance to the deities.

These roles certainly had their counterparts in Maya cities of the Classic Period, although the details of sacrificial practice and priestly hierarchy probably differed. From the very beginnings of settled life in Maya lands, it appears that priests specialized in knowledge of astronomic cycles and seasonal change. They became specialists in time, maintaining control over the recurring patterns of religious life by setting dates for festivals and becoming repositories of dynastic history. They developed the elite skills of writing and reading and, by the Classic Period, were closely associated, if not synonymous, with the scribes and stonemasons who were so revered for their written art.

Left: Wearing facepaint, elaborate costumes and headgear and carrying ritual staffs, Mixtec priests advance to sacrifice.

Above: The goggle eyes of the rain god can be seen on this ceramic figurine of a splendidly attired priest from Teotihuacán.

TEMPLE WOMEN

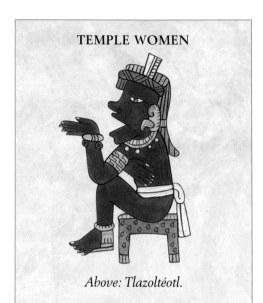

Above: Tlazoltéotl.

There were many opportunities for women in Aztec religious life. The major goddesses were served by cadres of female priests. For example, priestesses of the fertility goddess Tlazoltéotl heard confessions from those wishing to own up to sexual wrongdoing. The priestess of Chalchiúhtlicue, goddess of rivers and ocean, performed a rite of blessing for newborn babies, sprinkling the infant with holy water. Priestesses also represented and impersonated their patron during religious festivals. During the festival of Huey Tozoztli ('Major Vigil'), the priestess of corn goddess Chicomecóatl pronounced a blessing over farmers' supply of seeds.

In Ochpaniztli ('Clearing'), the harvest celebration, the Chicomecóatl priestess sacrificed and flayed a female victim and donned her skin as a suit. With another priestess, appearing as the fertility goddess Toci, she then hurled fistfuls of corn into the crowd. Farmers kept the seeds for planting next season.

Some priestesses, the *maqui*, served as temple prostitutes. They were visited by young warriors, travelled with the army on campaign and even marched into battle. Their divine patron was Xochiquetzal, goddess of flowers.

MANY PRIESTS, MANY TASKS

While the top-level priests were all members of the *pipiltin* nobility in Aztec society, members of any class could become rank and file priests. There was a range of opportunities for priests. Top-level sacerdotal administrators supervised the ranks of priests, the priestly schools, the performance of ritual and the practical management of temple finances and landholdings. Elite serving priests led worship in the Templo Major and main temples and performed major sacrifices on important religious feast days. Other sons of the nobility lived as monk-like attendants and celebrants in the great temples. Each painted his body black or wore a long, black-hooded cloak. They were celibate and often fasted for festivals. Their hair was matted with blood from the cuts they made to their head during rites of autosacrifice.

Right: The elaborate ritual costume, headgear and jewellery worn by Maya priests are depicted in delicate detail on a stela from the mid-8th century AD.

Some priests were members of the army and marched into battle alongside high-ranking soldiers in the centre of the army's battle line. They carried images of Huitzilopochtli and other deities. Others worked in *calmecac* schools, where all the teachers were priests. Some were the learned artist-scribes who expressed their vast knowledge of astronomical cycles and ritual worship in codex books. Others were shaman-diviners, gifted with spiritual vision, the capacity to interpret it and the gift of spirit and body healing.

CHAPTER FIVE

EVERYDAY LIFE

The day started early for Mesoamericans: the people of Tenochtitlán rose before dawn. When the morning star, Venus, appeared in the sky, drums and conch trumpets sounded from the Templo Mayor and the temples that were the focus of religious life in each locality. The *tlatoani*, his relatives and the nobles, priests, farmers, fishermen, hunters and merchants all awoke. Many took a steam bath to refresh themselves. For most, breakfast was a few tortillas or tamales, perhaps a cup of *atolli* or maize soup. Labourers carried a few more maize snacks to work for a midday meal.

In a Maya village or city of the Classic Period, the first hours of the day were markedly similar. The majority rose before dawn, took a steam bath, ate a maize breakfast and made their way to the fields, artisan-workshop or other place of work grasping a few tortillas for later sustenance.

After a long day's labour, most workers were home before dark. They ate their largest meal, again based on maize, at this time. Some accounts suggest that labourers, hungry from their labours in the fields, ate as many as 20 large tortillas at evening meal. Men and women usually ate separately, squatting or sitting on the floor. Afterwards, lighting their homes with pine torches, both men and women often settled down to craft-work, perhaps chipping simple tools from flint or making pots for their own use. Merchants, by contrast, sometimes hosted elaborate feasts, while in noble houses evenings of poetry and music might be laid on in gardens and patio areas giving on to luxuriously appointed dining areas.

Left: A page from the Mixtec Codex Zouche-Nuttall depicts the wedding of Lady 3-Flint to Lord 12-Wind.

LIFE IN THE HOME

In Tenochtitlán, the *tlatoani's* divine magnificence was reflected in the splendour of his elegantly decorated palace, surrounded by gardens containing ponds, walkways, an aviary and even a zoo. Members of the *pipiltin* nobility also had palatial residences with a *temazcalli* or steam bath and expansive gardens, while wealthy merchants and craftsmen expressed their social standing in fine, but much smaller houses. The home of a common family was a single-roomed hut, or a few rooms clustered around a courtyard. Walls were usually of adobe or wattle and daub, although some wealthier commoners lived in stone buildings.

Multiroom houses contained one or more bedrooms, a living room with a central hearth and perhaps a bathroom. Single-room huts provided little more

Below: Aztecs lived on or near the floor, sitting on reed mats to eat and work at weaving or toolmaking close to the hearth.

than a space for sleeping, with the family hearth often situated outside beneath a canopy. The family might keep a turkey or a small dog in a pen alongside the house or a few birds in a cage. Many households also had a small garden called a *xochichinancalli* ('flowerbed among the reeds') for growing vegetables, flowers and healing herbs. All houses had a shrine to the ancestors. The location as well as the size of a family's home depended on their wealth and social standing.

WORKING FROM HOME

Home was a place of labour for women, who spent long hours spinning, weaving and cooking. They span thread from maguey agave, henepen or cotton using a handheld drop spindle, working it into woven cloth using a loom strapped on the back and held in the lap. When not weaving or sewing, they ground maize for hours using a rolling stone or pestle at a low table called a *metatl*. With maize dough they made tortillas on a large clay disc laid over a fire on three hearthstones.

Above: This modern reconstruction of an Aztec working family shows a farmer bringing home crops while his relatives weave and attend to the children.

Poorer families generally lived farther away from the city centre. They often lived in single-room huts, whereas the better off families lived in stone buildings nearer the city's ceremonial precincts and major markets. Aztec houses had little or no furniture: people worked, sat and ate on the floor. They usually slept on woven reed mats.

The men worked in the *chinampa* fields or took their boats, nets and harpoons out fishing on the lake. They taught their sons how to fish and encouraged them to try their luck at catching birds. If the conscription call came, they could be forced to go on military campaign in the army or perhaps to serve as labourers in a vast building construction project designed to express the might and celebrate the religious devotion of the 'people of the sun'.

Left: The kind of thatched hut typically occupied by Maya peasants is depicted amid trees in a detail from a temple mural.

WITHIN THE CORNER POSTS

In the lowlands of the central Maya region, the typical commoner's house was built on a low platform of earth or rubble, with walls of stone, mud blocks or adobe built around four wooden corner posts and a roof of pole and thatch. Sometimes only the lower half of the wall was made of long-lasting materials such as stone or adobe, and the upper part was filled in with straw or reeds. The house contained one or two rooms at most.

Builders often laid out three or four of these small constructions around a central courtyard. According to Bishop Diego de Landa, the Maya of Yucatán split these houses lengthways by building an internal wall. In the rear, private part they built bed frames of branches and saplings over which they laid mats as mattresses. Here they slept, using cloaks as coverings.

The front part of the house functioned as a kind of porch, and provided a cooler place to sleep in hot weather. In some areas a family group might have used several small buildings arranged around a central yard: one for storing food, tools and equipment, one for sleeping, one as a living area, one as a shrine, one as a workshop for making stone tools – and a small hut with a central fire heating stones for use as a steam room. Some Maya villagers stored food and water in pits called *chultunes* dug in the ground.

As among the Aztecs, the majority of men were away from home for long hours working in the fields or hunting. At home, the women worked ceaselessly spinning, weaving, grinding flour, preparing food, tending to the garden and the needs of the turkeys or dogs they kept for meat.

Any cloth that was not needed, together with surplus vegetables or other items that could be spared from the garden were taken to the nearest market to be sold or to barter for items which the family did not make themselves.

At times of sowing and harvest the division of labour shifted, so that women went out to assist their menfolk in the fields with the extra seasonal work.

FAMILY NETWORK

People tended to live in family or extended family groups. At Tikal, an extended family often lived in houses arranged on the north, south and west sides of a courtyard and facing east towards a fourth building on a higher platform. This probably contained a shrine to the ancestors and, beneath the floor, the graves of the most revered among past family members.

All members of Maya settlements lived in the same pattern of buildings. Wealthier members such as nobles, traders, military leaders and the king lived in increasingly splendid versions of the basic buildings.

Below: Carving on an archway in Labná depicts a simple, one-roomed thatched hut.

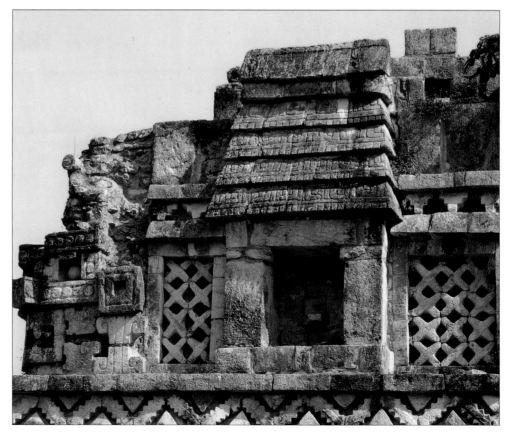

THE MATCHMAKER'S ART

Among the Maya of Yucatán at the time of the Spanish Conquest, girls and boys who reached puberty went through a ceremony named the Descent of the Gods. The sacred rite, performed by a priest with the help of local elders, set the young apart from their childhood. From that day onwards, they were considered to be members of the adult community.

Girls were then judged to be ready for marriage. Their mothers taught them the skills necessary for married life and instructed their daughters in modesty. This included showing her how, when she met a man on a path, she should turn away and present her back to him, so that he could pass easily and undisturbed. The young woman was also instructed that, if she came to the well with her cousin or another man, she should keep her eyes gently lowered as she brought him water.

In some Maya communities, sons left the parental house and moved into a communal building set aside for unmarried men. There they played dice and games with small balls and beans. It was not unknown for these young men to bring prostitutes home and they paid for their services with a handful of cacao beans. Unmarried men marked themselves out by painting their skin with black dye. They avoided tattoos, which were only permitted to husbands.

MARRIAGE PLANNING

Marriages were generally arranged, either by the father or by a professional matchmaker called an *ah atanzah*. The ideal wife would be a woman of the same social level and from the same village as the son. Marriage plans were often agreed between families while the son and daughter to be wed were still children; the families then began to live as in-laws even though the marriage might be some years off.

Before any marriage agreement was made, both families consulted the priestly astronomers who made sure that there was no ill omen attached to the prospective couple's dates of birth or to the day proposed for the wedding ceremony. Marriages were permitted between first cousins, but some unions were taboo. For example, a man could not marry a woman who carried the same surname or patronym.

Left: Xochiquetzal, ('Precious Flower') was honoured by the Aztecs as a goddess of love, domesticity and the flowers of the earth.

Above: Chalchiúhtlicue, who presided over the prolonged wedding ceremonies of the Aztecs, is usually shown wearing jade.

The marriage ceremony was held in the house of the bride's father. The couple wore new robes woven for the occasion by the two mothers. After the wedding the new husband and wife lived in the house or the group of houses occupied by the bride's family for about six or seven years. The husband's new in-laws benefited from his labour throughout this time and, indeed, by custom could evict him from their home compound if he refused to work.

After this the couple moved to live adjacent to the husband's father, often in a newly built house within the complex. Commoners had one wife, but wealthier men could wed several women. Members of the elite in Classic Period Maya cities such as Tikal took many wives and also kept women outside wedlock as concubines.

DEATH AND DIVORCE

A couple could divorce simply by one partner repudiating the other. Younger children of the wedding would remain with the mother, while older children tended to go with the same-sex parent.

A man might divorce his wife if she proved unable to have children or if she failed in duties such as making food or preparing his evening bath. Any remarriage took place without ceremony, as wedding rites were reserved for first marriages. A man seeking a new union would simply visit the house of the woman he had chosen. If she was agreeable she would prepare him a meal. Widows and widowers were expected to mourn the lost partner for a year before remarrying. A widower could not marry his dead wife's sister or mother.

CHALCHIÚHTLICUE'S BLESSING

Customs were not very different among the Aztecs. Weddings came under the protection of river and ocean goddess Chalchiúhtlicue. Young Aztecs married in their late teenage years or perhaps their early twenties. The young man's parents arranged his marriage after consulting with members of the extended family or kin group. They sent a professional matchmaker to the parents of the chosen young woman. The matchmaker presented his case on four consecutive days, after which the parents of the young woman were expected to announce whether they accepted the marriage offer or not.

The marriage ceremony lasted four days. On the evening of the first day, the bride was bathed and dressed in fine robes, before her kinswomen decorated her legs and arms with red feathers and painted her face with a paste containing tiny, shimmering crystals. They offered

Left: A scene from the Codex Becker *shows the wedding of a Mixtec noble couple. Faint footsteps lead to their future offspring.*

her words of wisdom about the life she was preparing to begin, then the strongest one lifted the bride on to her back and carried her through the streets to the house of the husband's parents.

Inside, amid scenes of celebration, the couple sat side by side on a marriage mat, while elders lit a fire in the family hearth and burned offerings of copal incense, which sent up sacred clouds of smoke to attract the gods' blessings. The groom's mother produced a wealth of robes and mantles as gifts for her prospective in-laws. Then a matchmaker approached the couple and tied the groom's cape to the bride's skirt and the groom's mother fed first the bride and then the groom with

four mouthfuls of tamales, a dish prepared of meat and corn husks. This ceremony marked the couple's union: next they were led into the bedroom to consummate their marriage, while the gathered relatives made merry.

Feasting continued for four days. At the end of this time, a series of formal speeches concluded the celebration. First, the most respected elder female on the new husband's side reminded the new wife of her duties and of the need to be trusting, humble and hard working. The mother of the bride spoke next, to her new son-in-law, asking him to remember that he owed his wife a duty of love, hard work and self-sacrificing attention.

Below: The bride arrives at her wedding on the back of her matchmaker (bottom centre) and is shown, later, seated on a mat.

A CHILD IS BORN

When a pregnant woman went into labour, her midwife would lead prayers to the goddess of childbirth – Tlazoltéotl among the Aztecs and Ix Chel among the Maya – to ease the woman's pain and bring a healthy baby. The midwife mixed herbs and grasses to produce a sedative mixture that she fed to the mother. She then gently laid a warm stone on her straining belly. Among the Aztecs, when the baby was born the midwife would utter a series of battle cries in praise of the exhausted mother who had fought long and hard with her offspring in

labour. Then the midwife would speak to the baby, greeting the new arrival as if it were a voyager who had completed a long and difficult journey, encouraging the infant to settle among its family, declaring that life in the world was short but a man or woman had many duties, the most important of which were to work hard and to honour the gods.

The midwife would next cut the baby's umbilical cord and store it safely, before giving the baby its first bath, explaining in a reverent voice that pure and cleansing waters were the gift of Chalchiúhtlicue, the consort of Tláloc the rain god and goddess of springs, rivers and the sea. If the baby were a boy, he was expected to keep the umbilical cord until adulthood and carry it to a distant battlefield, where it was his duty to bury it; a girl would bury her umbilical cord beside the family hearth.

Left: Heavy with the power of fertility, this statue of a pregnant woman was made in Nayarit, West Mexico, c.200BC–AD200.

Above: Power over the beginnings of life. This almost abstract face is believed to be that of the Huastec goddess of childbirth.

After its first bath, the newborn was ready to receive visitors. Many members of the extended family came to pay their respects. One after another, they would make reverent declarations of respect for

A NOBLE WELCOMING
Among noble and wealthy Aztecs, a baby's arrival was celebrated with a lying-in that lasted up to three weeks. Visitors came from great distances – some important families even received ambassadors from foreign states. The hosts provided splendid gifts of the finest woven cloaks and embroidered skirts for their prominent guests. Food, *pulque* and other drinks were provided for all who came to pay their respects.

the mother, the midwife and the newborn baby. Visitors were greeted with food and drink. Priestly interpreters of the *tonalamatl* book of the sacred calendar would arrive to interpret the ramifications of the baby's precise minute, hour and day of birth for its prospects and future behaviour.

Much depended on which gods were influential at the child's birth. If the omens were bad, the interpreters offered advice as to how parents and baby could improve the infant's prospects. They also set the date for the baby's bathing ritual: this would normally be four days after the birth, but could be delayed or brought forward if the divine influences on that day were not good.

A BATHING CEREMONY

On the appointed day, the midwife conducted the bathing ceremony in the presence of parents and extended family. She laid a basin of water on a reed mat and surrounded it with miniature tools appropriate to the baby's sex and the family's standing and profession. If a boy child had been destined for the army by the *tonalamatl* priests, the midwife would lay out a small bow and arrow on top of an amaranth-dough tortilla intended to represent a warrior's shield. If he were the son of an artisan, then she would lay out tiny implements representing the father's profession, the path that lay before the boy as he grew. For a female baby, the midwife would place a tiny skirt together with spinning instruments to represent a woman's work.

The midwife then circled the basin in an anticlockwise direction as she spoke to the baby, before she bathed him or her and presented him or her four times to the heavens and to the cleansing water provided by blessed Chalchiúhtlicue. Any older children in the family were next sent out into the street to publicly announce the name chosen for the

Left: The young boy represented by this terracotta statuette, made in Veracruz c.AD550–850, learned to wear headdress, earrings and necklace before clothes.

newborn. The baby was dried, dressed and laid in its cradle while the joyful mother, the father and the assembled relatives celebrated the birth with feasting and music.

A WEB OF DIVINE INFLUENCES

The Maya keenly believed the minute, hour and day of a baby's birth in the ritual calendar set the child's temperament, determined its prospects and brought with it religious and ritual responsibilities – acts that were necessary to limit or bring to fruition the divine influences at work in the moment of birth.

Among the Cakchiquel and other southern highland Maya, babies were given the name of the day in the 260-day calendar on which they were born. Among the Yucatec-speaking Maya at the time of the Spanish Conquest, each baby took four names: a name chosen by a

priest following a divining ceremony; the father's family name; the family names of father and mother together; and lastly a familiar or nickname.

So developed was the shared aesthetic sense among the Maya that mothers and fathers were willing to work on the baby's body to make it conform to common ideals of beauty. To produce the flattened forehead that was widely admired they bound the baby's head between flat pieces of wood, one pressed against the forehead and one against the back of the skull. After several days encased in this way, a baby's skull was flattened for the remainder of life. The Maya also admired a cross-eyed look, so a mother would tied resin balls to the hairs that fell down towards the eyes of the growing baby to encourage the child to focus on the resin balls.

THE FIRST YEARS

Aztec parents brought their children up to be hardworking, dutiful and self-disciplined. As toddlers grew older, their parents taught them various domestic tasks. At around the age of three, daughters were taught by their mothers to spin and weave, to grind maize and to make tortillas. At the same age, boys began to help around the house, for example, by fetching and carrying water. When boys reached the age of six or seven years, they began to spend their days with their fathers at the lakeside, learning to fish and to gather reeds. If the family made their living by a specialized craft such as pottery or basketmaking, the mother or father would begin instruction in its techniques when the child was aged eight to ten years.

The Aztecs were not averse to using corporal punishment to bring their children into line, although codex accounts suggest that they avoided doing so until the child was around eight or nine years old. The Codex Mendoza shows parents punishing backsliding or lazy children by pinching them on the ears or arms, pricking their skin with the thorns of the maguey cactus, spanking them or binding them up and laying them in a cold, damp place. The most unusual punishment depicted was forcing a child to inhale the burning odours of roasting chilli peppers by holding him or her over a fire on which chillies had been scattered.

AZTEC SCHOOLS

Children progressed to school when they came of age. Scholars are uncertain whether this was at 7, 10 or 14 years. Children of commoners went to the *telpochcalli* ('young person's house') that stood beside their local temple. In sizeable cities there was a *telpochcalli* for each *calpulli* or residential ward. Girls and boys were taught separately. They learned history, public speaking, dancing and singing and received religious instruction. Boys also underwent rigorous military training, while girls learned to serve in the temples of the city. An Aztec education emphasized a young person's duties and responsibilities: he or she was encouraged to find fulfilment in serving the gods, the state, the *calpulli* and the family livelihood.

Sons and daughters of the nobility were educated separately from commoners, in establishments called *calmecac*. They received instruction in religious ritual, in following the sacred calendar and

Left: The Codex Mendoza *shows discipline of 7–10 year-olds. At 7, a boy is taught to fish while a girl learns to spin; beneath, the children are threatened with maguey spikes at age 8, then pricked with the spikes at 9, and bound and beaten at the age of 10.*

LEARNING IN MAYA LANDS

The Maya of the Classic Period ran similar elite schools to train the younger sons of royalty and the highest echelons of the nobility as artist-scribes. Some elite Maya scribes were women, so these elite schools must either have accepted female pupils or have operated sister establishments for princesses and the daughters of the nobility.

Less privileged Maya were educated at home in the skills of domestic living and of the family livelihood. For the first three years both boys and girls spent their time almost exclusively with their mother, but from the age of four or five years they began a wider life. At this stage a boy would have a white bead tied in his hair as a sign that he was ready to accompany and begin learning from his father, while a girl had a red shell tied to a string around her waist. Boys went with their fathers to the fields and on hunting trips, day by day picking up the skills they would need in adult life.

Below: A potter in Tlatilco, Mexico, made this striking and well proportioned ceramic child's head c.400BC.

Above: The Codex Mendoza *depicts 11-year-olds being forced to inhale chilli smoke; at 13, the boy transports rushes by canoe while the girl grinds maize for tortillas.*

interpreting the *tonalamatl* and in understanding and conducting the main festivals of the Aztec religious year. They also learned military theory, agriculture and horticulture, astronomy, history and the skills of architecture and arithmetic. Students at *calmecac* were also taught and practised the skills of high oratory and of reading and writing. They graduated to become such leading figures of state as judges, military commanders, bureaucrats and priests in the most important temples. A few very able children of commoners were also selected to enjoy the benefits of this elite form of education. There was one elite school for girls and one for boys in each city. Students were expected to follow religious fasts, to perform penances and to take purifying sacred baths. Their teachers were priests.

THE GIFT OF THE MAIZE GOD

Throughout Mesoamerica the staple food was maize. Its preparation was laborious: first it was soaked with lime or ash, then boiled until its skin could be pulled off; afterwards it was ground to a paste with a grooved rolling stone on a long flat stone the Aztecs called a *metatl*. This dough was baked as tortillas (flat, thin cakes) on a circular clay dish supported over the fire by three hearthstones. Maize was cooked with chilli pepper and honey in a soup-like stew the Aztecs called *atolli* and in tamales – mixed with peppers and vegetables or sometimes meat, then wrapped in cornhusks and baked on the cooking plate.

Below: A ceramic Zapotec funerary urn from a Monte Albán tomb depicts the corn god with an animal-mask headdress.

A Maya villager woke to a breakfast of maize water, then left for the fields carrying several balls of ground maize encased in leaves. At night, refreshed after his agricultural labours by a steam bath, he was served tortillas. In Atzec lands a peasant's midday meal consisted of the maize soup *atolli* and his reward for his work in the evening was to dine on tortillas topped with beans, other vegetables and chilli sauce.

FEASTING ON FLESH

Richer members of the Aztec community ate a more elaborate diet, but it was always based on tortillas and tamales. Successful merchants laid on magnificent feasts for their fellows to boost their professional standing. During the festival of Panquetzalíztli, held in honour of the Aztecs' tribal lord Huitzilopochtli, these feasts included the flesh of slaves provided by the merchants to be sacrificed at the temple – served with tortillas, tamales and other maize and bean delicacies. According to the records of the Spanish churchman Bernardino de Sahagún, the *tlatoani* or ruler of Tenochtitlán faced an array of 2,000 dishes every day. This combined basic and luxury foods – tortillas, tamales, turkey, venison, quail, rabbit, hare, rat and many fishes, plus fruits in great variety.

VEGETABLE VARIETY

To supplement their maize, Mesoamericans grew the grain amaranth, called *huautli* in the Aztecs' Nahuatl language. The Aztecs ate a wide range of vegetables including many types of bean, squashes, onions, sweet potatoes (called *camotli*) and a root vegetable

Above: The Tudela Codex (1553) *shows a woman pouring chocolate from a height to give the drink a frothy head.*

called *jicama*, which resembled the turnip. It was added to vegetable stews, steamed or thinly sliced and eaten raw with a spicy chilli and salt seasoning. They also added peanuts and popcorn to their diet. Among fruits they ate the green tomato (called *tomatl*) and the red tomato (*xictomatl*), the avocado (*ahuacatl*), the custard apple, the zapote, the guava and the chirimoya.

The poor ate whatever meat and fish they could add to their diet. The Maya ate deer, home-raised and wild turkeys, iguanas, armadillos, rabbits, peccaries (a pig-like mammal), squirrels, porcupines, monkeys, macaws and other birds and rodents including agouti, paca and doubtless rats. Those among the Maya who lived in coastal, riverside and lakeside areas ate fish and shellfish while others

Above: On a painted plate from the region of Tikal, an enthroned ruler is being served a cup of the chocolate drink.

made do with dried fish transported by traders. In Tenochtitlán and other Aztec cities, the menfolk caught fish and birds, and they probably hunted rabbits and deer in the countryside. Families raised turkeys and dogs in small pens and birds in cages if they could afford to do so. Sometimes the women-folk traded home-woven cloth and flint tools or obsidian blades made at home by their husbands for deer or rabbit meat at the market.

SEASONINGS AND DRINKS

As well as chilli peppers, Mesoamericans used coriander, sage and the herb dogweed (*chenopodium*) for seasoning. Among other flavourings, they prized vanilla very highly, finding it in the pods of a species of orchid.

The wealthy greatly enjoyed the chocolate drink the Aztecs called *xocolatl*. A man making the drink would grind roasted cacao beans then sometimes mix the powder with dried corn. He would add cold water and beat the liquid until it foamed, then add pods of the vanilla orchid or spoonfuls of honey. The Maya also used a flower called the ear flower (identified by scholars as *Cymbalopetalum penduliflora*) as a flavouring for chocolate drink. In carved and ceramic representations of elite groups, one noble figure is often depicted holding a bundle of these ear flowers.

Xocolatl was a drink of rulers, princes and nobles: some sources suggest that Moctezuma II and his court consumed 50 jugs of the drink every day. The Maya served it in tall cylindrical vases from which they poured it into shallow calabash drinking cups from a great height to generate froth. In AD749, a king of Piedras Negras celebrated the 20th anniversary of his accession with a chocolate-drinking ceremony with leading members of the nobility and an ambassador from Yaxchilán. The event was commemorated in a carved wall panel. Chocolate was also drunk by Maya parents and matchmakers during elite marriage negotiations and it was served at high-class weddings.

Throughout Mesoamerica, people drank an alcoholic drink made from the fermented sap of the maguey agave together with a bush root called pulque wood. The drink was called *pulque* by the Aztecs. They celebrated the goddess Mayáhuel as the divine patron of the drink.

In Aztec lands, *pulque* was officially allowed only to nobles, the ill and the elderly and to warriors brave in battle. There were fierce laws against public drunkenness, enforceable by the death penalty if a person were discovered drunk three times.

Bishop Diego de Landa, describing religious ceremonies celebrated each month by the Maya, suggests that public drinking and intoxication was part of religious ceremonial. Celebrants indulged in a sacred wine called *balche* made from the bark of the balche tree together with water and fermented honey. It was left to steep for some time, during which a prayer was intoned to the spirits of all animals and plants in the surrounding wilderness. It was said to induce feelings of tribal unity and togetherness.

Right: A Huastec statue celebrates corn goddess Chicomecóatl. She was also known as Chicomolotzin ('Seven Ears of Maize').

CLOTHES AND HAIRSTYLES

In Maya lands, commoners, nobility and royalty all wore the same basic clothing but wealthier people possessed far more ornate and elaborate versions of the outfit worn by the peasants.

MAYA MALE WARDROBE

The male Maya peasant wound a cotton loincloth between his legs and several times around his waist. The cloth, called *ex* in the Yucatec tongue, was woven on the home handloom and was around five fingers in width. More elaborate versions of the *ex* were decorated with feathers at each end and, when worn, these hung down colourfully before and behind. Elite men wore loincloths embellished with geometric designs and the heads of deities. Nobles often wore a belt from which they hung jade deity masks and plaques. They might also have worn a god mask on the chest together with a jade-bead necklace.

When he needed protection from the elements, a man wore a square cotton robe over the loincloth. It was held up by knots on the shoulders. This piece of clothing, called a *pati* in Yucatec, was worn plain by the poorest, but was decorated with elaborate embroidery when worn by wealthier members of the community. Rulers often wore a jaguar skin or a *pati* sewn with quetzal feathers to signify their exalted status.

Maya peasants wore deer-hide sandals (*xanch*) tied between the toes and around the ankles with cords of hemp. Nobles wore extremely elaborate sandals with long ties and large heel covers decorated with images of ancestors and deities.

Above: The magnificence of a Maya lord's headdress and chest plate is recreated in this terracotta figure, made c.AD100–650.

Left: Twin statuettes made in Oaxaca AD1150–1250 represent Mixtecs wearing elaborate ear and face jewellery.

MAYA FEMALE WARDROBE

Women in Maya communities wore a loose cotton garment called a *huipil*. In some communities, the *huipil* was a waist-length blouse, worn with a skirt; in others it was a loose, untailored shift-like dress with head and armholes. The *huipil* blouse is worn to this day by Maya women in the mountains of Guatemala: each community has its own distinctive embroidered geometric design. The loose-fitting *huipil* dress is still worn by Maya women in Yucatán, where traditional embroidered designs decorate the hem and the area around the arms and neck. The 16th century authority Herrera, who reported on the Maya for the Spanish crown, wrote that in his era women wore a loose sack-like dress like the Yucatán *huipil*, together with a cotton headdress. Bishop Diego de Landa wrote that Maya

Above: Musicians and court attendants at Bonampak wear relatively simple costumes but extravagant masks and headdresses.

women wore a simple skirt and a cotton cloth wound around the torso to cover their breasts. Women sometimes also wore a petticoat beneath the *huipil* or skirt, and a shawl over it.

HAIRSTYLES AND BODY ART

Men shaved a small area at the crown of the head, but otherwise kept their hair long, winding it in a plait around the head with the 'tail' dangling down the neck. Luxuriant tresses of black hair were the pride of Maya women, and mothers instructed their growing daughters in caring for their hair and in the many different hairstyles worn. Men and women experimented with body paint and tattoos: the designs worn by women were more delicate than those sported by their husbands and brothers. The colour of body paint could be significant: black indicated that a man was a bachelor, black and red meant a warrior, while black and white was reserved for prisoners. A prayer would be offered for men painted turquoise blue, for they were bound for a fate of ritual slaughter under the priest's sacrificial knife.

Low-ranking men and women wore simple loop earrings made from stone, shell, bone or wood. They embellished their appearance with lip and nose plugs. Elite figures, on the other hand, wore lip plugs, earrings and nose plugs made from obsidian, jade or stone. They also wore a variety of necklaces, collars, bracelets and knee or ankle bands made of jade, feathers, sea or river shells, crocodile teeth and the teeth or claws of the majestic jaguar. After the arrival of metalworking among the Maya in around the 9th century AD, the elite began to wear ornaments and decorations of copper or gold.

ONE ROBE FITS ALL

Among the Aztecs, clothing was also similar among all classes, with the higher social ranks wearing more elaborate garments. Peasant farmers and fishermen often went barefoot and wore a simple loincloth or *máxtlatl*, adding a cloak or *tilmatl* that was knotted over the

Right: Just 14cm (6in) tall, this figurine shows the headdress in great detail.

shoulder when necessary. Among the poor these items were woven from maguey agave fibres, but the wealthier wore cotton. The *tilmatl* might be decorated with animal designs or geometric patterns or have a coloured border. Leading nobles' robes were sometimes feather-covered, bordered with rabbit-fur, dyed turquoise or decorated with jade beads, seashells and pieces of gold. Those in highest authority were permitted to wear a richly coloured waistcoat or *xicolli*.

Nobles wore sandals (*cacli*) usually made of animal skin or woven plant fibres. As among the Maya, these had pronounced heel covers to protect the back of the foot. They also had rubber boots.

Aztec women wore a skirt called a *cúeitl*, wound about the lower body and tied at the waist with a fabric belt. There were regional variations in upper garments. In Tenochtitlán, women wore a waist-length shirt called a *huipil*: the word that is used for the similar Maya garment by scholars is in fact from the Aztecs' Nahuatl tongue. Elsewhere, women tended to wear a cape called a *quechquémitl*.

BEATING THE ODDS

According to Spanish chroniclers, the Aztecs were devoted gamblers. All Mesoamerican games had religious overtones because they saw the entire universe as structured by and charged with divine meaning. Even the apparently chance events of a sporting contest or a gambling pastime were open to interpretation and might provide guidance from the gods.

THE BALL GAME

By far the greatest devotion was reserved for the ball game. It was played in various forms from at least the mid-second millennium BC in Mesoamerica. Two teams of players on an I-shaped earth or stone court tried to send a hard rubber ball through a stone loop set high on one or both walls – or in some versions into the 'end zone' behind their opponents – using elbows, hips and legs. The game was rich in religious symbolism. The ball might be identified with the sun, or the match interpreted as a re-enactment

Above: The test of daring called voladores. *Later, the men will swing upside down around the pole on the end of the ropes.*

of sacred battles between the Aztec gods Quetzalcóatl and Tezcatlipoca or between the Maya Hero Twins and the lords of the underworld. Spectators gambled on the outcome of matches. The game must have been an exhilarating spectacle, played at high speed by very skilled and brave performers wearing elaborate protective costumes. Nevertheless, the ball game was so deeply coloured by its many religious overtones that it was more a religious ceremony than a public sporting contest.

THE BEAN GAME

Another ancient Mesoamerican game of chance and skill, called *patolli* by the Aztecs, was played on the ground using a cross-shaped board of 52 squares painted on a mat or scratched into plaster or clay. Players moved blue and red pieces around the board according to the throw of dice, with the aim of moving all one's pieces to the centre of the cross. The game that developed into *patolli* was played at least as early as the 7th century AD, when a

Left: On the feast of Xocotluetzi, young men competed in climbing the pole to be first to take hold of symbols hanging there.

board was marked out on the floor of the Zacuala residential building in Teotihuacán. About 100–200 years later, no fewer than three boards were marked on the plaster floor of the Palacio Quemado at Tollán.

The cross-shaped Aztec board appears to have been a simplification of an older design incorporating a cruciform shape and squares. *Patolli*, like the ball game, was played throughout Mesoamerica. The Maya marked out playing boards at many ancient sites including Tikal, Uaxactún, Piedras Negras, Chichén Itzá, Palenque and Dzibilchaltún.

In their version of the game, the Aztecs used inscribed kidney beans as their dice – their name *patolli* derives from the Nahuatl word for kidney bean. Both players and onlookers placed wagers: according to a report by Diego Durán, a noisy group would gather around the game and bet on the players. Wealthy merchants and members of the nobility risked large amounts of gold and precious jewels on the outcome; others bet what they could afford. Desperate gamers are said to have bet their house or even their freedom on the result. Durán's report indicated that the game was called *totoloque* and that both playing pieces and dice were made of gold, but scholars believe he must have been mistaken on this last point.

Winning or losing was in the hands of the gods. Durán wrote that players would pray to Macuilxóchitl, god of pleasure and of games, and cast incense into a nearby brazier before making a throw. Sometimes priestly diviners would be asked to interpret the outcome of a throw or of a game. The mat was portable, so the game could be played anywhere, even in the streets. Spanish chroniclers' accounts suggest that *patolli* was played with remarkable and noisy fervour at all hours of night and day in Tenochtitlán.

The Aztecs also played a game resembling checkers on a mat or board marked with squares, using black and white pieces.

POLE GAMES

Two remarkable tests of skill and strength centred on descending or climbing a tall pole. One was a contest associated with the festival of the god Huehuetéotl. Several men competed to be first to reach the top of a very tall pole and grasp an icon of Huehuetéotl that had been placed there.

Another game, dubbed *voladores* ('flyers') by the Spanish conquistadors, involved five men. The five players clambered to the top of a pole. Four attached themselves by one ankle to ropes that were wound elaborately around the pole while the fifth settled himself with flute and drum on a wooden platform at the top of the pole.

As the drummer-flautist played his musical instruments, each of the four flyers leapt headfirst from the pole. Falling upside down, the men would swing round and round by the ankle very fast and getting closer and closer to the ground as the rope unravelled. Just before the flyer smashed his head on the ground, the man would pull himself up on the rope with his hands. This meant that he landed feet-first on the ground – and the momentum then carried him forward at a fast pace. An image from the *Codex Borbonicus* depicts the men circling the pole on ropes to the beat of the drum,

while a priest standing on the steps of a nearby temple pyramid calls down a blessing on the proceedings.

This test of skill as performed by the Aztecs is still attempted in the early 21st century in the Gulf Coast region of Mexico.

Above: Diego Durán gave a full account of patolli *in the* Codex Durán. *This image, from that codex, is of a variant of the game.*

Below: These columns are all that remains of Tollán's Palacio Quemado, where three patolli *boards were marked on the floor.*

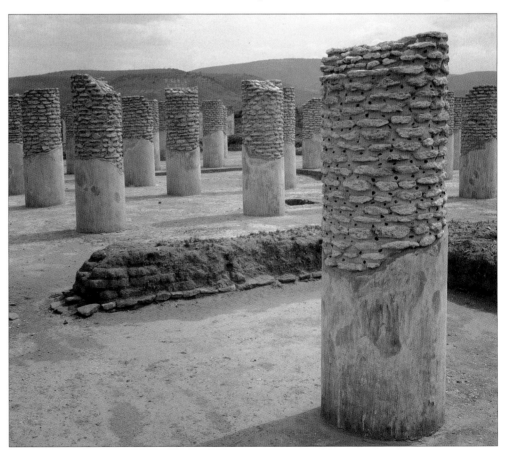

THE BEAT OF THE DRUM

For the Aztecs, music, dancing and singing were among the highest arts. Musicians aspired to be like the great Toltecs of Tollán, masters of every craft and creative art who were celebrated for composing from the very deep places of their hearts and so making music divine. The Aztecs valued dance and music both in profane and sacred contexts, not only as a form of recreation and communal celebration such as in naming ceremonies for children or at marriage feasts, but also as an act of religious devotion, an integral part of ceremonies honouring the gods.

Below: Dressed for ceremonial performance. This carved whistle is from Nebaj, Guatemala, c.AD300–900.

THE SONG HOUSE

Both these forms of music and dance were taught to the young. In the *calmecac* schools of the nobility – where the teachers were priests and where pupils were fledgling rulers, scribes and men of religion – sacred music and ritual dances were taught. In the *telpochcalli* schools frequented by commoners, the future workers of the empire were instructed in love songs, war songs and profane dances. Each of the *telpochcalli* was equipped with a special area called a *cuicalli* ('song house'), consisting of a courtyard surrounded by rooms. The school's highly respected music teacher would place his drums in the centre of the yard and the children would be put through their paces as he played and instructed them in the steps of the dance.

The Spanish churchman Gerónimo de Mendieta, writing in the 16th century, reported that Aztec nobles kept a composer as part of their domestic staff. The composer would write new songs and dances for religious festivals, but also to mark secular events such as a war triumph, a noble wedding or the accession of a new ruler.

DRUMS AND PIPES

Aztec music was stronger on rhythm than on melody: musicians created a strong beat on drums, rattles and rasps. There were two main types of drum: the *huehuetl*, which stood upright, consisted of animal skin stretched over the ends of a carved wooden frame and was played with the hands, while the *teponaxtli*, which was laid horizontally on a circular base, was split to form a double tongue that the drummer hit with rubber-headed hammers to produce a two-tone note. Other musicians complemented the drummers' rhythm with rattles and scrapers made from notched human or animal bone. Wind instruments included conches (large seashells) and flutes, whistles and trumpets (usually made of

Above: This impressivve example of the Aztec huehuetl *('vertical drum') or war drum is carved with warrior imagery.*

clay). Dancers contributed to the music with hand-held gourds filled with seeds, or with anklets of seashells.

The Maya also led their music with rhythm. They had a wide variety of drums. The *tunkul* was, like the Aztec *huehuetl*, an upright drum: the Maya version was made from a hollowed tree trunk and was often as tall as the drummer's chest, with a deerskin stretched over the end. A second Maya drum was identical to the Aztec *teponaxtli*, with two wooden tongues played with hammers, while

Right: Sacred steps in the round. Aztec dancers encircle a minimalist orchestra in this image from the Codex Durán.

another was made from a tortoise shell and played with the palm. Bishop Diego de Landa reported that this tortoise drum gave issue to a very doleful sound. A fourth drum was made from clay and shaped like two vases set base to base, with a membrane at each end. Musicians also played panpipes, conch shells and trumpets of clay or wood. They also had flutes carved from hollowed human leg bones, deer bones and reeds or fashioned from clay. Dancers tied copper, gold or silver bells to their wrists, legs and waist and played a small hand-held drum, called a *pax*, as they danced.

STREET ENTERTAINERS

Music and singing accompanied street entertainments provided by jugglers, acrobats and clowns. Troupes of entertainers laid on dances and comic entertainments for the elite at the courts of rulers and on the spacious patios of noblemen's houses, but also for the commoners in marketplaces, on streets and even outside the cities in small villages. Since trade was performed by barter and currency was little used even at market, they doubtless performed for their supper or for a supply of tortillas, beans and vegetables to take away for later consumption. Hernán Cortés took a troupe of acrobats with him back to Europe, where they performed at the imperial court of Charles V in Spain.

Right: A Mixtec figurine celebrates Macuilxóchitl, patron of the ball game and of the board game patolli, *and god of music.*

FESTIVAL OF THE MUSIC GOD

Macuilxóchitl, who was associated with gambling in his guise as god of pleasure and of games, was also considered to be the patron deity of musicians. He was connected to flower god Xochipilli and to the calendrical day-name '5-flower'.

Macuilxóchitl was sometimes shown with a symbol like a butterfly in place of his mouth. In his role as music god, he might take the form of a turtle. Before his feast day in Tenochtitlán, devotees fasted then covered themselves with jewellery and symbols of the god. According to Bernardino de Sahagún, the ceremony included songs and dancing to the resonant beat of a drum, before worshippers made offerings of animal blood and specially baked cakes to Macuilxóchitl. At the climax of the feast-day celebration, Sahagún reported, priests put a company of slaves to death to satisfy the music god's thirst.

LYRICS AT THE FEAST

Aztec poets found an enthusiastic audience for their work at elite banquets in the leading cities of the empire. Rulers, princes and nobles shared a love of metaphorical language and lyrical self-expression. Masters of verse and philosophical reflection recited their poems in the patio areas of palaces and noble homes, to the accompaniment of music on flutes and drums, while stars danced overhead in the deep blue of night. Most members of the elite classes, including rulers such as Netzahualcóyotl of Texcoco and Tecayehuatzin of Huexotzingo, were poets.

GENRE POETRY

The verses came in a range of genres. One group, known as *xochicuicatl* ('flower songs'), focused on the pleasures and consolations of nature's beauty for those afflicted by suffering. Another group was

THE POET NEZAHUALCÓYOTL

Nezahualcóyotl, ruler of Texcoco, was celebrated as a warrior, wise king and writer of laws. While his forebears and contemporaries were devoted to many gods, he built a temple to a single deity he called Ipalnemoani ('The One By Which We Live') or Tloquenahuaque ('The One Who is Always Near'). He was also a celebrated and sensitive poet, who often examined the pain humans feel due to the changes brought about by the movement of time – which was called *cahuitl* ('the power that departs from us') in the Nahuatl language.

One of his poems declared: 'What can put down lasting roots in this place of change? Everything here is only passing. Even the most precious creations, of jade and turquoise, end in pieces, crumbling to dust.'

yaocuicatl ('war songs'), which expressed a fierce joy in conflict and traced the movements of the mind and heart in battle. *Xopancuicatl* ('spring songs') celebrated the new life of the fields in spring, reminding listeners of the spirit's quickening when maize shoots return after winter. A fourth type were *icnocuicatl* ('orphan songs'). They described the pleasures of life, while recalling the ephemeral nature of all pleasures. One declared: 'The time will come for us all to go, by day or by night, down into the mysteries of death. Here on earth we have time to know ourselves, briefly we pass over the earth's surface.'

The language of the Aztec poets was rich in metaphor. Their poetry was 'song and flowers' bloom'; when a poet

Left: Xochipilli, god of poetry, flowers and souls, was also a symbol of summer. This image is from the Codex Vaticanus.

Above: An unusual portrait of a standing coyote, this stone carving was made by a Totonac sculptor and found at Ihuatzio.

stepped forward to speak he entered into the 'flowering space', the 'spring arena' or the 'house of blooms'. He called political and temporal power 'the place on the mat'.

Tenochtitlán was 'eagle and cactus place' because the México/Aztecs had traditionally founded the city at the spot where they saw an eagle on a cactus, in fulfilment of their god Huitzilopochtli's promise. The city was also 'home of white willows' in reference to the trees that grew there and 'place of darts' because of weapon production in the city.

Poets celebrated warfare as 'shield and dart', 'a singing of shields', and as 'the place where the shields' mist clears'. Poets often spoke of self-knowledge in terms of 'knowing his face'. In Mesoamerican philosophy, the face was seen as the place in which the self resided. Aztec poets could find employment within the religious establishment, as composers of the many hymns – in honour of gods such as Huitzilopochtli, Centéotl, and Tláloc – sung as part of the great religious ceremonies. They also wrote epic poetry, for example the narratives of the birth of the god Huitzilopochtli, of the creation of the world and succession of five world eras, of the many gifts to humankind and the heroic actions of the god-prince Quetzalcóatl.

PUBLIC DEBATE

Another body of literary figures, who may also have been poets, were the *tlamatinime* ('the Ones who Know'). They produced prose works called *huehuehtlahtolli* ('statements of ancient knowledge') that contained philosophical questions, along with statements about duty, death and honour. Sometimes these works were read and debated in public ceremonies. One takes the form of an address by a father to his daughter, in which he warns his offspring that the world is a place of suffering, exhaustion and disappointment, of pain caused by burning sun and winds sharp as obsidian blades. However, he adds that the bitter taste of life is sweetened by compensations such as sensory pleasure, laughter, physical strength and bravery.

A VOICE AT COURT

We have little evidence of the role of Maya scribes in producing poetry and secular writing other than official documents such as the tribute lists, marriage papers or the genealogical histories. However, we know from reports by Diego de Landa and other post-Conquest sources that the Maya enjoyed communal celebrations involving both sacred hymns and secular music with dancing.

The revered *ah ts'ib* or *ah k'u'hun* of Classic Period Maya cities, who proudly wore his pens in his long hair as a status symbol and badge of office, was celebrated for his facility both with language and with images. This exalted figure sat with rulers and their intimates at great state occasions and must surely have given right expression to the feelings of the group in songs and poems. A people that so appreciated the visual arts and music are likely to have been an appreciative audience for the skilful use of words.

Below: This chocolate goblet is decorated with an image of a Maya prince enjoying the drink.

115

CHAPTER SIX

SACRED CULTURE

Teotihuacán's Temple of Quetzalcóatl, adorned with vast heads of a feathered serpent, was set in a compound containing a plaza large enough to hold a significant proportion of the city's 100,000-plus population. At Chichén Itzá, the Pyramid of Kukulcán also gave on to a vast plaza and was aligned in such a way that thousands of spectators could watch the sun create an astonishing serpentine pattern of light and shadow at spring and autumn equinox. Throughout Mesoamerica, sacred centres were laid out with spectators in mind. At the top of steep steps, positioned scores of metres above the crowd, priests and rulers in bright costumes celebrated the gods in choreographed acts of sacred theatre.

Often this theatre presented acts of sudden or extreme violence – such as slicing open a victim's chest and wrenching out his palpitating heart. However, the sacred drama of religious life also included gentler elements such as dances in celebration of ancestors during the festival of Tlaxochimaco or making corn effigies of the god Xiuhtecuhtli and eating tamales with greens during the festival of Izcalli. Equally, many acts of religious celebration centred on astronomical and seasonal events and effects (as in the equinoctial light show at Chichén Itzá) or on marking the passage of time. Festivities accompanied the end of each *katun* of 7,200 days in Maya cities of the Classic Period such as Tikal and Uaxactún.

Left: The great palace at Palenque commanded views of the city's sacred buildings and ceremonial areas.

THE GAME OF THE GODS

The ball game called *tlachtli* by the Aztecs and *pok-a-tok* by the Maya goes far back into the Mesoamerican past. By the time of the Aztecs it was already at least 2,000 years old, for it was played in Mexico in the mid-second millennium BC. An earthen ball court, 80m (260ft) long and 8m (26ft) wide, at Paso de la Amada in the coastal region of Soconusco, Chiapas, was in use *c.*1400BC and is the oldest court yet discovered in Mesoamerica.

Scholars believe that the game, which was played with a rubber ball, may have originated in the coastal lowlands adjoining the Gulf of Mexico. This was the land of

Below: The ball game's connection to blood-letting fertility rites is plain in this carving from Veracruz depicting a player decapitated after losing a match, with snakes of lifeblood coming from his neck.

rubber and the area in which the Olmec civilization developed in the second to first millennium BC, named in later years from the Nahuatl word *olli* ('rubber'). The design of courts changed over time. The ball court was usually shaped like an 'I', with a thinner central section between two wider end zones. Raised walls usually ran down the sides of the central section and, in many courts, a stone hoop was set in each side wall.

RULES OF THE GAME

Two teams of between two and eleven men each played with a hard, solid rubber ball about 15–20cm (6–8in) in diameter – slightly smaller than a human head.

Players tried to keep the ball moving using only the head, hips, elbows and knees. A team scored points – or in some variants won the match – when one of its players sent the ball through the hoop on the side wall. Stone markers were set at various points of the court, and in some versions players could also score points by hitting these markers or by sending the ball into their opponents' end zone.

The rules must have varied a good deal in different eras and various types of court. In the murals of the Tepantitla residential building in Teotihuacán, artists depicted both the traditional ball game and players competing with hand bats, so the city's residents must have known a bat-and-ball variant of the sport.

Archaeologists also report that at Teotihuacán teams played the traditional ball game on open ground with a few markers to indicate the limits of the pitch and the end zones. The courts had no sidewalls or stone rings and so players

Left: This ceramic figure, found at a site in Nayarit, Mexico, takes part in a variant of the ball game played using hand-held bats.

cannot have scored points by putting the ball through the hoop. Few pitches dating from before AD1100 have been found with side rings on the walls. This element of the game appears to have been an addition of the Postclassic Period.

The ball game was always a great spectacle. The oldest known court, at Pasa de la Amada, was laid out between banks of benches for spectators. In the Aztec era it was customary for the winners of the game to seize the belongings of the watching crowd – rich pickings, given that the elite turned out bedecked in jewellery and fine robes. There must have been quite a scramble to escape from the seats when the ball passed through the hoop on the side wall and the winning players suddenly poured into the crowd.

A SACRED NARRATIVE

From ancient times the ball game had major religious and ritual significance. Scholars report that the game represented a sacred narrative of the sun god's descent into the underworld, victory there and subsequent ascent as the maize god. Some suggest that a match was played as part of the fertility rites after crop planting, to bring on the rains that fed the maize plants. Carved panels on ball courts often represented maize or cacao plants.

Above: El Tajín had no fewer than 12 ball courts. One court had walls carved with a defeated ballplayer awaiting death, the sacrificial knife poised above his head.

In Aztec lands, the game was associated with the divine history of Quetzalcóatl, the Plumed Serpent god, his descent into the underworld of Mictlán, his outwitting of Mictlantecuhtli and his ascent as the planet Venus. In one version of the myth of Quetzalcóatl-Topiltzin in Tollán, the god played an epic ball game against the god of darkness and fate, Tezcatlipoca, only to lose when the dark lord transformed him into an ocelot.

In Maya regions, the game was an enactment of the exploits of the Hero Twins Hunahpú and Xbalanqué, who played the ball game in the underworld Xibalba against the lords of that place before rising to the heavens as the sun and the planet Venus. It celebrated the divine twins' defeat of the powers of death. Some writers suggest that the ball represented the sun and that the players' attempts to keep it off the ground were part of religious rites designed to honour the sun and maintain its life-giving position in the sky. The ball game represented the ongoing struggle between the powers of light and those of darkness.

SACRIFICIAL GAMES

The ball game was also associated with blood sacrifice. Among both Maya and Aztecs, defeated players could be put to death at the end of the match. Some Maya court complexes included staircases: the defeated captain was tied in the shape of a ball and hurled down the steps to death, in celebration of the gods' descent to the underworld. Some authorities suggest that battles may have been re-enacted through the ball game and that kings or nobles among the prisoners of war were sacrificed at the close of the proceedings.

Rulers either played the game or donned the protective clothing worn by the players for ritual performance. A panel at La Amelia in Guatemala shows the King of Dos Pilas wearing a ball game outfit of kneepads and belt, while a ball court carving at Copán represents the king as a ball-playing Hero Twin. Like the board game *patolli*, the ball game could be an act of divination. In some accounts, Moctezuma II was defeated in a match against Netzahualpilli, the ruler of Texcoco, who had prophesied that a foreign race would govern Tenochtitlán. Moctezuma's defeat was one of many ill omens that unsettled the ruler before the arrival of Hernán Cortés.

Below: Players face up for a round of the ball game in an image from the Codex Borbonicus. *The Nahuatl word* tlachtli *also meant the I-shaped court on which it was played.*

CYCLES OF TIME

Mesoamericans believed the universe was constructed according to a sacred pattern that could be read in the movements of the stars, and of time through its units of hours and days. Priests and astronomers kept astonishingly accurate track of time using the movement of the stars as their measure. The long, recurring patterns of the night sky provided a physical template of the invisible patterns of time.

OBSERVING TIME IN THE SKIES
These highly skilled astronomers apparently used the simplest of observational equipment, judging the movements of the stars with the naked eye against

Below: One of the windows in the Caracol tower at Chichén Itzá is aligned to the setting of the sun on the vernal equinox.

notches cut in a pair of crossed sticks. Sacred structures and complexes of buildings were laid out to honour celestial and calendrical events such as solstices and equinoxes and to aid in their observation. For example, the Pyramid of the Sun at Teotihuacán was aligned to mark the sun's daily east–west passage and the equinoctial rising of the Pleiades constellation on the horizon.

At Uaxactún the pyramids and temples labelled Group E by scholars were precisely arranged to enable astronomical observation to be made and celebrated. On the western side of a plaza stood a single pyramid, while opposite, on top of a platform on the eastern side, were three temples – E-I (at the platform's northern edge), E-II (in the platform's centre and so due east of the pyramid) and E-III (at

Above: A detail of a stone carving from Chichén Itzá represents Noh Ek (Great Star), the symbol of the planet Venus.

the platform's southern edge). An astronomer standing on top of the pyramid on the western side of the plaza would have viewed the sun rise directly above temple E-I on the June 21 solstice, directly above temple E-III on the December 21 solstice and precisely over temple E-II on the midpoints of 21 March and 23 September. This remarkably precise layout was the prototype for other building complexes in Maya cities of the Classic Period.

INTERSECTING CYCLES
Astronomers plotted the 584-day cycle of the planet Venus and its interaction with the 365-day solar pattern and calculated that the two intersected every 2,920 days – equivalent to eight solar years or five Venus cycles. Occasions on which holy cycles interconnected in this way were doubly sacred and were the occasion for grand ceremonies. Another example is the intersection once every 52 solar years of the *tonalpohualli* day count and the *xiuhpohualli* year count. The end of a 52-year cycle – called a 'bundle of years' by the Aztecs – was a time of potential

calamity, with the prospect of universal dissolution should the gods choose not to inaugurate a new bundle of years. The new cycle in turn was a time of renewal and optimism, in which pyramids and ceremonial buildings might be refaced with stone and householders rebuilt or refurbished their homes.

THE MAYA LONG COUNT

The Maya also marked time using a longer-running measure that scholars label the Maya Long Count. Dates were marked on stelae, stone thrones and other monuments in Maya cities of the Classic Period to commemorate royal births and accessions to the throne, battle victories, ritual sacrifices of rival leaders and so on.

Time was counted forward from a date zero that corresponds to 11 August 3114BC in the Gregorian calendar and dates were carved in five units of decreasing size: 144,000 days (*baktun*), 7,200 days (*katun*), 360 days (*tun*), 20 days (*uinal*), and 1 day (*kin*). Kings set up monuments to mark the end of each *katun*, which was a time of public festivity. The elite and people of Uaxactún held a *katun*-end festival in AD357 – or 8.16.0.0.0. in the Long Count. Rulers also erected monuments to mark the halfway point in a

Below: This pyramid is one of the temple-observatories of Group E at Uaxactún, aligned to view sunrise on the solstices.

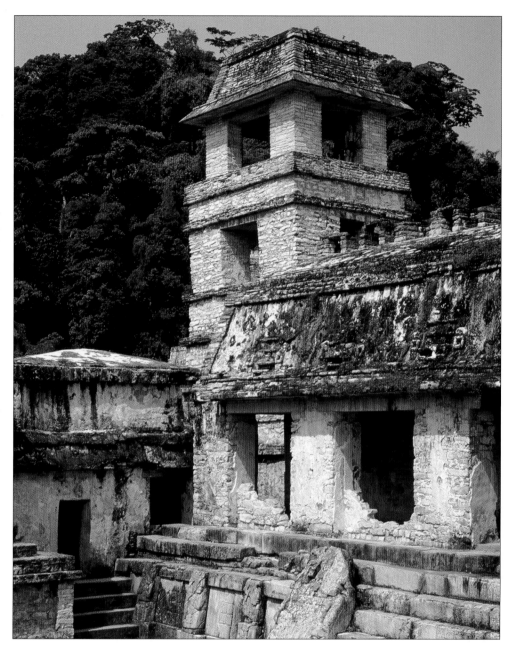

Above: The four-storey tower in the Palace complex at Palenque was probably used as an observatory by the king's astronomers.

katun – a period of 3,600 days known as a *lahuntun*. At Piedras Negras and Quiriguá, rulers even marked the passing of the quarter-*katun* timespan of 1,800 days (*hotun*).

Katuns came in cycles of 13, totalling 93,600 days or around 256 years. Each *katun* of the 13 was identified by number and associated with a set of prophecies: diviners, rulers and ordinary people expected a *katun* to contain events and conditions similar to those in a past *katun* of the same number.

This temporal repetition could be bad or good, unwelcome or welcome. Kings at Tikal in particular went to great lengths to emphasize their connection through the cycle of *katuns* to an earlier period of material wealth.

THE HOLY COUNT

Certain numbers had profound religious symbolism. Three was a holy number because the universe had three layers: the heavens, the terrestrial plane and the underworld. Thirteen, the number of planes in the heavens, was also sacred, as was nine, the number of layers in the dark underworld. Divine figures had power over each of these layers. According to Yucatec-speaking Maya, the gods of heaven were *oxlahuntiku* (combining the words for 'god', *ku*, with that for 'thirteen', *oxlahun*) and the lords of the underworld were *bolontiku* (from 'nine', *bolon*).

HOLY WORLD, SACRED SKY

Ancient religious life in Mesoamerica was focused on the fertility of the earth and led by shamans who assumed animal form to undertake spirit voyages. In the religious tradition that grew from these roots, the earth and heavens were sacred, patterned with divine meaning.

NATURAL AND SUPERNATURAL

Mesoamericans saw no clear distinction between the material world in one place and the spirit world in another. The physical world of deserts, rivers, seas, mountains, storms, maize plants, great trees, wild animals and people was built according to the sacred template that also structured the movements of celestial planets and the cycles of time. Diviners could interpret earthly events and celestial movements in terms of time's patterns and future events. The movements of celestial bodies such as the sun and Venus gave sacred meaning to the physical forms of the earth. For example, some Maya traditions understood the four directions in terms of the movements of the sun. The east was the place of

Above: This stone turtle was carved by an Olmec craftsman before 200BC. The Maya believed the earth rested on a turtle's back.

the sun's morning emergence from the underworld and the west the place of its evening descent to the dark Xibalba, place of death. The north was the sun's full power at the zenith, its position at noon, while the south was identified with

Below: Mesoamericans saw sacred wells, such as this one at Chichén Itzá, as an opening into the underworld of the spirits.

SACRED PLANTS

In Aztec lands tobacco was called *yetl*, and was said to have been created in the celestial realms for the gods' enlightenment. Priests smoked the plant in animal-headed clay pipes in an attempt to call on the god whose animal form was depicted by the pipe bowl. For example, a pipe with a dog's head might be used to summon Xólotl, the twin form of Quetzalcóatl, who took the shape of a dog.

In Maya ceremonies in Yucatán, priests rolled great cigars of tobacco and drank a wine made from the bark of the balche tree. Experts report that they used wild tobacco with a nicotine content of 16 per cent, a full 16 times stronger than that smoked in typical Western cigarettes.

Mesoamericans also held holy a number of hallucinogenic mushrooms (for example, *psilocybe aztecorum*) as well as the maguey cactus, whose fermented sap was made into the alcoholic drink *pulque*.

Above: A wall painting at Chichén Itzá, c. AD900, depicts the ancient plumed serpent god known to the Maya as Kukulkán.

the darkest hour of midnight, when the sun fights for its very life with the lords of the underworld.

In the night sky, the Maya saw the Milky Way as a vast two-headed sky serpent, with one head giving issue to life and the other the source of death. The serpent appears to have been an embodiment of the supreme Maya god Itzamná or Hunab Ku. In this form, Itzamná gave issue from one mouth in the east to the rising sun, bringer of life, while from his second mouth in the west death came with the swallowing of the sun. The Milky Way was also a pathway to the underworld. In Yucatec it was called *Zac Beh* ('The White Path') and was understood to be the road followed by the spirits of the deceased as they travelled to the underworld to face a series of demanding tests.

Mesoamericans saw mountains as sacred; a physical form for the celestial home of ancestors according to Maya traditions, a source of life according to Aztec beliefs. The Aztecs identified mountains as the places of the rain god Tláloc's stores of water, the origin of the maize plant discovered in the mountain's heart by Quetzalcóatl and the place of the tribal lord Huitzilopochtli's birth. A cave in a rocky, dusty mountainside was

a place of burial, an entrance to the sacred earth and a place of access to the land of the revered ancestors.

Aztec and Maya cities replicated these sacred physical forms in stone. The temple was a holy mountain and its entrance was a sacred cave. The ball court, also like a holy cavern, represented an entrance to the underworld.

ANIMAL ALLIES

The sacred patterning extended to the world of animals. Many creatures were held to be holy because they were forms of the gods. Tezcatlipoca might be the majestic jaguar or the cunning coyote; Huitzilopochtli was eagle, hummingbird or macaw, Quetzalcóatl – or Kukulcán in Maya lands – was quetzal as well as divine serpent. The turtle, the crocodile and the snake were images of the fertile earth.

Mesoamericans also believed that humans had animal protectors or familiars known as *nahual* in the Aztec language and as *way* by many Maya groups. These were

Right: This figure made by a Remojadas potter in Veracruz, c.600–900AD, wears a jaguar-head belt and may represent a shaman.

the creatures whose forms shamans might adopt. They would do this upon entering a state of instructive spiritual ecstasy under the influence of one of the plants held to be sacred for their power to transport seekers beyond the boundaries of everyday consciousness.

THE HEALING ARTS

To the Aztecs healing was sacred: their main word for doctor, *teopati*, combined *patli* ('medical arts') and *teo* ('holy'). Aztec creation narrative explained the cause of sickness. At the start of the fifth or current world age, the existing race of humankind was made from the bones of the men and women who had lived in the fourth world age. These bones had been languishing in the underworld, but the Feathered Serpent god Quetzalcóatl ventured into that dark realm to rescue them. However, the Feathered Serpent was tricked during his escape from the underworld and dropped the bones, which broke into many pieces. He carried the remains to the home of the gods, where all the divine lords and ladies agreed that the bones should be ground to a powder, then moistened with the gods' blood and mixed to a paste. From this paste the first people of the fifth world age were made. People suffered illness, old age and death because they were originally made from broken bones. However, they had a special calling to serve the gods because they were fashioned from the gods' blood.

THREE SPIRIT CENTRES

People were made according to the same divine template that structured all parts of the universe. Just as the universe had a tripartite structure – with the heavens above, the terrestrial plane in the middle and the underworld beneath – so three spirit centres existed within the human body. The first, residing in the head, was *tonalli* ('hotness'). This was the counterpart of the soaring heavens.

When a body lost *tonalli*, death followed – and so a corpse was cold. People dissipated *tonalli* by self-indulgence in sex or drunkenness. They could boost it by bravery in battle and by living an austere, self-restrained life. Doctors sometimes prescribed herbal fragrances to increase a patient's *tonalli*. In the natural way of things, *tonalli* increased with age and old people were respected for having a strong *tonalli*. When a shaman or diviner embarked on a spirit voyage, it was his *tonalli* that left his body and entered another realm.

The second spirit centre, *teyolia*, was the counterpart of the terrestrial plane and was situated in the heart. *Teyolia* was the source of our thoughts, creative impulses and human personality. Tenochtitlán's noble poets were rich in the quality of *teyolia*. This, too, was weakened by sensual indulgence. The *teyolia* was akin to the Western idea of the soul in that it departed the body at death and travelled to its fate in the afterlife – the underworld for most, but one of the levels of heaven for those who had been sacrificed, killed in battle, died giving birth or suffered various watery deaths associated with the rain god Tláloc.

The third spirit centre, *ihiyotl*, situated in the liver, was the counterpart of the underworld. Energy, life's breath and

Left: The Florentine Codex *(1575–77) depicts various Aztec medical procedures, including a cure for haemorrhoids, treating a fever and the binding of a broken leg.*

passionate desire were the products of *ihiyotl*. Lazy people, who lacked drive and the power to achieve things, were understood to have a badly functioning *ihiyotl*.

A HEALTHY BALANCE

The three parts of the universe were perpetually held in balance by natural order, by the four cardinal directions and by the tree of life that majestically rose in the centre of the universe connecting heaven, earth and underworld. Doctors taught that the way to health lay in safeguarding the good functioning of the three spirit centres of the body and ensuring a natural balance between them. An unexpected reverse or accident might damage one of the centres and cause illness or disturbed behaviour. For example, a shock resulting in emotional turmoil would be expected to damage a person's *ihiyotl*.

SPIRITUAL HEALING

Throughout Mesoamerica healing combined knowledge of herbal remedies with trust in the power of shamans and diviners to seek and remedy the causes of health problems. In addition, all peoples of Mesoamerica put faith in the power of public bloodletting and sacred ritual to

satisfy the gods and avert disease, famine, earthquake and other natural disasters. Physical and spiritual were intertwined: illnesses or disturbances might have physical or spiritual causes and could be treated with spiritual or physical means, or both. A doctor might tell a woman with a severe cold that she had suffered damage to her *tonalli*. He could use his knowledge of herbal medicine to prescribe a fragrance to boost her *tonalli*. Equally, he might seek out the spiritual cause of the malaise by sending her to a diviner.

Above: A Mixtec codex celebrates the god of medicine. Aztecs revered Patécatl, who was also god of drunkenness, as lord of medicine.

The diviner would seek to discover whether the damage to the woman's *tonalli* was caused by a curse from one of the gods. Sometimes the diviner might take hallucinogenic mushrooms, peyote or morning glory seeds to bring on a trance in which he could discover the cause and find a way to appease the god in question. He might throw coral seeds and seek answers from the movement of sensations in his body.

Aztec doctors were divided broadly into those treating physical symptoms, the *teopati*, and those seeking and addressing spiritual causes, *tictli*, men who could read the divine patterns and structures of the universe. The medical specialists were expert in herbal medicine, the *tlametpatli*, who drew on their ancient healing art to treat problems including heart trouble, stomach sickness and breathing disorders. In markets across the empire, *panamacanis* sold mixed herbal remedies.

Left: A detail from the Florentine Codex *shows a plant used to treat fever. Healers administered bitter medicines wrapped in chocolate paste to patients.*

SACRED THEATRE

Large-scale public sacrifices on the steps of temple pyramids made a powerful statement of secular power as well as of religious devotion. In Tenochtitlán, visiting dignitaries witnessed an over-whelming proof of the city's great power, which was sufficient to build the vast sacred arena, mobilize a cadre of magnificently attired priests and musicians and bring to sacrifice a vast army of prisoners.

RITES OF SACRIFICE

The crowds which gathered for the ceremony celebrated the power of the gods who demanded and were worthy of such ritual; the glory of the ruler who could command such a display; and – a central

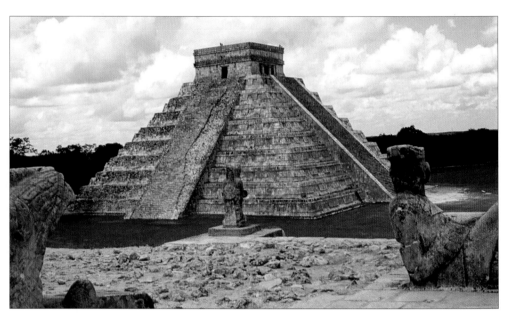

Above: At Chichén Itzá the Temple of the Feathered Serpent – viewed here from the top of the Temple of the Warriors – was an awe-inspiring setting for sacred ritual.

mystery of their religion – the fact that life was dependent on sacrifice. Just as, in Aztec belief, the gods had sacrificed their blood to the creation of humans in the current age and then again to set the sun moving in the sky, so human blood was a necessary offering to maintain sacred order and balance in the cosmos.

Public rites of sacrifice brought the gods to visible life on the temple steps or in sacred processional. A priest or ruler dressed as the god or goddess honoured became that divine form. A priestess wearing a jade skirt was Chalchiúhtlicue in Tenochtitlán, while a Maya ruler might embody the maize god or Chac, lord of rains. Equally, victims destined for sacrifice were considered by the Aztecs to be *ixiptla* ('in the gods' image'). They were believed to contain within their frail human bodies the awesome power of creation and destruction that belonged to the gods,

Right: A detail from the Codex Mendoza *(c.1541) shows part of a sacred ritual as a priest plays drums and sings hymns.*

making possible the re-enactment of the primal scenes of divine sacrifice through which this world's sun and people were brought into being.

The Toltecs and their followers in Tenochtitlán and Chichén Itzá greatly escalated the use of ritual slaughter in religious ceremonies. From the era of Tollán onwards, human sacrifice had a much greater role.

RITUAL SONGS

The Aztecs sang hymns to honour their gods during religious ceremonies. Sacred songs have survived to the goggle-eyed rain god Tláloc, to flower god Xochipilli, to strong-limbed maize deities Chicomecóatl and Centéotl and to the war lord Huitzilopochtli. The hymn in praise of Xochipilli declares that the sacred quetzal bird sings its joy in the flower lord during the dark hours of midnight, while the worshipper makes his song at dawn, adding that praise will rise to Xochipilli from Tláloc's temple.

Tláloc's hymn praises the god as a magician and envisages ancestors at rest or playing at ball in the misty paradise of Tlálocan. Huitzilopochtli's hymn celebrates him as the sun god, who lives among the clouds and the cold air, who as he spreads the brilliance of light stirs a passion for war in the hearts of men. The song, which was probably declaimed by two singers in a stirring answer and response, hails Huitzilopochtli as the instigator of sacred conflicts that result in the defeat and capture of many prisoners for holy sacrifice.

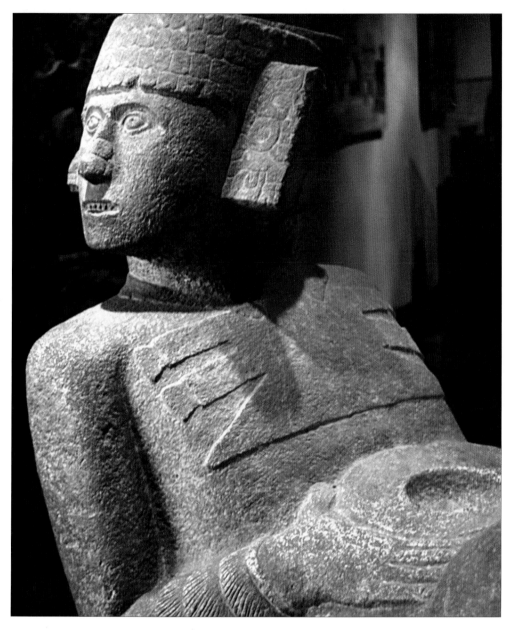

particular musical ceremonies in which they specialized. De Landa described one dance in which two men led the steps. One hurled reeds at the other, who exhibited great skill in catching them, all the while following the steps of the dance. Another dance witnessed by de Landa was a sacred war dance, in which as many as 800 men carrying small banners followed a complex pattern of steps in perfect unison. In Tenochtitlán, the leading warriors, priests and members of the *pipiltin* nobility engaged in a sacred dance with their divine ruler at the climax of enthronement ceremonies that began the rule of a new *tlatoani*.

Below: In the gods' image. A Maya funerary urn, c.AD250–900, represents a fearsome-looking priest dressed in ritual costume.

Above: Offering plate. A chacmool from Tenochtitlán holds the hollowed dish used to display the hearts of sacrificial victims.

INCENSE AND DANCING

Ceremonies were accompanied by the burning of incense, usually copal resin, but also the resin of the rubber and chicle trees. Worshippers believed that as the smoke rose it became food for the gods and goddesses. In sacrifices to placate the rain god, his human petitioners told that the clouds of incense had the power to attract the dark, rain-heavy clouds for which they prayed. Before burning, cakes of resin were painted turquoise blue, the colour of sacrifice. When worshippers could not provide a jaguar or alligator for animal sacrifice, the incense was sometimes moulded into the shape of an animal heart. In the Cenote of Sacrifice at Chichén Itzá, a worshipper made an offering of an incense ball containing a cake of vegetable material in the shape of a human heart.

Music played an important role in the theatre of the sacred. Large bands of musicians took part in sacred processions and sacrificial ceremonies, playing clay and shell trumpets, drums and rattles, and creating a mournful howl with conch shells. The celebrated murals at Bonampak represented a 12-man orchestra as part of a procession: they played tortoise-shell drums, ceramic trumpets and seed-filled gourds.

Among the Maya, group dances were very serious and highly sacred. According to Bishop Diego de Landa, groups of men and women danced separately and had

THE ROUND OF FESTIVALS

The Aztecs believed that they were dependent on the gods for the sun's rising every morning, and wove rites of religious observance into the very fabric of daily life. Each of the eighteen 20-day months had at least one festival honouring the gods. These were not all of equal importance to an individual. People with skilled occupations, for instance, had their patron gods and observed ceremonies with particular attention at the time

Above: Sacred serpents and presiding deities are detailed in one of the 56 almanac pages of the Maya Madrid Codex.

Left: A statue of Xipe Totec from Veracruz c.AD900–1200 shows a priest who is wearing a flayed skin.

when their patron was celebrated. Among the people of the empire, so many of whom worked on the land, the more ancient fertility-based cults of such gods and goddesses as Tláloc, Chalchiúhtlicue and Centéotl would probably have had more impact than the newer cult of Huitzilopochtli, which was associated with the elite.

CYCLE OF AZTEC FESTIVALS

For a farmer in the Tenochtitlán *chinampa* fields, the festivals associated with the stages of the agricultural year loomed largest. In the first month of the Aztec year (14 February–5 March), worshippers at the festivals of Atlcaualo ('The Ending of Water') and Cuauhitleua ('The Lifting of Trees') made offerings to maize goddesses Chicomecóatl and Xilonen. These included sacrifices of children.

In the second month (6 March–25 March), during the festival of Tlacaxipehualiztli ('Skinning of the Men'), sacrificial victims were killed and skinned in honour of Xipe Totec, god of spring and germinating seeds. The god's priests wore the skin of a victim over their own face and body. In the fourth month

(15 April–4 May), as part of Huey Tozoztli ('Major Vigil'), priestesses of Chicomecóatl performed rites to bring the gods' blessing on farmers' seed supplies.

In the eighth month (4 July–23 July), the festival of Huey Tecuilhuitl ('Major Festival of the Lords') celebrated the appearance in the fields of the first shoots of maize and particularly honoured Xilonen, the goddess associated with these shoots. Offerings were made to a young woman who took the form of Xilonen for the duration of the festival.

Harvest was celebrated in the eleventh and twelfth months (2 September–21 September; 22 September–11 October'), in the festivals of Ochpaniztli ('Clearing') and Teotleco ('Coming of the Gods and Goddesses'). In the first of these, a female victim was killed and flayed in honour of Xilonen-Chicomecóatl and her skin worn by a priestess of the goddesses, in grim echo of the festival of Tlacaxipehualiztli. The second festival was a simpler celebration of the harvest.

No doubt overshadowing all these festivals in the mind of the farmer was the one that marked the end of a 52-year cycle of the 260- and 365-day calendars and the beginning of a new cycle. It usually occurred once only – if at all – in a lifetime. On the night in question, the most senior priests sacrificed a victim on Mount Huixachtlán ('Place of the Thorn Trees'), cut his chest, then tore out his heart and in his gaping chest cavity lit a new fire signifying the new cycle of years. If the new fire did not take, according to religious teaching, it showed that the gods did not consent to allow a new cycle to commence and the current age of the world, in which the Aztec empire had grown to glory, would end.

Below: A deity consumes the flesh of a sacrificial victim in a detail from an Aztec tonalamatl book of days.

CYCLE OF MAYA FESTIVALS

The Maya laid out large and important complexes of buildings in major cities of the Classic Period to celebrate equinoxes and solstices. Occasions such as the year's shortest and longest days were charged with sacred meaning and were the focus of ritual public celebration.

Our main source for detailed knowledge of the festivals of the Maya year is the account given by Bishop Diego de Landa of religious ceremonies in 16th-century Yucatán. As with the Aztec calendar, the year ended with five days of ill renown when people tried to avoid activity. The new year and beginning of the first month, Pop, was celebrated by sweeping houses and replacing all household tools and utensils. The second month, Uo, was the time for fishermen, hunters, doctors

Above: A flint sacrificial knife symbolically stops the life breath in a ritual victim's skull. This offering is from Tenochtitlán.

and priests to celebrate their patron gods; the priests performed acts of divination using the sacred books to read the fates for the coming year. In the fifth month, Tzec, beekeepers made offerings to Hobnil, one of the four *bacabs* said to support the creation in the four cardinal points. They burned incense and prayed to be granted large amounts of honey. In the sixth month, Xul, offerings were made to Kukulcán, the Feathered Serpent. A great procession with feather banners culminated in offerings of food at Kukulcán's temple; devotees stayed at the temple for five days, while jesters toured the town putting on performances and collecting contributions that were then divided between the nobility, the priests and the jesters themselves.

During the eleventh month, Zac, hunters made offerings to atone for the blood they had spilled as they went about their work. In the thirteenth month, Mac, a large-scale sacrifice of animals was performed in honour of Itzamná and the four rain gods or Chacs to ensure plentiful rainfall to feed the maize plants in the approaching rainy season. In the sixteenth month, Pax, a war ceremony was held that culminated in feasting, drinking and sacred dances.

THE CULT OF VIOLENCE

Mesoamericans saw conflict as a sacred and ubiquitous element of life. As the sun rose each morning, it slaughtered the moon and stars that had proudly ruled the night sky just as, the Aztecs said, proud Huitzilopochtli had killed the moon goddess Coyolxauhqui and his four hundred brothers in the first moments of life. The shedding of sacrificial blood was a sacred duty; a way of maintaining universal order by honouring the blood sacrifice offered by the gods that had brought the current world age into being.

Sacrifice and warfare were intimately connected; indeed, military conflict was a sacrament. Warfare was celebrated as an opportunity to demonstrate character, bravery and power and as a means of feeding the gods' thirst for blood. A major impetus for warfare was the need for sacrificial victims.

Below: A detail from the late 16th-century Codex Magliabechano *shows a bloody sacrifice in honour of Tezcatlipoca during the Aztecs' 13th month, Pachtontli.*

Among the Maya, commoner prisoners may have been made into slaves, but nobles, leading warriors and – most significantly – rival rulers were destined for ritual public sacrifice. The Maya considered human sacrifice to be a necessary rite for major events such as the inauguration of a new king's reign, the first use of a new temple or building and the announcement, birth or blessing of an heir to the throne.

KILLING KINGS

In Classic Period Maya cities, a special decapitation ceremony was reserved for the despatch of captured kings and rulers. Such a sacrifice was recorded in carving by a glyph called the 'axe event' by scholars. A ball court marker erected by King Kan II of Caracol commemorates the sacrifice by 'axe event' of a Caracol ruler in AD556 in the rival city of Tikal, a sacrifice that sparked a conflict between Caracol and Tikal. The

Below: Sacrificial ritual mirrored the ferocity of the wild. This jaguar statue is from Chichén Itzá.

conflict ended in a Caracol victory in AD562 and, probably, in the sacrificial beheading of Tikal ruler Double Bird. The decapitation sacrifice may have occurred as the climax of a ritual enactment of the ball game, which celebrated the triumph of the Hero Twins in defeating the lords of Xibalba.

Among the Maya of the Postclassic Period in cities such as Chichén Itzá, victims were painted turquoise blue, the colour of sacrifice, and led up the temple steps to the sacrificial platform wearing peaked headgear. There, high above the crowds watching in the plaza below, the sacrificial stone was painted turquoise and four assistant priests, also dressed in this brilliant colour, held the victim over the stone while the main priest or *chilan* carved open the victim's chest and wrenched out his heart. The *chilan* then smeared statues of the gods being honoured with the heart blood of the sacrificial victim and wiped the blood on his own skin. He cast the body down the steep steps into the plaza, where it was skinned by helpers. The skin was given back to the *chilan*, who put it on as a 'suit' and danced before the crowd.

The Maya of Chichén Itzá had adopted the Mexican sacrificial practice, presumably the one followed by the Toltecs. Aztec priests of this era also tore the heart from the chest of a sacrificial victim. After

Above: A ritual victim's death was highly honourable. The Codex Duran *(1570–81) shows a team of Aztec priests extracting a human heart on the sacrificial stone.*

holding it up in offering to the sun god Tonatiuh, they threw it at the image of the god being celebrated, Huitzilopochtli or Tláloc, which in time became covered with the blood of the victims. In the plaza below, the audience in this theatre of sacred violence watched the rite and saw blood run down the steps of the temple platform while the bodies of the victims were cast down to tumble over the slick steps until they reached bottom.

DEATH BY RITUAL CONFLICT

Both Maya and Aztecs also performed sacrifices through ritualized conflict. In the Aztec festival of Tlacaxipehualiztli ('Skinning of the Men'), held in the second month in honour of Xipe Totec, Aztec warriors bearing clubs fitted with razor-sharp obsidian blades attacked victims tied to a sacrificial stone who were armed only with a club decorated with feathers. The warriors slashed at the defenceless 'combatants' until their blood ran freely into the earth.

A similar stylized conflict was performed as a rite of sacrifice by the Maya. The victim was stripped naked, painted turquoise blue and dressed in the peaked headdress associated with sacrifice. He was tied to a post while warriors danced around him, each bearing a bow and arrows. A priest took blood from the victim's genitals and made offering of it to the gods. Then the warriors began to shoot, sending a hail of arrows at the chest of the victim until he slumped lifeless on the spot.

A graffito drawn in Temple II at Tikal depicts a similar sacrifice of a victim tied to a sacrificial post and slain by a magnificently attired warrior-priest who is using either an arrow or a spear.

REVERENCE FOR ANCESTORS

Long after its decline from power, the city of Chichén Itzá was a major destination for pilgrims from throughout Maya territories. They came to offer sacrifices in the great Cenote of Sacrifice and to wonder at the magnificent temple of Kukulkán, the immense ball court and the vast hall of the thousand columns. Here, as in highland Mexico, the present seemed unable to match the achievements of the past.

The México/Aztecs who founded Tenochtitlán were part of a wave of incomers from the barren north. Insecure as newcomers and as nomads with no evidence of past achievement, they attempted to find glory by association through linking themselves to the Toltecs and Tollán, even claiming that they had spent some years among the holy ruins of that city during their southward migration; the older ruined city of Teotihuacán the Aztecs saw as a place of the gods, site of sacred events at the start of the current world age. They made pilgrimages to both Tollán and Teotihuacán, bringing offerings to place in the sacred spaces of those cities, adding their own religious structures on the hallowed ground and also removing items left by the ancestors and carrying these objects back to sanctify sacred buildings in Tenochtitlán.

Aztec mourners buried two people with pottery from Tenochtitlán and Texcoco in part of the Ciudadela at

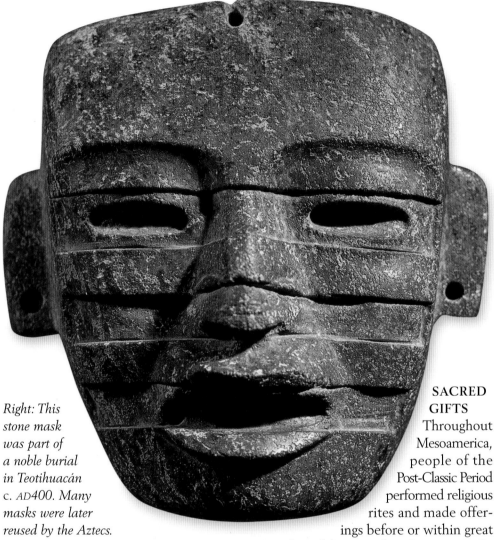

Right: This stone mask was part of a noble burial in Teotihuacán c. AD400. Many masks were later reused by the Aztecs.

Teotihuacán; Aztec architects even built a pyramid-platform over and encompassing the pyramid-temple of Quetzalcóatl there.

At Tollán Aztec religious visitors made similar burials and ceramic offerings, and also built residential quarters and sacred structures on top of the ceremonial centre of the Toltecs. Funerary masks from Teotihuacán graves were laid as offerings within the Templo Mayor in Tenochtitlán.

Left: The scale of Teotihuacán's sacred architecture overawed later Mesoamericans. Surrounding the Plaza of the Moon, once a scene of ritual worship, are eleven temples.

SACRED GIFTS

Throughout Mesoamerica, people of the Post-Classic Period performed religious rites and made offerings before or within great sacred sculptures of earlier times. In Morelos in the 13th century pilgrims made offerings before the great 2,000-year-old Olmec carvings at Chalcatzingo: local Tlahuica builders erected stairways and platforms to a height of 30m (100ft) to create a sacred space before the carving known as Monument 2, which represents a reclining figure with two people wearing elaborate ceremonial garb approaching him and one moving away. At Monté Albán, Mixtec pilgrims buried their rulers and in the grave known by archaeologists as Tomb 7 left magnificent offerings of gold and silverwork. Maya pilgrims conducted religious ceremonies and left ceramic effigies in the ruined temples at the Classic Period site of Dzibanché, Quintana Roo.

A SACRED TRADITION

In venerating ancient objects, reusing them and making offerings of them in tombs and temples, the peoples of the 12th–15th centuries AD were following a very well-established Mesoamerican religious tradition. Many centuries earlier, at Classic Period cities such as Tikal, Uaxactún and Cozumel, devotees made offerings of Olmec figurines, masks, plaques and objects used for drawing one's own blood. Maya nobles or rulers in this era wore Olmec greenstone pieces as sacred amulets.

A PILGRIMAGE GONE WRONG

In 1536 Ah Dzun Xiu, descendant of the Xiu dynasty that had been ousted by their rivals the Cocoms at Chichén Itzá in the 13th century, determined to lead a pilgrimage to make human sacrifices at the Sacred Cenote in the city of his ancestors. The king, who now ruled in the city of Mani, had been convinced by a recent hurricane, plague and smallpox epidemic that there was a pressing need to appease the gods. He asked for a guarantee of safe passage through the lands of his traditional enemy, Nachi Cocom. The lord of the Cocoms granted the request but plotted violence. When Ah Dzun Xiu, his son, nobles and trains of sacrificial victims arrived in Cocom lands, they were lavishly welcomed with feasting and entertainments that lasted for four whole days. But on the fourth evening, the hosts turned suddenly and viciously on their guests and slaughtered every last one. The gods had their sacrifice, but without the ceremony that had been planned. The episode served further to divide the Maya of Yucatán and paved the way for victory in the region by a force of Spanish conquistadors.

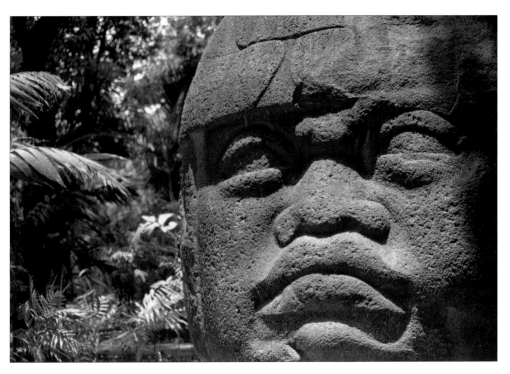

PILGRIMS TO THE PYRAMIDS

Surviving documents from the 16th century indicate that the Aztecs used the Teotihuacán pyramids not just for reverent worship, making offerings and blood sacrifices, but also as a dramatic setting in which to execute criminals. One account reports that on the Teotihuacán pyramids Tenochtitlán priests set up images of the underworld god Mictlantecuhtli, of the moon goddess Coyolxauhqui and of Tonacatecuhtli (Lord of our Sustenance), the male aspect of the primeval god of duality Ometéotl. The priests came in the company of the *tlatoani* once every month in their calendar – that is, every 20 days – to seek the gods' continued blessings on the growing empire. Priests and worshippers also sought guidance at oracle shrines in the ancient city. Aztecs deeply respectful of the achievements of the past also visited the ruins of the fortified city of Xochicalco, in western Morelos, where they reverently viewed the carvings of serpents, hieroglyphs and humans on the Pyramid of the Feathered Serpent.

Aztec potters and stonemasons expressed their devotion to the sacred power of the past and respect for the achievements of their ancient forebears by imitating bygone styles. At Tenochtitlán a group of heads of the *xiucóatl* ('fire-serpent') accompanied by calendrical dates is a homage to Xochicalco's Pyramid of

Above: Many generations of Mesoamericans revered their Olmec forebears. This head of an Olmec king is now at Villahermosa.

the Feathered Serpent. Sculptors also produced statues celebrating sacred images from Teotihuacán, while builders copied the proportions, murals and decorative style of Teotihuacán when constructing the five diminutive buildings in Tenochtitlán called the Red Temples. The nearby House of the Eagles, which lay just to the north of the Templo Mayor, was a detailed celebration of the achievements of Toltec stonemasons, sculptors and woodworkers.

Below: Many sacred structures at Chichén Itzá were built to honour the architecture and religious culture of the Toltecs. This is a detail of the Platform of the Eagles.

WHERE THE ANCESTORS GO

The Aztecs were taught not to fear death. Life and death were one aspect of the sacred duality that structured the universe, a duality also expressed in oppositions such as day and night, hot and cold, light and darkness.. Life was not easy, suffering was inevitable and death was inescapable. Many deaths were celebrated as honourable, for example, dying in giving birth, in battle or in a rite of human sacrifice. For the Aztecs it was a matter of honour to embrace death with equanimity and with a certain pride.

DAY OF THE DEAD

The Aztecs' positive attitude to death has carried through into modern Mexican celebrations on the Day of the Dead.

The Day of the Dead is celebrated on the Roman Catholic Church feasts of All Saints' Day (1 November) and All Souls' Day (2 November). The first day is usually set aside to remember those who died in childhood and infancy, with departed adults celebrated on the second day.

At home people build small altars in memory of the dead and load them with food, drinks, cakes and sweets – including sweet rolls called *pan de muerto* ('death bread') adorned with dough pieces shaped like bones, and breads called *anima* ('souls'), as well as a cup of the traditional maize soup (*atole*) and for adults beer, tequila and cigarettes. The altars are lit by candles and perfumed with traditional copal incense. The dead are expected to return to share once again in the sensual joys of life on earth. At the family burial plot, relatives gather to hold celebrations including dancing, singing and feasting at the graves of their departed. These festivities are complemented by an open-air Roman Catholic mass.

FLOWERS BLOOM

Each year the people of Tenochtitlán held the festival of Tlaxochimaco ('Coming Forth of Flowers') in honour of ancestors and, in particular, in celebration of the lives of those who had died in the last year. In the first days of the festival, the people gathered wild flowers in the fields near the city and carried them to the temple as an offering to the ancestral tribal god Huitzilopochtli and to Tezcatlipoca, one of the gods of death. They performed ritual dances in memory of the deceased.

The Maya, by contrast, were profoundly fearful of death despite the fact that it was as frequent a visitor among them as it was among the Aztecs. Far from celebrating those who had departed the earth, the bereaved made great demonstrations of their grief with wails of despair by night and floods of tears by day.

Funerary customs also varied among the cultures of Mesoamerica. The ancient way, which was followed widely in the

Above: These figures are part of a procession of gods and goddesses painted on the walls of a noble burial chamber (Tomb 105) in Monte Albán, probably in c.AD500–750.

Below: A skull decorated with shell and jade was laid in the tomb of an Aztec noble who went fearlessly to the spirit world.

settlements of Oaxaca, in Teotihuacán, in Veracruz and throughout Maya regions, was to bury the body in a shroud with a funerary mask for the wealthy and a range of offerings connected to the person's livelihood when alive. The Toltecs and their followers in the Postclassic Period, including the Aztecs, preferred cremation. The body was wrapped in bandages and tied in an upright, seated position before being burned; the resulting ashes were then buried with funerary offerings. Some members of the Aztec elite, however, were granted burial.

RICH AND POOR BURIALS

The burials of rulers, nobles and the wealthy were considerably richer than those of commoners. Elite graves in Classic-Period Maya cities were rich in offerings of jade and serpentine, in funerary masks, jewels and splendid clothes.

In some special cases a pyramid-temple might be erected or an existing structure refashioned to encompass a tomb for the deceased king. A high-ranking scribe would be buried with the pens and other equipment he used to ply his elite trade.

Commoners were generally buried beneath the floor of their houses. In time, as relatives died and were buried alongside them, the house would be abandoned and used as a family shrine. According to Bishop Diego de Landa, a commoner in Yucatán would be buried in his cotton robe with a few grains of maize or jade beads in his mouth. These would sustain or support him on his voyage along the white road of the Milky Way to the underworld.

Above: Zapotec nobles were buried. Urns such as this one, found in Tomb 113 in Monte Albán, were not used to contain ashes and must have had a ceremonial use.

SACRIFICED IN DEATH

From the 10th century on, the Mixtecs broke open the graves of Monte Albán's former Zapotec rulers and used them to bury their own elite. They left magnificent grave offerings in gold and silver. Slaves and dogs were killed and interred to mark the rank of their former master.

Sacrificial burial appears to have been a Mesoamerican practice as far back as the time of Teotihuacán. A series of burials beneath the Pyramid of the Feathered Serpent contain 137 bodies with hands tied behind the back. Scholars believe they were killed as an offering to the gods upon the completion of the pyramid *c*.200AD.

Left: The snake, a complex symbol of new life and of the earth, is depicted consuming a human skeleton in a carving from Tula.

PART TWO

ART AND ARCHITECTURE

A carved bone found in the tomb of King Ah Cacau (*r.* AD682–734) beneath Temple I at Tikal depicts the hand of an artist-scribe emerging from a gaping monster's mouth. This monster-mouth was an established Mesoamerican image for the entrance to the spirit realm of the underworld – and the carving indicates that the Maya believed artistic ability and inspiration to have a divine source. Certainly the Maya of the Late Classic Period, in which this bone and the great majority of delicately painted polychrome vases were produced, celebrated their artists as a gifted elite. These exquisite vases – some of the finest produced in any world culture – were often signed by the artists who painted them.

The México/Aztecs, too, revered their artists, whom they called 'Toltecs' after the founders of the city of Tollán/Tula. In the Aztec Nahuatl tongue *tolteca* meant 'artist', and the word for artistic ability was *toltecayotl*. In the years of the Aztec empire, there was no distinction between artists and craftsmen: *tolteca* included artisans such as carpenters and weavers. They were seen as divinely blessed: their task was to seek sacred meaning in their heart and express this truth in their work. If they worked in this way, they would truly be like the Toltecs, whose city of Tollán was remembered as place of beauty and artistic excellence.

This survey of arts and crafts begins with a discussion of the main styles of architecture and a survey of the great cities. It describes the work of potters, weavers and featherworkers, then looks at stone and wood carving, metalwork, jewellery-making, mural painting and the production of painted codex screenfold books. It ends with a discussion of Mesoamerican aesthetics.

Temple I or Great Jaguar Temple, from the terrace of the northern acropolis of the Maya city of Tikal, was once painted red and adorned with moulded plaster masks.

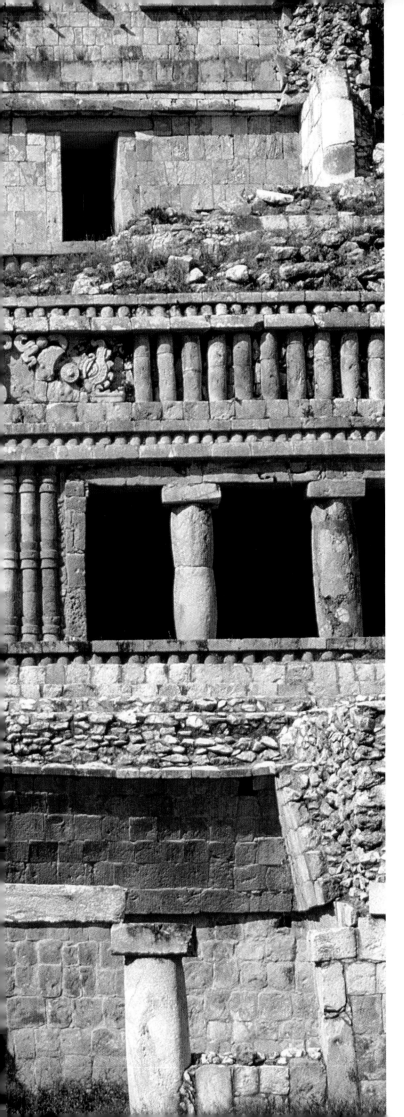

CHAPTER SEVEN

PALACES, TEMPLES AND SACRED CENTRES

Archaeologists generally distinguish between two types of Mesoamerican public building: 'palaces' and 'temples'. Palaces are usually long, low residential and administrative buildings that contain many rooms, small windows, niches above doorways and carved benches. Temples are usually built on top of tall stepped pyramid-platforms, with very limited interior space, and are topped with tall roof combs masonry structures that support a decorative facade. Scholars see palaces as utilitarian, and temples as sacred spaces reserved for ritual activity.

The distinction is helpful, but must be used with some caution since these words are only labels applied retrospectively by historians. Many palaces were used for administrative functions – such as meetings of council groups, or collection and storage of tribute – in addition to being the residences of kings or leading nobles. They contained shrine rooms and areas used for religious ritual such as autosacrifice – the letting of one's own blood. 'Temples', meanwhile, were used for varied purposes in different places and at different times. Some buildings, such as the five-storey palace in Edzná or the Great Palace of Sayil, appear to have combined sacred and utilitarian functions.

Left: In the middle of the three levels of the Palace at Sayil, a pair of columns divides each of the wide chamber doorways.

FROM HUTS TO TEMPLES

A decorative frieze on the Nunnery Quadrangle at Uxmal gives a stylized representation of a simple hut, the kind of dwelling inhabited by millions of Maya householders. A similar image was carved on an ornate archway leading to a group of palace buildings at Labná and was represented in murals painted at Chichén Itzá. The images depict the front of a single-storey oblong dwelling with a square central doorway and a thatched roof.

The Maya generally erected buildings on raised platforms: even the tall pyramids constructed to support temples can be seen as building platforms functionally. For a simple dwelling, however, the platform was low, built of earth or rubble covered in adobe plaster (a thick mixture of mud and straw). The great majority of Maya houses were built mostly if not entirely of perishable materials and so did not survive to be examined by historians. However, archaeologists can trace the remains of domestic building platforms and so plot the arrangement of houses within settlements. However, the actual building methods used by the Maya to raise their houses remain a matter of educated conjecture, based on the frieze and mural images described above and on the building methods employed today by modern descendants of the ancient Maya.

MAYA BUILDING METHODS

Scholars believe that ancient Maya house builders first set up four sturdy corner posts, then created a lattice of thin sticks between them and covered the lattice-work with adobe plaster. In hot regions,

Above: This Aztec terracotta model represents the 'sacred mountain' of a steeply stepped pyramid topped with a temple.

builders might well have left the walls unplastered, allowing breezes to pass through and cool the inhabitants. The shape of the plot was usually rectangular, but could have rounded ends. In some areas, where building stone was readily available, builders laid stone building platforms for houses, or even built the lower parts of the walls in stone before covering them with adobe or lime plaster.

This tried and tested design was the template for all Maya buildings. Stone temples were more elaborate and permanent versions of the ancestral hut. Elements of the primitive house were reproduced in palace and temple: for example, builders in stone used the same square-shaped door with wooden lintel

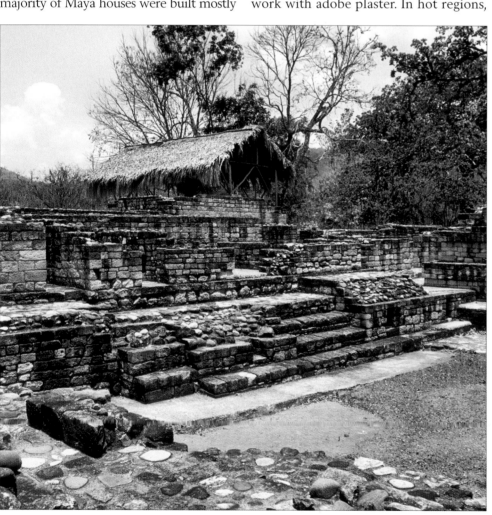

Left: Maya dwellings often consisted of small buildings arranged around a central courtyard. This example is in Honduras.

that had been developed over generations by house builders. The sinuous lines of rope or creeper that tied the straw wall-padding in place in the family hut were reproduced in the ornamental carving on the friezes of sacred buildings and palaces.

TEMPLE MOUNDS

The earliest temples, of *c*.2000BC, were probably almost indistinguishable from ordinary dwellings – the gods naturally lived like humans. However, priests and their builders set the gods' buildings apart from village dwellings by raising them on higher platforms than those used for domestic structures. The platforms grew higher and higher over time. The practice of rebuilding temples on the same spot, over and encompassing their predeces-

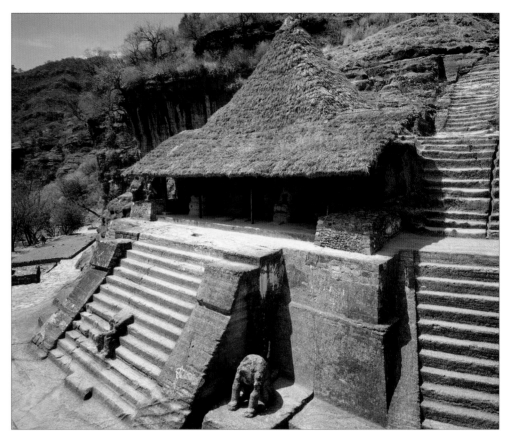

sors, became a hallowed architectural custom. As the temple mound or platform grew taller and taller, builders had to add a new architectural element – one or more access stairways to enable priests and other ritual contributors to reach the temple at the top of the platform. The temple-platform began to resemble a great hill, entirely appropriate for a people who regarded mountains as sacred.

AZTEC BUILDING

Houses varied from simple, single-room huts with wooden walls and a straw thatched roof to large and elaborate stone mansions with flat stone roofs supporting herb gardens. Remains indicate that walls were made of wooden planks, latticework plastered with adobe, sun-dried adobe bricks or stone. In the marshy lakeside terrain of Tenochtitlán, even basic houses were often raised on stone building platforms to provide firm foundations

The design of the simplest housing similarly remained the template for palace buildings and the temples atop the steep pyramid-platforms. Images drawn for Friar

Left: The simple thatched hut occupied by Maya peasants was celebrated in stone in the archway at Labná (c.AD600–900).

Above: The Aztec Temple of the Eagles at Malinalco was cut c.AD1500 from mountain rock near modern Tenancingo.

Bernardino de Sahagún's *General History of the Things of New Spain* (completed 1569) depict an Aztec house made of wood and straw, one built from stone with a straw roof and one built entirely of stone. Another shows a nobleman's house with an elaborate decorated frieze.

RAW MATERIALS

Builders made use of locally available stone and other materials. In the southern Maya region, there was generally a shortage of easily worked rock for construction. Even major buildings were often made from adobe blocks, although at Copán labourers quarried and used local trachyte and at Quiriguá they worked with marble, sandstone and rhyolite.

In the central and northern Maya regions, builders had access to large amounts of limestone that was easy to cut into blocks. The limestone could also be burned to produce lime for making plaster.

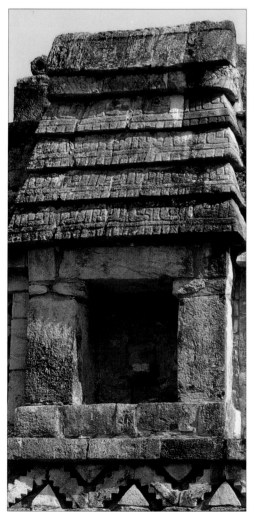

BUILDING STYLES:
FROM TEOTIHUACÁN TO TIKAL

The architectural style of Teotihuacán was widely influential across Mesoamerica for many hundreds of years. In particular, the city was known for its *talud-tablero* construction, which alternated an upright rectangular section (*tablero*) with a sloping section (*talud*). The *tablero* had a recessed central part.

In Teotihuacán, the style was particularly developed in the Ciudadela or Citadel area of the city, which included the Temple of Quetzalcóatl and 15 other stepped pyramids, as well as two elite residential buildings and an 11-hectare (4.4-acre) open plaza. The Teotihuacános used *talud-tablero* construction only for sacred buildings. At Teotihuacán, the upright *tablero* was always larger than the sloping *talud*, but elsewhere these ratios varied.

Archaeologists do not know for sure where the style originated, although some

Below: Architectural styles such as 'Puuc', 'Chenes' and 'Usumacinta' take their names from the regions in which they developed. This map also shows the main mining areas for certain raw materials.

suggest that immigrants to Teotihuacán from Tlaxcala might have brought a taste for and expertise in this type of building with them. Tlaxcalans, who also brought agricultural expertise in cutting terraced fields and irrigation with dams and canals, were using a form of *talud-tablero* construction in their civic and ceremonial buildings before 300BC, well in advance of the first major sacred buildings at Teotihuacán.

VARIATIONS ON A STYLE
The *talud-tablero* style was used very widely. At Kaminaljuyú *c.*AD200–400 builders either from or influenced by Teotihuacán built a ceremonial centre using *talud-tablero* construction. The style was also used in the Lost World complex at Tikal. At Xochicalco the Temple of the Feathered Serpent played a unique variation on the style by reducing it to the single component of the design: in profile, the temple presents one large sloping *talud* topped with a single *tablero*. Another variation on *talud-tablero* was developed by the builders of the Pyramid of the Niches at El Tajín in Veracruz:

Above: The archway at Kabah, Yucatán, is a good example of the corbelled vault or 'false arch' which looks like an inverted V.

there are six *talud-tablero* levels, with each sloping *talud* topped with a vertical *tablero* containing several niches, and at the top of each *tablero* there is an additional 'flying' reverse *talud*. At Tollán the El Corral temple consisted of two *talud-tablero* levels. The style was revived in the Temple of the Feathered Serpent at Chichén Itzá, which has nine *talud-tablero* tiers. The Aztecs built two small *talud-tablero* buildings in their sacred precinct at Tenochtitlán as an explicit tribute to the sacred city of Teotihuacán.

RAISING THE TEMPLE PLATFORM
In Maya lands builders usually constructed pyramid-platforms from earth and rubble and faced them with cut stone. These platforms usually had four faces with either one stairway or four stairways, one on each face, providing access to the temple on the summit. In some sites, several buildings were built on a single platform, in which case archaeologists usually call the platform an 'acropolis'. The platforms rose from generation to generation, for it was customary to build new platforms and temples over and enclosing the existing sacred structures. The roofs of Maya temples were typically decorated with tall facades of stucco

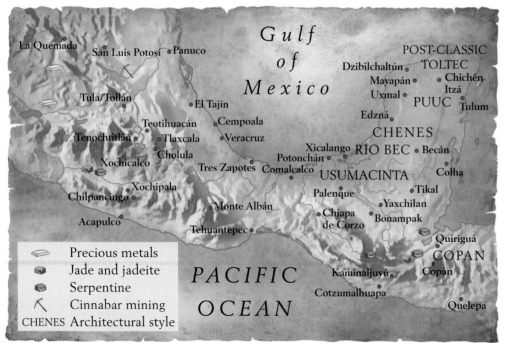

Precious metals
Jade and jadeite
Serpentine
Cinnabar mining
CHENES Architectural style

Gulf of Mexico

La Quemada San Luis Potosí Panuco
POST-CLASSIC
Dzibilchaltún TOLTEC
Mayapán Chichén Itzá
Uxmal PUUC Tulum
Edzná
Tula/Tollán
El Tajín
Teotihuacán Cempoala CHENES
Tenochtitlán Tlaxcala Veracruz Xicalango RIO BEC Becán
Cholula Potonchán Comalcalco
Xochicalco Tres Zapotes USUMACINTA Colha
Xochipala Palenque Tikal
Chilpancingo Yaxchilán
Monte Albán Chiapa de Corzo Bonampak
Acapulco
Tehuantepec
Quiriguá
COPAN
PACIFIC Kaminaljuyú Copán
Cotzumalhuapa
OCEAN Quelepa

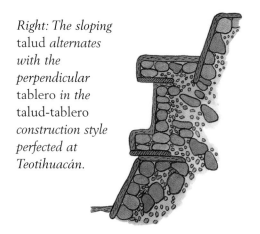

Right: The sloping talud alternates with the perpendicular tablero in the talud-tablero construction style perfected at Teotihuacán.

moulding or mosaic sculpture, usually supported from behind by masonry structures called roof combs. In the mortuary temples of Tikal, the roof comb element contained a portrait of the king buried in a vault beneath the temple platform.

Maya builders of the Classic Period generally relied on the corbelled vault – called the 'false arch' by architectural historians – to support the roof. This structure, which resembles an upside-down V, is created by laying inward-projecting blocks on top of one another: the blocks successively narrow the gap between walls until a single stone can bridge the gap at the top of the arch. (This contrasts with a true arch, whose use was never developed by the Maya, in which the keystone at the top anchors the other stones and creates a structurally much stronger unit.) Corbelled vaults need the support of thick walls beneath them. Maya buildings with false arches had severely reduced interior space given their outer size. Walls were generally made of rubble covered with stone.

BUILDING STYLES

A number of regional styles developed in Maya lands. The sacred buildings of Tikal epitomize the central Petén style, which is characterized by vertiginous pyramid-platforms each topped by a temple with a tall masonry roof comb, a single doorway and thick rubble-filled walls.

At Palenque, Yaxchilán, Piedras Negras and Bonampak the Usumacinta style was characterized by buildings with thinner walls and three or more doorways. At Palenque, for example, builders could erect thinner walls with several doorways

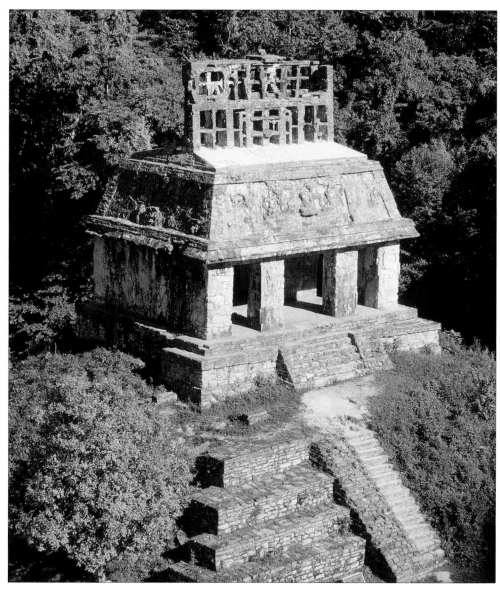

Above: Stucco carving on vertical temple-top roof combs was used to convey dynastic information, as here at Palenque.

because they had replaced the tall vertical facades used in the Petén style with inward-sloping facades that were partly supported by the vaulting of the roof. They also made lighter latticework roof combs rather than the solid masonry ones of the Petén region. Within, the buildings often had two parallel rooms divided by a wall that also helped to bear the roof's weight. A benefit of using thinner walls was that the buildings were considerably lighter and more airy within.

Another regional style of monumental architecture developed at Copán and Quiriguá, where temples, palaces and platforms were decorated with elaborate stucco modelling. A distinctive feature was the building of 'reviewing stands',

which were large platforms with wide access stairways. In the reign of King 18-Rabbit (AD695–738)at Copán, artisans began to create carved stone decorative elements in place of stucco; these were generally painted over with plaster.

Below: From the time of the Toltecs onwards, chacmool sacrificial figures were placed outside pyramid-top temple sanctuaries.

143

A LOVE OF DECORATION: YUCATÁN

The ornate modelling and façades at Copán had counterparts in styles developed farther north in the Maya region. In the Río Bec style, used in the southern Yucatán peninsula in the late Classic Period, builders put decoration and style before function. They erected vast constructions that were essentially reverent imitations of the great pyramids at sites such as Tikal: lofty towers with non-functional steps, doorways that led nowhere and 'false temples' built of solid rock for appearance only. Their buildings had elaborate façades incorporating mosaic masks, which often featured a long-snouted deity believed to be the rain god Chac.

Examples of the style are found at Becán, Xpuhil and Río Bec, in the region north of Calakmul. For example, the building known to archaeologists as Structure 1 at Xpuhil has towers supporting solid temple-like structures with roof combs. Buildings with the appearance of monumental sacred architecture clearly brought prestige to settlements such as Xpuhil or Becán, even if the temples and pyramids could not be used.

The related Chenes style took decorative elements a stage further, creating building façades dominated by decorative masks. In some of these, the entire façade represented a divine face with the doorway as the god's mouth. Chenes-style buildings were raised in the late Classic Period at sites slightly farther north in the

Left: The Temple of the Magician, Uxmal, rises to an imposing height against the night sky. Its western stairway climbs to a sanctuary whose entrance is a god's mask.

Yucatán peninsula. On the building known as Structure II at Chicanná, the façade represents the face of a god; perhaps the primordial creator Itzamná. The doorway is a serpent mouth, with two stylized eyes and fang-like projections above the opening. The structure gave its name to the settlement, for Chicanná means 'house of the snake's mouth'.

PUUC ELEGANCE

Further north again, the Puuc style developed in the Puuc region in north-western Yucatán. Builders preferred to limit decoration to the upper façade and to keep the lower half of walls plain. They built walls of lime concrete and faced the lower part with limestone veneer. Craftsmen applied pre-cut decorative elements to the upper façades in a repetitive pattern, whose elements were sometimes divine masks or serpents, but were more often abstract patterns such as lattices, fretwork and columns. In developing this style, which appeared at the close of the Classic Period (c.AD800–1000), Puuc

Above: Intricate decorative patterns and masks of the Maya rain god Chac on the upper walls of the Nunnery Quadrangle at Uxmal are typical of the Puuc style.

builders may been influenced by the repetitive decorative patterns used by their counterparts at Mitla and other sites in Oaxaca.

Splendid examples of the Puuc style are found at Uxmal in the Governor's Palace and the buildings of the Nunnery

'THE MAYA REVIVAL'
The US architect Frank Lloyd Wright was greatly impressed with the elegance of Puuc structures and applied the style in several public buildings erected in the 1920s. These created a vogue for a Maya Revival movement in architecture that encompassed other architects including Robert Stacy-Judd, Alfred Bossom and Richard Requa. Stacy-Judd used Maya inspiration in building the ironically named Aztec Hotel in Monrovia, California, in 1924–25. Requa's Maya Revival buildings included the Federal Building in San Diego (1935).

Quadrangle, both of which combine a plain lower wall with intricate decorative designs in the upper façade. The city of Uxmal demonstrates that these architectural styles developed alongside one another and were not mutually exclusive, for the shrine on the first terrace of the Temple of the Magician, at the top of a steep west-side storey, presents its west-facing entrance as the mouth of a divine mask in pure Chenes style.

At Kabáh, which was connected to Uxmal by an 18km (11-mile) *sacbé* causeway, the Temple of the Masks uses masks of the rain god Chac as the repetitive element on the façade. The building is identified as Puuc style by archaeologists, although its façade is entirely covered

Below: The Castillo and Group of the Thousand Columns typified the Chichén Itzá style copied in later Yucatán cities.

with the pattern of masks and so does not feature the plain lower half and decorated upper half typical of pure Puuc. The Great Palace at Sayil and the Palace Arch at Labná are other fine examples of the Puuc style.

TOLTEC ARCHITECTURE

At Chichén Itzá, archaeologists identify two main groups of buildings, with largely distinct styles. The southern group – which includes the Nunnery buildings, the Akabdzib, the House of the Deer, the Red House and the celebrated circular Caracol – is built largely in the Puuc style. The northern group – which includes the Temple of the Warriors, the Group of the Thousand Columns and the great Castillo or Temple of the Feathered Serpent – pioneered a new architectural style in the Maya region, featuring buildings with colonnades. The style exhibited a strong

Above: Sacred entrance. The creator god's face – with fangs and eyes above the door – sanctifies Structure II at Chicanná.

influence from the monumental architecture of sites such as Tollán (Tula) in highland Mexico.

This style became the prototype for building in the Postclassic Period that followed the collapse of Chichén Itzá. The Chichén Itzá style was influential, for example, in the construction of building at Mayapán and Tulum, although the 'copies' were of much poorer quality than the magnificent originals at Chichén Itzá.

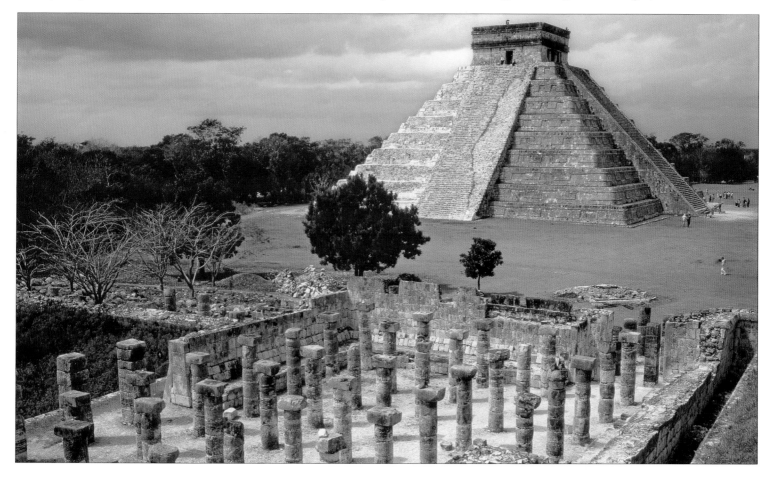

HIDDEN MEANINGS IN SACRED BUILDINGS

At the heart of Tenochtitlán, the Aztecs built up the Templo Mayor over many years on the same sacred site, each new pyramid-temple encompassing its forerunner. The first temple on the site was raised as early as the city's foundation *c.*1325, while improvements and enlargements continued until 1502. This was in line with hallowed Mesoamerican building practice. The great Pyramid of the Sun at Teotihuacán was built in the 1st–2nd centuries AD over a sacred underground cavern and a ground-level shrine, while builders at Tikal, Uaxactún, Chichén Itzá and countless other ceremonial centres followed the same custom, raising their ceremonial structures ever higher, like great mountains, as they built over and on the temples of their ancestors.

In Tenochtitlán, the Aztecs identified the Templo Mayor as a recreation of the holy mountain of Coatépetl on which their tribal god Huitzilopochtli was born. In a number of Maya cities, also, temples were explicitly identified as holy mountains. Stucco masks representing mountains (called *witz*) often flanked the stairways on these structures. Just as a cave in a mountainside was a point of access to the spirit world, so the temple entrance high on a sacred mountain gave access to the supernatural regions.

SACRED TEMPLATE

In Tikal and other cities, architects of ceremonial centres followed a template based on the four cardinal points and three levels of the universe: earth, heaven and underworld. While north was associated with the celestial realm, south was the way to the underworld. East was the place of the rising sun and west, the place of its descent into darkness, represented the earthly realm, governed by time cycles such as the daily pattern of the sun's rising and setting. Buildings in east, west and north were often placed to form a triangle, with the fourth, southern position in the sacred pattern implied.

The scholar Clemency Coggins showed how at Tikal the Twin-Pyramid groups erected to celebrate the end of a *katun*

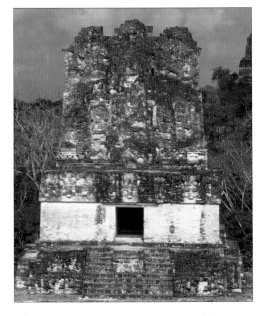

Above: Holy mountain top. Rising 42m (138ft) above the forest floor, Tikal's Temple II outreaches even the towering treetops.

(7,200-day period) were laid out according to this template. These groups consisted of pyramids with four stairways at east and west, with a building containing nine doors lying to the south and a roofless enclosure containing a stela and 'altar' or 'throne' to the north. While the east and west pyramids celebrated the sun's daily cycle, the nine-door southern building represented the underworld, which had nine levels. The northern building was uncovered and so gave access to the sky, the celestial realm of the ancestors. In this place, as if connected to and blessed by his dynastic forebears, the king stood – represented by the stela that named him and the throne stone that celebrated his power.

HOLY NUMBERS

The numerical patterning of Mesoamerican cosmology was regularly celebrated in architecture. Just as the southern

Left: Worshippers gather in the plaza for a katun-ending ceremony at one of the Twin-Pyramid Groups in Tikal.

building of the Twin-Pyramid groups at Tikal contained nine doors to represent the nine layers of the underworld, so the 50m (164ft) Temple I at the same site had nine levels. So did the 30m (98ft) Temple of the Feathered Serpent at Chichén Itzá.

The numbers of 365-day and 260-day calendars similarly gave sacred meaning to ceremonial buildings: the Temple of the Niches at El Tajín in Veracruz had 365 niches, while the four staircases of Chichén Itzá's Temple of the Feathered Serpent each contained 91 steps which, when added to the single continuous step at the base, made 365. The Temple of the Masks at Kabah had 260 masks.

RITUAL FURNITURE

In Tollán, Chichén Itzá and Tenochtitlán, adaptations of sacrificial ritual called for specialized pieces of sacred furniture. One was the *chacmool*, carved in the form a reclining figure thought to represent the god Tláloc, with a receptacle on his chest into which a sacrificial victim's heart could be deposited. Another was the skull rack on which the heads of decapitated victims were displayed. These pieces of ritual furniture were used, and might indeed have been invented, by people in

Above: In Frederick Catherwood's engraving Chichén Itzá's Temple of the Feathered Serpent is notable mainly for its mountain-like bulk. But archaeological clearing revealed its intricate design, with 365 steps to match the days of the solar year.

the northern reaches of Mesoamerica at La Quemada and Alta Vista in Zacatecas state and at Cerro de Huistle in Jalisco. This people, identified by scholars as belonging to the Chalcihuites culture, built a court with colonnades, using both square and round columns, a plaza with pillars and a very large I-shaped ball court. They carved militaristic images of warriors with shields and weapons and they used skull racks as well as – at Cerro de Huistle – an early form of the *chacmool*.

Scholars believe that the sites predated the rise of Tollán and the Chalcihuites culture might therefore have been the precursor of many of the militaristic sacrificial rituals of the Toltecs and their followers at Chichén Itzá and Tenochtitlán.

Below: Twin shrines occupied the summit of the Templo Mayor in Tenochtitlán. This chacmool demanded sacrificial blood outside the shrine of rain god Tláloc.

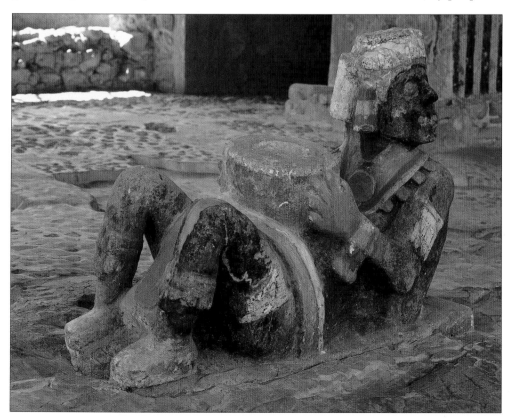

THE IMPACT OF COLOUR AND SOUND

To a worshipper in the Great Plaza of the Citadel in Teotihuacán, the Pyramid of the Feathered Serpent rose vast against the blue sky, presenting a great wall of red, its moulded plaster decoration depicting snakes, feathered serpent heads and goggle-eyed, fanged masks picked out in green, blue and white.

At Tikal, a nobleman in the Great Plaza gazing up at the great temples of the North Acropolis would see towering red-painted buildings adorned with moulded plaster masks. Mesoamerican sacred buildings, which are today remarkable for their size, structure and setting, in their prime also created a major impact with bright colouring and detailed stucco decoration.

The Pyramid of the Niches in El Tajín makes an extraordinary impression because of the contrast of light and shadow in the 365 apertures of the structure. Archaeologists report that its appearance in its prime would have been even more remarkable, for they have found traces of the dark red paint that originally coloured the interior of each niche and of the bright turquoise that bordered each one. Colour played a crucial role in the theatre of the sacred that Mesoamerican ritual centres generated. Priests, and sometimes victims, donned

brilliant plumage and costumes. Among the Maya, victims destined for sacrifice were painted turquoise. Their blood splashed brilliant red on the *chacmool* or sacrificial stone.

COLOURED MESSAGES

The use of coloured paints enhanced the messages of divine, dynastic or military power represented by sacred and other ceremonial buildings. The twin temples atop the Templo Mayor in Tenochtitlán were painted in bright colours as a way

Above: Traces of wall colouring remain on one of the palaces at Kabah. The city was linked to Uxmal by a sacbé *roadway.*

of identifying their divine patrons. The northern shrine to Tláloc was painted blue and white to signify his powers over water, while the southern shrine, to Huitzilopochtli, was red to celebrate his control of war and sacrifice.

At Palenque, the detailed stucco images in the roof comb of the shrine that tops the Temple of the Inscriptions pyramid were painted in bright colours to make them clearly visible to crowds in the plaza below.

At Kabah, near Uxmal, each of the myriad repeating heads of the rain god Chac that adorn the 50m (150ft) length of the Temple of the Masks was originally painted in turquoise, green and red, creating what must have been an overwhelming impression.

At Tollán, the great carved warriors that once supported the temple roof atop the Temple of Tlahuitzcalpantecuhtli were painted in bright colours to emphasize their bulk and power.

Left: Uaxactún's Pyramid E-VII-sub was originally decorated with red stucco and large masks, perhaps of the underworld god.

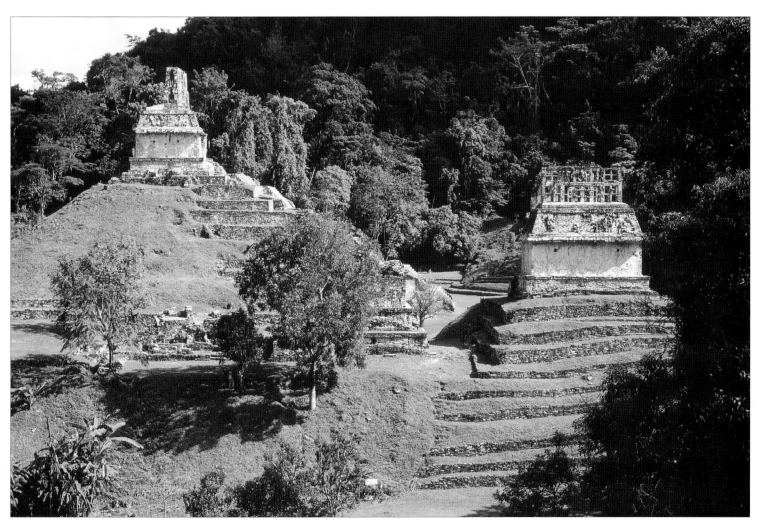

SOUND EFFECTS

Recent scholarly work has suggested that ritual complexes and sacred arenas might have been designed with acoustics in mind. The architecture of the Temple of the Feathered Serpent at Chichén Itzá appears to reinforce the sound of a voice declaiming at the top of the building: a

Below: A modern reconstruction of Teotihuacán's Temple of Quetzalcóatl shows the colours that greeted worshippers.

crowd watching and listening in the plaza beneath would have been able to hear the words of a priest making a ritual speech in praise of the gods or celebrating the undying power of the state. If so, the builders would have had knowledge of a building acoustic science that is now lost among architects.

David Lubman has reported that when a person standing in the plaza before the pyramid-temple claps his hands, the pyramid steps reflect back a sound like a descending bird-call – a sound that is a remarkable imitation of the primary call of the sacred quetzal bird. The quetzal was associated with the god Quetzalcóatl/Kukulcán, who is celebrated in the temple. Lubman argues that the steps were carefully designed to produce this echo. The lower steps combine a narrow tread and tall back, making a high-pitched 'chirp' echo, while the upper steps create a deeper echo like a whoop. Together they form a descending sound highly reminiscent of the quetzal's call. Lubman adds that the echo is a little ragged

Above: Solar blessing. At winter solstice the setting sun's rays lit on dynastic carving in Palenque's Temple of the Sun (right).

because the pyramid steps are no longer covered with plaster, as they would have been in ancient times. When the pyramid was newly built, the echo effect would indeed have been striking.

LIGHT EFFECTS

The Temple of the Feathered Serpent possessed another remarkable secret. Its builders positioned it so that at spring and autumn equinox, sunlight creates an undulating pattern of light and shadow on the steps, a celebration in light of the divine serpent in whose honour the temple was raised.

Alignments at Palenque produce light effects that celebrated the divine standing of the ruling dynasty. The Temple of the Cross is aligned so that at winter solstice, the setting sun will illuminate carved scenes and appear to bless the dynasty they honoured.

ARENAS FOR A SACRED CONTEST

The magnificent Great Ball Court in Chichén Itzá is Mesoamerica's largest, measuring 68m by 166m (225ft by 545ft) including the surrounding structures. Its pitch is I-shaped, opening out into wider end zones. The playing surface, 36m by 146m (120ft by 480ft), is enclosed by vertical sidewalls 8m (26ft) in height, each of which bears a circular ring halfway up its surface.

Chichén Itzá's Great Ball Court was part of the city's northern complex of ceremonial and sacred buildings, which archaeologists have dated to AD900–1200. The city contained no fewer then 13 ball courts, the largest number at any Maya centre and more even than at the other great Mesoamerican centre of the game, El Tajín in northern Veracruz, where there were 12 ball courts.

As elsewhere, the game at Chichén Itzá had important ritual and sacrificial elements. Relief sculptures on the walls of the court depict a newly victorious ball player who has just decapitated his defeated opponent: he holds the victim's

Below: The ball court at Monte Albán is an example of the earlier court design, with sloping sidewalls and without wall rings.

head aloft in triumph, while blood cascades from the headless corpse. The Great Ball Court carvings depict a total of 14 ball players, each with a skull attached to his belt. This iconography identifies them as lords of the underworld, Xibalba, against whom the Hero Twins played ball in Maya religious narrative.

SACRED IMAGES

Similar bloodthirsty rituals were carved in stone at Yaxchilán, where relief images on the steps of the structure known as Temple 33 depict King Bird Jaguar, his father and predecessor Shield Jaguar and his grandfather, another Bird Jaguar, playing the ball game with balls made from the bound bodies of captives. Scholars suggest that the images refer to an ancient Maya religious narrative known as *Ox Ahal* ('The Three Victories'), which told of human heroes who in time immemorial defeated and beheaded three lords of the underworld. The panel depicting Bird Jaguar playing the ball game makes reference to the narrative, which survives in the Quiché Maya *Popol Vuh*. One of the courts at El Tajín had vertical walls carved with a defeated ball player awaiting death, the sacrificial flint knife poised.

Above: Points were scored by hitting the ball through the ring. This court is at Uxmal, where – as in many cities – the court was positioned to connect north and south.

WATCHING THE DEADLY GAME

Ball courts usually provided seating for spectators. The oldest known ball court in Mesoamerica – found in 1988 at Pasa de la Amada in Chiapas, Mexico – had side-banks with benches 30cm (1ft) tall and 2.4m (8ft) deep. Thousands of years later, the Aztecs also built their courts with spectator seating.

Many courts had rings mounted on the walls. Sidewall rings were found on courts at Tollán, and in many highland Mexican sites of the Postclassic Period, including Tenochtitlán. This contrasts with most earlier courts – for example, at Monte Albán, Copán, Cerros and Tikal – that had low sloping sidewalls and no surviving wall-mounted rings.

The earlier courts often had markers indicating the centre of the playing area, so dividing the pitch into two equal halves. Some courts had niches at the ends in diagonally opposite corners. These were found, for example, in the courts at

*Right: Copán's Great Ball Court –
dedicated in 18-Rabbit's reign (AD695–738)
linked the Great Plaza to the north with the
palaces and temples to the south.*

Monte Albán and at Tollán. Scholars
are unclear of their purpose. The rules of
the ball game clearly varied in different
eras and locations. At Chichén Itzá
and in other courts of the Postclassic
Period, the object appears to have
been to score points by driving the
ball through the sidewall rings. On
other courts, players may have scored
points by making the ball bounce in their
opponents' endzone.

*Below: The Great Ball Court at Chichén
Itzá, seen here from the south, was
overlooked by the Temple of the Jaguars.*

IMPORTANCE OF POSITION

The ancient ball court at Pasa de la
Amada was unusual in that it was not
linked to a ceremonial centre: it appears
to have been built in the heart of an elite
residential area with no temples or ritual
areas nearby. In many later settlements,
the ball court played an important role
within the sacred patterning of a city's
ceremonial centre. A court was often
placed between the northern realm of the
celestial ancestors and the southern region
associated with the underworld. The
court, like the open plaza and the mouth
of the pyramid-top temple, represented
an entrance to the underworld. A ball
court in Tikal's East Plaza performed this
function in a three-point north-west-east
design based on the North Acropolis and
Temples I and II. At Cerros, in Belize, the
ball courts (dating to 400–150BC) were
positioned to consolidate the north–south
alignment of the ceremonial centre.

THREE PARALLEL GAMES

Tikal's oldest ball court, laid out in the
Great Plaza's south-east corner, contained
a unique triple court, which had three
pitches within a single complex. This was
built to the south-east of the Great Plaza,
beyond a ravine. It stood beside a sweat-
bath. These buildings, called *temescals*,
were closely associated with the ball
game. They might have been used for
cleansing rites as part of sacred ceremonial connected with the game.

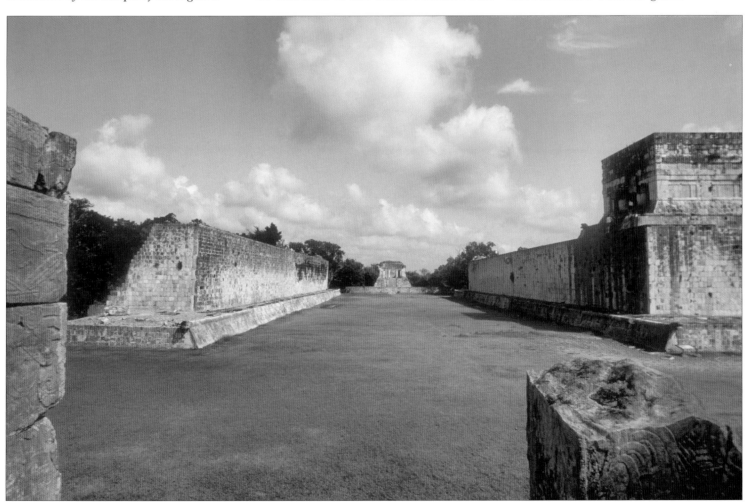

PALATIAL STYLE OF MAYA RULERS

Palenque is unique among the Maya cities of the Classic Period in giving a central position in the city to the royal palace and administrative area. In most cities, the 'sacred mountains' of temple-platforms and mortuary monuments took pride of place, adjoining or enclosing plazas and open spaces that held stelae celebrating the achievements of royal rulers. At Tikal, for example, the central structure was the ceremonial Great Plaza bounded by royal mortuary shrines, to the north in the form of the North Acropolis and, to east and west, in the form of Temple I and Temple II respectively. The palace buildings were situated to the south of the main plaza in the Central Acropolis and farther south again in the buildings known to archaeologists as Group G, which lie alongside the causeway laid to connect the centre to the Temple of the Inscriptions.

HOME OF A KING

At Palenque, the palace stood on a raised platform, 10m (33ft) in height and measuring 80m by 100m (260ft by 320ft). It commanded views of the city's sacred buildings and ceremonial area and looked

Above: The square four-storey palace tower at Palenque had no counterpart elsewhere in the world of the Classic Maya.

beyond them across the river plain of the Usumacinta down to the Gulf of Mexico. The palace was home to King Pacal (*r.* AD615–83), whose ornate tomb was dug beneath his funerary monument, the Temple of the Inscriptions. His accession

was marked by a carved panel in the palace representing his royal mother, Lady Zac Kuk, in the act of passing the crown to him.

Pacal greatly expanded and improved the existing palace complex, which had been built by his predecessors from the 5th century onwards. Beginning in AD654, he laid a higher platform in the centre of the palace area and on it erected the structure called House E. This building later served as a throne room, in which three or more of his successors held ritual coronation ceremonies. Pacal constructed House C, to the north of House E, in AD661. Another palace building, House C, rose between two plazas, the East Court and the West Court, in the northern part of the palace. Directly south of the East Court the king raised another palatial dwelling, House B, also *c.*AD661, and directly to the east of the East Court he added House A around seven to ten years later.

Below: King and courtiers enjoyed elegant privacy in the interior courtyards of the palace complex at Palenque. The concrete roof rested on strong beams of sapodilla.

DYNASTIC BUILDING

Pacal's successors continued his work. His son Chan-Bahlum II (AD684–702) might have added Houses A and D at the far eastern and far western limits respectively of the building complex. Another building, House A–D, was probably added at the northern limit of the complex by King Kan-Xul II (AD702–711). He also built the rooms at the southern edge, including the remarkable four-storey tower that may have been an astronomical observatory.

The palace is luxurious throughout. Not only is it decorated with elaborate modelled stucco inside and out, but its builders used a modified arch that allowed spacious interiors , in marked contrast to the corbelled arch and narrow rooms found in many other Maya palaces and cities. When in use, the building was also brightly coloured. House E was painted white and also known as the

Right: Carving on the second storey of the Palace at Sayil features monsters and a rare deity known as 'the descending god', found only here and at Cobá and Tulum.

White House but the other parts of the complex were coloured a dark red with details in blue, green and yellow. The complex contains 85 'windows' in the T-shaped form of a Maya calendrical day-sign that scholars call 'IK': its translation is 'wind-breath' or 'breath of life'. The 'windows' might not have been built for the usual purpose, for they were generally set rather too high in the wall for people to look through them comfortably. Nevertheless, they allowed light to enter and also had a decorative function. In the East Court, the king received

Above: This view of Palenque's palace is from the top of King Pacal's mortuary monument, the Temple of the Inscriptions.

ambassadors and fellow rulers. Its walls were decorated with carved inscriptions detailing Pacal's military successes and representing the many foes and rivals he had humbled and made captive.

A PALACE-TEMPLE

At Copán, King 18-Rabbit (AD695–738) erected a building that archaeologists believe was a combined palace-temple complex – known to archaeologists as Temple 22 – on the northern edge of the East Court of the Acropolis, the southern part of the city centre. Like many Maya temples, it was adorned with *witz* (sacred mountain masks) at the corners. In the Maya city of Edzná in Campeche, builders raised a pyramid temple platform that was also a palace: the five-storey structure had lower levels designed with many rooms, doorways and windows like a palace, but also a temple building on the flat fifth level that was accessed by a frontal staircase.

THE AZTEC PATTERN OF ELEGANCE

Aztec rulers lived in splendour, at a very great remove from the humble dwellings of their subjects. Their palaces were large and splendid, but took the same basic form as the dwellings occupied by the nobles and the middle classes: several rectangular rooms arranged around a courtyard or patio. They were unusual, however, in having a second floor: only nobles and rulers were permitted to build two-storey dwellings. Palaces contained administrative and storage rooms as well as living quarters for the ruler, his wives, concubines, guards and servants. Royal residential areas in Aztec palaces were generally reserved for the upper storey, while council rooms, courts, war chambers, arsenals, storage rooms and other administrative buildings were laid out on the ground floor. Extensive patios and pleasure gardens, well planted with trees and watered by streams and fountains, stocked with abundant wildlife, covered vast areas.

Below: Many of Teotihuacán's elite residences were decorated with murals. This owl fresco is from the Tetitla complex.

Above: In Teotihuacán the Quetzalpapálotl Palace, at the south-west corner of Plaza of the Moon, may have been priestly quarters.

A PICTURE OF ROYAL LIFE

According to Fernando de Alva Ixtlilxóchitl, writing in the early 17th century, the palace of Netzahualcóyotl, ruler of Texcoco, covered an area of more than 80 hectares (200 acres). A celebrated image from the 16th-century *Mapa Quinatzin* depicts the palace complex in Texcoco. Netzahualcóyotl holds court with his son Netzahualpilli in the throne room overlooking a large patio-courtyard

DESIRE FOR PRIVACY

Although an Aztec palace contained many public rooms such as stores and courtrooms that could be accessed even by commoners, the *tlatoani's* own quarters were reserved on the upper storey and contained many secluded outdoor patios and gardens in which the ruler and his intimates could associate with their noble peers in quiet and privacy. The divine aura of the ruler, which dictated that he must eat alone and could not be addressed with full eye contact, needed to be protected.

There were certainly ancient Mesoamerican prototypes in Teotihuacán and Tollán for setting the palace alongside centres of public life such as the marketplace and ceremonial area, but equally in the 'palaces' of Monte Albán, there was a prototype of an elite building with many stairways, corridors and secluded patios – a design intended to safeguard the privacy of rulers and nobles.

in which several men – either allied rulers or the leaders of Texcoco's communities – are in earnest discussion. Behind them on one side is an extensive network of rooms for storing imperial tribute, while on the other side of the patio are temple rooms containing shrines. On either side of the throne room are administrative chambers, one used for counting and storing military supplies and the other a courtroom for the city's judges.

Opposite these rooms at the far side of the patio is a splendid area for receiving ambassadors from rival and allied cities and a large meeting house set aside for discussing matters of war. This pattern is typical of Aztec-era palaces and similar to the design of Moctezuma's splendid building in Tenochtitlán.

Above: A fresco detail from the Tetitla residence in Teotihuacán contains a floor plan for a palace building.

PALACE PROTOTYPE

The unknown builders of Teotihuacán, who exercised such an enduring architectural influence on later Mesoamericans, constructed a palace compound in the 1st–2nd century AD of the kind built about 1,200 years later by the Aztecs. The palace at Teotihuacán was part of the great Ciudadela or Citadel complex that also contained a vast plaza and the Pyramid of the Feathered Serpent. It lay at the junction of the main thoroughfares that divided the city into four and sat directly opposite a large marketplace. Similarly, in Tenochtitlán the *tlatoani's* palace occupied a position adjoining the main square and temple precinct in the heart of the city.

The Ciudadela palaces lay on the north and south sides of the great Pyramid of the Feathered Serpent. They consisted of groups of low-lying apartment buildings gathered around open patios – the very pattern that Aztec builders would later use in their own designs.

Opposite the Ciudadela, the open space that archaeologists believe was a marketplace was flanked by other low-lying palace-style buildings that were probably administrative buildings needed to monitor and control the vibrant trade on which the city thrived. By the era of Tenochtitlán, the two 'palace' functions – ruler's residence and administrative compound – had been combined.

The monumental Ciudadela complex built *c.*AD100–200 was a new departure for the Teotihuacános, who had previously laid out buildings in groups of three on an ancient sacred pattern. Scholars believe that the new style might have marked the beginning of a new political era, an attempt by a powerful new leadership in the city to distance themselves from a possibly despotic former regime.

The Ciudadela celebrated the authority and power of the state, with its palaces adjoining open spaces for the gathering of residents and centralization of trade. Later Mesoamericans learned a great deal from this association of elite residences with monumental architecture.

THE BURNT PALACE

At Tollán, the Toltecs erected twin palace-administrative buildings adjoining the Temple of Quetzalcóatl. To the east was the Palace of Quetzalcóatl and to the west was a much larger three-halled structure, now known as the Burnt Palace because much of it was lost to a fire. Like its predecessor at Teotihuacán and its successors at Texcoco and Tenochtitlán, the palace building probably hosted meetings, was used to greet notable visitors and was a state storeroom for items of trade and tribute. Once again, the building adjoined both a plaza and a large area that scholars believe was a marketplace.

Below: At Tollán these pillars are remains of the colonnades that once graced the Palacio Quemado or 'Burnt Palace'.

THE MAGNIFICENCE OF MOCTEZUMA

Moctezuma's palace in Tenochtitlán was a statement in stone of the *tlatoani's* divine magnificence. Surrounded by extensive gardens containing ponds, courtyards, an aviary and a zoo, the palace was a residence fit for a ruler so magnificent that none of his subjects were permitted to look him in the eye.

ROYAL CITY WITHIN A CITY

Spanish accounts report that Moctezuma's palace had more than 300 rooms, which were arranged around internal courtyards. Legal documents concerning landholdings suggest that the emperor's city complex covered 4 hectares (10 acres). An administrative building as well as a royal home, the palace contained military council rooms, a throne room and reception areas for greeting ambassadors and political visitors, legal apartments used by judges as courtrooms, two armouries and large areas for storing

Below: A reconstruction of Moctezuma's two-storey palace in Tenochtitlán reveals extensive courtyards and gardens within.

tribute from around the empire. According to an account by the conquistador Bernal Díaz del Castillo, the palace contained extensive areas for storing cacao, feathers, gold, jewels, cotton and foods that had been received as tribute payments. There were also rooms for accountants managing the wealth generated by tribute and taxation.

The vast building contained libraries, music rooms and areas for craftsmen retained to work for the emperor. There were also permanent quarters for the rulers of Texcoco and Tlacopán, the Aztecs' allies in the Triple Alliance, together with guest rooms for visiting notables from states within the empire. The importance of the lakeside town of Chiconauhtla, derived largely from its control over the straits connecting the lakes of Zumpango and Xaltocán with Lake Texcoco, was reflected in the fact that the ruler had the right to keep an apartment in the imperial palace

The Tenochtitlán palace complex was arranged over two floors, with the *tlatoani's* quarters on the upper floor and

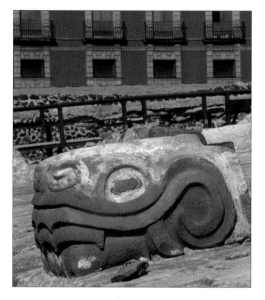

Above: A serpent-head Tenochtitlán foundation stone was uncovered by archaeologists in Mexico City.

state or administrative rooms and servants' living space on the gloomier ground level. An image from the *Codex Mendoza* (*c.*1541) represents the two-storey building with a courtyard and steps leading to an upper-floor reception room in which the dazzling Moctezuma himself sits in state. On either side of his quarters stand apartments for leading allied rulers. Below on the ground floor lie two meeting rooms, in one of which four judges discuss an important case, while the other is kept for councils of war.

PALACE COURTROOMS

Friar Bernardino de Sahagún's description of the palace in Tenochtitlán indicated that legal administration worked on three levels for nobles, military and commoners. In one room of the palace court, legal experts heard noble disputes and complaints of wrongdoing. Their sanctions included banning an offender from the palace complex, banishing a person from the city or ordering his execution by stoning, hanging or beating; chopping off the hair was a lesser punishment, but greatly feared because it would make a leading member of the *pip-iltin* nobility look like a shaven-headed *macehual* or commoner.

In a palace room named the *tecpilcalli*, leading members of the military dispensed their own justice. In the *teccalco* chamber, commoners could bring disputes and complaints to judgement. The *tlatoani* himself heard difficult cases and took advice from the three most senior judges or *tecuhtlatoque* before passing judgement. Judges faced the strictest sanctions – including execution – if they were found to be corrupt.

ANCIENT AMENITIES

There were more than 100 bathrooms in the *tlatoani's* palace. Several times a day the ruler washed and changed his clothes: he discarded his garments after wearing them once. He lived in great splendour on the palace's second floor, with his two wives and 150 concubines, together with legions of guards and attendants. His servants were housed in their own luxurious apartments.

A large part of the palace was given over to kitchens and food stores. At every meal some 300 guests were served from an extensive menu designed to stimulat-

Below: This stone, once part of Moctezuma's elegant Tenochtitlán palace, shows evidence of having been worked by an Aztec mason.

ing the most jaded palate. Such was the *tlatoani's* splendour that dinner guests were forbidden to watch him engage in activities such as eating: he consumed his food in isolation behind a golden screen. Delicacies to tempt the royal diners included frogs served with green chilli peppers, sage-doused locusts and a helping of prickly pear served with fish eggs from the great lake of Texcoco.

In the patios of the royal palace complex, acrobats and musicians practised. The gardens contained ten pools stocked with waterfowls that feasted on fish. Hernán Cortés wrote to King Carlos V of Spain that these birds were so numerous they required 110kg (250lb) of fish each day. In the zoo, royal jaguars, coyotes and

Above: The Codex Mendoza *(c.1541) shows Moctezuma sitting on the upper floor of his two-storey palace, between apartments for visiting dignitaries. Before the building, one man departs while four litigants present a case to the judges in the lower right-hand chamber. The lower left-hand chamber is identified as the war council room.*

serpents were kept in regal luxury. Some were fed on human flesh carried from the temple complex nearby.

Throughout the palace, servants, guards and administrators burned incense and sweet-smelling woods in their braziers to mask the smell of decaying body parts that the breeze sometimes carried across from the temple quarters.

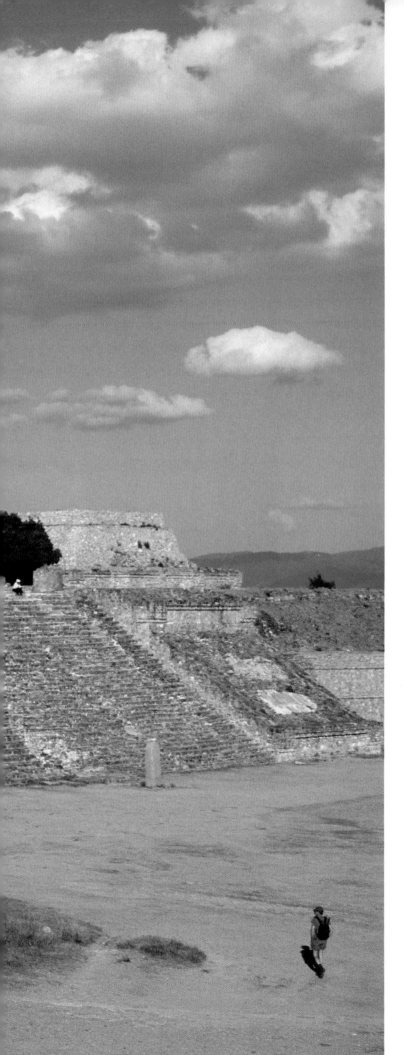

CHAPTER EIGHT

BUILDING THE CITIES

The builders of great Mesoamerican centres looked for inspiration in the cities and sacred buildings of the past. They paid homage to the achievements of their ancestors by reproducing their styles: Teotihuacáno *talud-tablero* construction spread across Mesoamerica – being used, for instance, in Tikal, Kaminaljuyú, Xochicalco, El Tajín and Chichén Itzá. Great cities of the past were also places of pilgrimage or sacred occupation.

Cities had a unifying function, linking cultures and peoples across centuries, but also connecting people within a region. A city was the focus of its area, providing employment in outlying artisanal areas or an outlet for the excess agricultural produce of the region's farmers. For instance, Tikal provided a means of living for a vast outlying population of some 60,000; Teotihuacán similarly supported a large outer area of rural settlements, some growing food, others working local flint or obsidian; Tenochtitlán was the focus of an extensive area of *chinampa* farmlands.

A city also created connections between areas across great distances: from before the start of the Classic Period, Mesoamerican trade was driven by the needs of wealthy city populations and religious elites for rare or exotic products. Long-distance trade driven by the vast population of Teotihuacán, for instance, forged links across many thousands of kilometres between the Mexican highlands and settlements such as Tikal or Kaminaljuyú.

Left: The North Platform bounds the northern edge of Monte Albán's Plaza, at the heart of Mesoamerica's first true city.

SACRED TOWNS:
SAN LORENZO AND LA VENTA

Settlers first occupied the plateau that became the Olmec centre of San Lorenzo, near the Gulf Coast of Mexico, *c.*1500BC. Their descendants began public building works about 250 years later. A group had grown wealthy and powerful controlling the farming of fertile lands alongside the local Coatzacoalcos and Chiquito rivers and perhaps by managing trade in obsidian, greenstone and basalt from resource-rich uplands nearby. The leader of this group was able to command and reward the labour needed to build a sacred ceremonial centre.

Below: Stela 2 at La Venta shows an Olmec monarch dressed as a player with the bat used in some versions of the game, after c.*1000BC.*

SACRED CENTRE
Beginning *c.*1250BC, hundreds of workers built up and levelled the plateau. On its top, 50m (160ft) above the surrounding countryside, they laid out a series of pyramids and rectangular courts on a north to south alignment, oriented precisely 8 degrees west of true north – probably to line up with the rising of a star or planet at a ritually significant time such as an equinox. They used clay and earth to make these buildings, but imported basalt from the Tuxtla mountains 70km (10 miles) away to line a remarkable series of drains that were connected to fountains and artificial ponds. These were made from skilfully shaped interconnecting pieces of basalt.

Above: On Altar 5 at La Venta, a king or shaman-priest wearing a jaguar headdress holds a 'were jaguar' baby – an infant with snarling jaguar features.

SACRED FIGUREHEAD
The king may have been worshipped. Eight colossal basalt carved heads erected at San Lorenzo were probably portraits of the settlement's rulers. Some of the heads were more than 3m (10ft) tall and weighed 20 tons. The king's power derived not just from his wealth, but also because he was a sacred figurehead, guarantor of his people's safety and of the

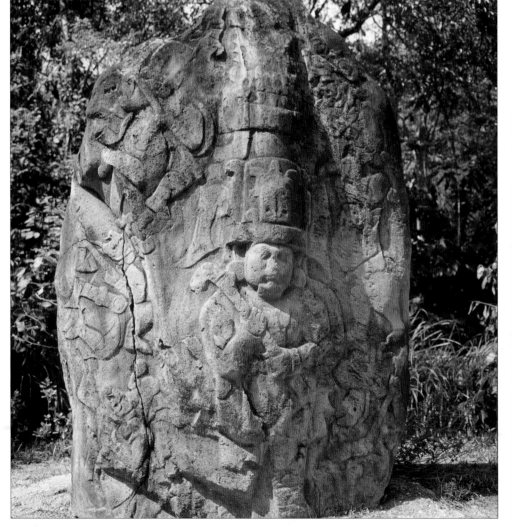

RELIGIOUS PIONEERS IN TWIN OLMEC SETTLEMENTS
Olmec remains at San Lorenzo and La Venta suggest that the inhabitants of these temple towns were pioneers in many facets of Mesoamerican religious life. The Olmec worshipped a feathered serpent deity together with a rain god and revered jaguars and eagles as well as crocodiles and sharks. They also practised the rites of autosacrifice, in which a worshipper expelled his or her own blood: stingray spines and other items – perhaps including shark's teeth – were used to induce blood flow. Generations of Mesoamericans would follow the Olmec lead in these matters.

continued fertility of their maize fields. The buildings and monuments of San Lorenzo were erected before 900BC. While the site appears to have been a busy trading settlement after that date, its people did not feel the need to raise further pyramid-mounds or to carve new stone thrones or heads. Some time during the years 900–700BC, axe-wielding men smashed the Olmec heads and thrones of San Lorenzo and buried the remnants in ditches. The violence done to the statues suggests that this was an act of vandalism by invaders, but the careful collection and hiding of the remnants in ditches might indicate that it was a piece of elegiac destruction by Olmec who wanted to set their own age apart from the past.

Pottery remnants from the years after 700BC suggest that at this time San Lorenzo was occupied by people originating in Maya regions of Chiapas and Guatemala. In the years 600–400BC, the inhabitants of the settlement probably built a ball court. Archaeologists have discovered two elongated mounds running in parallel that they believe are the side walls or spectators' stands of a ball court.

AMID THE MARSHES: LA VENTA

From *c*.1150BC onwards, Olmec builders constructed another centre at La Venta, about 60km (35 miles) north-east of San Lorenzo and just 12km (7 miles) inland from the Gulf coast. They chose a salt mound amid freshwater marshland, in an area where villagers had already been living for more than a millennium, supporting themselves by fishing, hunting, gathering and growing maize in the fertile soil.

La Venta's builders raised a ceremonial centre of mounds and plazas, aligned like those at San Lorenzo precisely 8 degrees to the west of true north. The tallest of these, called Complex C by archaeologists, is an earthen mound 32m (105ft) high. Some scholars have suggested that it was intended as a recreation of a sacred volcano. Others have likened its shape to that of the pyramid in the Group E complex at the later Maya city of Uaxactún, which may have been structured in four quadrants to celebrate the cardinal points and which was aligned precisely to the sun's rising on sacred equinoctial dates. In front of the mound, running northwest, lay an elongated plaza. Beyond the plaza lay a further sacred arena (named

Left: Olmec religious life appears to have centred on worship of the ruler and his ancestors. This colossal basalt head, from La Venta, may represent a departed king.

Above: The four sides of La Venta Altar 5 are carved with shaman-kings holding 'were jaguar' babies. The 'were jaguar' may have been venerated as an image of the rain god.

Complex A by archaeologists) containing a court enclosed on two sides by basalt columns, ten further mounds, several platforms and a buried serpentine mosaic pavement measuring 4.5 by 6m (15 by 20ft) and representing the face of a jaguar, beneath which many sacred offerings were laid. Above the pavement, at ground level, lay a sarcophagus of sandstone carved to represent the earth monster in the form of a crocodile floating on water.

Both La Venta and San Lorenzo were relatively small in size. With around 1,000 people resident in each at their peak, the settlements are perhaps better called towns than cities. For many years archaeologists concentrated on the ceremonial role of La Venta and San Lorenzo, but recent work has established that the sites were residential as well as religious centres. At La Venta, living quarters lay to the north-east of the main ceremonial complex. At San Lorenzo the network of drains may have been used functionally by the town's inhabitants, or may have played a role in religious ceremonies celebrating the life-giving power of the waters that fed the maize plants.

CITY OF THE ZAPOTECS:
MONTE ALBÁN

An elite group among the Zapotec inhabitants of the highland Valley of Oaxaca founded the settlement of Monte Albán *c.*500BC. It was located in a dominant position on a flattened mountain ridge between two peaks, with good views down all three arms of the valley. In its early years, the settlement consisted of three residential districts and contained up to 7,200 people. The ridge had no agricultural land, and Monte Albán's residents lived on the produce of the three arms of Oaxaca valley: Tlacolula to the east, Etla to the north and Zaachila

Below: A plan of Monte Albán's Main Plaza. The plaza was laid out and paved in white stucco by Zapotec labourers c.300BC.

to the south. Produce was distributed at a market on the flattened ridge. The settlement grew rapidly. Home to 15,000 people by *c.*200BC, Monte Albán had become Mesoamerica's first city.

Major building works had begun about a century earlier, *c.*300BC. An army of labourers flattened the uneven mountaintop and laid out a plaza paved in white stucco.

The Temple of the Danzantes, adorned with carvings of defeated war captives, arose in the south-west corner of the plaza. The city's elite commissioned stone tombs for their burials and builders produced increasingly elaborate masonry graves, some of which were distinguished by corbelled roofs.

Above: Looking north across the expansive Main Plaza at Monte Albán, Building H looms in the foreground.

A MATURE CITY

Monte Albán was a thriving city for several centuries. In the period AD500–750, its population rose as high as 24,000. The city spread over two adjacent hilltops, covering 6.5km (4 miles), and contained 14 residential areas. Each had its own plaza, while the city's elite rulers and administrators lived in 14 'palaces' arranged around the city's main commercial plaza. In these years, labourers erected a great pyramid 15m (50ft) in height and more than 100m (325ft) in length at the south end of the main plaza. Carved stelae at the four corners appear to commemorate a state visit by emissaries from Teotihuacán, perhaps on the occasion of the building's ceremonial dedication. At the northern end of the plaza, builders constructed a hall with fine colonnades that gave on to a low-level patio backed by tall pyramids.

The city specialized in crafts, making elite produce from obsidian and seashells: The workshops lay to the north-east of the main plaza in an area of noble dwellings. The elite of Monte Albán appear to have valued seclusion and privacy. Noble dwellings were secluded, with central patio areas sometimes accessed by long corridors and through a number of intervening rooms. The main plaza was largely cut off from other parts of the city.

Mound X

North

Platform

Main Plaza

Ball Court

System IV

Building H

Building L

Gallery of the Slain Captives

Structure J

Conquest Slabs

Stela 5   Stela 4

Stela 12

Stela 13

Stela 3

Stela 6

South

Stela 2

Estela Lisa

Stela 1

Stela 7

Platform

Stela 8

CAPITAL OF THE BALL GAME:
EL TAJÍN

The settlement of El Tajín in the Gulf Coast region of northern Veracruz was established in the early Classic Period, when it had trading links with the great metropolis of Teotihuacán. The celebrated remains, which include the Pyramid of the Niches and no fewer than 12 ball courts, date from much later – the 9th–11th centuries AD. These remnants are a small part of the city that once stood here: ruins untouched by archaeologists and so still covered in foliage stretch for 5km (3 miles) into the low hills of the surrounding tropical rainforest.

PYRAMID OF THE NICHES

Builders erected the ceremonial centre that contains the Pyramid of the Niches in the flat southern part of city. The six-tier pyramid supports a temple on its flat top, making seven levels in all, with progressively fewer niches in each level. The bottom tier contains 88 niches, the second has 76, then the levels contain 64, 52, 40 and 28 while the temple has 17 – making a total of 365, one for each day of the solar year. Close by, the builders set out two ball courts. One is decorated with bas-relief carving depicting the sacrificial slaughter of a ball player.

Below: Building 3 stands directly west of the Pyramid of the Niches in central El Tajín. It makes use of niches and Teotihuacáno talud-tablero *architectural elements.*

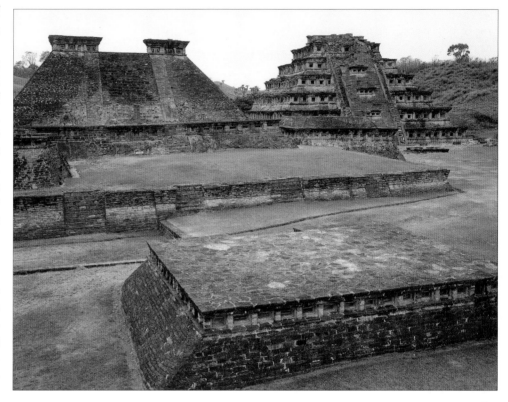

Above: The buildings of El Tajín were at one time covered with polychrome stucco. The niches of the Pyramid of the Niches were painted red with turquoise borders.

Labourers cut terraces into the small hills to the north of the ceremonial centre and laid out an extensive residential area. They raised elite homes or palaces with colonnades, rooms with corbelled vaults and fine roof combs. They built walls to separate the residential district – known as Tajín Chico – from the ceremonial area to the south and from the king's palace complex to the west.

HOME FIT FOR A KING

Skilled stonemasons cut splendid ornate reliefs in the Building of the Columns, one of the main structures in the royal complex, depicting images of military conquest and sacrificial ritual. The ruler shown most frequently in this area is King 13-Rabbit. Images represent toads as well as sacred serpents and royal jaguars. Glyphs indicate that the people of El Tajín followed the 260-day cycle as well as the calendar of 365 days celebrated in the niches of the main pyramid. The wet season in this part of Mexico hits hard: to prevent flooding and conserve

water, builders dug elaborate drains, underground waterways and tanks for storage. The city's 12 ball courts have led scholars to speculate that it might have been a centre for playing the ball game – perhaps a site used for grand enactments of sacred ritual linked to calendrical observations.

CAPITAL OF THE TOTONACS?

El Tajín might have been an early capital of the Totonacs, a people who rose to greater prominence in the Postclassic Period in Veracruz and the northern part of Puebla. In the 16th century, the Totonacs – who by then had their capital at Cempoala, some 150km (90 miles) south of El Tajín – had the distinction of becoming the first Mesoamerican people to join Hernán Cortés in his military action against Tenochtitlán.

THE PLACE OF THE GODS:
TEOTIHUACÁN

The great city of Teotihuacán – named
'the place of the gods' by the Aztecs –
was laid out from *c.*100BC onwards, on
an ancient sacred site in a region of highland Mexico where villagers had been
living since *c.*900BC. Builders erected the
first buildings in an area now called
Oztoyahualco ('Old City'), in the northern part of the valley about 1km (⅝ mile)
to the west of the land on which the
Pyramid of the Moon was later built.
They chose the Old City site, which had
little water, because it gave access to a
network of sacred caves and tunnels.

UNDERGROUND RITUAL
In the period AD1–150, the city's builders
reverently enlarged a natural cave beneath
the ground on which they would later
build the Pyramid of the Sun. They created an underground ritual site 100m
(325ft) long, with basalt roofing, walls
covered with mud plaster and water
channelled in for ritual use via a covered
drain made of stone. It led into four small
chambers. Next they built a small shrine
of stone and adobe bricks at ground level.

In the northern, original area of the
settlement, the builders laid out a series
of small plazas, each enclosed by three
temples. Archaeologists report that these

*Above: The city's axis, the 2.4km (1.5-mile)
Street of the Dead, runs 16 degrees east of
true north, linking the Pyramid of the Moon
and the Ciudadela complex in the south.*

*Below: Looking south from the Plaza of
the Moon, the Pyramid of the Sun rises
on the east side of the Street of the Dead.*

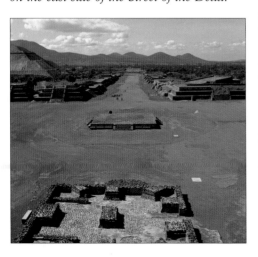

sacred constructions were associated with
access to caves and suggest that a series
of plaza-temple complexes, running
roughly south–west, probably followed
the line of the ancient subterranean caverns and tunnels. In all there are 20 of
these plaza-temple units, which have
been left largely untouched by archaeologists. Each might have been the original
settlement of 20 tribal or kin groups who
possibly united to found the city. In the
same period (AD1–150), farmers dug
the city's first irrigation system, a network
of simple canals excavated to spread the
waters of the Barranca de Cerro Colorado
among the farmlands at the western
perimeters of the expanding settlement.

CITY PLANNING
From the start the city was laid out
according to a clear design, divided into
quadrants by wide thoroughfares running
roughly north–south and east–west. The
north–south axis was oriented 16 degrees
to the east of north to align both with the
peak of Cerro Gordo and, according to
some scholars, with the point at which
the Pleiades set at that time. The Pyramid
of the Sun, located on the east side of this
north–south line, was the first sacred

building erected in Teotihuacán, in the 1st century AD. The original structure was later rebuilt, but archaeologists report that in its first version the pyramid was very nearly as tall as the majestic final building, which rose to a height of 66m (216ft). The original pyramid might have supported twin temples, as did the pyramid built at Cuicuilco, also in the Valley of Mexico, and many later Mesoamerican pyramid/temple-platforms.

The city grew very fast. In AD150 it was home to as many as 80,000 people and covered 20sq km (7sq miles). The population continued to grow – reaching a peak of 100,000–200,000 by AD500 – although the city did not expand far beyond this ground area. Large numbers lived in and farmed outlying rural areas beyond the city limits.

When finished, the north–south thoroughfare was 40m (130ft) wide and 2.4km (1½ miles) long. It was lined on both sides with low-lying buildings identified by archaeologists as elite residences or palaces, but which the Aztecs believed

Below: The small stepped pyramids flanking the Plaza of the Moon are dwarfed by the 66m (216ft)-tall Pyramid of the Sun.

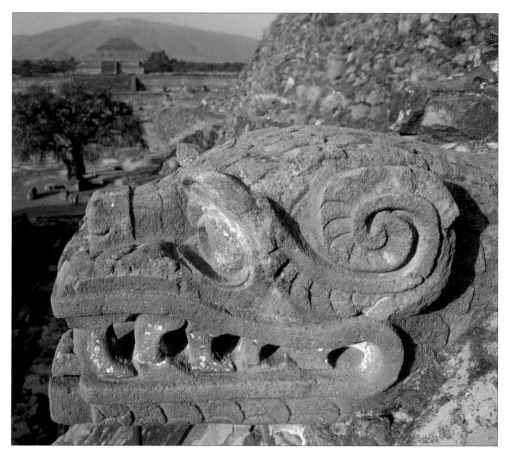

were the tombs of their ancestors – leading them to call it the Street of the Dead. At the northern end of the street lay the Pyramid of the Moon, 43m (140ft) in height. It faced and gave on to an open square known as the Plaza of the Moon. In its south-west corner the elite residential building known as the Palace of Quetzalpapálotl was built in AD500–750. One of Teotihuacán's plaza-temple groups, the Plaza of the Columns, lay to the west of the Street of the Dead, a little to the north and on the opposite side to the imposing Pyramid of the Sun. Both the Sun and Moon pyramids were flanked by smaller pyramids and gave on to plazas, which might also have been intended to form plaza-temple groups of the kind typical of Teotihuacán.

Heading south, the street is flanked by palace buildings and sacred structures and gives access via side streets to areas of residential apartment buildings. An extensive collection of apartments, temples, plazas and platforms on both sides of the street is known as the Street of the Dead Complex. These were magnificent buildings, constructed of the finest materials and provided with mica floors.

Above: At the southern edge of the city centre, a serpent's head honours the Feathered Serpent Quetzalcóatl on the god's temple in the Ciudadela complex.

IN THE CITADEL
Further south, the Street of the Dead gave to the east on to the city centre, the Ciudadela, a vast, enclosed square structure of platforms, roughly 400m (1,300ft) square and incorporating 15 pyramids, two palaces, an 11-acre (4.4-hectare) plaza and the magnificent stepped pyramid-platform Temple of Quetzalcóatl. Opposite the Ciudadela, on the west side of the Street of the Dead, was another vast enclosed area called the Great Compound that was probably the city's main marketplace. Its northern and southern edges consisted of long platforms supporting apartment buildings thought to have been the homes of the city's administrators and bureaucrats. The large western avenue led directly out of the compound heading west, while the eastern avenue began at the eastern edge of the Ciudadela, behind the Pyramid of Quetzalcóatl. The Street of the Dead continued southwards beyond the Ciudadela and the Great Compound for 3km (2 miles).

TOWERING MONUMENTS:
TIKAL

In the dense jungle of the Petén region, Tikal began to expand from a village *c.*500–300BC. By 300AD it was a major city, celebrating in stone the achievements of a great dynasty of kings. At its greatest extent in the 8th century AD, the city – with extensive environs covering about 16sq km (6sq miles) – was home to a population of 60,000.

CYCLICAL REBUILDING
The building of Tikal was a massive feat of construction. The main temples, tombs, ceremonial buildings and elite residences covered 2.5sq km (1sq mile). Moreover, most of the city's main buildings were refashioned and reconstructed many times. By Mesoamerican tradition, new structures were erected directly above and encompassing their predecessors. In Tikal, the building of the North Acropolis, a collection of pyramid temple-tombs, began as early as 250BC. Over the centuries the Acropolis floor was re-laid 20 times, so that the final layer was a full 10m (33ft) higher than the first. Scholars believe that the city must have supported a full-time force of stonemasons, sculptors, painters and labourers to carry out this cyclical building and rebuilding.

The centre of the ceremonial complex was the Great Plaza. To its north lay the North Acropolis, burial ground of kings. Many times rebuilt, it consisted in its final form of a large rectangular platform, 100m by 80m (325ft by 260ft), supporting eight royal temple-tombs built *c.*AD250–550. Subsequently, four further temples were built on a second platform along the southern extremity of the North Acropolis, giving via stairways on to the Great Plaza.

TWIN MORTUARY MONUMENTS
Facing one another on the eastern and western sides of the Great Plaza rose Temple I and Temple II. Temple I, which climbs in nine terraces to a height of 50m (164ft) on the eastern side, was built as

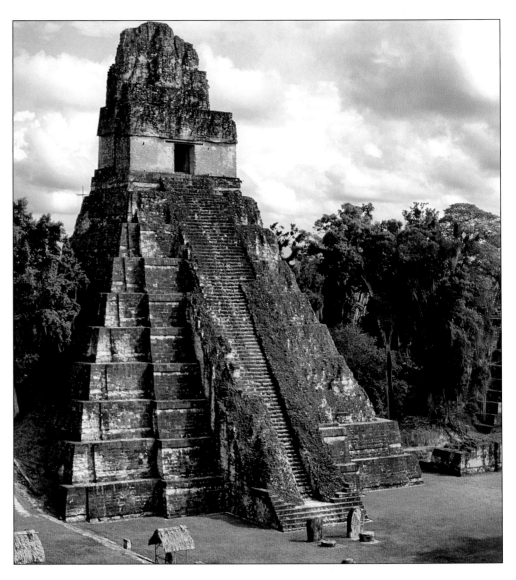

the funerary temple of King Ah Cacau (AD682–734). He was the first member of Tikal's dynasty to be buried outside the North Acropolis. Temple II, rising in three levels to a height of 42m (138ft), supports a sacred building that might have been set up to honour Ah Cacau's queen: the remains of a wooden lintel from this temple bear a portrait of a royal woman.

To the west and east of the Great Plaza lay other plazas. Behind Temple I lay the East Plaza, containing a ball court and a rectangular collection of buildings thought to have been used as a market. From the East Plaza, a *sacbé* known to archaeologists as the Mendez Causeway

Above: The stairs leading to the summit of Temple I rise at an angle of more than 70°.

led south-east past a collection of palaces now called Group G for 0.5 km (0.3 miles) to Temple VI. This temple is also known as the Temple of the Inscriptions because stonemasons carved a record of Tikal's dynastic history on the rear and sides of the roof comb that rose above its summit temple. Labourers built Temple VI during or just after the reign of Ah Cacau's son, Yax Kin (AD734–46). A stela celebrating Yax Kin's accession was erected at the foot of the great pyramid. South of the East Plaza was the Central

Acropolis, a vast palace containing buildings arranged around courtyards. This was probably the official residence of Tikal's ruling dynasty. Farther south beyond one of the city's many reservoirs rose Temple V, Tikal's second tallest structure at 57m (185ft), the temple-tomb of an as yet unidentified ruler. This southernmost region of the ceremonial centre also included another area of royal tombs, the South Acropolis, and the Plaza of the Seven Temples, which in addition to seven temple-shrines gave on to numerous palaces to south and west. It contained a triple ball court, with three pitches, which is unique in Mesoamerica. Beyond this plaza to the west, labourers built the Lost World complex, which contained a platform on its western edge and three platforms on its eastern side aligned with equinoctial sunrises – like the Group E arrangement of pyramids in the Maya city of Uaxactún.

Behind Temple II, a *sacbé* now known as the Tozzer Causeway led westwards to Temple IV, 70m (230ft) high and the tallest building in Tikal. This structure was built for King Yax Kin (AD734–746). Two surviving wooden lintels above the

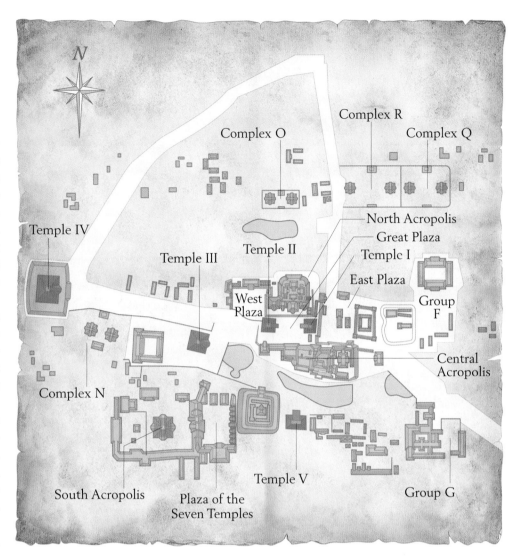

Above: Four sacbeob *(causeways) link groups of sacred buildings in central Tikal.*

Below: This view of the North Acropolis is from the heights of Temple I.

doorway to the temple-shrine on the summit of the artificial mountain record the date 9.15.10.0.0. in the Maya Long Count (AD741). A *sacbé* now called the Maudslay Causeway ran north to a collection of twin pyramid groups.

Temple III, which lay to the south of the Tozzer Causeway, was the last pyramid temple erected at Tikal. It was probably the mortuary shrine of King Chitam (AD768–794). A stela erected at its base was carved with the date 9.19.0.0.0. (AD810). Only one later dated monument was raised at Tikal, a stela of 10.2.0.0.0. (AD869) in the Great Plaza. By the end of the 9th century the city had been abandoned to the encroaching vegetation and to groups of squatters.

TWIN PYRAMID GROUPS

At Tikal, several rulers erected twin pyramid groups to mark the close of a *katun* or period of twenty 360-day years (a total of 7,200 days). The groups consisted of

two pyramids, each with a flat top and four access stairways, symmetrically arranged on the west and east edges of a plaza, with an enclosure containing an altar and a stela on the plaza's northern edge and a building with nine doorways on its southern edge. These groups have been found only at Tikal, save examples at Yaxha and Ixlu. The first at Tikal was erected in the early years of the 6th century AD in the East Plaza and reused several times. In the late 7th century AD, King Ah Cacau (AD682–734) erected a twin pyramid group to celebrate the end of the first *katun* following his accession. Its altar was marked with the date 9.13.0.0.0. (18 March AD692). From this occasion until AD790, a new group was erected for each *katun*-ending. The largest (known as Twin-Pyramid Group 4E-4) was built in AD771 by King Chitam.

PACAL'S GLORY:
PALENQUE

The city of Palenque at the northern edge of the Chiapas highlands in Mexico, site of the ornate 7th-century tomb of King Pacal that is one of the glories of Mesoamerica, was distinctly different from Tikal and other great Maya cities of the Classic Period.

It contained no forests of carved stelae, no wide ceremonial plazas, no great *sacbé* or causeways, no acropolis of royal tombs. Its buildings were adorned with stucco sculpture and carved reliefs that pioneered naturalistic portraiture of royal figures. It gave pride of place at the centre of the city to the royal palace, home of the living king, rather than – as at Tikal – to temple-tombs housing the remains of divine ancestors.

Palenque appears to have risen to a position of power in the reign of King Pacal (*r*. AD615–83). Most of the surviving parts of the city date from his reign or later and the oldest surviving use of the city's emblem glyph was cut during his time.

PACAL'S PIONEERS
Pacal began a major programme of building in AD647, raising the temple Olvidado ('Unnoticed Shrine'), around half a kilometre to the south of the palace in the city centre. His architect-builders pioneered the use of the thin walls and numerous wide doorways that would become a distinctive feature of Palenque architecture. The temple, standing on an

Above: The lid of Pacal's sarcophagus shows the king falling down the cross-shaped Tree of Life into the underworld.

escarpment and reached by four stretches of stairs linked by platforms, had three doorways giving on to two inner rooms. Inscriptions on the north façade, carved within round cartouches, identified the king as the son of his father, Kan-Bahlum Mo', and of his mother, Lady Zac-Kuk.

THE KING'S PALACE
Pacal proceeded to develop the palace complex. On the large palace platform originally constructed by his predecessors, he built the royal residences identified as Houses E, C, B and A and laid out the expansive East Court. He commissioned sculptors to decorate the palace walls with stucco portrait masks, hieroglyphs, supernatural symbols and sacred scenes. To the south he began work

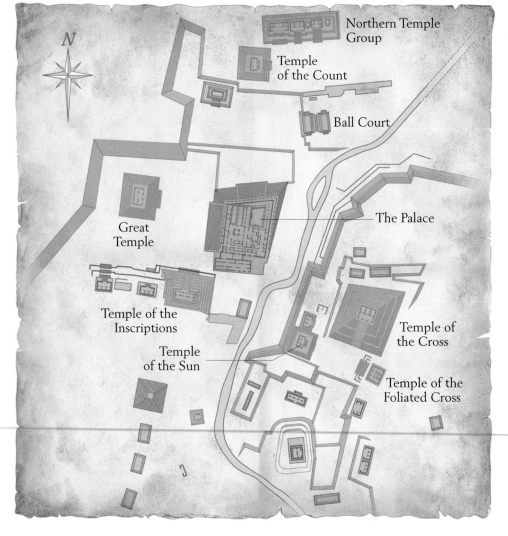

Left: In the eastern part of the city centre, the temples of the Cross, the Foliated Cross and the Sun celebrated Pacal's dynasty.

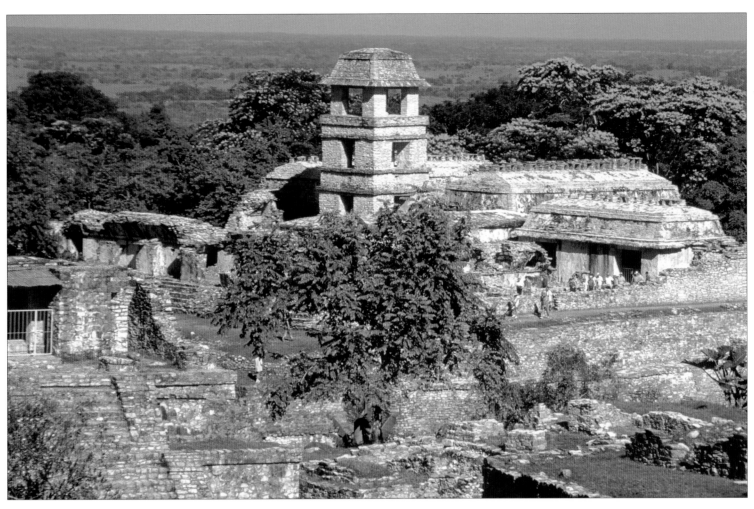

Above: The Palace tower at Palenque commands wide-ranging views of the green Chiapas countryside.

on the great Temple of the Inscriptions, beneath which his tomb was prepared, ready for his eventual death in AD683.

Pacal's son Chan-Bahlum (*r.* AD684–702) completed the Temple of the Inscriptions, which rose to a height of 25m (82ft) and was topped with a temple containing five wide doorways and a roof comb. The portions of the temple facing the court were decorated with painted stucco reliefs that depicted the new king receiving his divine sanction to rule from great Pacal.

POWER OF THE ROYAL LINE

Next, Chan-Bahlum erected three shrines – the Temple of the Cross, the Temple of the Foliated Cross and the Temple of the Sun – facing one another across a plaza in the eastern part of the city centre. They each represented one of the three levels of the Maya universe. The Temple of the Cross, situated in the north, was linked

to the heavens; the Temple of the Foliated Cross, in the easterly direction of the rising sun, was associated with the earth; and the Temple of the Sun, in the westerly direction of the setting sun, was identified with the underworld. They contained carvings celebrating Chan-Bahlum's links to his divine father.

A panel in the Temple of the Cross showed Pacal and Chan-Bahlum on either side of the ceiba world tree that the Maya believed connected the three levels of the universe. The carving in the Temple of the Foliated Cross depicted the pair on either side of a giant cob of maize bearing human heads, a reference to the Maya creation myth in which the gods Huracán and Gucumatz made the first humans from maize. The image in the Temple of the Sun presented Chan-Bahlum and his father adopting a martial pose, one to each side of a battle shield adorned with spears and the jaguar god of the underworld.

Archaeologists have not found Chan-Bahlum's tomb, but many believe it may lie beneath the Temple of Cross since this

was the northern member of the group and burials were generally laid in the direction of the north.

Chan-Bahlum II's brother, Kan-Xul II, rebuilt the palace complex and may have erected the curious four-storey tower that was probably an astronomical observatory. This structure has no counterpart anywhere else in the Maya realm. Scholar Linda Schele has suggested that the tower was built as a tribute to King Pacal. An observer standing at the top of the tower at the winter solstice would see the sun set directly on to the Temple of the Inscriptions, thus going down into the underworld by way of Pacal's tomb.

With Kan-Xul II's reign the great building work of Palenque came to a close: the king was captured in AD711 by the rival city of Toniná and, after a long captivity, was beheaded there. Before the century was out, Palenque became one of the first Maya cities to cease cutting dates in inscriptions and so enter the historical silence of the celebrated collapse of the 8th and 9th centuries. The last inscribed date at Palenque was AD799.

169

CITY OF THE JAGUAR KINGS:
YAXCHILÁN

Yaxchilán was built on a hill overlooking a bend in the Usumacinta river in Chiapas, Mexico. The city's origins lie in the 4th century AD, when it may have been founded as a satellite of Tikal, but it was developed primarily by two kings of the 8th century: Lord Shield Jaguar (*r.* AD681–742) and his son Bird Jaguar (*r.* AD752–68). From the date of its investigation by Sir Alfred Maudslay, the British gentleman-scholar hailed as the 'father of Maya archaeology', Yaxchilán has been celebrated for its magnificently carved door lintels, some of which have been on display in the British Museum in London since Maudslay had them shipped to Europe in 1882.

TOMB FOR A QUEEN
The city's main ceremonial area lies on an artificial terrace above the Usumacinta. The large plaza runs parallel to the river. On its south side, Lord Shield Jaguar built a structure known to archaeologists as

Below: A detail shows the stone lintels of Yaxchilán's palaces. The remains of a stone throne lie before the building.

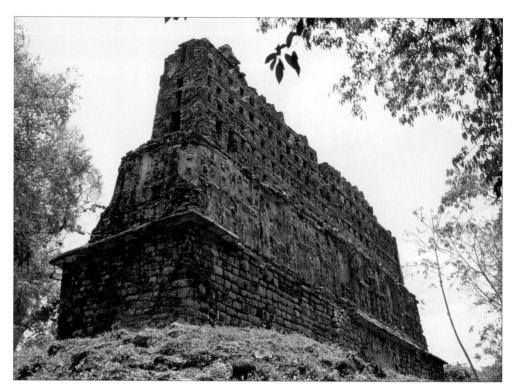

Above: Stucco sculptures once decorated the roof of Temple 33. Standing on high ground, the vast temple dominates the city centre.

Temple 23, or the Queen's House, that was dedicated to his principal wife, Lady Xoc, in 9.14.14.13.17 (726AD), the 45th year of his 61-year reign. This building contains celebrated door-lintel carvings of Lady Xoc performing rites of ritual bloodletting by running a spiked cord across her tongue; of Lady Xoc having a sacred experience through the Vision Snake of King Yat Balam, founder of the dynasty; and of Shield Jaguar, accompanied by his wife, donning battle garb as he prepared to set out in search of sacrificial captives. Temple 24, erected on the western edge of the Queen's House, recorded her death in AD749 and almost certainly contains her grave.

Earlier, in AD732, the king dedicated Temple 44, also known as the War Memorial as it commemorated a series of noble captives taken by Lord Shield Jaguar. Among other sacred structures erected by Shield Jaguar was Temple 41, at the summit of the hill that rises behind the ceremonial terrace. This structure commemorated celebrations of a sacred solstice in 9.15.9.17.16 (AD741).

STRUGGLE TO SUCCEED
Lord Shield Jaguar was succeeded by his son Bird Jaguar. The succession was not without its difficulties. Bird Jaguar was not the king's son by his principal wife, Lady Xoc, but by another royal bride, Lady Evening Star, who is thought by scholars to have come originally from Calakmul. Whether because the succession was contested by a son of Lady Xoc, or because Bird Jaguar's connection to the royal line of Calakmul made him unpopular, there was a gap of ten years between the death of Lord Shield Jaguar in AD742 and the coronation of Bird Jaguar in AD752. Afterwards these difficulties contributed greatly to construction in Yaxchilan's ceremonial quarter: Bird Jaguar erected many buildings and stelae promoting his right to the throne and, once his position was secure, poured his construction efforts into securing the succession of his son Chel Te.

In the course of these projects, Bird Jaguar III rebuilt most of the ceremonial centre and also extended the city to the south-east. Before his time the main plaza was crossed by gullies, but he had the area flattened and smoothed. In a reign of 16 years, he built 12 sacred buildings and raised 33 monuments. Much of the work complemented that of his father. He built a new hilltop structure, Temple 40, alongside Shield Jaguar's Temple 41 and in front raised a carved stela that celebrated both his father and mother and made reference to the solstice celebration of

Below: Bird Jaguar wears an elaborate costume and headdress and holds the manikin sceptre, symbol of royal authority.

AD741 in which, as a prince, Bird Jaguar had shared duties with his father. Alongside Temple 23, which his father had built to honour Lady Xoc, Bird Jaguar erected Temple 21, which was adorned with lintels representing Bird Jaguar and his wife enacting the same scenes celebrated in the lintels of the earlier temple. One showed Bird Jaguar watching a wife letting blood from a tongue, another showed a wife encountering the Vision Serpent and a third showed Bird Jaguar in his military glory.

LINTEL RECORDS
Behind Temple 23, Bird Jaguar built another sacred building, known as Temple 33, where the steps were carved with scenes of rituals involving the ball game: one showed Bird Jaguar enacting a sacrifice with noble victims bound in the form of balls from the ball game. On the lintel above the temple doorway, Bird Jaguar rose in his full glory at his accession, dressed in the costume of a Maya king and holding the *manikin* sceptre. Other lintels at the temple depict Bird Jaguar and his son performing a ritual and Bird Jaguar again in the company of a leading noble. Many of the nobles of Bird Jaguar's reign are represented in door-lintel carvings and on stelae: scholars suggest that the king may have needed support in order to consolidate his position and so was forced to share status with these lords by including them in the historical record.

THE ELEGANT CITY:
COPÁN

The great Maya city of Copán in western Honduras – celebrated in particular for the ornate, almost florid style of its sculpture – lay at an altitude of 700m (2,296ft) in a river valley surrounded by mountains. This attractive, well-watered, fertile spot alongside the river Copán was the site of villages from at least 1000BC.

FIRST STAGES OF THE ACROPOLIS

The city developed and rose to prominence in the 5th–8th centuries AD, when it became capital of the most powerful state in the south-eastern Maya region.

Below: The city's extensive ceremonial centre was laid out on a north–south axis on the west bank of the River Copán.

The ceremonial and sacred centre of the site measured some 300m by 600m (984 by 1,968ft). In the southern half was a raised platform known to archaeologists as the Acropolis, built up over generations and incorporating two great courts and a number of temples. In the northern part lay a ball court, a celebrated stairway carved with hieroglyphs detailing dynastic history and the vast Great Plaza, site of numerous stelae and carved 'altars' or thrones. *Sacbé* or causeways left the great plaza running north–east and west: to the north-east lay an elite residential area known to archaeologists as Las Sepulturas.

Copán's kings in the 8th century claimed to be part of an unbroken dynastic succession of 18 monarchs running

Above: A decorative mask, perhaps of the sun god, adorns the Stairway of the Jaguars (AD200–900) in the East Court.

back to the founder they identified as Yax Kuk Mo' (c.AD426–37). In his reign, the buildings of the Acropolis structure – first laid out before AD400 – were added to and expanded.

SHRINE TO THE CITY'S FOUNDER

One of the Acropolis buildings, subsequently built over and called the Papagayo, appears to have been a shrine to Yax Kuk Mo': it contained a stela that identified the dynasty's second king as the son of the founder and recalled rites performed by Yax Kuk Mo' on an auspicious date in 9.0.0.0.0. (AD435). Contemporary with the Papagayo structure, the first of several version of the Copán ball court was laid out to the north of the Acropolis.

The Acropolis was established at its final size by as early as c.AD450–500. At this time, a higher platform occupied the south-eastern quarter of the Acropolis, while the northern part consisted of a lower area of elite residential and administrative buildings arranged around three adjacent courtyards.

Great

Plaza

Altar L

Middle
Court

Ball
Court

Court of the
Hieroglyphic
Stairway

West Court

Altar Q

East
Court

Royal Residence

N

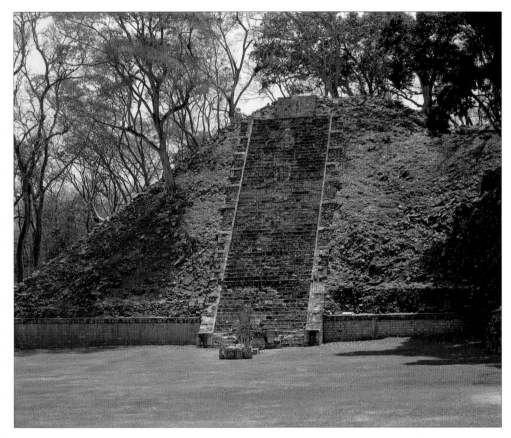

The seventh king of the dynasty, Waterlily Jaguar, may have built a two-level platform that arose in the mid-6th century AD at the eastern edge of the Acropolis's East Court. Hieroglyphs on one of its stairs named the king and reported that he built a palace, called the House of Mah Kina Yax Kuk Mo, on the southern edge of the Great Plaza.

Also around this period, builders on the Acropolis raised a two-storey temple with many rooms known to scholars as Rosalila. Its façade was covered with brightly painted stucco carving of birds and the god Itzamná.

Almost the whole of the 8th century AD was taken up with the reigns of two kings, Butz' Chan (AD578–628) and Smoke Jaguar (AD628–95). In their reigns, Copán developed into a powerful city state with wide influence.

Smoke Jaguar may have begun the final restructuring of the Acropolis. To celebrate the calendar period-ending of AD652, he erected a series of stelae at both the eastern and western limits to the valley of Copán. These may have been intended to mark the limits of his territories or may have been aligned with astronomical events.

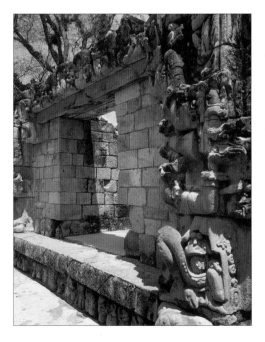

CLAIM OF GREATNESS

Smoke Jaguar's successor King 18-Rabbit (AD695–738) carried out a great deal of construction work in the central part of the city. King 18-Rabbit erected a great temple-palace, identified by *witz* ('sacred mountain') masks in its decorative carving as a holy peak, on the northern edge of the Acropolis East Court. This was the last of several royal structures on the site. He laid out a series of stelae bearing his portrait in the Great Plaza. One of these, Stela A of AD731, was inscribed with the emblem glyphs of Tikal, Calakmul and Palenque as well as that of Copán and has been interpreted as a statement of Copán's status as an equal among these illustrious states.

King 18-Rabbit also built or completed the building of the Great Ball Court, the final version of several courts constructed on a site north of the Acropolis. An inscription on its eastern wall recorded the ball court's completion as 9.15.6.8.13 – a day in AD738. Just 113 days after this date, the king was captured and executed by

Left: Temple 22. The main door was carved to represent the mouth of the Witz or sacred mountain – and so was seen as an entrance to the spirit realms of the underworld.

Above: The Hieroglyphic Stairway contains 63 steps carved with 2,500 glyphs recording the history of Yax Kuk Mo's dynasty.

King Cauac Sky of Quiriguá. The scholars Linda Schele and David Friedel have suggested that 18-Rabbit probably met with disaster during a campaign intended to furnish him with sacrificial victims for the ritual dedication of the ball court.

To the south of the ball court, the later King Smoke Monkey (AD738–49) began the Hieroglyphic Stairway that recorded the kings of the dynasty to that date. He also built a council house, believed to have been used for meetings of lineage officials, which was dedicated in AD746. His successor Smoke Shell (AD749–63) completed and dedicated the Hieroglyphic Stairway in the first year of his reign.

The 16th king Yax Pac (AD763–820) commissioned and dedicated the monument known as Altar Q, which bore the images of all 16 kings of the dynasty and featured the first king, Yax Kuk Mo' handing the sceptre of power to Yax Pac. He also built the structure known by archaeologists as Temple 11 facing north across the plaza bounded by the Hieroglyphic Stairway towards the Great Plaza.

PRIDE OF THE TOLTECS:
TOLLÁN

The celebrated home of the Toltecs was an extensive city encompassing some 13km (8 miles). Its population of up to 60,000 was spread out in outlying areas and lived by farming, mining basalt, making chert tools and working obsidian. The ceremonial area at the centre was precisely laid out 18 degrees east of north. It contained two pyramids, two plazas, a council hall and two ball courts.

The most important structure, facing on to the main plaza from its eastern edge was the one known as Building C. This was once a pyramid temple platform, but Aztec pilgrims dismantled the temple and removed the stone facing. All that remains is the small mountain of rock and earth that formed the core of the pyramid, together with a few pieces of carved stone. Scholars believe that the temple would have been a modest two-room building with an antechamber and a shrine, but do not know which god was honoured there.

Below: Sacred snakes feast on human skeletons on the coatepantli *or serpent wall that runs along Building B's north side.*

IN QUETZALCÓATL'S HONOUR

To the north of the plaza, Toltec builders erected a five-stepped temple pyramid sacred to Quetzalcóatl. On the top of the pyramid the temple roof was supported by columns, some in the shape of warriors 3.5m (11ft) tall. Before the temple, a reclining *chacmool* would have been placed. The warrior figures were broken up and cast into a ditch, perhaps by looters, but have been reassembled and returned to their place of duty on the top of the pyramid.

Stonemasons cut panels to face the tiers of the pyramid. They represented a human head emerging from a monster's jaws, an image tentatively identified as Quetzalcóatl Tlahuizcalpantecuhtli, the god in his form as Venus the Morning Star. They also showed eagles, jaguars and coyotes consuming human hearts. Traces of paint sometimes show that these would have been painted bright colours.

THE BURNT PALACE

To the east of the temple lay a secular building that archaeologists call the Palace of Quetzalcóatl or Edificio 1, while to the west was a vast building measuring 59m

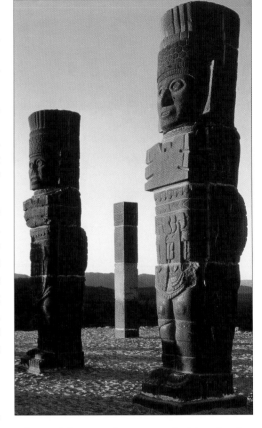

Above: Atlantean figures on the Temple of Quetzalcóatl. Their eyes and mouths were probably inlaid with obsidian or shell.

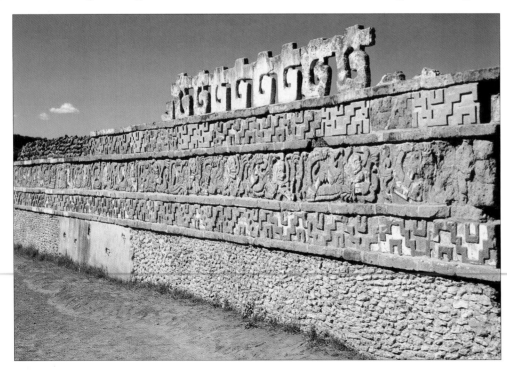

by 91m (200ft by 300ft) and called the Palacio Quemado – or 'Burnt Palace', because it was largely consumed by flames. Its builders set it out in three halls with colonnades that face south on to a long gallery. The Burnt Palace was probably an administrative building used for meetings, receptions and storing trade and tribute items. Gamblers would have gathered there to play *patolli*: three boards for the game are marked on the floor.

In the west of the central area lay a ball court and the space between the main plaza and the court was probably the marketplace. In the centre of the main plaza stood a square shrine around 1.7m (5ft 6in) tall, built in the *talud-tablero* style of Teotihuacán and with one staircase on each of its four sides.

TWIN STYLES:
CHICHÉN ITZÁ

The main buildings of Chichén Itzá were laid out in two styles in different areas of the city. Three structures, mainly in the Puuc architectural style, later called the Nunnery, the Annex and the Iglesia occupied the southernmost part of central Chichén Itzá. The Akabdzib, a building in similar style to the east of this group, has been dated to *c.*AD869. To the west lay the Casa Colorado or 'Red House', with a frieze commemorating noble bloodletting ceremonies in AD869 and AD870.

North-east of the Nunnery group, lay the curious circular building later called the Caracol (from the Spanish for snail) because the spiral staircase within it was held to resemble a snail's shell. A stela found on the building's upper platform dated it to AD906. It may have been a circular temple or an observatory.

THE NORTHERN COMPLEX
A *sacbé* ran northwards from the Caracol to the northern group of buildings, comprising the Temple of Kukulcán, the Temple of the Warriors, a ball court and the Group of the Thousand Columns. The complex was arranged precisely 18 degrees east of true north.

Above: Puuc-style buildings were in the south, Toltec-style structures in the north.

HOLY WATERS
The city made use of two major *cenotes* or natural wells formed when the limestone rock in the area collapsed to reveal water gathered beneath. One, the Xtoloc *cenote*, lay in the centre of the city, to the east of the causeway linking the Caracol to the northern platform. The second, the *Cenote* of Sacrifice, was the site of human sacrifice and other ritual offerings and lay to the north of the northern platform.

Left: Puuc-style carving on the facade of the Nunnery represent the the earth monster and the long-nosed rain god Chac.

HILL FORTS:
CACAXTLA, XOCHICALCO AND TEOTENANGO

In the central highlands around the Basin of Mexico, three fortified hilltop settlements flourished from the 7th and 8th centuries AD onward, at the time that Teotihuacán and Monte Albán were in decline. Historians believe that as the powers of Teotihuacán and Monte Albán waned, the highland cities began to reassert their influence. The cities of Cacaxtla, overlooking the Tlaxcala valley, Xochicalco in western Morelos and Teotenango in the Toluca valley exhibited a common style in the use of glyphs and counting systems. The first two cities largely faded from prominence after AD900, but Teotenango was an important independent centre until its conquest by the Aztec *tlatoani* Axayácatl in 1476.

CACAXTLA
Celebrated for its mural paintings, Cacaxtla rose to prominence after *c.*AD650 in a well-appointed hilltop location that had been occupied since the Preclassic Period. The hill on which Cacaxtla stood

Below: The South Plaza at Teotenango appears to have been laid out as a homage to the Ciudadela or Citadel in Teotihuacán.

would have been an obvious choice for settlement, for it enjoyed a plentiful water supply from its own springs and was an easily defended position commanding views of the Tlaxcala valley and beyond.

Archaeologists have discovered that there were at least five stages of construction at Cacaxtla. Its builders laid out the ceremonial site on the hilltop on a rough north–south axis. They erected a palace, temple-shrines, altars and several corridor-like structures. The corridors were part of a distinctive construction thought to be associated with the system of defences: a series of long, low buildings arranged around patios over several levels and joined by staircases, which would have been easily defended in times of conflict.

Cacaxtla's patios and doorways were the sites of human offerings, mainly of babies and children: 208 skeletons have been found, including those of 199 infants. These scores of young lives were probably offered as dedication sacrifices when the buildings were completed. In the sacrifices the bones were scattered randomly, together with obsidian points and scrapers, shells, figurines of animals,

Above: On Xochicalco's Temple of the Feathered Serpent, Quetzalcóatl is represented with consuming jaws.

bone needles and jewellery such as ear spools and nose plugs. From the main patio of the ceremonial area, steps led up to an elongated chamber with seven entrances painted with vividly coloured murals depicting battle scenes. The conflict might portray a ritualized bloodletting. Warriors wearing Teotihuacán-style outfits defeat others identified as Maya by their deliberately deformed heads. Some of the Maya are naked and painted turquoise blue, the traditional colour of sacrifice.

A stairway from the chamber led to a structure now called Building A by archaeologists, which was dominated by four large painted figures on either side of the doorway. One figure, believed to represent the moon, is depicted as a jaguar-man releasing drops of life-giving water from a sceptre on to the prone body of a jaguar-serpent. Another figure, in similar costume, pours water from a pot marked with symbols of the rain god Tláloc.

In the south-west of the ceremonial centre builders erected what appears to be a temple to Venus the Morning Star (Tlahuizcalpantecuhtli). On either side of a doorway artists painted two large figures, each wearing a five-pointed half-star that was a well known symbol of Venus.

XOCHICALCO

At Xochicalco, builders cut deep ditches, walls and ramps to fortify much of the lower part of the hill and laid out the residential and ceremonial areas of the settlement on terraces cut into the upper slopes. They built causeways to connect areas of the site and to link the city to

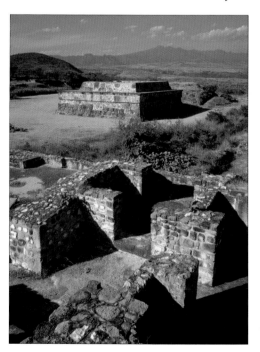

Above: This blue-skinned toad appears in Cacaxtla's Red Temple. The plant behind him bears 'fruit' of human heads.

nearby settlements. One connected the ceremonial and residential hilltop to the ball court, which was laid out on the lower hill with rings on the side walls.

In the main ceremonial area, artisans carved the Pyramid of the Feathered Serpent with images of high-ranking warriors and lists of places that paid tribute to the city's military hierarchy, together with Feathered Serpent reliefs and glyphs relating to fire ceremonies and to the ritual calendar. About 30m (100ft) south of the pyramid, workers built a sacred structure now called the Temple of the Stelae, because it contained three expertly carved stone posts, each bearing a human face and a set of glyphs. Scholars still debate the meaning of these stelae. Some suggest that they represent sky and fertility deities and were used in

Left: The Temple of the Feathered Serpent stands in the centre of the main square in Xochicalco, laid out on a terraced acropolis.

agricultural rites. Others claim that they were, like the carving on the pyramid, a celebration of Xochicalco's military might. The stelae were deliberately damaged and broken, then buried in pieces, but scholars have gathered the fragments and put them back together.

TEOTENANGO

At Teotenango the land falls away sharply from the hilltop on three sides, while on its northern edge labourers erected a vast defensive wall. On the hilltop, from about AD750 onwards, settlers laid out a large ritual and civic area with a number of plazas, altars, temple platforms, a ball court, residential areas, streets and markets. The builders were clearly influenced by Teotihuacán and paid tribute in their own construction to the architecture and sculptural achievements of that great city. In particular, the South Plaza at Teotenango, enclosed by low buildings with stairways, appears to be a reproduction of the great Citadel at Teotihuacán. Teotenango's highest building was the Temple of the Serpent, adorned with serpent carvings.

TARASCAN STRONGHOLD:
TZINTZUNTZAN

The Tarascans laid out their capital, Tzintzuntzan, beneath wooded highlands on the shores of Lake Pátzcuaro in Michoacán, western Mexico, at an altitude of 2,130m (7,000ft). An army of labourers, probably prisoners or workers provided as tribute by peoples humbled in the course of the Tarascans' empire-building wars, created a vast east-facing terrace measuring 440m by 260m (1,440ft by 850ft). Here they built, in line, five temples on terraced circular platforms. The temples have been destroyed but the platforms, called *yácatas*, remain. They were faced with great slabs of stone.

Nearby, the Tarascans' labour force raised a building now known as El Palacio, with many rooms arranged around a patio together with a roofed, narrow gallery defined by rectangular pillars. This might have been a royal palace or a residential area for elite priests, conveniently situated close to the temples supported by the *yácatas*.

A KING'S TEMPLE BURIAL?

The *yácata* temple mounds might also have been mortuary monuments. Archaeologists found graves they believe to be sacrificial burials of servants in the mound they call Yácata V. One grave, in the south-east corner, contained five women, buried with copper ornaments,

Below: The yácatas *were faced with stone veneer, which does not survive here. Some 40,000 people once lived in Tzintzuntzan.*

bells and ritual vessels. Another, in the north, contained nine women buried with arms linked together and accompanied by rich deposits including obsidian lip plugs, turquoise ear plugs, silver tweezers and gold earrings, along with copper bells and axes. The burials might have been made to accompany one of the Tarascan kings on his voyage into the afterlife. The royal grave probably lies nearby, but has not yet been found.

HOME OF THE HUMMINGBIRDS

The Tarascans were skilled producers of gold and silver jewellery and of copper axe heads. They and their predecessors in western Mexico were the pioneers of metalworking techniques in Mesoamerica, using knowledge and skills passed along trade routes into western Mexico from Colombia and Peru. They were the only Mesoamericans to use metal weapons.

The Tarascans were also known for their high level of skill in weaving, in particular for making mosaics of feathers using the plumes of local hummingbirds. Their capital's name, Tzintzuntzan, meant 'home of the hummingbirds'.

Above: Circular platforms or yácatas *survive at Tzintzuntzan without the temples that once stood on top of them.*

TARASCANS DEFEATED

Tarascan skill in making weapons, together with great martial spirit, kept all-comers at bay. Even the imperial Aztec army in the reign of Axayácatl (1469–81) did not succeed in defeating the people of Tzintzuntzan in 1479. However, in 1522 the Spanish adventurer Captain Olíd, who had served under Cortés in the siege of Tenochtitlán, took the Tarascan capital without a struggle.

When Cortés had been marching on Tenochtitlán in 1519 he had sent emissaries to Tzintzuntzan asking for military help. Rather than send a reply, the king ordered his priests to sacrifice the Spaniards to the gods. However, the Europeans had unwittingly brought a hidden weapon, for a smallpox epidemic swept through the ranks of the Tarascans and carried off the king. When the Spanish returned three years later, the new king did not dare to fight the soldiers who had brought down the Aztecs.

CITY OF PRIESTS:
MITLA

The elegant palaces of Mitla, which lie at an altitude of 1,480m (4,855ft) on the eastern edge of the Tlacolula valley in Oaxaca, were built on an ancient settlement inhabited by Zapotecs from as early as 1200BC. Mitla rose to prominence in the Postclassic Period following the decline of nearby Monte Albán. From *c.*AD900 the Mixtecs left their mark on the site. Archaeologists have found numerous Zapotec tombs at the site, which they believe was a sacred burial place. Its Zapotec name was Lyobaa ('Site of Burials'), while the name of Mitla was Nahuatl for 'Realm of the Dead'.

A CITY LAID OUT
The city was laid out in five groups of thin, elongated structures arranged around rectangular courtyards. Beneath the South Group, which was on the southern bank of the Rio Grande de Mitla, archaeologists found a collection of cruciform tombs with elite burials in them. The

Below: The Hall of the Columns still bears traces of its original colour. It takes its name from the stone pillars standing within it.

other buildings were arranged on the rocky hillside opposite. To the west lay the Arroyo Group and the Adobe Group, while the Group of the Columns sat in the east and the Churches Group occupied the north-east of the settlement. Gravediggers laid out more tombs beneath the Group of the Columns.

INFLUENTIAL MOSAICS
At Mitla, Zapotec craftsmen arranged cut stones in a mosaic to form a decorative fretwork and other geometric patterns on façades and door frames. Architectural historians believe these designs might have been influenced by the development of geometric decoration patterns in the Puuc style of north–central Yucatán.

The Zapotec builders used beams to support the roofs, which were gently sloping, so that rainwater would drain off into the courtyards. They made the walls of mud and stone and covered them with plaster or trachyte.

The Group of the Columns was divided into north and south courtyards. From the North Court there was access through a hall named for its six huge

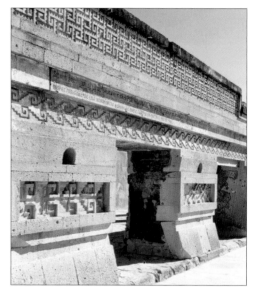

Above: The intricate geometric carving on the outer walls of the Hall of the Columns is remarkably well preserved.

columns to an enclosed courtyard surrounded by four rooms. Historians believe this was the residence of Mitla's priestly elite. The courtyard decorations represent Quetzalcóatl in the form of a stylized celestial serpent. Some of Mitla's rooms were decorated by Mixtec painters.

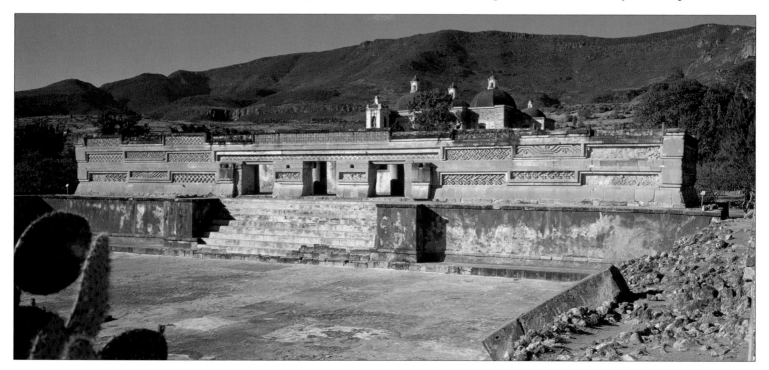

CENTRE OF THE WORLD:
TENOCHTITLÁN

Like the Teotihuacános before them, the Aztecs laid out their capital in four quarters – according to legend, on the command of the tribal lord Huitzilopochtli himself. At the centre stood the vast ceremonial precinct containing the Templo Mayor. Nearby was the great imperial palace and the vast market square of Tlatelolco. Causeways 3.5m (12ft) in width left the island city to north, west and south, connecting the mainland. On the island the causeways became great thoroughfares that terminated in the sacred complex at the city's heart. Fresh water was carried into the city by aqueduct from Coyoacan.

Each of the *capultin* or tribal groups had its own land, with sacred precincts and temple. There were 12–15 *capultin* in each of the four quarters. Major rites and important celebrations were held in the main ceremonial precincts. People moved about on foot or by canoe along the canals that crisscrossed the city.

THE TEMPLE GROUNDS
The sacred quarters of Tenochtitlán were enclosed by a wall in a large square area about 365m (1,200ft) on each side. The wall was known as the *coatepantli* ('Serpent Wall'), because its outside was carved with snake images. At the eastern end the Templo Mayor rose to a height of 45m (150ft), supporting twin temples. On the northern part of the temple platform stood a shrine to Tláloc, with a *chacmool* before it, while on the southern part was the holy place of Huitzilopochtli, before which stood a blood-drenched sacrificial stone.

Climbing towards these temples from ground level, a priest first took a staircase decorated with painted stucco designs honouring the Feathered Serpent Quetzalcóatl and with frogs, which were symbols of Tláloc. The steps led him to a lower platform, on which a vast stone carving of moon goddess Coyolxauhqui was set in the floor before the steps to the Huitzilopochtli shrine. From this place steps rose steeply to the temple above. When a victim's body was cast down from the shrine of Huitzilopochtli, it would fall on the features of the god's mother, Coyolxauhqui. The Templo Mayor was flanked by other sacred structures. To the north were the military

Left: Scholars now believe the temple north of the Templo Mayor to have been the warriors' quarters, the House of Eagles.

House of the Priests

Unidentified Temple

N

Temple of Quetzalcóatl

Temple of Tláloc

Ball Court

Templo Mayor

Temple of Huitzilopochtli

Tzompantli

Temple of Tezcatlipoca

Temple of Xipe Totec

quarters of elite warriors, called the House of Eagles, while to the south rose a temple to Tezcatlipoca. West of the Templo Mayor stood a circular temple holy to Quetzalcóatl in his guise as wind god Éhecatl and beyond that, at the western limit of the ritual enclosure, was a ball court.

THE TEMPLO MAYOR OVER TIME

The first temple was built c.1325, the year of the city's establishment. According to the foundation legend, the México/Aztecs built a rudimentary platform and temple from wattle and daub to honour Huitzilopochtli in the very spot at which they saw an eagle consuming a snake on a cactus, in fulfilment of a divine prophecy. Archaeologists have not been able to uncover evidence of this lowest-level structure. They do know that by c.1390, a temple building about 15m (50ft) tall stood on the site. It already supported twin temples to Huitzilopochtli and Tláloc, approached by twin staircases.

Around 1431, three years after the foundation of the Triple Alliance of Tenochtitlán, Texcoco and Tlacopan, the Aztecs built a much larger temple on the same site, entirely enclosing the previously existing structure.

They made further improvements in 1454, under the rule of Moctezuma I (1440–69), adding decorative elements and making many offerings. In particular, builders added a new staircase to the western face of the pyramid and skilled

Above: The vast Templo Mayor, 45m (150ft) tall, dwarfed the rounded temple of Quetzalcóatl-Éhecatl that stood before it.

craftsmen laid a greenstone sculpture of Coyolxauhqui at its foot. This was the forerunner of the celebrated Coyolxauhqui stone, which artisans carved in 1469 under the rule of Axayácatl (1469–81).

Later rulers Tizoc, Ahuítzotl and Moctezuma II demonstrated their devotion by making improvements and additions to the temple in 1482, 1486 and 1502 respectively.

A SACRED SPOT

The México/Aztecs built up their capital in a sanctified setting on twin islands in Lake Texcoco. Setting the city on an island had great religious significance, for it made Tenochtitlán a recreation of the México/Aztecs' legendary northern place of origin, Aztlán, which they believed was

Left: The Codex Durán *represents the twin shrines, to Tláloc and Huitzilopochtli, that occupied the top of the Templo Mayor.*

Right: Sacred precinct in the heart of the city. Hernán Cortés drew this map of Tenochtitlán to send to Charles V.

land surrounded by water. It also meant that the city was a microcosm of the earth itself, a tribute to the gods' creation, for in Aztec cosmology, the earth was surrounded, like a great island, on all sides by water.

WATERWORKS

Tenochtitlán's development was due in no small part to their success in reclaiming the marshy shallows of western Lake Texcoco for *chinampa* fields, and later taking control of the established fields in the southern lakes of Chalco and Xochimilco. In the reign of Moctezuma I (1440–69), labourers built a vast 15km (10-mile) dyke to prevent the salt waters of the northern and eastern part of Lake Texcoco from polluting the freshwater areas that they were farming.

181

CHAPTER NINE

POTTERS AND WEAVERS

As royal wife Lady Xoc knelt before her kingly husband Shield Jaguar, drawing a spiky rope across her tongue to make a sacred offering of her blood, she wore an exquisitely decorated *huipil* cotton garment. The carver of this celebrated 8th-century scene on a limestone door lintel from Temple 23 in Shield Jaguar's city of Yaxchilán paid great attention to detail – and gave a tantalizing glimpse of the highly developed art of Maya weaving.

Of the work of Mesoamerican potters, weavers, basket-makers, mat-makers and feather-workers covered here, only pots survive in large numbers. This is partly because woven textiles and basket-work naturally decay while ceramic products survive unless smashed, but also because many pots were saved from everyday breakage by being put to sacred use as temple or tomb offerings. Yet although most Maya and many Aztec creations in cloth and basketwork have not survived, we know that they were intricately made and decorated. We have evidence of carved and painted images – both of people wearing woven textiles and of decorative schemes derived from textile and basket patterns. A basket shown in a mural in Chichén Itzá's Temple of the Jaguars, for example, was highly elaborate in construction and decoration. Clothes represented in carvings on Classic Period Maya stelae, in the Bonampak murals, on painted Maya pots, in Aztec statuary and in painted codices give an idea of the range and quality of Mesoamerican woven materials.

Left: The musicians shown taking part in a procession at Bonampak wear elaborate headdresses and costumes.

MILLENNIA OF POTTERY

Mesoamericans produced pottery for 4,000 years, from the beginnings of settled life in villages *c*.2500–2000BC until the Spanish Conquest of 1519–21. They made a variety of wares in many different finishes, reaching the apogée of their craft in the delicate portrait plates and vases made in the Maya cities of the late Classic Period. As Mesoamerican artisans produced such a range of pots, plates, cups, vases and ritual vessels, this survey is only able to select a few highlights and distinctive developments.

*Below: Sea hunter. A cormorant closes in on a fish in the decorative scheme of this Maya cylinder vase (*c.AD700–900*).*

BEGINNINGS

The first Mesoamerican potters might have picked up the necessary skills from South American incomers, for people in Ecuador and Colombia were making ceramic pieces about 1,000 years earlier than their counterparts in Mexico and Guatemala.

Early potters might have taken their basic forms from those of everyday containers . For example, neck-less jars with wide, globular bases were probably based on the shape of gourds.

From these first days in *c*.2500–2000BC (during the early Preclassic Period), Mesoamerican potters experimented with decoration. They added colour-slips (additional layers of clay) and polished the surface. They made incised patterns of dots and lines and used hand-modelling, adding faces or heads to the shoulders of jars. They experimented with painting pottery and using 'resist' or negative patterns to provide a contrast to the main colour and they tested the effects of different firing techniques.

In these early times, potters began to make anthropomorphic figures that probably represented the gods in rites at the household shrine. These figures were produced in considerable numbers right through to the Spanish Conquest.

A DEMAND FOR RITUAL WARES

By *c*.1000–400BC (the middle Preclassic Period), potters were producing tripod bowls, spouted vessels, tall-necked jars sometimes bearing handles on the neck, and cylindrical incense burners.

Artisans first produced polychrome (many-coloured) vessels by applying coloured paints in yellow, red, white and black after the vessels had been fired. They also used bichrome (two-coloured) slips or additional layers of clay on vessels. Incense burners were the first Mesoamerican ceramics to have a specialized ritual function.

Around 400BC–AD250 (the late Preclassic Period), pottery decorated with sinuous parallel lines negative to the main colour – known as Usulutan ware – was popular in Maya lands. Artisans made the pattern by applying parallel lines of wax to the pot. These melted away during firing to reveal a secondary colour beneath. Potters further developed the use of modelled decorations on vessels and their handles, particularly on incense burners. Bowls with toad decorations and clay models of mushrooms are identified by scholars as celebratory of mind-altering substances ingested by shamans, who valued a secretion of toad glands as well as certain mushrooms for their capacity to

---

METHODS OF PRODUCTION

From the first days of Mesoamerican pottery onwards, many householders who lived by farming probably made simple pots for their own use at home. If they developed their skills, they may have produced extra pots or plates to be sold at market. Around 250BC–AD1, towards the end of the Preclassic Period, some of these home potters began to specialize in particular forms such as vases, plates or pots. By the start of the Classic Period *c*.AD250, certain skilled artisans had become specialist potters who, while working from their home, made their living entirely by ceramic production and no longer worked the land. Soon after this time, elite groups appear to have established workshops of potters in cities, to supply wealthy and royal circles with the elegant handmade pottery they admired. From *c*.AD800–900 onwards, light-industrial centres were established to produce wares using moulds for distribution across wide areas. All these methods of production coexisted.

transform consciousness during spirit adventures and acts of divination. During the years c.AD250–550 (the early Classic Period), polychrome decoration became dominant in Maya lands. Artisans used geometric designs or bands of diminutive images in red and black on an orange/cream background. The potters of Teotihuacán were influential at this time: their small containers and brightly painted cylindrical pots with tripod legs were widely traded and copied.

PORTRAIT PLATES AND VASES
Around AD550–800 (the late Classic Period), potters and scribe-artists in city workshops of the central Maya region produced justly celebrated vases, tripod dishes, cups, pots and incense burners painted with portraits, scenes of court life and glyphs. Then in AD800–900 the spread of militaristic Putún Maya merchants from their homeland in Tabasco was accompanied by the fine-grained pots known to historians as Fine Orange Ware.

Right: This flanged and lidded bowl (c.AD250–550) is typical of Maya vessels with geometric decoration produced in the early Classic Period.

These appear to have been early examples of light-industrial production, for they came in standard sizes and with decoration produced using moulds.

In AD900–1250, artisans in the Pacific coastal regions of south-western Guatemala began to fire pots in pit kilns that were able to generate high enough temperatures to produce a glazed finish. The pots, decorated with moulding and carving, are known by historians as Plumbate Ware. They were the only glazed pots produced in Mesoamerica, although from the Classic Period on, potter-artists in Maya cities had been able to achieve a glaze-like finish. They did so by painting pots after firing and decorating them with a clear, unknown wash – perhaps a kind of resin – that scholars call 'Péten gloss' due to its use by potters from cities in the Péten region.

In 1250–1521 Maya artisans in the southern highlands made and traded simple wares decorated with black and red designs on a cream or white base colour. Scholars call these pots 'Chinautla Polychrome'. Another distinctive development was the mixing of talc in clay, which produced a slightly reflective sheen and a

Above: Rain and lightning god Cocijo was a favourite subject for ceramic funerary urns among the Zapotecs who worshipped him.

cooking surface – on, for example, *comales* (tortilla griddles) – with certain non-stick qualities. Products made with this mixed clay were found throughout the highlands of the southern Maya region, where the Quiché and Cakquichels rose to prominence at this time.

IN AZTEC LANDS
One of the many aspects of the market in Tlatelolco that astonished the Spanish conquistadors was the vast display of beautifully finished ceramics. In the Aztec era, craftsmen produced a wide range of pottery for use in both sacred and utilitarian contexts. For sacred use they made incense burners, braziers, censers, urns, figures of gods and goddesses, goblets, votive vessels and model temples. For everyday use they made plates, cups, bowls, jugs, pitchers and other vessels.

Many of these utilitarian objects could also have had a sacred function, since they were included in offerings at the Templo Mayor, in graves at Teotihuacán, at Tollán or in other temple settings. The elite polychrome ceramics used in the *tlatoani's* palace and by members of the nobility were made in Cholula and parts of Oaxaca. Aztec-era potters also made fired-clay flutes and ceramic rattles.

FIGURES OF CLAY

Potters at Remojadas in the region of Veracruz produced very distinctive hollow clay figurines in the 8th–9th century (the late Classic Period). These craftsman, part of the 'Veracruz culture' associated with the city of El Tajín, were inheritors of an ancient Mesoamerican tradition. From as early as *c.*2500BC, at the beginning of settled village life in Mesoamerica, early craftsmen and women were making female figurines associated with cults of the land's fertility. One of these figures, dating from 2300BC, was found in a household fireplace at Zohapilco at the eastern end of Lake Chalco in the Valley of Mexico.

In the 2nd millennium BC, Olmec craftsmen made baby-face figurines called 'dolls' by some early archaeologists. These were beautifully produced hollow figures, with a surface coating of white, representing chubby figures with legs outspread and the face of a baby. The figures probably had some religious use associated with Olmec cults seemingly focused on the were-jaguar, a jaguar-faced human – often resembling a baby – thought by scholars to stand for the earth.

Olmec baby figurines were exported far and wide from centres such as La Venta and San Lorenzo using the Olmecs' extensive trading networks.

SHAMANIC RITES

About 1100BC, craftsmen made and used large numbers of handmade ceramic figures in the Valley of Mexico, in the villages of Tlatilco on the western side of Lake Texcoco and Tlapacoya beside Lake Chalco. Some were clearly used in association with shamanistic rites: they represented shaman-priests and weird two-headed creatures or three-eyed monsters that were perhaps the product of ecstatic visions and spirit-journeys following the consumption of mind-altering substances. Others were caught in such scenes of home life as mothers nursing babies or religious festivities

Above: This smiling boy (c.AD750–900) is typical of 'Remojadas figurines', with outstretched arms and wide, ecstatic grin.

and other celebrations involving cavorting acrobats, musicians and players of the sacred ball game.

Figurines such as this were produced in all parts of Mesoamerica in the Preclassic Period, but their use appears to have gradually died out towards the end of that era before reappearing in the mid-to-late Classic Period. Scholars have suggested that since the figurines were probably used in pre-temple religious rituals, they would not have been needed or welcome when formal religious life centred on temples became the norm. The new religious elite would probably

Left: These figurines made in Veracruz c.AD1200–1520 may represent ritual victims. The man (right) seems to be taking a hallucinogenic substance. Victims were drugged so that they seemed calm when going to their deaths.

have been keen to destroy all materials connected with rituals which they would have seen as outmoded. Archaeologists at Monte Albán, for example, report that hand-modelled figurines associated with household shrines disappeared from residential remains about the time that the building now called Mound X, identified as the city's first public temple, was erected some time after *c*.300BC. It is unclear precisely how and under what conditions the practice of making and using figurines resurfaced.

STYLIZED TEOTIHUACÁN FIGURES

In Teotihuacán *c*.AD400, craftsmen used moulds to make articulated figures about 25–30cm (10–12in) in height. In stark contrast to the highly naturalistic representations of the later creators of the Veracruz Remojadas figurines, the Teotihuacános produced stylized figures with triangular-shaped faces, which generally have openings in the top of their heads. They also made non-moveable figures set in unusual postures. Scholars have not established a context in which these figures could have been used, beyond suggesting that they might have played a role in survivals of ancient village-based fertility celebrations in the wide spread of village communities around the metropolis of Teotihuacán. Then about AD650–700, Teotihuacáno craftsmen began to produce larger mould-made figurines representing nobles and deities on thrones.

RELIGIOUS ECSTASY

There was certainly significant Teotihuacáno influence in the Veracruz region, so the tradition of mould-made ceramic figurines in the great metropolis of highland Mexico might well have fed into the marvellous flowering of clay-figure moulding represented by the late Classic Period Remojadas craftsmen.

The gifted modellers at Remojadas made clay images of men, women and children, some attired as ball game players, some dressed as warriors. One distinctive form represented men – and more often women – with

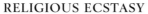

Left: Veracruz figurine c.*AD250–500 represents a club-wielding warrior with skin blackened for battle.*

Above: A Veracruz potter of c.*AD500–950 fashioned this statue of a priest wearing a jaguar god headpiece and costume.*

outstretched arms and elegant, wide-faced features, their mouths open and drawn in a broad smile or laugh, their teeth visible within their mouths.

The Remojadas potters produced highly naturalistic work. They decorated some figures with black asphalt paint to emphasize the features and details of the figures' often elaborate dress; other figurines they painted in many colours. Some scholars argue that the figures are in a state of religious ecstasy, having taken mind-altering substances. Others suggest that the laughing individuals are sacrificial victims whose unusual demeanour has been produced by swallowing hallucinogenic drinks intended to enable them to hide their terror and assume a joyful demeanour as they go to their deaths. The figures are typically about 30–45cm (12–18in) in height. The Toltecs at Tollán also produced mould-made clay figurines of people and animals, as did craftsmen at Xochicalco.

MODELS FROM THE WESTERN ISLE

Maya potters developed great artistry in moulding clay figurines in the middle to late Classic Period (*c*.AD400–900). A large collection of exquisitely modelled figures was found in graves on the limestone Island of Jaina, just off the west coast of the Yucatán peninsula.

The island was a flourishing sea-trading and fishing centre for many centuries. In addition to its port and trade facilities, it contained two modest ceremonial centres named El Zacpool and Zayosal, together with a ball court and cemeteries in which the clay figurines were found. The buildings were simple, made of an earthen core that was faced with an irregular pattern of stones, then plastered with stucco and painted.

RULERS' GRAVEYARD?

Scholars are uncertain whether the splendid clay figures and wealthy grave offerings were laid in the tombs of rich local merchants, of priests and sacerdotal assistants at the ceremonial centre

Below: This kneeling figure, 15cm (6in) in height, is one of many Jaina Island models that represent ball players.

or of nobles and rulers from inland cities such as Uxmal and Kabah. Because the island's ceremonial buildings were modest, it would appear most likely that cemeteries were the graves of elite groups from the mainland rather than of locals. Jaina lay just off the coast and could be reached by foot through swamps at low tide. Because the island was on the western coast of the peninsula, the sun dropped behind it each night as it sank into the underworld Xibalba. Accordingly, some scholars argue that Jaina might have been chosen as the site for an elite cemetery because symbolically it lay on the path to the underworld.

Older figures found at Jaina, dating from before AD650, are generally solid and hand-modelled. After *c*.AD650, potters began to produce hollow figures made using moulds, perhaps in emulation of the Teotihaucáno craftsmen who were making hollow-mould figures from *c*.AD400–500 onwards. Some of the later Jaina artisans were not happy to rely solely on moulds and combined the new technique with older traditions producing, for example, a figurine with a mould-made torso but a handmade head. Many of the figures are musical instruments. Some, with holes bored in the back, are whistles. Others contained clay pellets and could be used as rattles.

PORTRAITS IN CLAY

The Jaina figures are generally 20–30cm (8–12in) tall. Some figures are highly naturalistic portraits – perhaps of the nobles in whose graves they were buried. They depict proud warriors with scarred or tattoed skins, wise old men, beautiful maidens and elderly matrons. Other statuettes represent less than idealized figures taken from life such

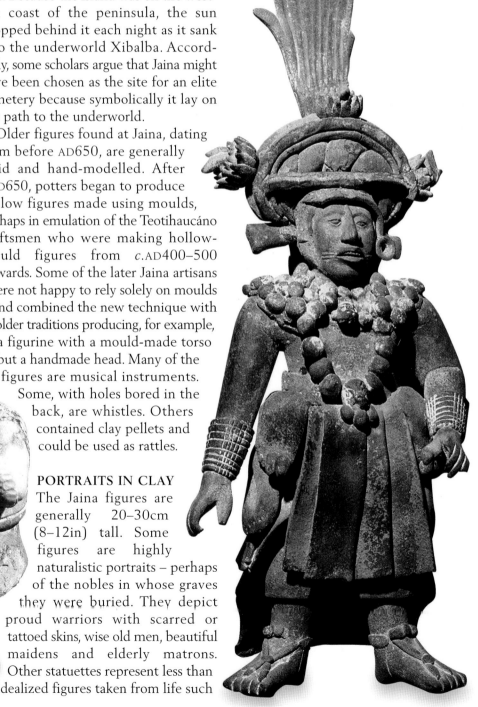

Below: The potters who made the Jaina Island models worked with great skill and delicacy, as evidenced in the attention to detail in the feather headdress, necklace, bracelets and ear decoration on this figurine.

Right: The Jaina Island tomb figures give us an invaluable insight into the clothes and headgear worn by Classic Period Maya.

as invalids, dwarfs, drunks and hunchbacks. One 7th–9th-century figure represents an old man who has lost his wits to drink. He holds a flask beneath his arm and has a look of unseeing stupefaction on his face.

Some of these models are careful representations of figures involved in religious ritual. One such 7th–9th-century figure represents a naked man with his hands tied behind his back, who would appear to be a noble prisoner bound for ritual sacrifice following capture during a war campaign launched by a rival city against his own. Another figurine depicts a ball player wearing protective belt and holding the ball prior to the start of a ball game. Other Jaina Island figures represent a shaman or priest in a trance.

IMAGES OF GODS

Some figures show gods and goddesses – usually divinities associated with the underworld. One such statue-pair from the 8th–9th century AD represents an elderly, lecherous man who is trying to raise the skirt of a beautiful maiden: scholars identify the man as a treacherous underworld lord and his consort as the moon goddess Ix Chel.

Another statue-pair represent a woman who is standing behind and over a seated male, almost enveloping him in her cloak. This may be a celebration of the protective power of Ix Chel in her role as mother goddess. A deity who is represented several times among the Jaina models is a figure called the Fat God, a squat full-faced man with a feathered headdress and very tall helmet.

The Jaina Island figurines were painted in bright colours. Curiously, the potters did not work hard on reproducing the feet or hands of their subjects, which were often finished without attention to detail, but they put great effort into reproducing individual physiognomies and styles of clothing as well as adornment with jewellery, headdresses and body art such as tattoos.

The figures have been an invaluable source for historians seeking information about details of Maya court life – such as elite clothing. The finest of the figurines are the older, solid ones made before *c.*AD650. Experts declare them to be among the finest pieces of their kind in all the Americas. Because so many of the figures were of warriors, some argue that the island cemetery might have been reserved for members of the military elite, or for rank and file members of the army who had won particular glory in battle.

Below: Scholars believe that this cloaked Jaina Island figure with mysterious headdress may represent an elite priest.

CERAMIC CULTURES

Fragments of pots, plates, bottles and jars generally provide the bulk of remains discovered by archaeologists when investigating living areas such as house platforms or household waste areas. In graves and temple offerings elite pottery forms are also well represented. The distribution of types of pottery and methods of decoration in different regions across spans of time gives a clue to the movements of people and influence. For this reason, archaeologists and historians often identify cultures by the type of pottery remains they left.

MANY-COLOURED SCENES OF COURT LIFE

The painted vases, plates, incense burners and drinking vessels produced in the Maya cities of c.AD550–800 in the late Classic Period were probably decorated by the highly educated noble artists usually referred to as scribes. Many of these vessels bore glyphic writing that gave the names and titles of the people represented and identified other elements of the image. Sometimes the glyphs provided an entire dynastic history for the ruler who was depicted sitting in state, conferring with his scribes and advisers, celebrating an anniversary of his accession or enjoying the chocolate drink.

EXPERT POTTERS

Some vases were incised with images and glyphs rather than painted, and in these cases the delicate lines were almost certainly cut by the same artists who were such skilled carvers of stelae and lintels.

We do not know whether specialist potters created the plates, cups and vases and then handed them over to be decorated

Below: Ceramics such as this painted vase from the Sula Valley, Honduras, accompanied elite burials in their tombs.

or whether the scribal artists were also responsible for making the pots. Some of the surface effects and colouring on painted vessels were achieved by expert manipulation of oxygen levels during the firing of the pottery and in these cases the scribal artists responsible for the final appearance of the vessel must have been involved in its firing.

Scholars believe that many of the scenes depicted on pictorial vases were taken from screenfold books. The scribal artists must have developed an expert judgement in order to transfer the elegant proportions of composition and neat glyph-work to the curved surface of the vase being worked.

There is very little evidence that the scribes first marked out the designs before painting over them, for this would have left visible marks beneath the final design.

Scholar Michael Coe has suggested that the artists might have marked out the design in charcoal, which would have disappeared when the vessel was fired, but this can be no more than speculation.

Above: Deities were often shown in attendance at the scenes of religious ritual and court life represented on vases.

ROYAL FUNERAL RITES

Examples of elegantly painted Maya ceramics of the late Classic Period include the vessel known to archaeologists as the Altar Vase, found in the Usumacinta-region city of Altar de Sacrificios. According to scholar R.E.W. Adams, the image painted on the vase represents a funeral held in AD754 following the death of a royal woman of middle age.

Six dancing figures on the vase are believed to represent three visiting dignitaries from other cities, each accompanied by a *way* or spirit companion. The visitors, who had travelled from nearby Yaxchilán, from mighty Tikal and from an unidentified city in the highlands of the southern Maya region, laid offerings of fine ceramics in the royal tomb. The Altar Vase itself was laid in the grave of a young woman sacrificed in honour of the deceased princess or royal wife.

An image on the vase of a young woman performing rites of autosacrificial bloodletting might be a portrait of this young victim, who was herself probably a junior royal.

At Uaxactún archaeologists found a magnificent cache of painted ceramics in a stone tomb containing the corpse of an elite figure, probably a king. The corpse, buried in the building known as Structure A-I, was laid along the sanctified north–south axis used for ceremonial centres, with its head to the north. Next to the skull was a vase painted in the 8th century AD with a scene of court ritual using black and yellow against a red-orange base colour. The scene shows a king enthroned beneath a feathered shade held by an attendant. The king faces two elaborately dressed visitors, their visible skin painted black, one carrying a spear and one holding a ritual object with three spikes that scholars call a 'knuckle duster'. A seated jaguar, mouth open in a roar or snarl, accompanies the two visitors.

In all, the tomb contained eleven exquisite pottery pieces, nine of them painted. A beautifully painted tripod plate depicting a dancer had a small hole bored in it – the result of a ceremony performed to free the soul of the plate so that it could travel with the spirit of the deceased king as he made his way to the underworld. Many other delicately painted ceramics were left as grave offerings in Tikal, Seibal, Altun Ha, Tayasal and other settlements.

HIGHLAND VASES
Painted vases of very high quality were also produced in the highlands of the southern Maya region. A vase found at Chama in the valley of the river Chixoy, Guatemala, depicts seven individuals in red, brown and black against a pink base.

Right: Elaborately attired priests, warriors or gods ring a beautifully finished vase from Honduras, made c.AD600–900.

Two main figures face one another, both painted black, one wearing a jaguar skin. Individual features are represented in detail, suggesting that these were portraits executed from life. The black paint on the main figures might be intended to identify the two main figures as merchants by linking them to Ek Chuah, the patron god of that group.

Many vases, plates and cups were signed by the artists who painted them. For example, a cup for drinking chocolate was signed by Ah Maxam, the noble scribe from Naranjo who decorated it. The glyphs he inscribed in black paint on a cream base describe the function of the vessel and identify Ah Maxam as scribe and member of the royal household.

POTTERY FOR BANQUETS AND TEMPLES

México/Aztec potters specialized in a range of fired-clay braziers sanctified by the images of gods and goddesses. They were positioned outside temples or before the altars of the gods and used for burning aromatic copal incense, a form of rubber latex called *hulli* and body parts of animal and human sacrifices.

SMOKE GUIDE
The braziers were painted in bright colours. One splendid painted clay brazier of *c*.1500 found in Tlatelolco celebrated male and female vegetation deities Xiuhtecuhtli and Chalchiúhtlicue.

A set of five braziers of *c*.1500 commemorated warriors who had perished in battles or been sacrificed and whose souls were believed to accompany the sun god in his daily passage across the heavens.

Hulli was burned particularly in rituals honouring the rain god Tláloc, for worshippers believed that the dark smoke it produced would summon dark, rain-laden clouds. Some authorities taught that the smoke from ceremonial braziers could

Below: These elegant goblets are typical of the high-quality wares imported to Tenochtitlán from the Aztec empire.

lead the soul of a deceased person to the afterlife. Large braziers measuring 40–100cm (16–40in) or more in height were made to be placed on the ground, but smaller versions about 20cm (8in) long were threaded with cords through the handles and waved by priests to spread sweet-smelling copal incense around the temple.

Potters also made long-handled painted clay censers, with a round fretwork head that contained coals and incense. Priests waved the censer to perfume images of the gods and goddesses.

Potters produced goblets for use in temple rites. The sacred vessels were filled with blood and connected by straws called *pópotl* to the mouth cavities of god and goddess statues.

Two imported Mixtec goblets of *c*.1500, decorated with skulls and three painted bands (representing the night sky), were found in a burial cache of ceramics laid beneath an area of Tenochtitlán known as El Volador, thought to be the southern part of Moctezuma II's great palace.

Above: This lidded vessel decorated with images of the rain god Tláloc was made by potters in Tikal in the early Classic Period.

Aztec worshippers created a large demand for votive vessels decorated with images of gods and goddesses such as Tláloc, Chalchiúhtlicue, Chicomecóatl and Xilonen to be placed in temple offerings. Potters also produced clay plaques which were perhaps intended for temple display or for use as offerings. One, dating from *c*.1500 and found in Culhuacán, represented the rites of the festival of Ochpaniztli, in which a priestess of the maize goddesses Xilonen and Chicomecóatl wore the flayed skin of a sacrificial victim.

TINY TEMPLE PRECINCTS
Clay-modellers produced miniature temple structures, typically 30–40cm (12–16in) tall, for use in home shrines. They were detailed reproductions of Aztec Postclassic Period pyramid-temples, complete with balustraded stairways on all four sides of the pyramid, a sacrificial stone at the top of the steps and a simple temple building, perhaps with decorated roof. One of three such temples found in Calipan, modern Puebla state, was even painted with a red line down one stairway to represent the blood of sacrificial victims. The temples were probably placed on home shrines alongside small

clay figures of corn, rain and fertility deities and used in rites linked to the festivals of the agricultural year. However, the temples were also used to honour other gods: the three models found in Calipan were made in honour of the fire god Xiuhtecuhtli, the earth mother goddess Toci and the war god Huitzilopochtli.

Potters in Puebla and Oaxaca specialized in large painted funerary urns with side handles. An important centre of production was the area known to historians as Mixtequilla Veracruzana in the south of modern Veracruz state where it borders Oaxaca.

These large vessels were also used to contain drink at ceremonial feasts. A mural at Cholula known as 'Los Belsilores' shows drinkers dipping their tankards into the large urn-like vessel. After being used in this way, they would probably have been placed in a temple offering.

Below: Small clay models of deities and of temple-pyramids were used in home worship until Aztec times.

Above: An architectural decoration representing a forerunner of Tláloc was made in Teotihuacán c.AD100–500.

BANQUET WARE

The ruler and nobles of Tenochtitlán imported their high-quality ceramics. Potters in Texcoco produced a polished red ware that was used by the nobility at banquets, to make offerings in the temple and to accompany high-ranking individuals in their graves. In Cholula and in Mixtec crafts centres in Oaxaca, potters produced polychrome ceramics that were also popular in Tenochtitlán.

Many examples of Texcocan polished red wares were put in tombs or survived. A splendid red-ware vessel with painted black designs now in the St Louis

Museum is typical of the style. Art historian John W. Nunley has interpreted the shell-like black markings as representations of the maguey cactus leaf and suggests that the vessel was intended for serving the alcoholic drink *pulque*, which was made from the fermented sap of the maguey. He adds that the phallic outline of the vessel's spout was intended to emphasize and celebrate the drink's reputed qualities as an aphrodisiac.

The nobles favoured painted tripod plates with elegant decoration in many colours. The legs of the plate often represented snakes, eagle heads or jaguar claws. A delicate cup made *c.*1500 for noble enjoyment was fashioned in the likeness of a flower, its long stem like four intertwining flower stems, and its bowl in the shape of a cluster of petals. Flowers were associated with the noble life: *pipiltin* nobility routinely held small bouquets of flowers to enjoy their scent and keep troubling smells at bay.

TENOCHTITLÁN'S LIFE-SIZE CERAMIC FIGURES

Aztec craftsmen produced remarkable fired-clay statues about 1.7m (5ft 4in) tall for the House of Eagles, a sacred precinct north of the Templo Mayor in Tenochtitlán. This was a notable development of the Mesoamerican tradition of making small clay figurines for use in worship. Aztec potters also followed this more modest path, making figures of deities such as Xipe Totec, perhaps 20cm (8in) tall. for use in domestic religious ritual and in temple offerings.

SUN COMPANIONS

A pair of life-sized statues representing eagle-warriors were mounted on a bench in the House of Eagles, which was used for penitential retreats and rites of autosacrificial bloodletting in which worshippers cut ears, cheeks or penis to offer blood to the gods. The statues were originally covered with stucco and decorated with a design in white paint that reproduced the eagle feathers worn into battle by these elite warriors. Each statue was made in four segments – the head and helmet; the torso and arms; the groin; and the lower legs. Archaeologists report that the eagle-warrior statues might have been images of the sun at dawn.

LORD OF THE UNDERWORLD

The House of Eagles also contained a pair of statues of Mictlantecuhtli, lord of the Aztec underworld Mictlán, also mounted on benches. One of the statues – 1.76m (5ft 7in) tall and 80cm (2ft 10in) wide – represented the hideous form of Mictlantecuhtli as a near-naked man with decaying flesh, bony torso and protruding liver, wearing a meagre loincloth, his hands vast claws, his mouth a terrifying grimace. Holes in the statue's skull would have held the dark curly hair associated with Aztec earth and death deities. Like those of the eagle-warriors, the statue was made in five pieces.

SKINNING OF THE MEN

Like their counterparts elsewhere in Mesoamerica during the Postclassic Period, Aztec craftsmen generally made smaller ceramic pieces using moulds. Four

Left: One of a pair of ceramic figures (c.1480) of underworld god Mictlantecuhtli, shown with exposed liver and grimacing mouth. Traces of the original white stucco covering are still visible. Like the warrior figure, above right, he stood in the House of Eagles in Tenochtitlán's sacred precinct. Here he stands on a tzompantli *(skull altar).*

Above: One of two life-size ceramic figures of eagle-warriors who stood in the House of Eagles, this was made c.1440–69.

figures found in Tlatelolco in 1968 celebrated the gruesome rites of the festival of Tlacaxipehualiztli ('Skinning of the Men') held to honour Xipe Totec, god of vegetation and germinating seeds.

The clay statues, each about 15cm (6in) high, represented priests and worshippers. Two warriors were seated on a bench, while two priests or other participants wore the skins of flayed sacrificial victims. An intermediate-sized statue, 97cm (3ft 2in) tall, of a Xipe Totec priest wearing the puckered skin of a victim was found in 1975 in the fortified city of Tepeji el Viejo in the mountainous southern part of modern Puebla state. The sacrificial statue, which was very beautifully made, had in its turn been sacrificed by being smashed. Archaeologists have reassembled the pieces to recreate the work.

BASKETWORK, MATS AND FURNITURE

The lakeside reedbeds of Mexico and Guatemala kept Mesoamerican basket-workers well supplied with raw materials. The makers of baskets and reed mats were practitioners of an ancient craft tradition and users of skills developed thousands of years earlier. Archaeological evidence shows that even before the beginnings of village life in Mesoamerica, hunter-gatherer groups made baskets, mats and sandals from reeds. In the Classic and Postclassic Periods, most working householders probably knew enough about reed-weaving to make their own simple mats and baskets for everyday use, just as they had sufficient rudimentary pottery skills to make their own pots, plates and cups.

Above: A detail from the list of Aztec tribute due from Tlatelolco to Tenochtitlán shows woven baskets of cacao and chia.

Specialist basket-makers made and supplied finer quality goods to those who could afford to barter for them at market. In the Aztec era, the reed-workers also made use of palm leaf, slats of cane and the leaves of the maguey cactus. They fashioned baskets in many sizes and shapes that could be used on *chinampa* fields, in the marketplace, in the household and even in the temple precincts for moving goods, storing food, secreting valuables or ritual items and keeping clothes away from dust and dirt. Other reed-weavers made *petlatl* mats and seats in fine weave for supply to nobles. Seats and low tables were generally restricted to wealthy households, while other folk used mats on the ground.

MAYA MATS AND BASKETS

The Maya of the Classic Period certainly used mats and baskets, but none has survived. An image of a basket carved on Lintel 24 in the city of Yaxchilán reveals how intricate Maya baskets could be. It combines three decorative schemes – a featherwork pattern, a twill design and a combination of frets and small squares – in a single item. The imprint of a Postclassic Period mat has been found on the floor of the shrine discovered beneath the Temple of the Feathered Serpent at Chichén Itzá. The pattern of its weaving is the same as that of mats still produced in the locality.

Mats were conceptually associated with political power. In Aztec society the *tlatoani* was known as 'the one who takes this place upon the mat'. For the Maya, too, the mat was the locus of authority. The title *ahpop* assumed by Maya rulers meant 'the one who sits on the mat'.

Below: A typically wide-eyed and grimacing Veracruz clay figurine of c.AD600–800 holds a woven basket full of produce.

NAPATECUHTLI, PATRON GOD OF REED WEAVERS

The Aztec reed-weavers' patron god, Napatecuhtli, was represented wearing a tall headdress crowned with a *quetzalmiahuayo* ('gathering of sacred quetzal feathers'). A band of the bark paper used to soak up blood in rites of autosacrifice was wound around his head, with bark-paper ornaments suspended from it.

Doubtless because reed-weavers gathered their raw materials at the lakeside, Napatecuhtli was also a god of water and was associated with the rain deity Tláloc. For this reason Napatecuhtli's face was generally covered with a serpentine Tláloc mask, in which curling snakes formed eyes and upper lip. His robes were also made of bark paper and hung to his feet. He carried a reed sceptre or *oztopilli* in his left hand and sinuous snake-staff in his right hand. A delicately rendered fired-clay vessel of c.1500 representing Napatecuhtli was discovered in 1996 in Tláhuac, Mexico Federal District.

RICHLY DECORATED ROBES

From sculptures such as door lintels and stelae we know that the rulers and noble elite of Classic Period Maya cities wore cotton fabrics with a rich weave and elaborate embroidery. Weavers made large amounts of cotton cloth in a variety of patterns. Only a few fragments of cloth produced by the ancient Maya have survived. A cache of chipped flints buried in the 6th–7th century Copán temple known to archaeologists as the Rosalila structure was wrapped in disintegrating fabric. A few pieces of white cotton cloth were discovered with late Postclassic pottery of *c*.1250–1500 at Tenam, a site in the eastern part of Chiapas. When archaeologists dredged the *Cenote* of Sacrifice

Below: Toltec warriors wore quilted cotton battle dress. This stone soldier, carved at Tollán, reproduces the costume in detail.

at Chichén Itzá, they found among the multitude of gold, silver and other precious offerings a few pieces of carbonized fabric with complex weaves.

AZTEC DESIGNS

In the Aztec empire, as in Maya lands, few pieces of cloth survived, but images in codices, in sculptures and in ceramics – together with the descriptions of Spanish invaders – reveal the rich variety of cloth and elegant decorative designs that were available.

As among the Maya, there were regionally distinctive designs. These were generally embroidered, woven, dyed or even painted on to the cloth. They were usually geometric designs, although some regions specialized in decorating with images of local animals or plants. The empire's finest textiles were those

Above: Used by Zapotec artisans., these loom shuttles carved from bones of the regal jaguar were placed in Monte Albán Tomb 7.

imported to Tenochtitlán from Veracruz. Huaxtec weavers, who were based in that region, produced highly prized white cotton cloth decorated with animal motifs.

Weavers made dyes from minerals, plants and animals. Red came from cochineal insects gathered in groves of nopal cacti – a useful sideline for agriculturalists. Blue clay and yellow ochre were other sources.

Purple came from the sea snail *Purpura patula*, found around the shores of Yucatán (see box). This snail was related to the Murex mollusc, found in the Mediterranean, from which the ancient Phoenicians made the 'royal purple' dye in classical Europe.

MAYA COLOUR CODE

Highland communities in modern Guatemala still follow ancient traditions in weaving practice, as far as historians can tell. These communities use handlooms to make cotton cloth and embroider this with cotton thread that has been dyed the required colour. Different communities have traditional designs. No two designs are identical, but they adhere to distinctive local patterns closely enough to be immediately recognizable. The meaning of the colours used also follows time-honoured ways. Red stands for blood, and blue sacrifice. Green-turquoise, the colour of the quetzal bird's magnificent tail plumes, is symbolic of royalty. Yellow, as the colour of maize, suggests food, while black stands for weapons – because it was the predominant colour of the obsidian used to make cutting blades for weapons. A deep purple colour derived from the sea snail *Purpura patula* found on the Pacific coast and carried inland by traders was highly esteemed.

COLOURFUL BATTLE DRESS

A celebrated portrait in the 16th-century manuscript *Codex Ixtlilxochitl* of Netzahualcóyotl, ruler of Texcoco, shows the colourful costumes available to the noble elite in Aztec Mexico. The portrait shows Netzahualcóyotl in ceremonial battle garb, bearing a blue shield, with long red tassels, on his left arm and on his head a blue headdress with white and red horizontal bands. These colours were matched in the blue of his tunic and the red of the protective binding on his upper arms. On his lower half he wears a flowing kilt in horizontal colour bands of white, red, green, yellow, red and green once more.

A page from the *Codex Mendoza* (*c.*1541) also made clear the bright colours worn by elite warriors for ceremonial dress. It depicts a selection of colourful outfits with elaborate feather headdresses and coloured shields decorated by *amanteca* feather workers.

Below: A modern Mexican hooked rug uses an Aztec design, incorporating images of birds and animals, and plant motifs.

FESTIVAL COSTUME

Clothes played an important role in religious ceremonies. At festivals, priests and priestesses, prisoner-sacrificial victims or commoners selected for sacrifice wore costumes that identified them as the god or goddess being honoured.

The costumes were often elaborate and highly coloured and so added to the spectacle and drama generated by these

Above: In August 2000, archaeologists excavating the Templo Mayor found this Aztec cloth in an offering to Tláloc.

public enactments of religious ritual. Colours and design elements added layers of religious meaning, a process well suited to representations of deities with many complex attributes, several of which they might share with other gods and goddesses.

For example, a celebrated statue of water goddess Chalchiúhtlicue (dated *c.*1500) found in Mexico City in 1824 wore the headdress that identified her as Chalchiúhtlicue, while her cape was embroidered with *chalchiuhtil* or jade symbols that were also essential elements of the goddess's outfit. However, she also wore a rattlesnake sash to hold up her lower garments and these associated her with maize goddesses and also with the earth goddess Coatlícue.

Statues like this one of Chalchiúhtlicue might have represented a deity or a priest/priestess impersonating a deity and showed details of festival dress. A few statues are naked or barely dressed figures and might have been dressed in brightly coloured real clothes as part of festival rites.

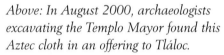

197

A GATHERING OF FEATHERS

Images in the *Florentine Codex* (1575–77) of Friar Bernardino de Sahagún depict highly skilled Aztec *amanteca* feather-workers at their job, sewing green quetzal feathers into elaborate headdresses for royal and priestly costumes, on to ceremonial shields and across temple banners. The emerald-green tail plumes of the male quetzal, gathered by specialist hunters in the tropical forests of Maya lands and imported to highland Mexico,

Below: Feather birds. These creatures on a painted terracotta brazier from Teotihuacán are stylized images of the sacred quetzal.

could be 1m (3ft 3in) long. It made a great visual impact when sewn around a headdress or added to its crown to make a tall *quetzalmiahuayo* (gathering of quetzal feathers). The feather-workers also used feathers from macaws, parrots, spoonbills and a range of other birds and made elite items of clothing, bracelets and magnificent costumes for dancing.

From at least the prime of Teotihuacán, in c.AD500, the transport of feathers was a major component of Mesoamerican trade. Other images in the *Florentine Codex* depict Aztec traders at market sitting alongside brightly coloured feather

displays. Feathers and feathered items were suitable offerings in temples because of their rarity and great worth. Quetzal feathers were additionally valued because of their length and, most importantly, because their colour resembled that of precious jade – the green of maize shoots and water, associated with Chalchiúhtlicue ('Mistress of the Jade Skirt'), and symbolic of life itself.

FEATHER-WORKING DEITY
The Aztec feather-workers, gathered in their own quarter of Tlatelolco, worshipped Coyotlinahual as their patron god. This deity was associated with Tezcatlipoca. In one version of the myth of Quetzalcóatl-Topiltzin as ruler of Tollán, when Tezcatlipoca arrived in the city of the Toltecs to bring about the fall of the Feathered Serpent through trickery and deception, he was accompanied by Coyotlinahual, who was identified as a magician.

EUROPEAN ADMIRATION
Feather-work was an unfamiliar craft to the Spanish invaders and one of the artistic achievements of the Aztecs and Maya that made the greatest impression on Europeans. (Although the conquistadors were keen to collect and send home Mixtec work in gold and silver, they admired it for its monetary rather than artistic worth and melted it down on its arrival in Europe.)

A magnificent example of the work of the most skilled *amanteca* was a *quetzalapanecayotl* ('quetzal-feather headdress') sent to King Charles V of Spain by Hernán Cortés in 1519 and now part of the collection of the Museum für Völkerkunde in Vienna, Austria. The vast headdress, which measures 1.16m by 1.75m (3ft 10in by 5ft 9in), contains 450 quetzal feathers adorned with gold appliqué and turquoise. It would have made a great impression, even from afar, when worn by priests of Quetzalcóatl in

Right: The Florentine Codex *depicts highly regarded* amanteca *craftsmen lavishing attention on a feather costume.*

processions and sacrificial rituals. Cortés collected a good number of featherwork items and sent a large consignment of them to Spain in 1522 but the precious cargo was seized by pirates.

NOBLE ADORNMENT
The Museum für Völkerkunde also contains a large fan, 1.19m tall and 68cm in diameter (3ft 10in by 2ft 2in), made from quetzal feathers and gold appliqué in the last years of the Aztec empire. Fans were used by rulers, nobles and elite *pochteca* merchants. These most elegant of Tenochtitlán's citizens provided a regular demand for the feathered fans produced by the *amanteca* of Tlatelolco. Nobles could be seen carrying a brightly coloured fan – feathered, for example, with the plumage of parakeets and hummingbirds – in one hand, and a bunch of flowers in the other. The fans were usually made with carved wooden handles.

Another fine survival of Aztec featherwork was a striking ceremonial shield, 70cm (2ft 3in) in diameter of *c.*1500, that depicted a creature some scholars identify as a long-tailed water beast called an *ahuítzotl* ('water-prickle creature'). Aztec legend had it that the *ahuítzotl* lay in wait for an unwary wanderer on riverbanks and lakesides, caught the wanderer in its tail and pulled him down to the depths of the water where he drowned. The beast's name was taken by the *tlatoani* Ahuítzotl (*r.* 1486–1502), who led vast sacrificial rituals for the dedication of the rebuilt Templo Mayor in Tenochtitlán in 1487.

Other historians have suggested that the beast on the shield is a coyote, an animal

Right: Amanteca *had many commissions from Tenochtitlán's religious hierarchy for feathered costumes worn in sacred ritual.*

form of the god Tezcatlipoca who was one of the patron deities of war, and that it might have been the mascot-symbol of an elite military order. The shield was made of reeds strengthened with lengths of wood and covered with animal hide. The craftsman stuck feathers of the spoonbill, oriole, macaw and cotinga to pieces of agave paper and glued these to the shield to create the design, adding quetzal plumes and more spoonbill and cotinga feathers around the rim. Strips of sheet gold emphasized the design.

MAYA FEATHERWORK
No examples of Maya feather-work have survived, but carved and painted images reveal the splendour of the capes, shields, headdresses, fans, spear pendants and other ornaments made by the Maya counterparts of the *amanteca*. At Piedras Negras, for example, Stela 12 depicts a

ruler wearing both feather headdress and feather robe. Similarly, in Chichén Itzá's Temple of the Jaguars, wooden door lintels were carved with images of featherwork. The murals at Bonampak also provide evidence of elegant Maya featherwork designs.

IN THE CHRISTIAN ERA
The native craft of feather-work survived the Spanish Conquest, after which featherworkers' expertise in making priestly headdresses and costumes led to their contributing to the wardrobe and paraphernalia of Christian priests. The Bishop of Michoacán remarkable mitre was made in *c.*1530–60 from maguey paper and cotton cloth with a delicate mosaic of feathers from hummingbirds, macaws, parrots, cotingas, spoonbills, tzinitzans and starlings depicting events from Christ's Passion and the Last Judgement.

CHAPTER TEN

THE CARVER'S ART

The monumental carved heads of Olmec kings in the 2nd–1st millennium BC were raised in rows in plazas or ceremonial areas, where their steady, inscrutable gaze would fall on any who approached. Likewise the carved stone pillars or stelae of Maya cities in the Classic Period stood in great public spaces, a statement of dynastic power. Sculpture in Mesoamerica took two main forms: free-standing monuments, such as Olmec heads or Maya stelae, and decorative elements on buildings.

In many cases carving on buildings was also for public consumption – for instance, the stucco deity masks that flanked access stairs on Maya pyramid-temples and the dynastic scenes carved on temple roof combs were both visible from the plazas below. In other cases – such as carving on door lintels at Yaxchilán or Piedras Negras or on stucco panels within temples at Palenque – these carved elements were intended for viewing close up and would have been seen only by members of the priestly and ruling elite. They still celebrated divine blessing on royal achievement and consolidated the standing of the dynasty, but did so by what historians call 'horizontal propaganda' within a single social level as opposed to 'vertical propaganda' from a higher level (of the rulers) to a lower level (of the commoners).

Left: The Toltecs developed the coatepantli *or serpent wall. At Tollán, it limited access to the main ceremonial area.*

THE KING'S HEAD:
OLMEC MONUMENTAL CARVING

The craft of Olmec stonemasons appears to have burst fully formed into the history of Mesoamerican carving. Scholars know no precedent in the region for the monumental heads, three-dimensional figures, colossal royal thrones and early forms of stelae or pillars that the Olmec produced from the 2nd millennium BC onwards. The only three-dimensional representations in Mesoamerica before the rise of the Olmec in the Gulf Coast region were the small clay figures found at many sites including the villages around the lakes of the Valley of Mexico.

SYMBOLS OF ABSOLUTE POWER
Seventeen Olmec monumental heads have survived. They are remarkably similar, with fleshy faces and foreheads gathered in a frown. All wear a tight helmet or cap that comes down to just above the eyes. Some 2–3m tall (6ft 6in–10ft) and weighing up to 20 tons each, their size alone makes

Below: Scholars believe that the Olmec could identify individual kings or the dynasties to which they belonged by interpeting emblems in their head dresses.

them deeply compelling, but they are also arresting in their naturalism; in the life-like detail of thick, slightly separated lips, the pupils of the eyes and the folds of flesh on the cheek. Simultaneously, their emotionless gaze makes them seem withdrawn and superior and is expressive of authority and absolute power.

MONUMENTAL FEAT
The heads were carved from large, smooth basalt boulders that occur naturally in the Tuxtla mountains around 80km (50 miles) from the Olmec temple towns of La Venta, San Lorenzo and Laguna de Los Cerros. The boulders were probably carved *in situ* in the mountains, then carefully wrapped and transported by river-raft to the ceremonial centres of these settlements, where hundreds of labourers assembled to move and erect the vast structures in rows.

Scholars believe that the heads were portraits in basalt of Olmec kings, perhaps the reigning lord or his most recently deceased ancestor, probably commissioned to mark funerals, coronation rites or important anniversaries of these

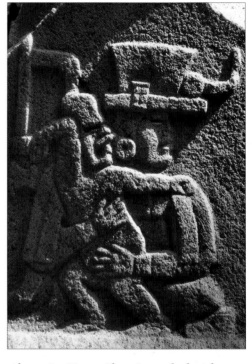

Above: La Venta Altar 5, marked with images of helmeted adults bearing 'were-jaguar' babies, was probably a royal throne.

Below: Olmec kings had power to deliver fertility, represented in this La Venta carving by the turtle shown above the ruler's head.

events. The headdresses are all different, marked with emblems that might have represented the king's name or that of the dynasty to which he belonged.

KNEELING BALL PLAYER?

Other notable Olmec stonework included a kneeling figure known as Monument 34 from San Lorenzo. Carved from basalt *c.*1100BC, the figure is 79cm (2ft 7in) high, with sockets cut at the shoulder that once held moveable arms and a carving of a concave mirror on his chest. Some scholars suggest that this kneeling male represents a player of the Mesoamerican ball game.

A statue carved at Laguna de Los Cerros *c.*1100BC is the only known standing figure carved by Olmec sculptors: the caped figure, nicknamed 'Superman' by scholars, stood 1.5m (5ft) tall.

More typical was a large greenstone statue of a seated man holding a baby that combined the features of a human infant with the square snout of a jaguar, an example of the 'were-jaguar' image commonly used by the Olmec and tentatively identified by scholars as an image of the rain god. This statue, found at Las Limas in Veracruz in 1965, is 55cm (22in) in height. On the knees and shoulders of the seated figure, the sculptor carved four profiled faces with distinctive features that may represent either four aspects of a deity or four distinct divinities.

Olmec craftsmen also carved several large stone thrones, which were once believed by archaeologists to be altars used in sacred ritual. Of these thrones, the most celebrated is the La Venta monument, which is known to archaeologists as Altar 4. This depicts a seated ruler in a bird headdress emerging from an opening in the front of the throne, holding a rope that connects him to a bound figure on one side of the stone. The same rope probably originally connected him to another figure on the other side, but this carving has been defaced. The

rope might indicate that the king had taken the other figure captive, or that the two were bound by dynastic links.

Archaeologist David Grove identified a buck-toothed ruler portrayed on Head 4 at La Venta as one of the bound figures represented on a throne at San Lorenzo. This suggests either that the two sacred towns had been at war and that a San Lorenzo king had captured a La Venta king, or that the monument celebrated

the kinship ties between the two ruling dynasties. On the La Venta Altar 4, a gaping jaguar's mouth was carved above the king suggesting that, in emerging from the niche in the stone, the king was coming forth from the heart of this regal predator.

Below: The posture and hand positions of this Olmec volcanic-stone statue led scholars to label him the 'standard bearer'.

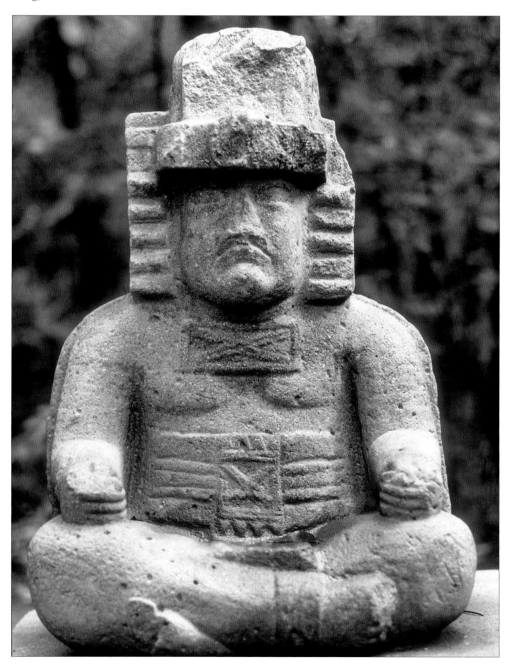

FROM THREE TO TWO DIMENSIONS:
THE FIRST STELAE

After *c*.500BC, Mesoamerican craftsmen moved away from the three-dimensional carvings of heads and seated or kneeling figures produced by Olmec artisans to concentrate largely on relief carvings in two dimensions. For more than 1,000 years, although potters continued to make clay figurines, relief carvings on panels, and thrones, slabs attached to buildings and stone pillars or stelae were the norm.

From the 6th century AD onwards, sculptors at the Maya city of Toniná created an unusual group of stelae that were carved on all four sides of the block, almost like a statue. Then in the 9th century AD, with the rise of the Toltecs – and perhaps in the Chalcihuites culture of northern Mexico, which some scholars now identify as a source of many Toltec practices and motifs – craftsmen returned to making this kind of monumental three-dimensional statue.

The Toltec-Maya at Chichén Itzá and the Aztec inheritors of Toltec power at Tenochtitlán were also enthusiastic practitioners of three-dimensional sculpture.

Below: The skeletal figure on this late Preclassic stone fragment from Izapa represents the underworld god of the dead.

Above: The deep relief carving of King Curl Head on Stela 10 (c.AD527) from Tikal has been eroded by time. Stela 10 stood on the North Terrace facing the Great Plaza.

CHALCATZINGO CARVINGS
The Olmecs had already demonstrated a great capacity for relief carving, evidenced in their high-relief work on stone thrones, in rock carvings and also in stone pillars or stelae. As early as 1100BC, craftsmen who were themselves Olmecs or who were working in the Olmec style cut elaborate reliefs in rocks at the trading centre of Chalcatzingo in the Amatzinac valley, to the south-east of the Valley of Mexico. One, dubbed 'El Rey' by historians, represents a king wearing an elaborate headdress, seated on a throne and holding a bar bearing a scroll design identical to the one carved on his throne, within a monster-mouth or cave believed to represent the entrance to the underworld. Art historian Esther Pasztory notes that the focus is on the importance of costume, equipment and location, as distinct from the monumental heads, which celebrated the power of the physical form.

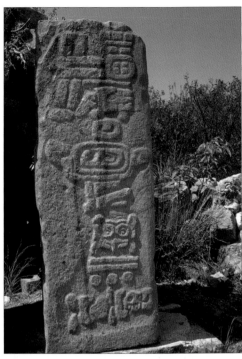

Above: Some Monte Albán stelae celebrated the achievements of individual rulers. They were carved with dates believed to be birth-dates taken by the kings as their names.

Olmec stelae similarly celebrated rulers in elaborate costume. The monument labelled Stela 2 at La Venta, for example, represents a figure in ceremonial attire apparently holding a sceptre, weapon or bat. Historians suggest that the image may depict a player of the ball game – perhaps a royal ball game player. The stela, 2.46m (8ft) tall, was carved *c*.1100BC.

RECORDING THE CYCLES OF TIME
The Olmecs' contemporaries in Oaxaca also excelled at relief carving. At San José Mogote, Zapotec craftsmen carved a stone slab representing a fallen figure and set it in the doorway of a ceremonial building where people would tread. In the carving, known to archaeologists as Monument 3, skilled and learned stonemasons cut the day sign 1-Earthquake from the 260-day ritual calendar between the feet of the figure, perhaps to record the name of the person represented or the date on

Above: Danzantes. Some 300 carvings of ritual victims or prisoners – once thought to be dancers – were displayed on Building J as a statement of Monte Albán's might.

which he was killed or sacrificed. Cut *c*.700–500BC, this is the oldest evidence we have for the use of the 260-day calendar in Mesoamerica.

Shortly afterwards, in *c*.500–200BC, Zapotec artisans at nearby Monte Albán carved loose-limbed figures on the structure now called Building L or the Temple of the Danzantes. Slabs bearing these carvings were probably arranged along the side of the building. The fluid carving of these figures – believed to be prisoners of war or sacrificial victims – includes scrolls emanating from the groin, probably representing the flow of sacrificial blood after the priests had mutilated the victims' sexual organs, or possibly celebrating rites of autosacrifice in which the depicted figures had cut their

own sexual organs to offer their blood. Scholars note that the stonemasons here represented victims rather than rulers, and as at San José Mogote, exhibited a concern with marking the place of the images within the cycles of time.

STELAE IN MAYA LANDS

At Izapa on the Pacific coastal plain of Chiapas, in the southern Maya region, craftsmen developed a highly influential style in carving stelae from *c*.300BC onwards. They cut images of scenes from religious narratives, in which human-animal figures interact in making offerings.

Scholars identify Stela 21 at Izapa (cut *c*.100BC–AD100) as the first representation in Mesoamerican carving of the act of sacrifice. The pillar depicts a standing figure holding the head of a newly decapitated victim, whose lifeblood pours forth in long scrolls both from the head and the prostrate body, while in the background

a ruler or noble passes by in a sedan chair carried by two porters. Another roughly contemporary stela, number 25, represents a man or hero from religious narrative standing on the ritually important right-hand side of a scene, holding a staff on which a magnificent bird perches and facing a crocodile with its nose in the ground and tail vertically in the air. The stone-carver gave the crocodile an explicit likeness to a tree and indeed added a bird in the 'branches' of its tail. Scholars cannot fully explain the scene, but the crocodile, normally an image for the earth, may be a representation of the ceiba cosmic tree connecting underworld and heavens through the terrestrial plane.

Craftsmen also cut stelae in this period at Kaminaljuyú in the Guatemala valley. They carved rulers, generally portrayed walking in profile wearing elaborate garb and headdress and holding objects of ceremonial or ritual significance.

SET IN STONE:
THE POWER OF MAYA KINGS

Craftsmen in settlements such as Izapa, Kaminaljuyú and Abaj Takalik in the southern Maya region were cutting glyphic inscriptions that probably included calendrical dates in the years *c.* 100BC–AD250 (the late Preclassic Period). Fragments of what might originally have been dated monuments survive, but none of the dates themselves have been found.

CHANGING PERSPECTIVE
In these early years, Maya sculptors represented rulers with feet, legs and head in profile, but the torso turned towards the viewer with both arms visible. At Tikal, sculptors began to experiment with the position of the figure. Stela 4, dated AD378 and recording the accession of King Curl Nose, is the oldest known pillar to show a figure turned entirely towards the viewer. Another Curl Nose monument, Stela 18 of AD396, is the oldest known Maya image of a seated figure facing the viewer. Another early carving of a figure looking straight out of the pillar, Stela 26 at Uaxactún, is dated AD445. This position was then found on stelae throughout the Classic Period, at sites including Palenque, Yaxchilán, Piedras Negras and Seibal.

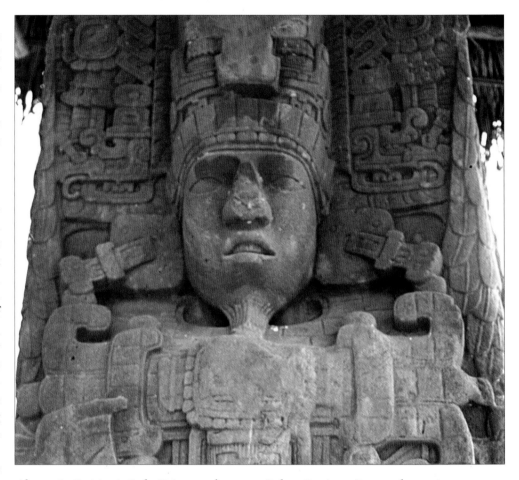

Above: At Quiriguá, Stela D is one of several in the Main Plaza bearing the face of King Cauac Sky (r. 724–84).

Below: Intricate Puuc-style carving surrounds a standing figure of the king on this monument from Kabah in Yucatán.

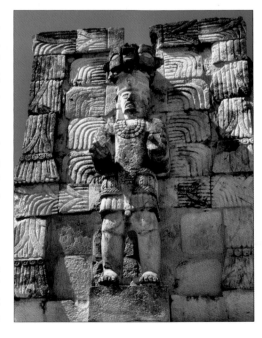

KINGS AND QUEENS OF CALAKMUL
The city of Calakmul, in south-eastern Campeche, contains 113 stelae – more than at any other Maya city. Some of these are unique in the Maya world in that they were raised in pairs that bear male and female portraits, understood to be the king and his queen. The first of these paired portraits were Stela 29 and Stela 28, raised by the city's second king in AD623. Another set, Stela 24 and Stela 23, were erected in AD702 by Calakmul's fifth king on the western edge of the city's Central Plaza.

Four stelae at Piedras Negras depict a newly inaugurated king in the position adopted on the celebrated Olmec Altar 4: seated cross-legged in a recess, facing the viewer. These four stelae were Stela 25 (dedicated in AD608), Stela 6 (AD687), Stela 11 (AD731) and Stela 14 (AD761). Each was an advance on its predecessor in terms of the success with which the carving was achieved, using progressively deeper recesses that permitted fuller development of the seated figure.

DEEP RELIEF
Images of kings facing out of the stela were most successfully developed by craftsmen at Copán and Quiriguá. At Copán, the carving on Stelae H (AD730)

ALL-ROUND CARVING AT TONINÁ

The stelae at Toniná, a city 50km (30 miles) south of Palenque, were unique in the Maya world in that they were carved in the round like statues. They were also unusually small, about 2m (6ft 6in) tall rather than the average for Maya stelae of 2.5–3m (8–10ft). Another carved structure at Toniná, known as Monument 122, features more conventional carving. It bears an image of King Kan Xul II of Palenque as a captive. Toniná's third ruler, who acceded to the throne in AD688, achieved a great coup in capturing Kan Xul II in AD711. Art historian Linda Schele suggests part of the tribute involved the despatch to Toniná of an elite sculptor from Palenque who was forced to carve an image of his defeated king.

Below: Many believe the deep-relief carving on Copán stelae to be the finest in the Maya world. Animal masks and complex regalia contrast with the serenity of the face.

Above: Quiriguá. The image of Cauac Sky on Stela E – which stands 10.7m (35ft) tall – is more than three times life size.

and Stela A (AD731) is extremely ornate and in very deep relief. At Quiriguá, Monument 5 (also known as Stela E and dated AD771) bears a splendid high-relief portrait of King Cauac Sky commemorating his victory over Copán. The largest known Maya stela, it measures 1.5m (5ft) wide by 10.7m (35ft) high and has an estimated weight of 65 tons.

CARVING THE GODS

Sculptors at Quiriguá moved on from stelae to carve large, unquarried sandstone boulders, subsequently known as zoomorphs, with images of sky divinities, earth creatures and kings.

One of these, Zoomorph P (also known as Monument 16), depicts a young ruler seated in the open jaws of a serpent representing the underworld and holds a shield with a sun god portrait and a sceptre of rulership. More than 3.4m (11ft) wide and 2.1m (7ft) high, the vast structure was typical of Maya sculptural aesthetics in its combination of natural and grotesque supernatural figures and the refusal to leave any space plain. The zoomorph was dedicated in AD795 and might have been cut to celebrate the accession of King Jade Sky.

THE WORK OF MAYA STONEMASONS

Maya carvers worked the rock that was locally available. For most this was limestone. At Quiriguá, Altar de Sacrificios, Toniná and a few other sites, stonemasons had access to sandstone, while at Copán they used a volcanic rock called trachyte. With a fine grain and predictable texture, trachyte was easy to carve and its availability at Copán was one important reason why that site rose to such prominence as a centre of the sculptor's art. The only drawback of trachyte was that it sometimes contained very hard flint

lumps. These were either hacked off, creating small depressions in the monument's surface, or left in place, forming small lumps. Elsewhere, stonecutters needed to work limestone and sandstone shortly after it had been quarried, for the rock was soft when first exposed but grew harder the longer it was in contact with the air.

ANCIENT QUARRYING

Labourers quarried rock by digging along the sides and ends of an oblong shaft of stone suitable for a stela. Then, probably using tree trunks as rollers and creepers as ropes, they hauled the shaft to the site where it was to be erected. There they dug a receiving hole and lined it with masonry, then pulled the shaft upright into the hole, probably by building a ramp of logs behind the shaft and using an A-frame fashioned from wooden beams to raise it. Once the shaft was in place, they built platforms around it on which skilled carvers set to work. They used round-handled, single-edged stone chisels 5–15cm (2–6in) and hammer stones up to 7cm (2¾in) across.

After the carvers were finished, their work was rubbed smooth using sand and water, then plastered and painted. Most stelae were painted a dark red or blue mixed with copal resin. This produced a long-lasting coating with a varnish-like finish. In some places, particularly where the relief carving was deeper, the paint remains visible, more than 1,000 years later.

WALL PANELS AND LINTELS

In addition to stelae, Maya sculptors excelled in cutting wall panels, thrones, stone lintels and decorative elements on buildings. Some of the finest examples of wall panels and thrones were carved at Piedras Negras, roughly midway between Yaxchilán and Palenque on the river Usumacinta. A wall panel carved in the year 9.16.6.9.16 (AD757) adorned a nine-

Above: Serpent warrior. On the Temple of the Warriors at Chichén Itzá, a soldier emerges from the jaws of a sacred snake.

level mortuary monument now called Structure O-13 by archaeologists. The panel represents the fourth king of the Piedras Negras dynasty making a ritual designation of his son as the royal heir.

Below: This limestone chacmool, *inlaid with shell and obsidian, was originally painted. He performed service as an offering stone for ritual victims' hearts at Chichén Itzá.*

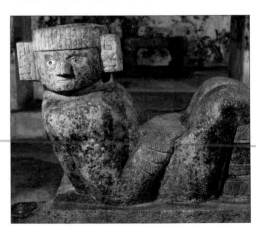

THE RULER'S ORNATE SCEPTRE
Maya kings were often represented on stelae and in other carvings holding 'the manikin sceptre', an ornately decorated staff symbolic of royal power: an example can be seen on Monument 16 at Quiriguá (carved in 795). Some centuries earlier, the influence of Teotihuacán on Maya sites had been seen in part by the carving of a Teotihuacano-style weapon, the spear thrower, on royal images: Stela 4 at Tikal celebrated the accession of King Curl Nose in 378 by depicting the king holding a spear thrower on his left arm beneath an image of the divine Maya patron of royalty, Bolon Tza'cab. Scholar Clemency Coggins demonstrated that the manikin sceptre symbol was formed by combining an image of Bolon Tza'cab with a carving of a spear thrower.

Above: Manikin sceptre.

Above: Delicate limestone carving of courtly consultation adorned the back of a royal throne dated AD747 and found in Chiapas.

The king is depicted on his throne, with his son and two other boys standing on his left and three elite visitors from Yaxchilán, including King Bird Jaguar, on his right. Piedras Negras stonecarvers also created a magnificent, bench-like throne that was placed in the main room of the palace in a position where it could be seen by subjects standing in the courtyard before the palace. The stonemason-scribes carved glyphs on three sides of the throne's front legs; the inscriptions reveal that the piece was dedicated to royal use in 9.17.15.0.0. (AD785).

The finest carved stone lintels in the Maya world were the depictions of King Shield Jaguar and his wife Lady Xoc on Lintels 24, 25 and 26 at Yaxchilán. These images of Lady Xoc performing autosacrifice by drawing a thorn cord across her tongue, of Lady Xoc experiencing a vision and of the king dressing for battle ,were raised in Temple 23, dedicated to the queen and the gods in AD726.

At Copán, stonemasons excelled not only in carving stelae and altars or thrones, but also in providing elaborate decoration for architectural elements such as stairways and a platform with monumental stairway that archaeologists call a 'reviewing stand'. On the Hieroglyphic Stairway, which was dedicated in AD756,

they cut more than 2,000 glyphs recording the city's dynastic history. The 63-step structure stood more than 20m (65ft) high and was 10m (33ft) wide, including its balustrades.

THE SEAT OF THE JAGUAR

In the 9th–10th centuries AD, rulers in the cities of the northern Maya region stopped commissioning carved monuments, instead employing stonecarvers to make decorative elements for sacred buildings. Artists at Uxmal produced an image of a head emerging from a serpent's jaws that was mounted in the façade of the base of the pyramid known as the House of the Magician. They also carved a new type of royal seat, the jaguar throne: a life-sized jaguar with flattened back on which the ruler sat. A jaguar throne has also been found at Chichén Itzá. Also at Chichén Itzá, under Toltec influence,

Right: This standard bearer was made for the Temple of the Warriors in Chichén Itzá.

stonemasons carved the reclining *chacmool* figures that were set before temples. The arched figures each include a vessel into which the heart of a sacrificial victim was placed.

The carvers also made standard bearers, seated figures about 1m (3ft 4in) tall that held a feather banner, and the upright warriors that archaeologists now call 'Atlantean figures'. These were used to provide the support necessary for door lintels and daises.

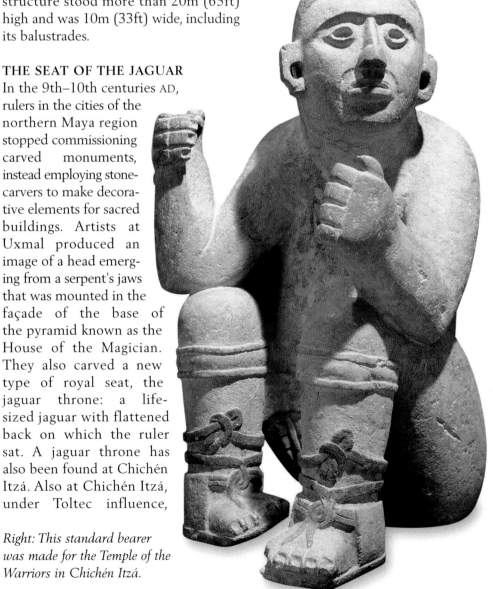

INTRICATE CARVING IN STUCCO

There was a long tradition in Maya lands of carving in stucco or plaster. From the late Preclassic Period (400BC–AD100), builders used carved stucco as a decorative element on sacred buildings.

PLASTER MASKS

At Cerros, in Belize, a temple-platform known as Stucture 5C-2 and built *c.*50BC included a long stairway flanked by four large painted plaster masks, one pair representing the rising and setting sun and the other depicting the planet Venus as morning and evening star.

At Uaxactún, a temple platform (H-sub 3) erected about the same time had a similar decorative layout. Four large masks representing the sacred mountain monster of Maya belief flanked the central stairway on the western face of the platform. In the lower two, the mountain was shown rising from the waters. The upper pair showed the mountain giving issue to the Vision Serpent that the Maya

Below: Awe-inspiring lord of day. This stucco mask from Kohunlich is of the sun god Kinich Ahau, a form of Itzamná.

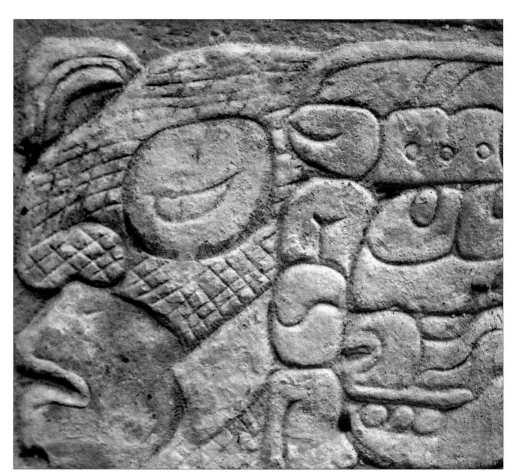

Above: Best known for murals, Bonampak also provides evidence of the well developed Maya art of stucco carving. A series of 130 stucco glyphs, like this one at Bonampak, were carved in Temple 18 at Palenque.

believed conducted shamans and initiates on spirit journeys along its many coils.

At the same site, the modestly sized platform known by archaeologists as E-VII-sub had a total of 16 stucco masks on its four faces. These masks represented the sun and Venus, as at Cerros. The platform served as an astronomical observatory in an arrangement of sacred buildings that historians call Group E, laid out to align with sunrise on winter and summer solstices. Similar masks were carved on sacred buildings at Tikal, Kohunlich, Lamanai and El Mirador in the late Preclassic Period.

RELIEF AT PALENQUE

The Maya tradition of decorative stucco carving continued into the Classic Period. It probably reached its apogée in the elegant relief panels and heads carved at Palenque in the 7th century AD. Here,

FROM STUCCO TO STONE

In the reign of King 18-Rabbit of Copán (695–738), when the centre of the city was transformed with the rebuilding of many structures and the erection of several monuments and much of the Acropolis took its final form, the king ordered the transition from stucco to carved stone for decorative elements on buildings. In their original form the stone carvings were covered with plaster and then painted. The underlying stone proved a much more durable material than plaster.

relief panels and other decorations took on the role, played by stelae in many other cities, of recording royal history and transmitting dynastic propaganda. The Group of the Cross temples built by Chan-Bahlum, son and successor of the great King Pacal, contained three large stucco relief panels. These represented scenes rich in religious detail celebrating the transfer of power from the deceased king to his son. On the roof of the Temple of Inscriptions, beneath which King Pacal was buried in a hidden crypt, stood a wide, five-doored temple. On its roof comb were stucco reliefs that similarly portrayed the new king being granted the right to rule by his father.

Left: The ancient sculptor who moulded this melancholy portrait for Palenque's Temple of the Sun achieved a moving naturalism.

Right: A noble profile carved in stucco at Bonampak shows the nose built up to join the forehead in line with the Maya ideal.

STUCCO MASTERPIECES

The crypt in which King Pacal was laid to rest was adorned with beautiful stucco reliefs representing nine figures variously identified by scholars as the nine lords of the night, the nine gods of the underworld or nine of the king's divine ancestors. On the crypt floor beneath the king's sarcophagus were two masterpieces of stucco carving: life-sized twin portraits of the king, one in his youth and the other in mid-life maturity. The heads, about 40cm (16in) high, portray an idealized image of the king. In line with Maya ideas of youthful beauty, the bridge of the nose of the youthful portrait is built up to connect to the forehead. However, the second head, of the middle-aged king, elegantly combined the ideal with the truth, for it reproduces the long face that the king had in other representations.

Scholars believe that Pacal's successor, Chan-Bahlum, probably ordered his carvers to produce actual rather than idealized portraits. An image of Chan-Bahlum on a stucco tablet from Temple IV shows him with a thick lower lip, an outsized nose

that went far beyond the Maya ideal and an expression of nervousness that is far different to the serenity accorded to Pacal. Similarly, fine stucco panels carved in House D in the Palenque palace complex during Chan-Bahlum's reign appear to show more realistic than idealized portraits.

ROSALILA MASKS

At Copán, stucco carvers reached great heights of achievement. Early buildings in the area later called the Acropolis were covered with elaborate stucco masks, but these were destroyed when the buildings were enclosed by later development. Nearby in the mid-6th century AD, a temple now called Rosalila by archaeologists was erected, its façade covered with fine stucco carvings. When, after many years, the building was encased by the next phase of construction, the masks and other elements were carefully preserved.

MEN AND GODS IN STONE:
AZTEC STONE CARVING

The years after *c*.AD900 in Mesoamerica saw a return to free-standing sculpture, an art that had not been practised since the time of the Olmec. Peoples of the northern Mexican Chalcihuites culture, the Toltecs of Tollán and those influenced by them at Chichén Itzá and elsewhere made three-dimensional Atlantean figures that supported temple roofs and door lintels, seated standard-bearer statues and reclining *chacmool* figures which were used to display and store human hearts in sacrificial ritual.

The Huastecs, a Maya-speaking people who inhabited the Gulf coast in northern Veracruz, also made monumental seated and standing statues that were a major influence on Aztec sculptors. Many of these anthropomorphic stone statues bore a second figure on its back, thought by scholars to represent an ancestral spirit companion. The Huastecs, who were particularly associated with the worship of Quetzalcóatl in his form as wind god Éhecatl, also built circular temples that might have inspired the building of the

circular Caracol at Chichén Itzá and which were certainly forerunners of the circular Éhecatl-Quetzalcóatl temple in the Aztecs' main ceremonial centre in Tenochtitlán. Having conquered the Huastecs *c*.1400, the Aztecs imported these styles in sculpture and temple architecture among the spoils of war.

GODS IN STONE
The Aztecs carved many stone figures of gods and goddesses with detailed iconography. This served to identify the deities and to suggest the complex attributes that they shared with other gods.

An 80cm (2ft 6in) stone statue of Xiuhtecuhtli, patron of the rulers or *tlatoque* (plural of *tlatoani*), depicted him wearing the *tlatoani's* costume: a diadem, *xicolli* ceremonial waistcoat, triangular loincloth that signified warrior status and sandals adorned with sun-rays at the heels. His mouth gave issue to fangs that were a symbol of the god's great age: Xiuhtecuhtli was so old that he had lost his real teeth. Xiuhtecuhtli was also a god of fire and associated with the sun: he was the Aztec form of the ancient god Huehuetéotl ('The Old One').

Above: This Aztec sculpture of Quetzalcóatl in his form as a coiled rattlesnake was cut from a single block of stone.

Such statues combined inconographic detail with naturalistic verve and a mastery of the human form. Seated statues of flower god Xochipilli depict a near-naked youth wearing only mask, loincloth and sandals. One, 115cm (4ft) tall, had flowers cut as if tattooed on the arms and legs. Some scholars suggest that these were images of plants with mind-altering properties used in divinatory rites. The statue was found in the 19th century in the village of Tlamanalco on the side of the sacred volcano Ixtaccíhuatl.

THE HUMAN FORM
Aztec sculptors also made beautifully realized statues of ordinary men and women. A female nude statue dated

Below: The Tizoc stone celebrates the military triumphs of the tlatoani *Tizoc, who took 14 towns for the expanding empire.*

Right: This cuauhxicalli *or eagle vessel, used for storing sacrificial victims' hearts, was sacred to Huitzilopochtli.*

*c.*1500 found in Texcoco and once called the 'Venus of Texcoco', together with several seated and standing statues of *macehualtin* commoner young men either naked or wearing loincloths, celebrated the youthful human form. Such statues might have been dressed in ritual costume that identified them as particular deities at festival time. A seated 33cm (13in) statue of a hunchback made *c.*1500 exhibited the sculptors' delight in naturalism and might also have been a tribute to Nanahuatzin, the disfigured and deformed god who rose to become the sun in the religious narrative of the first days at Teotihuacán. Hunchbacks and other people with physical deformities were well cared for in Tenochtitlán, but at times of solar eclipse might be chosen for human sacrifice because their bodies marked them out as the children of the sun god.

ANIMAL CARVINGS

Sculptors also represented the natural world, producing statues of dogs, coyotes, rabbits, jaguars, insects, lizards, fish, snakes, eagles, toads, pumpkins, squash and cacti. Many, while exhibiting the craftsmen's great naturalistic skill, had powerful sacred symbolism, since many gods and goddesses took animal form. Stone solar discs were carved and celebrated as symbols of the sun god Tonatiuh and of the current world age, which came under his rule and protection.

Aztec craftsmen reproduced Toltec forms such as Atlantean figures and *chacmools*. Archaeologists found a sculpted *chacmool* figure in front of the Tláloc shrine atop the early version (*c.*1390) of the great pyramid of the Templo Mayor in Tenochtitlán. The rather crude effigy was carved with Tláloc symbols, as was a later and more expertly carved *chacmool*

*c.*1502–20. A series of five stone warrior figures roughly 1.2m (4ft) tall found in Tenochtitlán possibly functioned as roof supports in the style of Toltec Atlantean figures. The five statues represented four male soldiers clutching spear throwers and wearing the triangular loincloth of the warrior and one female, wearing a skirt of arrows. Scholars suggest that they might have stood in the four cardinal points: males at east, south and north and the female in the west, a direction associated with women. The fourth male would have stood in the centre, the position of the world tree and the current world age, the spot occupied in Aztec cosmology by the great Templo Mayor itself.

TRIUMPHAL MONUMENTS

The Aztecs also produced monumental stone carving that celebrated the power of the gods, of the *tlatoani* and of the state. The celebrated Sun Stone, carved from basalt in the reign of Axayáctal (1469–81) with a diameter of 3.6m (12ft), commemorated the myth of the five world ages, the glory of the sun god and the power of the *tlatoani*. The Tizoc stone, a great cylinder 2.65m (8ft 8in) across and carved in 1481–86, celebrated the military triumphs of the Aztec army and in particular the *tlatoani* Tizoc (*r.* 1481–86) was depicted 15 times around the stone gripping a battle-weary victim by the hair, with a glyph beside each victim identifying the place of conquest. Another similar stone, 2.24m (7ft 4in) in diameter, was carved to celebrate the victories of Moctezuma I (*r.* 1440–69).

The Teocalli stone, carved in the shape of a pyramid-temple with front steps flanked by date glyphs, bore a 'temple' at the top carved with a sun disc and images of Huitzilopochtli to the left and Moctezuma II (*r.* 1502–20) to the right, both preparing to offer their blood in rites of autosacrifice. The stone, 1.23m by 92cm by 99cm (4ft by 3ft by 3ft 3in), was probably used as a royal throne. It was carved to celebrate the new fire ceremony that marked the beginning of a new 52-year cycle in 1507.

CARVING IN WOOD

The Maya called their stelae 'stone trees', suggesting that in the great cities of the Classic Period, dynastic monuments might once have been carved from tree trunks. There was certainly a flourishing Maya woodcarving tradition, as is evidenced by the few examples of wooden door lintels and beams that have survived.

DOOR LINTELS

The temples of Tikal were once graced by wooden door lintels. One of the surviving lintels, which once spanned a doorway in the building known as Temple IV, was carved from sapodilla wood with an arched serpent in the mid-8th century AD. From the serpent's mouth emerged an ancestral spirit, who might represent the dynastic founder, while above the serpent was the sacred quetzal bird of the Maya, its wings outstretched. Beneath the serpent's arched back was King Yax Kin (r. AD734–46), enthroned in splendour. The glyphic inscription declares that the king was shown celebrating a military triumph for Tikal on 26 July AD743. A slightly older lintel survives from Temple I, depicting King Ah Cacau (AD682–734) on the throne of Tikal, with a deity – perhaps his ancestral spirit – above him and a glyphic text celebrating military triumph over Calakmul on 5 August AD695.

Later wooden lintels survived in temples at Chichén Itzá and Uxmal. In the Temple of the Jaguars at Chichén Itzá, a carved lintel depicts a human figure surrounded by a feathered serpent and another figure within a spiked circular design representing the sun. US traveller John Lloyd Stephens (1805–52) discovered a carved sapodilla beam in the Governor's Palace at Uxmal and took it with him when he returned to the USA. Unfortunately, it was destroyed in a fire, much to the dismay of later scholars, who

might have been able to use the beam to date the beautiful building in which it was found.

SKILL OF THE WOODCARVERS

The beauty, detail and precision of the glyphic carving in wood was remarkable. The scribes carved the hard sapodilla wood while it was still green, for once

Above: A detail of an Aztec wooden drum of c.1500 shows an eagle-warrior who stands for the sun god Tonatiuh.

Below: Woodcarvers received military commissions for ceremonial weapons, such as this gold-covered spear-thrower.

cured it became as hard as metal. Scholar Michael Coe has suggested that the scribes first painted the symbols on the wood before cutting them with obsidian blades. Another surviving piece that demonstrates the skill of Maya glyphic carvers is a wooden box celebrating the memory of a late 7th century AD king of Tortuguero, a settlement near Tikal. The style of the glyphs closely resembles that on the Tikal lintels.

Maya woodcarvers almost certainly also made figures of gods and goddesses from wood, but none have survived, for they would have been easily and enthusiastically destroyed by Catholic churchmen. Images in the *Madrid Codex* depict the gods themsleves at work fashioning masks and figures from wood. This would seem to provide evidence that the craft was practised in Maya workshops.

A few examples of wooden figures of Aztec deities have survived. A seated statue of Macuilxóchitl of *c.*1500 depicts the god of music and gaming wearing his trademark crested headdress. Traces of paint show that the statue was originally red, but the inlay from the eyes and the ornament that once adorned his mouth are missing.

The statue was found in a cave, where atmospheric conditions were favourable to its survival. The same was true of a cedarwood fertility goddess figure of *c.*1500 which was discovered still in use for worship in a cave near the Toluca valley, Veracruz, in the 19th century. The figure wore the hairstyle which was conventionally adopted by married women and held her hands up to support the weight of her breasts, emphasizing her maternal role. Wooden statues of deities were called *cuauhximalli* by the Aztecs.

WOODEN DRUMS
Elaborately carved examples of both *huehuetl* upright drums and *teponaxtli* oblong drums have survived. A *huehuetl* drum, 98cm (3ft 2in) tall and elaborately carved with war symbols, was found in Malinalco

Above: A sapodilla-wood door lintel from Tikal Temple IV celebrates a military victory of King Yax Kin in July AD743.

– one of the mountain-top temples of the eagle- and jaguar-warrior elite – in the latter part of the 19th century. The carver cut the symbol for the current world age, Nahua Ollin (4-Earthquake), between an eagle-warrior and a jaguar-warrior. The glyph for war, *teoatl-tlachinolli* ('fire water') arises from the warriors' mouths. On the opposite side of the round drum the craftsman cut an image of an eagle-man that was almost certainly intended to be the sun god Tonatiuh himself. The lower part of the drum base was adorned with images of eagle- and jaguar-warriors in warlike procession.

A *teponaxtli* drum of *c.*1250 carved in the form of a jaguar was found in Puebla state in the late 19th century. Making these drums was the work of highly skilled specialists, who first hollowed the wood by burning, then finished the interior with chisel work. The top of the horizontal drum was split into two tongues and played with a hammer to produce a two-tone note.

Yet another example of a beautifully finished drum of *c.*1500 was carved in the shape of a reclining warrior from Tlaxcala shown with a copper-bladed axe.

Left: Mixtec craftsmen carved this delicate wooden jaguar and encrusted it with fine mosaic in c.1400–1520.

CHAPTER ELEVEN

PRECIOUS
WORK

In April 1519 Moctezuma II sent magnificent gifts of gold and silver to Hernán Cortés and his conquistadors. The collection – which included a solid gold disc as big as a cartwheel, together with an even larger disc of silver – was intended to honour the newcomers and to impress the Aztec emperor's power and wealth upon them. The gift also made a religious statement, for the gold and silver discs represented the sun and moon and celebrated the pre-eminence of the Aztecs – self-styled 'People of the Sun'.

The Spaniards, versed in a different culture, could not be expected to understand the religious message: the gift served only to fan their lust for Aztec riches. Some members of the invading group, including Cortés himself, certainly admired the craftsmanship of the pieces – he wrote to Charles V about Aztec jewellery that 'nowhere in the world could a smith have done better'. But many Europeans could not see beyond the dazzling monetary value of the silver and gold; predictably, the discs did not survive – they were melted down for their metal, the fate that awaited the great majority of gold and silver ritual items, ceremonial jewellery and other pieces sent back to Europe by the conquistadors. Cortés despatched several loads of Aztec precious metalwork, and these were among the items that astonished German artist Albrecht Dürer, who declared them to be 'strange and wonderfully worked objects' that thrilled his heart.

Left: God of spring and goldsmiths. This exquisite gold mask of Xipe Totec was an offering in Tomb 7 at Monte Albán.

AN IMPORTED CRAFT:
METALWORK IN MESOAMERICA

On 6 January 1932 Mexican archaeologist Alfonso Caso made a breathtaking find in a tomb at the Zapotec mountaintop city of Monte Albán. The grave had originally been laid out *c*.AD 500–750 with a large fore chamber leading into two rooms aligned east–west. These contained a stone carved with Zapotec glyphs and a number of funerary urns. The grave had then been reopened in the late Postclassic Period (*c*.1250–1500) by local Mixtec mourners, who buried nine skeletons with a magnificent tribute-cache of metalwork and jewellery. The grave, known as Tomb Number 7, contained no fewer than 121 golden objects, 24 silver objects and a large number of rings, necklaces and pendants. This find provided ample evidence of the Mixtecs' astonishing skill in metalwork and making jewellery.

LATE STARTERS
When compared to their South American neighbours, Mesoamerican craftsmen were late starters in metalwork. Native Mesoamericans did not make jewellery, ritual items, weapons or tools from metal until after *c*.AD800. As early as 2000BC, the inhabitants of the Andes mountains in South America had begun to develop metalworking techniques that slowly travelled northwards along marine and land trade routes. These techniques took almost 3,000 years to reach Mesoamerica, probably arriving roughly simultaneously in two separate areas: the northern Maya region of the Yucatán peninsula and, hundreds of miles to the west, coastal settlements in western Mexico.

Among the oldest metal objects in Mesoamerica is a small claw, *c*.AD550 in Panama. It is made of the alloy of silver, copper and gold known as tumbaga, and was buried in the ceremonial centre of Altun Há, on the coastal plain north of modern Belize City. Later, a hollow figure of a gold-copper alloy was deposited as part of a cache of valuables beneath Stela H at Copán. The stela was dedicated in AD782, although archaeologists cannot rule out the possibility that the cache was buried after this or added to at a later date. Only the legs of the figurine remain, but expert analysis of the casting and alloy suggest that it was imported from a site in the southern parts of Central America such as Panama or Costa Rica.

BEGINNINGS IN MEXICO
Archaeologists have established that in the earliest days of Mesoamerican metalworking, during the 9th century, artisans working with copper in western Mexico were producing the same items in the same way as their counterparts in

Left: One of the finds in Tomb 7 was this Mixtec gold pectoral or breast ornament representing the 'old fire god' Xiuhtecuhtli.

Left: This Mixtec gold earring was one of the hoard buried in Tomb 7 at Monte Albán. The Mixtecs' exquisite gold jewellery and other fine metalwork was admired and highly influential across Mesoamerica.

Another metalworking centre was established at Amapa, Nayarit, about 50km (30 miles) inland from the Pacific coast, on the river Santiago. Here artisans made copper rings, knives, needles, pins, axe-heads, beads, plaques, bells and awls.

In Michoacán the Tarascans worked local copper to produce small ritual figures, tweezers, open rings, needles and a large numbers of bells. They also made copper axe-heads that were used as a form of money.

In Oaxaca the Mixtecs began developing their metalworking expertise after AD900. They became the pre-eminent metalworkers of the Aztec age, when some Mixtecs worked as producers of jewellery and precious-metal items in Tenochtitlán, while others worked in their own centres in Oaxaca. México/Aztec craftsmen centred in Azcapotzalco also produced metalwork in the Mixtec style. They worked in gold, silver and tumbaga.

In the northern Maya region, metalworkers developed great expertise in repoussé work, hammering designs into a sheet of metal from the reverse side. Many repoussé pieces hammered from both gold and copper were found among the objects cast into the *Cenote* of Sacrifice at Chichén Itzá. They depicted scenes of conflict between Maya soldiers and warriors of the invading wave of 'Mexicanized' merchants.

THE GODS' GOLD

Gold was identified as *teocuitlatl* ('the gods' excrement') in the Nahuatl tongue, probably because it was found in nuggets, like the droppings of animals. Its colour meant it was also associated with the sun. Images of the gods sometimes represented them wearing the gold jewellery worn by rulers, warriors, nobles and priests. A stone casket of the late 15th century that belonged to the *tlatoani* of Tenochtitlán, Ahuítzotl (*r.* 1486–1502), depicted the god Tláloc wearing a necklace carved with the symbol for gold. A statue of Xochipilli of *c.*1350–1500 shows the god of flowers and music wearing a gold necklace.

Below: This Mixtec painted vase is of a human head laden with jewellery with pierced earrings and an elaborate headdress.

Ecuador. They were making needles, rings, tweezers, fishhooks, axe-heads for wooden-handled weapons and the sharply pointed pricking instruments known as awls. There is evidence that smelting and metalwork were carried out on the coast of Guerrero by *c.*AD900. In a settlement at Zihuatanejo, archaeologists uncovered slag pieces (the refuse separated from metal when it is smelted) and many bronze and other metal pieces in a find dated *c.*AD900–1100. The metal pieces included rings, bells and sheets of gold.

GOLDEN ORNAMENTS

Among the gold, silver and other precious items found in Tomb 7 at Monte Albán was a remarkable gold pendant, some 22cm (8.5in) long, made by Mixtec craftsmen c.1200–1500. This elaborate piece, an earring, was cast by the lost-wax process and consists of four detailed images set horizontally and beneath them four pendant elements. The four images represent, from the top: two gods playing the Mesoamerican ball game on an I-shaped court; a solar disc; a butterfly set in a square border that some identify as an image of a flint knife; and the crocodile earth monster. Some scholars interpret these as levels of the universe: the celestial realm of the gods, the sun, the moon (represented by the butterfly/knife) and the earth. Mixtec craftsmen were the masters of jewellery-making in the Aztec age.

JEWELLERY IN A SINGLE STYLE

The wearing of jewellery was strictly regulated in Aztec lands. Only elite warriors and members of the nobility were permitted to wear lip, nose, neck or ear ornaments in social intercourse, although gold and silver finery was also

Below: This Aztec butterfly nose-ring was probably worn by a statue of moon goddess Coyolxauhqui in the Templo Mayor.

Above: Aztec beaten gold arrows represent the xiuhcóatl *or fire snake wielded by Huitzilopochtli. They end in serpent mouths.*

used as part of the sacred costumes worn by priests. Jewellery was made in a single style across the Mesoamerican region – except among the Tarascans of western Mexico, who kept the Aztec world at bay. Scholars call this pan-Mesoamerican jewellery the South Mexican International Style. This style had three distinguishing features. First, its decorative elements were similar to the style of the codices or bark-paper books painted by the Mixtecs. Second, it was of very high technical quality, made by artisans expert in lost-wax casting and wirework. Third, its artisans favoured composite designs that combined metal and precious stones, more than one type of metal or that added pendant elements to pectorals or rings.

ANIMAL SIGNIFICANCE

A pair of 6cm (2.4in)-long ear ornaments, made by México/Aztec or Mixtec craftsmen c.1400–1521, represent bird heads emerging from solar disks and giving issue from their mouths to tassels and bells. Experts identify the birds as *coxcoxtli*, a woodland species associated with Xochipilli, god of flowers, music and games. A 15th-century gold finger ring made by Mixtec craftsmen is adorned with the head of an eagle crowned with an intricately reproduced feather diadem. The eagle's beak probably once held a pendant element or a bell. The body of the ring takes the form of a delicately imagined serpent. This ring is typical of

Mixtec output in representing common animals that had powerful sacred significance: the eagle is an image of Huitzilopochtli and the snake of Quetzalcóatl. Another Mixtec ring (c.1200–1521) represented both a jaguar head and a double-headed serpent, summoning the qualities of those powerful creatures for the wearer. Such rings were worn by members of the noble elite, in these cases perhaps by leading military figures, since the jaguar and the eagle both had important martial associations as the symbols of elite warrior groups.

Some jewellery represented the gods. A 6cm (2.4in)-long Mixtec gold pendant of c.1500 depicts Xiuhtecuhlti, patron of rulers and fire god, with the cylindrical elements in his headdress that were his

USING AND DISPOSING OF JEWELLERY

Jewellery was worn by members of the Aztec and Maya ruling and noble class for display and as part of ritual costumes in religious ceremonial. Precious items were offered in sacrifice, cast into the Sacred *Cenote* at Chichén Itzá, laid in a temple offering or provided as part of a cache interred during dedicatory rites for a building or stela. The best offering was the most precious: blood, the force of life. Jade, the colour of Chalchiúhtlicue and closely associated with life in the form of green maize shoots, was considered even more precious than gold or silver.

trademark; such cylinders were the sticks used to start a fire. The god's face bears a beard and from his mouth emerge two fangs, features that mark him as a primordial deity who has lost his teeth through age. From his ears hang two large circular ornaments that end in solar rays. These are appropriate as Xiuhtecuhtli also had solar associations and was identified as the Aztec counterpart of the Mixtec sun god

Iha Ndikandii. A Mixtec pectoral brooch of *c*.1500 also depicted Xiuhtecuhtli/Iha Ndikandii with these characteristic elements of fangs, beard and headdress with vertical cylinders.

LIP ORNAMENTS

Mixtec goldsmiths made elaborate lip ornaments for the Aztec warriors and nobles. A cast-gold lip plug in the shape of an eagle's head made *c*.1500 shows remarkable detailing in the feathers and beak of the bird. The plug was worn on the

Above: Sacred jade had connections to fertility. These jade-bead jewellery pieces were found in a tomb at El Otero, Mexico.

lower lip: its shaft was inserted through a hole in the skin and gum and held in place by a plate worn inside the mouth. Eagle lip plugs were probably worn by leading members of the eagle-warrior society. Such plugs must have been heavy. Another example, made *c*.1400–1500, had a cast-gold eagle head and gold plug for securing the ornament in the mouth, but the connecting piece was fashioned from rock crystal to make it lighter.

Right: An Aztec nobleman wearing this gold and crystal lip plug could carry the image of a sacred eagle on his lower lip.

55

55

WORK OF THE GOLDSMITHS

In his *General History of the Things of New Spain*, Friar Bernardino de Sahagún gave a lengthy inventory of the astounding wealth of gold, other rare metals and precious stones stored in Moctezuma II's treasury as items for ornamenting dancers and their costumes. These included gold models of plants, pelicans, sacred eagles and the *xiuhcóatl* fire serpent wielded by Huitzilopochtli. There was a turquoise disc set in gold, an eagle fashioned from greenstone and mounted in gold and a cylindrical crystal lip plug with feathers from the cotinga bird, also set in gold. The store also contained many articles made from jade and amber.

CELEBRATING WARRIORS

In wearing pendants or other images of warriors, an Aztec indicated that he or she was of good birth and a leading member of the nobility. A number of gold items have survived that celebrate or represent elite warriors. An exquisite pendant bell in the shape of an eagle warrior, made *c.*1500 by Aztec goldsmiths using the lost-wax technique, was worn on a chain or necklace. The bell, 9cm tall and 7.5 cm across (3.5in by 2.9in), consists of a hollow, pear-shaped gold vessel containing a copper pellet with eagle claws at the base. At the top of the pear shape, the warrior's head is enclosed in a battle helmet in the likeness of an eagle's beak, open to reveal the soldier's stern face. His arms are thin and feathered, giving them the appearance of wings. The left arms is bent to the front across his chest, where the soldier wears a pendant plaque in the warrior style. The right arm is raised beside his head and grasping a small, feather-trimmed shield, three dart-like spears and a staff – perhaps an *atlatl* (spear-thrower). Above the head there is a rectangular frame fashioned from gold wire. On the back of the helmet, two loops were used to mount the pendant on a chain when the piece was worn by a member of the fraternity of eagle-warriors in Tenochtitlán.

Right: A Mixtec pendant of c.AD1500 (described on pages 220–221), represents fire god Xiuhtecuhtli. The projections in his headdress are firesticks; the earrings are solar rays. He is usually shown bearded.

A Mixtec pendant of *c.*1200–1521 depicts another elite warrior in remarkable detail. The cast-gold figure, 8cm tall and 4.5cm across (3.1in by 1.7in), was worn on the chest or as a lip pendant. The figure wears a decorated headband and long, dangling earrings, together with a nose ornament, warrior-plaques on his chest and a lip plug from which a victim's head and three bells are suspended. His left hand holds a ceremonial shield, while his right grasps a pole that perhaps represents an *atlatl* spear-thrower or a staff of authority.

Another precious-metal warrior figure is a free-standing figurine made from tumbaga (a gold-coloured alloy of silver, copper and gold). The curious piece was found in a cache of gold objects in Texcoco. The figurine, made by Aztec metalworkers after 1346, stands 11.2cm tall and measures 6.1cm across (4.4in by 2.4in). The figure wears ornaments in the lip, ears and nose, together with a splendid headdress. His warrior's loincloth is covered with a skirt of pendant bells. In his left arm he carries a shield and weapons and in his right hand he holds a ritual object and another pendant bell. Cavities in his chest and the back of his head almost certainly once held precious stones. The eyes, now empty, were probably also inlaid with obsidian and shell. The glyphs 2-Rabbit and 3-Water, marked on his back, have puzzled scholars, for they have no obvious relevant meaning. Scientific tests on the metal suggest that it was cast in the period 1346–1570.

GOLD AS TRIBUTE

Mixtec and México/Aztec craftsmen used gold that had been supplied as tribute from subject regions of the empire. In regions such as Soconusco in western Chiapas, it was washed down from the hills and mountains in rivers and collected in the form of nuggets from the riverbeds. In workshops in the valley of Mexico, the metal was smelted at very high temperatures produced by craftsmen-labourers blowing through long tubes on to charcoal fires. Some goldsmiths worked in Moctezuma's palace in Tenochtitlán, producing goldwork exclusively for the *tlatoani* and his inner circle of nobles. These artisans were valued so highly that they were exempt from paying tax.

GOD OF THE GOLDSMITHS

Xipe Totec, worshipped by the Aztecs as the god of regeneration and of the green shoots of spring, was the patron deity of the Mixtec goldsmiths. Scholars believe that his cult, adopted by the Aztecs from the Mixtecs, had in turn been taken by the Mixtecs of Oaxaca from the region of Guerrero where some of western Mexico's very earliest metalworking centres were established in the 9th century AD. The breaking open of seeds in spring

Above: Golden deity. Mixtec goldsmiths produced delicate, lightweight pieces with intricate decorative and figurative elements. This breast ornament appears to make use of solar symbolism.

Xipe personified was perhaps considered to be like the breaking of moulds when goldworkers used the lost-wax method for casting.

Above: A delicately carved golden handle in the shape of a snake's head, made by a Mixtec artisan at Monte Albán, honours the sacred Mesoamerican serpent.

BELLS AND REPOUSSÉ DISCS

Among members of the Aztec nobility, metal bells with a good sound and a pleasing colour were highly prized. Many of the bells made by metalworkers were sewn on to nobles' outfits, so their resonance was highly valued. The creation of a good sound when walking was an important part of the overall impression that a nobleman made.

The colour of the bells was also significant, with silver and gold the preferred colours. The association of these colours with the moon and the sun had been established from ancient times among South American metalworkers and was passed into Mesoamerican belief and cultural patterns along with the metalworking techniques.

Metalworkers learned to make silver-coloured bells and other items by adding a little arsenic to copper and to make gold-coloured metal for artefacts by combining copper with tin.

Hernán Cortés reported on the widespread use of bells in costumes and other artefacts in his first despatch from Mexico. He described a bluestone mosaic headdress with many bells and gold beads, and a collection of animal heads with coloured skins that were hung with bells.

Small copper bells were widely made and distributed in Maya lands. They were worn by the death god Yum Cimil, who is also known to archaeologists as God A and are found on their own because they were probably hung on images of the god that have since been broken or disintegrated. The inhabitants of Quiriguá were using copper bells and ornaments in the period after c.AD800. These were almost certainly locally made.

SKILLED HAMMERWORK

Metalworkers in the northern Maya region developed particular skill in repoussé work, hammering intricate raised designs into copper, silver and gold from the reverse side of the disc. The work is stylistically close to the murals and carved reliefs of the early Postclassic Period at Chichén Itzá (AD1000–1250). One repoussé disc bears the image of a ruler with elaborate nose ornaments seated on a stone. He is wearing a magnificent feathered headdress and leaning forward in the direction of his extended left hand, which holds a pair of darts or small spears, while his other hand holds a ritual object. Several repoussé discs portray scenes of conflict between defeated Maya warriors and victorious warriors wearing and using Mexican-style equipment. One, 22cm (8.75in) in diameter, depicts two Mexican or Toltec-styled warriors driving Maya footsoldiers forward at the point of a feathered spear. The Maya warriors have the built-up upper noses characteristic of

Above: The skilful repoussé work can still be seen in remains of a gold disc recovered from the sacred cenote at Chichén Itzá.

their people and wear long nose ornaments, together with elaborate feathered headdresses. On the ground by the feet of the Toltec warriors, a sacred serpent, perhaps a representation of the god Quetzalcóatl, rears to give his blessing while the outer rim of the disc is decorated with a serpentine motif that also appears to incorporate the goggle eyes of rain god Tláloc. Another disc represents the mouth of a sky-serpent yawning to give issue to a Toltec-styled warrior. Some discs show sacrificial scenes, representing the highland Mexican rite of tearing the

CASTING BY THE LOST-WAX METHOD

Mesoamerican metalworkers used the lost-wax or *ciré-perdu* method to cast objects. To cast a statuette, a craftsman would first make a clay model then, after dusting this with charcoal, he would brush the shape evenly with melted wax. Once the wax had hardened, he would dust the surface again with charcoal before adding a second layer of clay. He would invert the object and heat it until the wax melted and poured out. Then he would set the mould right way up before filling it with molten metal. He would set the whole aside to cool. Later he would break the mould to reveal the cast-metal object.

Some objects in two metals were produced by two-stage casting, An example is the ornament historians call the Pectoral of Teotitlán del Camino, which is now held in Mexico City's National Museum. This combines gold and silver. The gold segment was cast first, then the silver part afterwards.

victim's heart from his chest. These were made in northern Yucatán using metal reworked from imported items.

OFFERINGS IN THE CENOTE

Archaeologists found a large number of metal offerings in the Sacred *Cenote* at Chichén Itzá. These include bracelets, necklaces, pendants, rings, bells, beads, earplugs, masks and disks decorated with scenes in elaborate repoussé work. They are made of copper and gold. The archaeological team also uncovered decorative metal elements from wooden objects such as ritual masks and ceremonial shields, in

Right: This delicate beaten gold nose ornament was found at Colima, Meixco.

cases where the wood had rotted away leaving only the metal. Many items had been broken or damaged as part of a rite designed to free the spirit of the object before it was offered. One gold sheet was rolled into a ball, but through academics' painstaking work has been restored to a condition in which it can be viewed and copied. It is decorated with an image of a triumphant Mexican warrior defeating two hapless local Maya in the course of the invasion of the Yucatán peninsula.

Many of the metal objects found at Chichén Itzá were imported items made in South America, the southern countries of Central America and the metalworking regions of western Mexico. Scientific analysis of the items dredged from the Sacred *Cenote* revealed that some of the pieces were made in Chiapas, Oaxaca, and the valley of Mexico, in Honduras, Panama and Colombia.

Above: Recovered from the waters. This gold shield pendant was part of a hoard of Aztec gold, probably looted by conquistadors from the palace of Axayácatl, then lost at sea and found in 1975 in deep water near Puerto de Veracruz. Eight bells hang from its base. It was cast by the lost-wax method. The horseshoe-like marks on the lower part are representations of a half-moon.

FACES OF GODS AND KINGS

An important strand of Olmec art was the carving of masks in greenstone, jade and other precious stones. Some have regular human features that scholars believe might have been portraits of rulers. Many others represent fierce animal faces with a snout. These may have been connected to the cult of the 'were-jaguar' that scholars identify as a possible image of the rain god. Members of the Olmec elite wore these fierce deity masks on their chests and in their headdresses during both religious and secular ceremonies. After death, rulers were laid to rest wearing these masks over their faces.

ANCIENT SHAMANIC RITES

Many scholars believe that the carving and wearing of animal-featured masks probably predated the Olmec to the people of the first villages in Mesoamerica. Shamans might have worn such masks during religious and divinatory ceremonies: the shamans were understood to take the form of fierce, snouted creatures such as the jaguar during their religious experiences. Perhaps the masks were worn more generally by the people during community festivities and gift-giving ceremonies in which wealthier members of the community – the members of a developing ruling class – redistributed some of their wealth as a way both of establishing their own status and satisfying the needs of the poor. The Olmec rulers apparently appropriated the tradition, commissioning and wearing masks of the most precious materials such as jade and greenstone. These were highly valued because of their green-turquoise colour, which had such powerful associations for Mesoamericans with fertility and life-giving waters.

MYSTERY OF THE MASKS

In Teotihuacán, carvers of serpentine, greenstone and other precious stones represented serene-looking human faces in masks. The masks often had eyes inlaid with shell, iron pyrite and other materials. They were certainly not portrait masks, for they had regular, slightly abstracted features.

Archaeologists have uncovered hundreds of these masks in the ruins of the ancient city. They were not worn during ritual or placed in graves, but might have been mounted on clay busts or bodies made of perishable materials. The busts or bodies were dressed in splendid costumes and worshipped as ancestors or as nature deities. Some authorities suggest that the masks were attached to corpse-bundles containing mummified bodies and venerated in a sacred setting.

In the same period, craftsmen in Maya regions were also carving masks of jade and other precious stones to be placed in elite graves. At Calakmul an elite figure identified from glyphs by scholar Joyce Marcus as Long-lipped Jawbone was

Right: Precious green. This Mixtec greenstone mask has undeniable power, although it does not aim for naturalism.

buried before *c*.AD500 wearing a jade-mosaic mask, with a second laid on his chest and a third worn on his belt. A life-sized jade mask with inlays of shell and pyrite was buried at Tikal in the grave known to archaeologists as Burial 160 in *c*.AD527. A jade mosaic mask was laid over the face of King Pacal's corpse in his tomb at Palenque (*d*. AD683). It was found in pieces but has been painstakingly remade by art historians.

OLMEC HEIRLOOMS

Many Olmec portrait and deity masks were placed in graves and preserved throughout Mesoamerican history. In Aztec times they were treasured possessions passed down the generations as heirlooms. The Aztecs also collected Teotihuacáno and other masks and often reused them as grave offerings, sometimes adding their own mosaic work to the original artifact before placing it in a tomb.

Some 88 painted greenstone masks carved in the abstract style identified by archaeologists as Mezcala were collected and

Right: Face beyond death. This image of Tezcatlipoca is a human skull inlaid with turquoise mosaic.

placed in Chamber II of the Templo Mayor, Tenochtitlán. The style was associated with a culture that flourished near the Mezcala river in the region of the modern Mexican state of Guerrero from *c*.AD100–650, contemporary with Teotihuacán. Masks and figurines made by Mezcala craftsmen tended to have abstract features, indicated by circles, lines or depressions and raised areas in the surface. Some of the buried masks had the attributes of Tláloc, and scholars believe that the large offering was made to honour the rain god's helpers, the *tlaloque*.

The Aztecs themselves carved many masks in greenstone, obsidian, jade and other stones. Priests, priestesses and other impersonators of deities wore the masks in temple ceremonies.

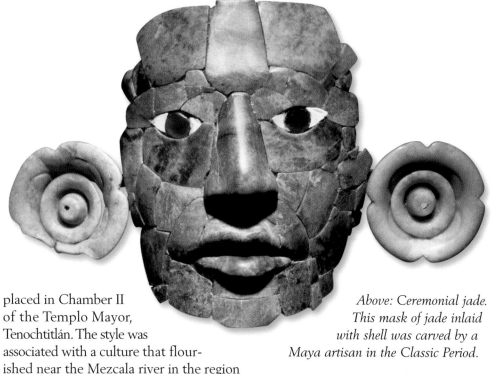

Above: Ceremonial jade. This mask of jade inlaid with shell was carved by a Maya artisan in the Classic Period.

Sometimes, as in Teotihuacán, the masks were attached to sacred bundles, to represent the face on the divine body. A splendid Aztec greenstone mask of Coyolxauhqui, moon goddess and sister of Huitzilopochtli, was probably decorated with ornaments and worn on the chest during ritual performances. The mask, made *c*.1500, was carved with images of bells on the cheeks that celebrated the goddess's name ('Lady with Bells on Her Face'). A diorite mask of Chalchiúhtlicue, carved *c*.1500, was probably attached to a sacred body. It included carvings of a quetzal-feather crown, marks representing face paint on the cheeks and, on the rear, an engraving of the glyph '8-Grass', one of the goddess's names in the ritual calendar.

DEATH MASKS

Craftsmen in Tenochtitlán and other cities also made masks that were buried with the deceased, presumably to provide individuals with a face for the spirit world after the cremation of the corpse. A very fine stone portrait mask carved *c*.1350–1500 and representing the features of a fresh-faced young man was dedicated to Quetzalcóatl in his guise as wind god Éhecatl by an image of the seated wind god together, with a carving interpreted as '9-Wind', one of the god's names in the ritual calendar.

227

SHELL AND PRECIOUS STONE DECORATION

Mesoamerican craftsmen excelled in fine mosaic work using turquoise, onyx, mother-of-pearl, malachite, jade, marine shells and other forms of inlay. From Olmec times, deity and funerary masks carved from precious stones were sometimes decorated with mosaic covering or inlaid with obsidian, onyx and shell to represent the eyes.

A magnificent Teotihuacáno mask of *c*.AD450 was covered with turquoise across most of the face, with inlays of shell for the eyes and obsidian for the eyeballs. Red spondylus or mollusc shell added a geometric nose ring, outlined the eyebrows and added a central forehead glyph that scholars believe once identified the person or deity celebrated in the mask itself.

This mask was found in an ancient grave in Malinaltepec, modern Guerrero province, in 1921. It was probably carried there by traders from Teotihuacán.

Below: At Palenque artists made exquisite mosaic masks, such as this late Classic Period jade piece (c.AD600–900).

TIKAL TREASURES

Two superb Maya jade mosaic vessels were buried at Tikal in the 8th century AD. One was laid with the body of King Ah Cacau (*r.* AD682–734) and a rich selection of jade jewellery, shells, pearls and jaguar skins in the grave known as Burial 116 beneath Temple I. The vessel was constructed from jade pieces tacked with jade pins around a cylinder of wood; its lid bore a portrait believed to be of the king himself. A second, similar vessel was laid in the grave now called Burial 196, within the comparatively modest Temple 73 at the south-western corner of Tikal's Great Plaza. Other items in the tomb, including the inscribed spine of a stingray and a named drinking cup, suggest that the tomb was associated with Ah Cacau's successor, Yax Kin (*r.* AD734–46). However, many scholars argue that the tomb is too modest to be that of so great a king as Yax Kin and that it might be that of his far less celebrated son (AD766–68), known to scholars only as the '28th Ruler'.

In the 14th–16th centuries, Mixtec craftsmen were renowned for their mosaic work as well as for their metalwork. One of Moctezuma II's tribute lists reveals that each year Tenochtitlán received ten turquoise-mosaic masks made by skilled artisans in Oaxaca. Tribute of turquoise-mosaic ceremonial shields was also sent from Oaxaca to Tenochtitlán each year.

FACE OF THE GODS

A number of Aztec-Mixtec mosaic-encrusted deity masks have survived. One celebrated example is a mask of the god of darkness and fate Tezcatlipoca. This

Above: A human skull inlaid with turquoise and ivory mosaic was among the gold offerings found in Tomb 7 at Monte Albán.

was fashioned *c*.1400–1521 from a human skull with a mosaic of turquoise and lignite inlaid in bands across the front, and eyes filled with white shell and black discs of iron pyrite. The inner part of the skull was lined with leather and the lower jaw hinged so that it could be moved when the mask was worn by a priest during religious ceremonial.

A turquoise-mosaic mask with serpents encircling the eyes and mosaic representations of feathers on either side of the eyes was made, probably by Mixtec specialists, on a cedar-wood base *c*.1400–1521. The mask was intended for priests of Quetzalcóatl or of Tláloc. The serpent eye-goggles were traditionally a symbol of Tláloc, while the feathers suggested the plumed serpent Quetzalcóatl. The mask, 17.3cm high and 16.7cm wide (6.8in by 6.7in), closely matches the description

given by Bernardino de Sahagún o
turquoise-encrusted mask despatched
a gift by Moctezuma II to Hernán Cor
in 1519. Sahagún reported that the m
would have been worn with a tall plu
of quetzal feathers.

Another Tláloc mask, of *c.*1500
made of turquoise, malachite, mother-o.
pearl, jade and red and white shell laid
on a wooden base. The mask, with the
rain god's elongated snout and tall headdress, was 29cm (11.4in) tall. Scholars
suggest that this sacred Tláloc likeness formed the top of a priest's staff or
ruler's sceptre.

A magnificent Aztec wooden pectoral
covered with turquoise mosaic and shell
inlay represents the double-headed sky
serpent that was one of the symbols of
the feathered serpent god Quetzalcóatl.
The pectoral, made *c.*1400–1521, measures 20.5cm by 43.3cm (8in by 17in)

*Below: On this unique double-headed Aztec
serpent pectoral, turquoise mosaic is attached
to the wooden base using resinous gum.
White and red shell mark the mouth.*

*Above: This Aztec helmet decorated with
mosaic of precious stones was probably
made by a Mixtec artist* c.AD*1400–1520.*

and was worn by priests of the feathered
serpent god Quetzalcóatl or by the ruler
himself – Quetzalcóatl was one of the
patrons of Mesoamerican kingship. Its eye
sockets, now empty, were probably once
inlaid with shell and iron pyrites. Some
scholars suggest that the pectoral was
worn during ritual celebration of the birth
of the Aztecs' tribal god Huitzilopochtli,
whose birthplace Coatepec ('Serpent
Mountain') was represented by the towering bulk of the Templo Mayor in
Tenochtitlán.

In the Aztec era, mosaic craftsmen also
applied their expertise to the making of

elaborate handles for sacrificial knives.
The handle of one splendid knife depicts
an eagle-warrior in a mosaic of turquoise,
shell and malachite laid on wood; the
blade is of chalcedony. The crouching
warrior holds the handle or *ixcuac*
between extended hands, while his face
emerges from the open bird's beak.

MOSAIC ON WOOD
Throughout Mesoamerican history, artisans probably also cut deity and portrait
masks from wood and then added fine
mosaic overlay. Few of these precious
objects have survived. Some, made by
Aztec-Mixtec craftsmen in the 14th–15th
centuries and preserved in desert conditions near Tehuacan in the modern
Mexican state of Puebla, give an indication of the style and quality of the work.

One of the masks found in Puebla
retains all its original turquoise covering,
and part of the onyx inlay in the eyes and
mouth. The find in Tehuacan also contained several once-splendid mosaic
ceremonial shields, some with all the
mosaic decoration now sadly worn off.

CHIPPED AND CARVED STONES:
ELABORATE OFFERINGS

Maya artisans chipped and cut stones, blades and flints with elaborate skill. Obsidian and flint blades and the remarkable decorative chipped flints known by scholars as 'flint eccentrics' were sacred objects, buried in large caches beneath temples and monuments.

Above: An Olmec jade piece was carved in the form of a canoe c.500BC. Sacred markings are visible at the ends.

FLINT ECCENTRICS
Some eccentrics are fashioned to represent human heads in profile. A number of chipped flints found at El Palmar, Quintana Roo, were probably once the heads of ritual staffs. One represents a human figure, with elaborate headdress, protruding lips perhaps intended to suggest a lip plug and a large ornament on

Below: This carved Maya jade pendant, 12cm (5in) across (c.AD850–1250), was found in the Sacred Cenote at Chichén Itzá.

the back. The 6th-century Copán temple that archaeologists call the 'Rosalila structure' contained a large cache of chipped flints, including a number of human profiles. Scholars believe that these may once have been the heads of the 'manikin sceptres' carried by Maya rulers as a sign of authority. Other flints are chipped to represent leaves or the form of the symbols of office called 'knuckle dusters' by scholars and held by notable court attendants in murals and painted scenes on vases.

CARVED FIGURES AND PLAQUES
From the days of the Olmec, Mesoamerican craftsmen cut small pieces of jade and other stones with remarkable delicacy and precision. An Olmec jade bead found in Chiapas was fashioned in the shape of a human head, while another small jade found at Necaxa in modern

WORKING JADE
Technically, Maya jades are jadeite, a very hard mineral with a chemical composition distinct from that of nephrite, the material carved in Chinese jades.

Mesoamericans gathered jadeite from streams and rivers in the form of pebbles, rocks and even sizeable boulders. Skilled craftsmen used a sawing motion with cords to cut and deepen lines in the hard rock, drilling holes with bones or pieces of hardwood, in both cases using water and sand or tiny stones to aid in cutting. The precision, delicacy and artistic flair of their work is astonishing.

Partly because the rock was found in streams, but more significantly because of its typical mottled green to blue-green colouring, jadeite was associated with water and fertility among the Aztecs, and with water and rain deities such as Chalchiúhtlicue and Tláloc.

Above: An Olmec jade figurine, found at La Venta and made c.1200–200BC, is believed to represent the god of the maize plant.

Puebla state was cut in the shape of a crouching tiger. In Maya lands, archaeologists found several delicately carved figurines in jade and other similar stones during excavations at Copán, Chichén Itzá, Uaxactún and other sites.

The small, carved heads were often worn as pendants. One found at Chichén Itzá bore a date in the Maya Long Count equivalent to AD674. Scholars believe that traders brought it to Chichén Itzá from Piedras Negras, its probable place of origin. A cross-legged human figure beautifully fashioned from fuchsite, a stone similar to, but softer than jade, was deposited in an offering at Uaxactún beneath a stairway at the structure archaeologists call Temple A-XVIII. The figurine had linked forearms, rounded belly, rectangular eye sockets originally painted red and a large left ear – its right ear was apparently damaged. Holes drilled in the stone probably gave such ornamental pieces ritual meaning.

At Palenque, a carved jade figurine of the Maya sun god Kinich Ahau was placed within King Pacal's sarcophagus

in the royal tomb beneath the Temple of the Inscriptions. A substantial jade head of the same god, found in a king's tomb at Altun Há in Belize, weighed 4.42kg (9.7lb), making it the largest Maya sculpture in this precious stone.

CELTS, PLAQUES AND PECTORALS

A 4th-century jade celt or implement, probably worn as a belt decoration, was carved with the Maya Long Count date 8.14.3.1.12 (17 September AD320) and with a full-length portrait of Tikal ruler Moon Zero Bird. The celt, known by scholars as the Leyden Plaque, celebrated Moon Zero Bird's 'seating' or accession to the throne of Tikal on the marked date in AD320. It depicts the king, in full ceremonial costume with celts and deity masks hanging from his belt, trampling on a captive depicted in a style similar to that used for images of captives on Tikal monuments. The plaque, one of the oldest dated Maya artefacts, was probably taken from King Moon Zero Bird's tomb at Tikal in ancient times. It was found in 1864 at Puerto de Barrios near the river Motagua in Guatemala.

A blue-green jade plaque, 30cm (12in) tall, was carved by a leading jade-craftsman of the late Classic Period Maya world. It represents a king on a throne, his body facing forwards but head in profile, wearing a serpent headdress from which emerges a figure with an unsettling, grotesque face. Before the throne a second figure kneels in supplication, while

Right: An Olmec adze, or type of axe, from Veracruz is carved with the features of the sacred jaguar.

a speech scroll coming forth from the king's mouth indicates that he is declaring his identity and mighty achievements or else offering prayers to the gods on behalf of his people. The beautifully worked piece, found in Teotihuacán, was perhaps offered as an elite gift or else traded for valuable goods.

A splendid jade pectoral cut by Mixtec craftsmen c.AD1000 bears witness to the continued popularity of this precious stone for ceremonial and sacred objects.

CHAPTER TWELVE

IMAGES, SYMBOLS AND WORDS

Mesoamerican wall paintings are filled with religious and political meaning. Sometimes accompanied by explanatory hieroglyphs, they are sacred statements, often dense with complex symbolism, intended to be 'read' and interpreted: celebrations of the gods' goodness in guaranteeing the fertility of the earth, of the power of the king and his ancestors or of the movements of time as evidenced by astronomical cycles.

Classic Period Maya-painted scenes include the humiliation or sacrifice of a defeated ruler, victory in battle, ceremonies of dynastic consolidation or acts of ritual bloodletting. Images represent action and carry narrative, while glyphs provide meaning and permanence by giving names and by setting the events in time.

In a parallel tradition, beginning in Teotihuacán and also finding expression in murals at Cacaxtla and in Caribbean Yucatán in the 13th–16th centuries, artists created symbolic religious scenes connected with the underworld, fertility and the cycles of the stars rather than dynastic or military events. In this tradition, glyphic writing played a much smaller role – there were no glyphic inscriptions at Teotihuacán. But scholars are convinced that religious symbols such as the five-pointed half-star Venus sign could be 'read' as part of a 'symbolic writing' by residents of Teotihuacán or Cacaxtla.

Left: Solar symbolism. A mural in Cacaxtla shows a man with eagle beak and wings who may represent the sun by day.

THE DATING OF EVENTS

The desire to record and celebrate the patterned movements of sacred time might have been the impetus that drove Mesoamericans to develop their glyphic system of writing. Many historians agree that the complex 260-day and 365-day calendars evolved before the earliest forms of writing, somewhere around the mid-first millennium BC.

CYCLES OF THE CALENDAR

As far as we know, written language was first used to identify people or to mark military triumphs by placing them within the cycles of the calendar.

The carvings often cited as the oldest piece of Mesoamerican writing are the hieroglyphs cut in the threshold of Monument 3 at San José Mogote c.600BC. These record the date 1-Earthquake from the 260-day calendar alongside an image of a prostrate figure.

The symbol is interpreted either as identification of the figure who, like many later Mesoamericans, had taken his name from the date of his birth, or as a

Below: Intricate calendrical hieroglyphs in the Palace at Palenque date the events depicted to AD644, during Pacal's reign.

record of the date of the victory in which he was taken captive or the day on which he was sacrificed.

Scribes or stonemasons using the dates of the 260-day and 365-day calendars could place an event precisely within a hallowed cycle of 52 years that the Maya called the Calendar Round. (This longer period represented the time that elapsed before a day in the 365-day year and a day in the 260-day year coincided: 18,980 days, or 52 solar years of 365 days.) Scribes who wanted to date events within longer spans of time needed a different measure. The dating system used on stelae of Maya cities in the Classic Period, known as the Maya Long Count, identified events both within the Calendar Round and within a span of years beginning on 13 August 3114BC. Historians do not know the significance of this date, but some have suggested that it marked the creation of the current world cycle, according to religious narrative.

The Long Count organized days in units of 20: *kin* (one day), *uinal* (20 days), *tun* (360 days), *katun* (7,200 days) and *baktun* (144,000 days). Given that the system was vigesimal – it used units of 20 rather than units of 10, as in decimal

Above: Stela at Sayil, dated AD800–950. Contemporaries could interpret details of the king's stance, costume and equipment.

calculation – the *tun* count should have been 400 (1 *kin* multiplied by 20 multiplied by 20), but the developers of the Long Count amended this to 360 to make it closer to the length of the solar year.

WRITING NUMBERS

Before creating the Long Count, the Maya must first have developed the concept of zero, so that some units in the count could be marked empty. Scribes and stonemasons indicated numbers by using dots for units up to four and a horizontal bar for the number five. They could write numbers up to 19 (three bars and four dots) using this system. For larger numbers they used the same symbols in horizontal layers, representing

Above: Divinely ordained cycles of time were plotted in calendrical charts. This is a modern reconstruction of an Aztec calendar.

units of 20. The lowest layer showed the number of units (1–19), the second showed the number of 20s, the third showed the number of 400s (that is 20 units of 20) and the fourth the number of 8,000s (20 units of 400).

On stelae, sculptors carved dates in vertical columns to be read from bottom to top, beginning with the largest unit.

The Long Count date on Stela 29 at Tikal used no zeros and was cut with the figures 8.12.14.8.15, meaning 8 *baktuns*, 12 *katuns*, 14 *tuns*, 8 *uinals* and 15 *kins* after the initial date of 13 August 3114BC, giving a date for the stela of 8 July AD292. Almost exactly 400 years later, in the same city, a mason cut the date 9.13.0.0.0. on the stone throne or altar associated with a twin-pyramid group set up by King Ah Cacau. This meant 9 *baktuns*, 13 *katuns*, 0 *tuns*, 0 *unials* and 0 *kins* after 13 August 3114BC: 18 March AD692.

Twin-pyramid groups were raised by Maya rulers in this period to celebrate the ending of *katun*-periods, which explains why the date in the inscription fell so precisely at the end of the 13th *katun*.

Below: Stela 9 at Tikal celebrates King Kan Boar. Both narrow edges of the monument are carved with an inscription that ends with his name glyph and that of Tikal.

DID THE OLMEC USE WRITING?

A tall column of basalt known as the Ambassador's Monument was found at the Olmec holy town of La Venta. Some historians claim this bears the very first evidence of writing in Mesoamerica.

Some time between *c.*1150BC and 500BC, stonemason-scribes carved one end of the column with the image of a walking bearded man (likened by scholars to an ambassador) alongside three signs (which appear to be glyphs) and one of which, a bird's head, might represent his calendar name. Olmec potters and carvers of ceremonial implements in precious jade and serpentine also incised symbols which might be glyphs, but scholars have been unable to break the code of the symbols.

Linguists suggest that Mesoamerican writing probably originated in a lowland environment like that occupied by the Olmec or the people of the central Maya region rather than the highland surroundings of the Zapotecs in Oaxaca. The glyphs represent predominantly lowland creatures such as the crocodile, the jaguar and the monkey.

REFERENCE BOOKS FOR PRIESTS

The chief scribes of Maya cities in the Classic Period were in charge of large libraries, containing a wide range of books written on bark paper or deer skin recording genealogies, arcane ritual and astronomical knowledge, medical information, and compendia of herbs, plants and animals. A mere handful of these books have survived natural decay over several hundred years and the book-burning zeal of the Spanish, who believed the sacred and even secular literature of the Maya and Aztecs to have been tainted by its association with sacrificial religion. Of the four surviving Maya codices, three date from the years before

the Spanish Conquest, with one probably made in the 17th century. The finest of the three pre-Conquest books is the *Dresden Codex* , so named from its location, since 1744, in the Royal Library in Dresden, Germany.

THE DRESDEN CODEX

Consisting of 39 pages of *amate* paper, with writing and images on both sides, the *Dresden Codex* contains almanacs of the 260-day calendar, with details of presiding deities and appropriate rituals, mathematical tables, descriptions of new year ritual celebrations and detailed charts of solar eclipses and cycles of the planets

Above: Gods, days and rituals. The intricately covered almanac pages of the Dresden Codex *are dense with meaning.*

Venus and Mars. Its scribes used very fine calligraphy, particularly in the Venus chart, which has tiny, delicate glyphs as small as 4mm (0.15in) high and 5mm (0.19in) across. According to the scholar Michael Coe, this is the most delicate fine-line work of any world manuscript, and it was written with a quill or with a reed pen rather than with the brush used for other Maya manuscripts.

The book was written by more than one hand. Variant scholarly accounts identify five or even eight distinct calligraphic styles across the 39 pages. In particular, the section on new year ceremonies on pages 25–28 of the manuscript is in a quite distinct and 'broader-brush' style, with glyphs more than three times wider than those in the Venus Table. Some scholars date the *Dresden Codex* to as early as AD1250. Others place its composition in about 1345.

Some scholars believe the book to be a copy of a codex produced during the Classic Period. It was in Vienna in the 16th century, having perhaps been found

---

THE 'WRIGHT CODEX'

The earliest known codex is not a book at all, but a ceramic vase around 25cm (10in) in height, which was discovered in a private American collection in 1991. On each of the four sides of the rectangular vase an artisan incised hieroglyphs and religious figures that appear to be reproductions of pages from a codex. Probably made in Guatemala c. AD600–900, the vase – known to

scholars as the *Wright Codex* – is as much as 700 years older than the most venerable existing Maya codex previously known. Its illustrations represent a man taking part in religious ceremonies, perhaps associated with his way or spirit companion. Scholars have hailed the vase as physical proof of their contention that the Maya used books throughout the Classic Period.

by Hernán Cortés in 1519 on the island of Cozumel. The shrine of moon goddess Ix Chel on Cozumel was an important pilgrimage site, and the book might have been brought there as an offering from an important city.

WORK OF A PROVINCIAL SCRIBE

The oldest surviving Maya codex is the *Grolier Codex* of *c*.AD1230. It is so named because, following its discovery in Mexico in 1965, it was first exhibited at the Grolier Club in New York City in 1971. The codex is a 10-page section of an original, probably twice as long, dealing with the 584-day cycles of the planet Venus. Its screenfold pages are painted on one side only. It contains little information beyond details of the day signs and deities associated with each phase of the planet's cycle and it was written without great care, perhaps in haste or by an unskilled scribe in a provincial setting.

One account of its provenance suggests that it was found in a wooden box with a sacrificial knife and a mosaic mask in a dry cave near Tortuguero, in the modern state of Chiapas. The book might have been used for reference by a provincial priest in the region of Chiapas or Tabasco, some distance from such contemporary centres of ritual religion and learning as Chichén Itzá.

CEREMONIES OF YUCATÁN

The *Paris Codex*, which takes its name from the French capital where it has been stored since 1832 in the Bibliothèque Nationale, probably dates to *c*.1450. According to historian Bruce Love, it might have been produced in the Itzá city of Mayapán. Analysis shows that its 11 double-sided pages were all written by one scribe. It contains information on cycles of *katuns* (periods of 7,200 days) and of *tuns* (360-day years) and on the importance of the larger 13-*katun* period, (containing 93,600 days or roughly 260 years), after which a new cycle of history was expected to begin, probably bringing a repetition of events in the previous 13-*katun* period. It also provides details of the gods presiding over the *katuns*, of the Year Bearers in the ritual calendar and of new year celebrations, as well as almanacs of astronomical cycles.

The fourth Maya codex is the *Madrid Codex*, which was probably produced in the 17th century in Yucatán.

Left: In the Codex Ferjérváry-Mayer, *a maize plant in the form of Chalchiúhtlicue is blessed by Tláloc, lord of the rains.*

Above: The Codex Ferjérváry-Mayer *is one of only nine* tonalamatl *reference books to have survived the Spanish Conquest.*

CALENDAR OF FESTIVALS

In Aztec lands, some fifteen pre-Conquest codices survived destruction in the early 16th century.

One example is the *Codex Cospi*. Written by Mixtec scribes in the period 1350–1500, it takes its name from its later European owner, the Marchese Ferdinando Cospi. Its 13 screenfold pages, made of coated deerskin, are painted on both sides and contain details of the ritual calendar and the Venus cycle as well as of sacrificial rites appropriate to the worship of different deities.

The *Codex Fejérváry-Mayer*, made before 1521 and also named after later European owners, is a *tonalamatl* reference book on the 260-day and 365-day calendars. It contains 22 double-sided pages of animal skin covered in white lime and painted with interpretations of the calendars. It also contains accounts of variously presiding deities, including the nine lords of the night and details of tribute in goods and labour which were required at different times of the year.

RECORD OF A VANISHING CULTURE

The majority of surviving codices were produced after the Spanish Conquest in the 16th century either by Spanish churchmen or by young Mexicans educated in colonial schools.

Many of these were based on eye-witness accounts or were reworkings of pre-Conquest manuscripts. Among the most celebrated and useful to scholars is the *Codex Mendoza*. This was composed

Below: Hieroglyphs are inscribed on the scales of the feathered serpent Quetzalcóatl in this detail from the Madrid Codex.

in the period *c.*1525–41, following a commission by the first Spanish Viceroy, Don Antonio de Mendoza. It is made of European paper and contains 72 pages written by a Mexican scribe in Nahuatl. Translations and interpretations have been added in Spanish by a bilingual author.

The first section starts with the building of Tenochtitlán and then describes the lives of nine Aztec rulers up to and including Moctezuma II, ending with an account of the Conquest. The second part contains an exhaustive tribute list of goods claimed by Moctezuma II from the empire of the Triple Alliance. A third section details customs of daily life among the Aztecs, including birth, marriage, education, state obligations, law and justice.

COPIED MANUSCRIPTS

A number of post-Conquest books appear to be copies of Aztec manuscripts. The *Codex Magliabechiano*, produced *c.*1521–1600 on European paper, includes illustrations of ritual outfits, a *tonalpohualli* sacred calendar and details of the sacred monthly festivals, together with images of funeral and sacrificial rites, autosacrificial bloodletting and ritual cannibalism. The *Codex Telleriano-Remensis*, written and illustrated by Mexican scribes and artists in Tlatelolco in 1555–61, combines an account of sacred festivals, a *tonala-matl* book of days used for divination and a chronicle of Aztec history.

The *Codex Ríos*, written and illustrated by Mexican Dominican friar Pedro de los Ríos *c.*1570–95, contains additions in Italian by another author which explain the ceremonies and religious traditions of the Aztecs. Its first section retells religious narratives and gives accounts of Aztec cosmology, while the second includes a *tonalpohualli* 260-day ritual calendar with a *xiuhpohualli* 365-day solar calendar. The third part details sacrificial and mortuary rites and provides information about calendrical day-signs, while the fourth contains post-Conquest historical accounts.

The style of drawing in the Ríos and the Telleriano-Remensis codices is very similar. Scholars believe they were both copied from a single pre-Conquest source.

ACCOUNTS BY CHURCHMEN

Two other important post-Conquest books classified as codices are the accounts of Aztec history and customs written by Spanish churchmen, the *Codex Durán* and the *Florentine Codex*. The *Codex Durán* is the name applied to the *History of the Indies of New Spain*. This

Above: A page from the Vienna Codex, *also known as the* Codex Vindobonensis. *Walking figures are gods or kings in action.*

('Book of Advice') contains a wealth of Maya religious narrative and astronomical knowledge including detailed accounts of the myth of the ball-playing Hero Twins. It was transcribed from sources written in hieroglyphs into the Roman alphabet by senior members of the Quiché Maya *c.*1554. It was then translated from the Quiché tongue into Spanish by Franciscan friar Francisco Ximenez in the 18th century.

The *Books of Chilam Balam* recorded the history and traditions of groups of Maya from north-western Yucatán and were named after a Maya shaman-seer of the late 14th century. They were written in the Roman alphabet and Yucatec tongue from hieroglyphic sources from the 16th century onwards.

was written in Spanish in 1570–81 by Dominican missionary Diego Durán. Spanish Franciscan friar Bernardino de Sahagún's *General History of the Things of New Spain*, also known as the *Florentine Codex* because of its association with libraries in the Italian city of Firenze (Florence), was written by scribes in Tlateloclo in 1575–77 in Spanish and Nahuatl. Both the Florentine and Durán codices contain detailed accounts of Aztec religious traditions, sacrificial rites, history and daily customs composed by their European authors on the basis of information gathered over many years among local survivors of the Spanish Conquest.

MAYA BOOK OF RITUAL

In Maya lands, one of the four surviving Maya codices is post-Conquest in date. This is the *Madrid Codex*, so called because it is kept in the Museo de América in the Spanish capital. It was long considered to be two separate manuscripts known as the *Troano* and the *Cortesianus*, but in 1880 Frenchman Léon de Rosny established that the two were sections of a single manuscript. The *Madrid Codex* contains 56 leaves, all except the first painted on both sides, making a total of 111 codex pages.

The *Madrid Codex* combines details of Maya beliefs about the four cardinal directions and their presiding deities with information about new year celebrations and detailed almanacs of the 260-day calendar. Like the *Grolier Codex*, it was apparently written in haste or by a lesser scribe, as it contains grammatical errors and careless penmanship. Scholar Michael Coe argues that as the *Madrid Codex* contains a piece of recycled Spanish paper among its bark-paper leaves, it must have been produced after the Spanish Conquest of Yucatán in 1542 that it was perhaps written in Tayasal, which retained its independence until 1697. Martin de Ursua, Spanish Governor of Yucatán, took Tayasal as part of a road-building project to link Guatemala and Yucatán.

Accounts of the history and religious traditions of particular Maya groups based on ancient sources were written down in the post-Conquest period. The *Popol Vuh*

Below: Stone workers hewing and crafting stone from Bernardino de Sahagún's General History of the Things of New Spain, *also known as the* Florentine Codex.

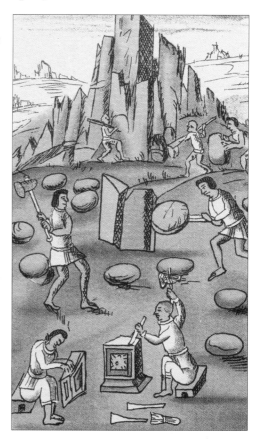

GLYPHS AND IMAGES

Sculptors of Maya stelae embedded their meaning in the image. Viewers were expected to understand the hieroglyphs in conjunction with the image portrayed. The image could be of a king with his defeated rival or of a ruler performing sacred rites of bloodletting. The hieroglyphs placed the event in the cycles of time and named the protagonists.

TYPICAL INSCRIPTIONS

A typical stela inscription began with detailed calendrical information, giving the precise day on which the event celebrated in the image took place. First it named the patron god or goddess of the month, then it gave the Long Count date and transcribed this same date into the

Above: Meaning in action. Divine rulers and gods adopt abstract postures in Mixtec-style codices. This page is from the Codex Zouche-Nuttall, *which may have been a gift from Moctezuma II to Hernan Cortés.*

Above: This cylindrical vase from Uaxactún is marked with a symbol and date that may record the owner's birth-date and name.

260-day ritual calendar, naming the god among the nine lords of the night who controlled that day and the phase of the moon that applied.

After this, an inscription might specify an event or anniversary of ritual significance that applied to the depicted activity, such as a *katun*-ending, then name the king and any other protagonist who had been involved.

Sometimes the glyphs giving the identity of the king would also name his ancestors or his offspring. At other times they would provide evidence of recent heroic activity. For example, various

glyphs identified the king as lord of five, ten or even twenty captives. Following glyphs might give dates for subsequent events such as the king's partaking in ritual bloodletting or sacrificial worship. The second date in an inscription would be given only in the 260-day calendar, since the historical context within the Long Count had already been established.

Above: The Maya used these glyphs to convey historical and dynastic information. From top left – 'was born'; 'acceded to throne'; 'event of taking captive'; 'taker of captives'; 'taken captive'; 'he'; 'she'; 'wife'; 'ruler's number in dynastic line'; 'king or queen died'.

NAMING

Some scholars liken the glyphs naming kings and dating their stelae to the name tags that the Maya inscribed on sacred and everyday items such as incised bones, ear ornaments and drinking vessels.

The practice of name-tagging was discovered by scholar Peter Mathews in 1979 when studying an ear flare from Altun Há, Belize. The ornament was inscribed with the phrase *u tup* ('this man's ear flare'), together with the name of the owner, who was a member of the royal family. Name tags were subsequently identified on incised bones from the tomb of King Ah Cacau in Tikal, and on plates, dishes and vases.

Scholar Michael Coe found a repeating pattern of hieroglyphs on elaborately decorated polychrome vases of the late Classic Period. This pattern, named the Primary Standard Sequence, amounted to a formula for naming and dating vases.

Generally painted around the outer rim of the vase or bowl or sometimes placed in a vertical column, it included up to 22 glyphs, always in the same order, but often with some missing and sometimes with as few as three glyphs. The sequence begins with several initial glyphs, sometimes including the head of the god Pawahtún, a four-fold god of the directions. This is thought to have functioned as a dedication of the vessel. Then came glyphs indicating whether the pot was carved or painted and identifying its shape, its use (perhaps for drinking or serving cacao), its owner and the artist who produced it. Sometimes the sequence also includes a date in the Calendar Round, which unusually referred to the date the object was made rather than the date on which the depicted events took place.

WORDS IN CODICES

In codices and in murals – just as in the inscriptions on stelae, stone thrones, zoomorphs and ceramics – words functioned to identify names and provide calendrical information, while images represented the activity that was being celebrated. In such pre-Conquest Mixtec books as the *Codex Zouche-Nuttall* or the *Codex Cospi*, illustrations were not designed primarily for aesthetic effect but to convey meaning.

Glyphs generally identified three key facts: dates, places and names. The human figures took a limited number of stylized postures, usually walking, standing or seated in profile and deity figures were usually shown in a flat, full frontal position. There was no attempt to achieve the naturalistic effects found in Classic Period Maya murals, stucco-work and polychrome vases and in Postclassic statuary.

Below: The highly prized role of the scribe could be taken by royal or noble women as well as by top-ranking men. This Maya ceramic shows a female scribe at work.

THE AGE OF BOOKS

In the Postclassic Period, the artistic style of Mesoamerica derived largely from that of codices. Ceramic decorations, mural images, representations on monumental state sculpture and decorative symbols in jewellery are all similar to illustrations in the codices. Because the largest number of surviving codices were written and painted by Mixtec scribes working near the city of Puebla, scholars call this the 'Mixteca-Puebla style'.

The style was not regional but far-reaching and even international. In Tenochtitlán, images carved on state monuments resembled pages from a codex. In Oaxaca, delicate jewellery figures and fine murals at Mitla had the 'codex style'. On the Caribbean seaboard at sites such as Tulum in eastern Yucatán and Santa Rita Corozal in northern Belize, 15th-century murals closely mirrored the appearance of Mixtec codices.

SACRED SYMBOLS:
OLMEC AND TEOTUHUACÁNO MURALS AND FRESCOES

Finds of superb murals in the sacred city of Teotihuacán, in Maya cities such as Bonampak and in highland Mexican settlements such as Cacaxtla provide evidence of a highly developed Mesomerican wall-painting art.

TRADITION OF WALL-PAINTING
The roots of this tradition date all the way back to the Olmec period, when artists decorated sacred caves with distinctive ritual imagery. In caves in the southern Sierra Madre mountains, modern Guerrero province, historians have found cave paintings representing kings, a stone throne, sacred serpents and a fierce jaguar.

The oldest of these paintings are probably those at Juxtlahuaca and Cacahuaziziqui, which date to *c*.1000–700BC. One of the images at Juxtlahuaca represents two men, one seated and the second standing in elaborate costume that includes a hooped tunic-skirt, jaguar skin and black cloak, together with a feather helmet. The standing figure holds a

Below: Were mural painters in Teotihuacán using a language of nature symbols? This strange bird adorned a residential complex.

Above: Sacred animals in the Jaguar Palace (c.AD400) in Teotihuacán were intended to bring bounty to the city's inhabitants.

serpent-like object in his left hand, while his right controls a ritual implement – perhaps a sceptre or a sacred tool like the 'knuckle-duster' seen in later Maya paintings. Other Juxtlahuaca paintings represent a jaguar with black outline and

a red-bodied serpent with fiery eyebrow and the distinctively Olmec cross (like the cross of Saint Andrew) on its face. Two figures painted at Cacahuaziziqui appear to have glyphs close to their mouths, as if representing speech.

At Oxtotitlán, near the town of Acatlán, artists created an intriguing set of cave paintings *c*.800–500BC. A large image of a ruler seated on a throne dominates the sacred cave. He wears an owl mask and feathered cape, together with a skirt bearing the Olmec claw-wing symbol. His left hand reaches vertically up, his right hand reaches down diagonally, while his left leg is drawn up and his right leg falls down before him. His throne represents a monster mask with open jaws.

A second image depicts a man, painted in black outline with outstretched right arm, standing behind and possibly performing a sexual act with a fierce-faced jaguar. A third mural at Oxtotitlán shows a four-petalled flower with a human face at the centre. This is suggestive of later cosmological images that represent the universe as a flower with a petal to north, south, east and west and the tree of life in the centre.

TEOTIHUACÁN MURALS

Among the people of Teotihuacán were skilled potters, makers of haunting masks and magnificent monumental architects. However, mural painting was without doubt the art in which they most excelled.

Teotihuacános created wall paintings from c.AD300 onwards, first decorating small structures lining the Street of the Dead. After c.AD500 they began to paint murals in the city's many apartment compounds and in the palace areas close to the Pyramid of the Moon and the Pyramid of the Sun.

Their style was almost abstract. They painted few narrative scenes such as battle victories or rites of sacrifice and no naturalistic portraiture, but used a wealth of stylized images and motifs taken from nature, such as shells, stars, coyotes, and jaguars. In recent years, scholars have argued that Teotihuacáno artists used these religiously charged signs as a form of symbolic written communication.

The artists first prepared the walls by applying a layer of clay, later adding a coat of lime mixed with sand and quartz. Once the surface was ready, the painters set to work, first applying a red background colour then drawing designs in black and a darker red. They filled in additional colours of blue, green and yellow as the last stage in the process.

THE GREAT GODDESS

Many murals contain images of the Teotihuacános' supreme deity, dubbed the Great Goddess by art historian Esther Pasztory. Like many Mesoamerican divinities, the goddess had dual aspects as both a beneficent giver of life and as an awe-inspiring force of evil. She was recognizable from her red and yellow zigzag band, her nose bar and her bird headdress. The murals of the Tepantitla apartment building show the goddess in her lifegiving aspect in a river setting, with water creatures and abundant growths of flowers. In the Tetitla building, meanwhile, she is seen in her evil aspect, with fangs and bestial claws.

The goddess clearly possessed fertility aspects, but otherwise had little connection to other female deities of Mesoamerica – her cult was apparently unique to Teotihuacán. Other gods represented in the Teotihuacán murals have closer links to those of the wider Mesoamerican pantheon. One is the storm god, with strong links to lightning and thunder and to the god the Aztecs called Tláloc. Another is the feathered serpent god whom the Aztecs called Quetzalcóatl. A third, an aged god represented as a crouching man supporting a brazier on his skull, was later known to the Aztecs as Huehuetéotl.

THE TECHINANTITLA COMPOUND

These paintings, produced c.AD600–750, are unusual for Teotihuacán in representing scenes of military life. They include a long procession of figures wearing a tasselled headdress associated with warriors and positions of power. Above and below the figures, a border consists of footprints. Eight of the marching warriors have glyphs painted by them, probably representing their names. Another section represented trees.

Below: Water falls from the hands of an early version of the pan-Mesoamerican rain god in a mural from Teotihuacán.

SCENES OF RELIGIOUS LIFE

Murals were painted at Cholula in the Puebla region of Mexico c.AD100–400, when the settlement was pre-eminent in its area and had close ties to both Teotihuacán and Monte Albán in Oaxaca. The earliest images are similar to some Teotihuacán wall paintings. They represent stylized insects with very large heads painted in red and yellow against black and other backgrounds.

THE DRINKERS

A more significant Cholula mural is one known to scholars as 'The Drinkers' and apparently representing scenes of ritual intoxication. Some 60m (200ft) across, the painting depicts a succession of humans – all wearing loincloths and some with headdresses or masks of fabulous creatures – together with several large drinking jars.

The figures are painted a light-orange flesh colour against a red background and rest on a blue-green band, beneath which are decorative elements including rhombuses. Some of the figures lift the vases up as if to pour out libations for nobles at a banquet, others hold drinking bowls. The drinking was probably of *pulque* (maguey cactus liquor) as part of a religious ritual. The figures are in loose, relaxed positions, probably because of the

Below: Staple food. In the Red Temple at Cacaxtla the muralist painted a maize plant that gives issue to human heads.

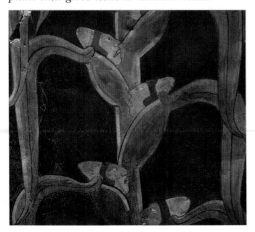

effects of the *pulque*, while their masks might be intended to represent the animal spirit companions that a shaman or spiritual adventurer would expect to meet during spirit voyages facilitated by *pulque* or other psychotropic substances. The mural was painted on the west-facing façade of a mortuary pyramid in which archaeologists found the rich burial of a man with Maya facial features.

Another Cholula mural, in a structure known to scholars as Building 2, represented shells and five-pointed stars, imagery found both at Teotihuacán and Cacaxtla and thought to be associated with fertility and the planet Venus.

A SYMBOLIC BATTLE?

A magnificent series of murals were painted in the hilltop settlement of Cacaxtla, above the Tlaxcala valley, c.AD655–835. These remarkable pictures, some of the finest in Mesoamerica, were discovered by looters in October 1975.

Overlooking the ceremonial area, the elongated structure known as Building B contains brightly coloured murals of battles or perhaps ritualized conflicts between two groups of warriors, who are clearly identified by their battledress. Some scholars focus on the geographical and cultural affiliations of the two groups. They identify the first group as Mexicanized Maya, who exhibit the influence of Teotihuacán in their battledress and equipment and who probably come from the Mexican Gulf Coast. They identify the second group as warriors from Maya lands farther east.

Other historians suggest that the conflict might be symbolic. The Mexicanized warriors sport equipment with jaguar symbolism while the central Maya wear nothing except bird helmets and body ornaments. The clash might be between night (represented by the jaguar, fearsome night predator and the form taken by the sun when it journeyed through the underworld during the hours of darkness) and

Above: At Cacaxtla drops of rain fall from a serpent sceptre wielded by a jaguar man. He is thought to represent the moon.

day (represented by the birds of the air). The images exhibit great naturalistic skill and painstaking attention to detail in their depiction of headdress and costume.

GODS OF THE SKY

Murals with complex religious symbolism adorn Building A at Cacaxtla, which is reached via a short stairway from Building B. These images consist of four large standing figures. On the south doorjamb of the entrance looms a black-skinned man, apparently dancing, who holds a conch shell from which a head emerges bedecked in jewels. On the south wall, another black-skinned man in eagle costume stands on a blue-green feathered serpent, holding a bright blue-green serpent sceptre from which flames emerge. On the north doorjamb of the entrance is a man with jaguar paws and skin, his head emerging from the open jaws of the jaguar. He wears a serpent headdress and holds a serpent in his left hand while, using his right arm, he up-ends a large jar decorated with the symbols of the rain god from which life-giving blue-green waters fall. From his belly emerges a maize or water-lily plant, bearing flowers.

On the north wall of the building another jaguar man holds a brilliant blue-green rain sceptre from which waters fall on to the body of a creature that is both jaguar and serpent. The scholar Maria Teresa Uriarte has identified these complex figures as images of the night sun (or moon) on the north wall and the sun by day on the south wall, with images of the rain god Tláloc/Chac on the north door-jamb and of Pahuantún or god N, a deity with links to the four directions and the underworld, on the south doorjamb. The main north and south wall images might represent the Hero Twins of Maya religious narrative as moon and sun, for in some accounts the twins rose to become these celestial bodies.

A third richly coloured mural adorns the structure at Cacaxtla dubbed the Temple of Venus by scholars. Artists painted a pair of blue-skinned figures, one to each side of the doorway. One badly damaged mural represents a female figure, with one breast visible, and the wall disintegrated where the other breast and her head would be. The other depicts a standing male with black hair, large protruding eye and arms upraised. Both wear jaguar-skin skirts beneath large, five-pointed half-star symbols of the planet Venus that hang from their waists. Both have bare feet, with white cloths tied around their ankles. One of the man's hands is not visible due to wall damage, but the other is in the shape of a jaguar's paw and in it he holds a five-pointed half-star. Behind him a scorpion's tail is visible and his arms are segmented like the tail. The images represent dual aspects of the planet Venus. Maria Teresa Uriarte suggests they might celebrate an astro-

nomical conjunction between the planet Venus and the scorpion constellation. The visible part of the Venus cycle had associations with the rainy season, so the planet and its deity therefore had links to water and fertility.

GOD OF THE UNDERWORLD

Another remarkable set of murals adorned the building known as the Red Temple at Cacaxtla. The muralists decorated the east and west walls of the temple, either side of a staircase. On the east wall they painted a feathered serpent rising behind a human figure who stands

Above: The opposing Cacaxtla image depicts the sun – an eagle man holding a fire-serpent and standing on an earth-serpent.

against a terracotta background over a bundle that might represent the travelling pack of a merchant, while before him grow a cocoa plant and blue-green maize plants that give issue to human heads. Among the plants is a toad with a blue-green body. The mural's border consists of serpentine figures and watery images in turquoise and yellow. Scholars suggest that the figure might be god L or the Old Black God, lord of the Maya underworld.

THE BONAMPAK MURALS:
A PRINCE IN LINE

The famous murals in the Maya city of Bonampak, on the River Lacanjá in the Chiapas region, were painted in the building now known as Temple 1 in the late 8th century AD. They celebrated the designation of the royal heir to King Chan Muan, a prolonged ritual that took place over 20 months from 14 December AD790 to 6 August AD792. Bonampak was greatly influenced by the larger centre of Yaxchilán, 30km (18 miles) to the north. The two centres may have been connected by a *sacbé* (sacred causeway) that archaeologists have discovered departing Bonampak and heading north. Alongside King Chan Muan and his heir, Yaxchilán royals are depicted taking part in the ceremonies as allies or overlords.

The murals adorn three rooms in the temple. They are painted on both the walls and the inner roof, with a band of

Below: A detail from the celebration scenes depicts senior figures from the court of King Chan Muan in intimate conversation.

Above: On the lower north wall of the first room, musicians and elaborately dressed gods or priests celebrate the heir's accession.

hieroglyphs running between them. The hieroglyph section contains Long Count dates giving precise dates for the events depicted. The artists probably intended the images to be viewed from the benches that are laid out on the floors of these rooms.

PRESENTATION OF THE HEIR
In the first room, the painting on the vault of the west wall depicts the young royal heir being presented to 14 white-robed noblemen of the court while his royal father and mother look on approvingly from a wide throne-stone. The vault of the north wall shows the king wearing a vast feather headdress, a jade pectoral and ear plugs. He is accompanied by two splendidly attired lords, apparently preparing for a ritual held, according to the hieroglyphic inscription, 336 days later than the initial presentation of the prince. The lower walls appear to depict this celebration, showing a band of musicians playing a wooden drum, trumpets, flutes, turtle shells and rattles, as well as a procession of masked and elaborately costumed members of the court, or perhaps priestly figures. One figure

appears to have crayfish pincers in place of arms. One wears the costume of the maize god, while a third is robed to represent a crocodile. Two members wear flowers in their headdresses.

VICTIMS FOR SACRIFICE
The second room depicts a battle fought to secure prisoners for ritual sacrifice, an important part of the heir-designation ceremony. The south, west and east walls are covered with battle scenes that vividly depict the chaos and carnage of conflict, with elaborately dressed soldiers fighting hand-to-hand, grabbing one another by the hair and thrusting spears forward threateningly. King Chan Muan is shown holding a jaguar-skin spear and a prisoner by the hair while standing alongside an allied ruler that scholars identify as King Shield Jaguar II of Yaxchilán. Both kings sport magnificent headdresses, wear jaguar-skin clothing and are protected from possible injury by a cadre of proud warriors. On the vaults above these walls,

Above: A battle scene from the second room shows fierce soldiers with extravagant headdresses facing down the enemy.

images represent the astronomical alignments that were found to be propitious for this great battle. On the southern vault, a turtle with three stars on its shell stands for the constellation of Orion. Other images represent different stars and the planet Venus.

The north wall of the second room depicts King Chan Muan presiding over the painful torture of captives destined for sacrifice to sanctify the heir-designation. One prisoner has already been killed and decapitated; his head lies on one of the platform-steps. Several nobles and two royal ladies flank the king at the top of the steps, standing beneath glyphs of their names. One of the women is Queen Green Rabbit from Yaxchilán. At the foot of the steps, warriors stand guard over the prisoners.

SACRED BLOODLETTING

Unfortunately, the murals of the third room have sustained quite serious damage, but enough is visible to reveal that they represent further royal scenes in the heir-designation ritual. In one painting, king and nobles in elaborate costume stand on a pyramid while musicians and dancers perform sacred rites in the plaza below them. A second painting depicts the royal family on a throne or dais within the palace performing autosacrificial

bloodletting as a way of seeking the gods' blessing on the prince of Bonampak. The king cuts his tongue with a spiked cord and collects the blood on bark paper. He will later burn the paper, both as an offering and as a way of summoning the Vision Serpent, along whose coils he might travel to encounter his way spirit companion, great royal ancestors or even the god and goddesses themselves.

The murals at Bonampak are valued for the insight they give, through their colourful and naturalistic representations of court ritual, into royal and religious life in Maya cities of the late Classic Period. Although they are an unusually complete survival, they are typical of the wall decoration used in many Maya palaces, religious and ceremonial structures. It was common practice to commemorate religious, dynastic and military events through wall painting.

Below: On the north side of the second room, King Chan Muan takes centre stage, wearing jaguar skin and holding a spear. At his feet prisoners of war endure torture at the hands of their captors.

WALL PAINTINGS AND MURALS

Fragments of murals survive at many Maya sites. At Tikal, small parts of murals dating to the 4th century AD have been found in the buildings architects call Group 6C-XVI, just to the south of the Lost World complex. One represents a human figure alongside a black circle marked with a glyph that has underworld associations. A second mural, known as 'The Mural of the Gamers', depicts eight human figures in two groups of four, walking in profile. Those whose heads are undamaged wear ribbon headdresses. Some authorities suggest that the figures in both murals are ball players.

At Xelhá near the coast of Quintana Roo, a mural in the substructure of the buildings called Group B depicts flying parrots and macaws. These images date to *c.*AD400–600. At Uaxactún, artists painted a mural *c.*AD450–550 to adorn a

Above: Mayapán's rulers commissioned murals in order to add to their city's status as it rose to eclipse Chichén Itzá.

room in the building called structure B-XIII. They depict scenes of noble life, showing groups of standing figures with fine headdresses and adornment. One group is seated within a building. Associated hierogylphs probably provide dates or names.

At Palenque, in House E of the royal palace, mural images of four-petalled flowers and geometric decorative designs have survived, along with a profile head of a noble or king wearing a splendid headdress containing a fish. These date from the 7th century AD.

At Yaxchilán only a single figure in profile and a few patches of colour remain of wall-paintings that once covered the interior of Temple 40, built during the reign of King Bird Jaguar (*r.* AD752–68).

MAYA TOMB PAINTINGS

From an early period the Maya painted the walls of tombs. A tomb dated to *c.*50BC in the North Acropolis at Tikal (Burial 166) has a mural with a red background and black outlines depicting standing figures with feather headdresses and deity masks, probably representing divine ancestors of the king or nobleman buried in the tomb. These are identified as the most venerable painted images yet discovered in Maya lands.

Several other Tikal tombs had paintings and glyphic inscriptions: Burial 48 is dated to AD457. Near-contemporary images in Tomb 1 at Río Azul in Guatemala, represent deity masks, serpents and watery features, and they can be dated to AD417 by a Long Count date in the accompanying inscription. At the same site, Tomb 19 (*c.*450–550) bears paintings said to represent the Jester god linked to the ruler's glyph 'ahaw'.

Below: This damaged mural from Tulum appears to be an image of the rain god, worshipped as Chac by the Maya.

HIGHLAND MEXICAN STYLE

At Chichén Itzá, fragments of mural were found on rubble pieces that once formed the inner walls of the Temple of the Warriors. They have been reconstructed to form two murals, one representing a military attack on a town and the capture of prisoners, the other depicting life in a coastal village. These are painted in a quite different style to the fluid, expressive naturalism of Maya mural painting that reached its apogée at Bonampak; instead, they are flat, two-dimensional and almost schematic. They apparently form part of the wave of Mexicanized culture and artefacts also represented by the appearance at Chichén Itzá of sacred furniture such as *chacmool* sacrificial figures and skull racks, of serpent-columns on buildings and of atlante carved warriors. The same schematic style, though

Below: Murals at Tulum and other cities of Postclassic Yucatán apparently return to the style and subjects of Teotihuacán art.

with rather more movement, is apparent in murals of fighting soldiers painted within the Temple of the Jaguars.

Wall paintings were also commissioned by the rulers of the city of Mayapán, which succeeded Chichén Itzá as the pre-eminent city of northern Yucatán after *c.*1250. Fine paintings discovered in 1997 in the buildings known as Structure Q160 and Structure Q80 exhibit a style reminiscent of the codex art of contemporary Maya and especially Mixtec painter-scribes. In Structure Q80, serpents are combined with geometric designs while anthropomorphic figures adorn Structure Q160.

INFLUENCE OF BOOKMAKERS

Murals at many sites on the Caribbean coast of Yucatán – including Tulum, Xelhá, Cobá, Rancho Ina and Tancah – exhibit this same codex-influenced style in the years after *c.*1250. They are different from earlier Maya murals in subject matter as well as in style. They do not represent scenes of military glory, dynastic succession and ritual sacrifice,

Above: War machine. In a mural from the Temple of the Jaguars, Chichén Itzá, the city's rampaging army engulfs a village.

but focus instead on themes of agriculture and the fertility of the earth, rebirth and astronomic cycles in an apparent return to the mural subjects of Teotihuacán style.

At Tancah, for example, within the building called Structure 12, a mural represents seven deities performing an agricultural rite in the company of the young maize god, who wears an ear of corn as a headdress. In Structure 1 at Cobá, a mural of the Postclassic Period shows a similar agricultural rite performed by deities included the maize god, the rain god Chac and the creator god Itzamná. Murals at Tulum adorn the Temple of the Frescoes and the Temple of the Diving God. In the latter, another scene of agricultural ritual represents two pairs of gods separated by the linked bodies of serpents. The mural is divided into the three cosmic levels of heavens, terrestrial plain and underworld.

SYMBOLISM AND NATURALISM

The artists of Teotihuacán produced representations in murals, pottery, masks and figurines that exhibited little interest in naturalism and far more in religious symbolism. Humans were anonymous members of a mass group: in masks, human features were often reduced almost to geometric shapes or hidden behind nose bars. Murals tended to represent people in profile, often in procession, moving towards a goddess or god figure who was shown full frontal. Many scenes were of animals, plants and deities, often involved in rites associated with fertility. These images did not glorify the military and political achievements of rulers, apparently focusing instead on deities and religious symbols.

In contrast, many Maya muralists, stucco sculptors and ceramicists of the Classic Period (AD250–900) excelled in naturalistic representations of the human face and body. At Bonampak, for example, the suffering of prostrate prisoners of war was depicted with deft and feeling naturalism in Room 2 of Temple 1. Images of court life on polychrome vases

and stucco carvings of King Pacal or King Chan Bahlum at Palenque are accurate and fluid representations of human expressions and gestures. (This is distinct from the much more stylized representations of royal figures produced by stonemasons on stelae and stone thrones.)

Images in Maya murals, ceramics and stucco focused on the beauty of the human body and face and of ceremonial attire such as the headdresses and costumes that also glorified the gods through sacred symbolism. Artists celebrated an ideal of human beauty in the stucco heads of King Pacal at Palenque and in the young maize god at Copán; in images of kings and courtiers on polychrome vases and in murals. This ideal consisted of a serene face with wide eyes, the bridge of the nose built up to join the forehead, full lips and smooth cheeks.

ROYAL PORTRAIT CONVENTIONS

Maya muralists and other artists generally stayed within established conventions of representation. They usually showed royal figures as exemplars of ideal beauty, not prone to ageing, in elegant costume

Above: Stone beauty. Maya sculpture probably reached its apogée in work such as this elegant head found at Copán.

and standing formally or occupying a regal seat. Artists had more leeway when it came to scenes of battle or those involving prisoners. The muralists at Bonampak took full advantage in representing an intense battle and subsequent presentation of prisoners to King Chan Muan in Room 2 of Temple 1. They showed soldiers and prisoners in many lifelike postures and expressions, prone and sitting, striding and thrusting, grimacing with pain and rolling their heads as if about to lose consciousness.

THE SHAPE OF A KING
Artists at Palenque made a limited departure from the tradition of idealizing the physical appearance of the ruling family. Doubtless on royal orders, they appear to have emphasized physical abnormalities peculiar to the ruling dynasty of King

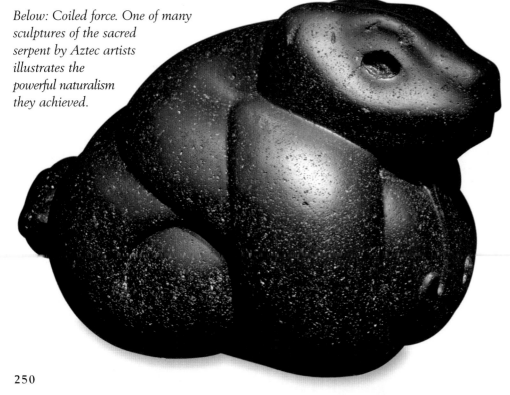

Below: Coiled force. One of many sculptures of the sacred serpent by Aztec artists illustrates the powerful naturalism they achieved.

Pacal. These included an outsized head and jaw, signs of the pituitary disorder known as acromegaly, seen in images of Pacal's mother Lady Zac-Kuk. Depictions of Pacal's son, Chan-Bahlum, on the Temple of the Inscriptions show him with six fingers on the left hand and six toes on both feet. One of Pacal's uncles had a club foot, and scholars believe that Pacal himself might have inherited this. In images Pacal's foot was stylized as a serpent, and from the early 10th century AD, a god with serpent feet, Bolon Dz'Acab, became established as patron of kings. King Chan Bahlum appears to have encouraged his sculptors and artists to pursue a more realistic style in portraiture, as evidenced by a portrait head of the king in Temple XIV which depicts him with natural features at odds with the Maya ideal.

These dual strands of Maya naturalism and Teotihuacáno symbolic art had a joint flowering in the remarkable murals of Cacaxtla, in Tlaxcala, which were painted in the 7th–9th centuries AD. Artists combined concern with

representing the human body in action (for example, in the Mural of the Battle in Building B) with a commitment to near-abstract scenes dense with religious symbolism (such as the murals possibly representing the sun and moon in Building A).

Artists of the Aztec era enthusiastically pursued naturalism in some statuary, but in painted work on vases and in codices followed the tradition of Teotihuacán.

Above: The artists who painted this mural in Tomb 105 at Monte Albán used symbolism reminiscent of Teotihuacán.

The codex art of the Mixtecs and Aztecs was reminiscent of Teotihuacáno murals in representing humans in profile in flat, almost schematic scenes. It differed in that it was often focused on the recording of dynastic history and the achievements of rulers, while Teotihuacáno art was intent on celebrating fertility through religious symbols.

The murals of cities such as Tulum, Xelhá and Cobá on or near the Caribbean coast of Yucatán in the 13–16th centuries returned to the religious-artistic themes of the Teotihuacános. It used a decorative style that was close to that of the Mixtec codices to celebrate fertility and astronomic themes using images of deities and religious symbols.

Left: The evocative impact of Teotihuacáno art is evident in this jade mask, probably intended for funerary use.

INDEX

administration 92–3, 154–6
afterlife 27
Ah Cacau, King 49, 50, 137, 166, 167, 228, 235
Ah Dzun Xiu 133
Ahuilzapán 26
Ahuítzotl 8, 56
Ake 13
Alta Verapaz 30
Altar de Sacrificios 29
aqueducts 8
archaeology 12–15, 189
architecture
  apartments 46, 48, 63
  building methods 140–1, 160, 179
  decoration 144–5, 148, 153, 179, 210–11
  houses 98–9, 140, 141
  orientation 37, 42, 43, 52, 60, 146, 160
  overbuilding 14, 46
  styles 14, 142–3, 145, 159, 175
art/artists 137, 191, 250–1
artisans 222
astrology 103
astronomy 9, 37, 45, 94, 100, 120
autosacrifice 170, 183, 209, 213, 247
Aztecs 7
  ceremonies 82, 85, 112, 126, 128–9
  Conquest 9, 11, 178
  cosmology 37, 213
  creation myths 8, 34–6
  empire 56–7, 74, 82, 92, 133
  mythology 27, 31
  origins 54–5, 56, 132
  respect for past 8, 11, 132–3, 159
  and Toltecs 52

ball game
  courts 53, 77, 150–1
  rules 110, 151
  sacrifice 118, 119, 171

symbolism 110, 118–19, 150
basalt 60, 202
baskets 86, 195
bats 33
bells 224
Bird Jaguar 170, 171
birds 32–3, 85, 87
Black Tezcatlipoca 35
Bonampak ('Painted Walls') 14, 15, 29, 246–7, 250
books see codices
Books of Chilam Balam 239
burials 134–5, 188
  masks 227
  reusing graves 159
  sacrificial 178
  tombs 44, 46, 248

cacao 35, 81, 83, 107
Cacaxtla 50, 176, 244–5
Cakchiquels 57
Calakmul 45, 49, 206
Calendar Round 234, 241
calendars 9, 103, 147, 163, 204–5, 234, 238
cannibalism 8, 106
canoes 31, 66
Caracol 48–9
Caribbean 29, 49, 65, 66
Catherwood, Frederick 11, 13
causeways 14, 45, 76–7, 167, 180
caves 40, 44, 123, 146

ceiba tree 30–1, 37, 68, 91
cenotes 29, 175, 196, 225
ceremonial centres
  buildings 26–7, 45, 52, 60, 160, 161, 172
  rituals 7, 117, 126
Cerro Gordo 27
Cerros 66
Chac 29, 36, 144, 148
chacmools 6, 7, 8, 9, 39, 127, 147, 209, 212, 213
Chalcatzingo 60–1, 204
Chalchihuites 65, 147, 204
Chalchiúhtlicue 8, 9, 29, 35, 100, 101, 102, 103, 198
Chan Maun, King 246, 247
Chan-Bahlum, King 169, 211, 251
change 9
Chichén Itzá 9, 11, 13–15, 39, 50, 52–3, 57, 66, 150
  architecture 145, 175
  fall of 55, 145
Chichimecs ('Sons of the Dog') 52, 56
childbirth 102–3
children 104–5
chinampa fields 28, 35, 80
Cholula 52, 70, 71, 244
cities 44–5, 159–81
Citlaltépetl 25, 26
climate 24–5
clothes 86
  Aztecs 109, 196
  festival 197
  Maya 108–9, 196
  nobility 68
  warriors 73, 90, 91, 197
  women 108–9
Coapexco 43, 60
Coatépetl 19
Coatlícue 12, 27
Cobá 30, 76
Cocoms 55, 133
codices 16, 88–9, 236–9, 241
  Codex Becker 101
  Codex Borbonicus 89, 111, 119
  Codex Cospi 237, 241

Codex Durán 111, 113, 131, 238, 239
Codex Fejérváry-Mayer 237
Codex Ixtlilxochitl 197
Codex Magliabechiano 130, 238
Codex Mendoza 69, 74–5, 104–5, 126, 156, 197, 238
Codex Rios 238
Codex Telleriano-Remensis 238
Codex Vaticanus 29, 114
Codex Zouche-Nuttall 91, 96–7, 241
Dresden Codex 236
Florentine Codex 72, 80, 84, 124, 125, 198, 238–9
Grolier Codex 237, 239
Madrid Codex 87, 215, 237, 239
Paris Codex 237
Selden Codex 56
Wright Codex 236
Columbus, Christopher 6
Copán 16, 29, 37, 47, 49, 93
  architecture 172–3
Cortés, Hernán 6, 69, 77, 113, 119, 163, 178
  Aztecs 9, 72, 82, 157, 224
  gifts 75, 217, 229
cotton 86, 183, 196
Coyolxauhqui 15, 130, 181
Coyotlinahual 198
crafts 42, 43, 44, 61, 86–7
creation myths 34, 35, 36, 124, 126
Cuicuilco 26, 27, 43, 44
Culhuacán 27, 54, 55
currency 73

dancing 112, 113, 117, 127
Day of the Dead 134
Díaz, Bernal 72, 82
diet 35, 40–1, 42, 84–5, 98,
    106–7
diplomacy 48
disease 57
divination 9, 94, 95, 119,
    122, 125, 129, 238
doctors 90–1, 124, 125
dogs 41, 71, 84–5
domestic animals 84, 98, 107
Dos Pilas 49, 51
drought 24–5
duality 9, 36
dyes 196

eagle warriors 32, 90
Edzná 139
Ek Chuah 83
El Chayal 46
El Mirador 44, 45, 46
El Petén 24, 25, 27, 55
El Tajín 50, 119, 150
    architecture 163

famine 25
farming 24,25, 31, 34–5,
    40, 42, 80–1
fatalism 9
feathers 64, 72–3, 86, 87,
    178, 198–9
festivals 113, 128–9, 134
fish 41, 84
flint 40, 48, 230
floods 25
forests 30–1
forts 176–7

games/gambling 110–11
gardens 81, 82–3, 98, 154
gifts 75, 217, 229
gods/goddesses 9, 23, 93
    animal form 32, 36, 122,
        123, 213
    birth 19, 27
    hunting 84, 85
    weather 25
gold 219–23
grave offerings 43, 44, 47,
    66, 135, 188, 218, 228
    reuse 8, 11, 132–3, 159
Great Goddess 243
Guatemala 6, 9, 13, 27
Gucumatz 34, 36, 169
Gulf of Mexico 6, 25

hairstyles 109
hallucinogens 94, 184–5,
    186, 187
healing 124–5
herbal medicine 83, 90–1,
    125
Hero Twins 32, 33, 37, 119
    , 150, 239
hieroglyphs 42, 173, 234
Huastecs 212
Huehuetéotl 111, 212
Huitzilopochtli 15, 19, 26,
    27, 33, 37, 43, 130, 146
human sacrifice 117, 119,
    126–7
    Aztecs 7, 8, 68, 85,
        106, 131
    Maya 9, 91, 94, 130–1
hunter-gatherers 34, 40
hunting 30, 32, 40, 41,
    84–5, 107
Huracán 25, 34, 36, 169
hurricanes 25, 57
hygiene 7, 180

incense 127
irrigation 31, 35, 46, 62,
    80, 81, 164
Isla Cerritos 66
Isle of Cozumel 13, 71, 237
Itzá 50, 53, 76

Itzcóatl 57
Ix Chel 67, 71, 102, 189
Ixtaccíhuatl 26, 28

jade 8, 49, 51, 220, 230–1
jaguar warriors 32, 90
jaguars 32, 33
    'were-jaguars' 186, 226
Jaina Island 66, 188–9
jewellery 108, 109, 218,
    220–3

Kaminaljuyú 45, 46, 47, 49
kings 44, 160
    death 9, 31, 130
    dynasties 48, 49, 93, 152,
        211, 246–7
    Maya 15, 31, 32, 45,
        46–7, 91

La Quemada 65
La Venta 42, 61, 161, 186
Labná 31
Lake Chalco 28, 41
Lake Chapala 28
Lake Texcoco 25, 28, 35,
    44, 54, 55, 56
Lake Xochimilco 28
lakes 28
law and order 156–7
libraries 236
literacy 89

Macuilxóchitl 111, 113
maize 40, 106
    creation myths 34, 169
    first use 28, 34–5
manufacturing 63, 65, 184
Mapa Quinatzin 74, 154
Mapa Tlotzin 31
markets 59, 62, 70–3
marriage 100–1, 107
masks 226–7, 228–9
Matacapán 63
matchmakers 100, 101
mats 86–7, 195
Maya 6, 83
    causeways 76–7
    ceremonies 83–4, 127, 129

Classic Period 13, 14, 92,
    97, 117, 250
cosmology 30, 169
creation myths 34
Long Count 45, 94, 121,
    167, 231, 234–5
'Maya collapse' 9, 51, 169
mythology 32
Postclassic Period 14
respect for past 9, 11
Mayapán 53, 55, 56, 57, 249
    League of 67, 71
merchants 68–9, 73
Mesoamerica
    climate range 24–5
    cosmology 9, 30, 33, 36,
        37, 120, 124, 125
    everyday life 97
    power structure 48–9
    social collapse 50–1
metalworking 87, 109, 178,
    217–25
Méxica/Aztecs 54–5, 56, 132
Mexico 6, 57, 84–5, 218–19
Mexico City 12, 24, 25
Michoacán 57
Mictlantecuhtli 194
Milky Way 123, 135
Mitla 56, 179
Mixcóatl 85
Mixtecs 6–7, 45, 56,
    132, 135
    codices 241

crafts 73, 218, 220–1, 223, 228
Moctezuma I 25, 56, 57, 82–3, 156–7, 181
Moctezuma II 6, 56, 69, 75, 82, 107, 119, 181, 217, 222, 228, 229
monkeys 33
Monte Albán 6, 24, 43, 44, 46, 48, 50, 179
Monte Negro 45
moon 8, 71
mosaics 179, 228–9
Mount Coatépetl 19, 27, 146
mountains 26–7, 123, 146
murals 57, 233, 242–9
music 112–13, 126, 127

Nakbé 43, 45
name-tagging 241
names 103
Nanahuatzin 35, 213
Napatecuhtli 195
Netzahualcóyotl, King 82, 114, 154, 197
Nevado de Toluca 26
nobility 44, 45, 79, 92, 98, 104–5
numbers 121, 146–7, 234–5

Oaxaca 6, 34, 42–3, 44–5
obsidian 44, 62
    tools/weapons 41, 60, 87
    trade 46, 49, 51, 53, 62

Olmeca-Xicalanga 50
Olmecs 6, 24, 42, 132–3, 160–1, 186, 235
    carving 45, 202–3
    masks 226–7
    trade 59–61
Ometeotl 36
Oxtotitlán 242–3

Pacal, King 8, 15, 31, 49, 93, 152, 153, 168–9, 211
Pacific Ocean 61
palaces 139, 140, 174
    Aztec 98, 154–5, 156–7
    Maya 152–3, 168
Palenque 12, 13, 15, 29, 49, 51, 152, 248
    architecture 168–9, 210–11
Panquetzalíztli 73
Pawahtún 241
Piedras Negras 16, 208
pilgrimage 8, 11, 57, 62, 70, 132–3, 159
plazas 117, 152, 166
    Teotihuacán 48, 117
pochteca 68
poetry 114–15
Popocatépetl 25, 26, 28
Popol Vuh ('Book of Advice') 33, 34, 150, 239
population 42, 48, 51
    cities 44, 46, 50, 81, 165, 166
pottery 46, 62–3, 87, 184–5
    Aztec 194
    banquets/temples 192–3
    clay figures 43, 66, 186–9, 194, 202
    Maya 190–1
priests/priestesses 7, 94–5, 120, 126
pulque 32, 90–1, 107, 122, 193
punishment 73, 104
Putún Maya 50, 55, 75, 76
pyramids
    Chichén Itzá 117
    Cholula 70

Palenque 15, 168–9
Pyramid of the Moon 12, 27, 133, 164, 165, 243
Pyramid of the Niches 53, 148, 163
Pyramid of the Sun 120, 133, 146, 164–5, 243

Quetzalcóatl 32–3, 37, 122, 149, 229
    ball game 119
    creation myths 35, 36, 124
    death/reappearance 26, 52
    Éhecatl 26, 212, 227
    Mixcóatl 85
    Toltecs 52–3
quetzals 30, 32–3, 64, 87, 149, 198
Quiché 29, 33, 36, 55, 57, 75, 93
Quiriguá 13, 29, 51

18 Rabbit, King 51, 143, 153, 173, 210
rabbits 32
raiders 53, 54–5
rain
    Chac 29, 36
    Tláloc 15, 25, 26, 33, 35, 36, 37, 43, 192
religion 36–7
    commerce 71
    festivals 95, 117, 126–7
    hymns 126
    murals 244–5
    numbers 121, 146–7
    sacred gifts 132
    women 95
Remojadas 186, 187
Rio Azul 45, 47
rivers 28–9
rubber 118

sacred structures 120, 142, 146–7
    light/sound 149
    ritual furniture 147

see also ceremonial centres; pyramids; temples
sacred symbolism 76–7
salt 53, 66
San José Mogote 42–3, 44, 61, 86
San Lorenzo 42, 60, 61, 160–1, 186
schools 104–5, 112
scribes 16–17, 88–9, 94, 95, 105, 115, 236
settlements
    development 42, 43
    early 40–1, 60
    waterside 29, 41
shamans 32, 122, 123, 124, 125, 184, 186, 226
shells 67
Shield Jaguar 170, 171, 183, 209
slaves 65, 68, 71, 73
snakes 33, 36–7
social structure 42, 79
    Aztecs 90, 92, 98, 100
    Maya 91, 92–3, 99, 101
    Quiché 93
soldiers 90–1
Spanish 6
    Aztecs 7, 8, 9, 217
    smallpox 178
    vandalism 11, 89, 236
spies 69
statues 212–13
stelae 17, 37, 91, 204–5, 206, 208
    inscriptions 16, 45, 240
Stephens, John Lloyd 11, 12–13, 214

stone carving 226–7, 230–1
  Aztec 212–13
  Maya 204, 206–7, 208–9
  Olmec 202–3, 204
  Zapotecs 204–5
stucco 44, 210–11
sun 36, 118, 119, 122, 128, 130
  Aztecs 37, 213, 217
  creation 8, 36, 126
  death/rebirth 9, 23, 36, 118
  world ages 19, 35, 37
Sun Stone 12, 213

Tabasco 24, 25, 42
Tarascans 7, 55, 56, 57, 178
Tehuacán Valley 34, 40–1
temples 7, 123, 139, 140–1
  Chichén Itzá 39, 126, 132, 142, 149, 214, 249
  Monte Albán 162, 186–7, 205
  Palenque 148, 149, 169
  Temple of the Masks 148
  Templo Mayor 11, 13, 15, 19, 27, 37, 43, 146, 148, 180–1
  Tikal 13, 27, 45, 148, 166–7, 214
Tenoch 54, 55
Tenochtitlán 7, 12, 25, 33, 37, 68, 70, 81, 82
  architecture 8, 156–7, 180–1
  Conquest 11, 163, 178
  origins 33, 55
Teopantecuanitlán 61
Teotenango 176, 177

Teotihuacán 6, 8, 12, 27, 44, 62–3, 132
  architecture 46, 142, 148, 155, 164–5
  art 187, 243, 250
  decline 48, 50
  growth 46
  Street of the Dead 27, 46, 62, 165
Tepanecs 54, 55, 56
Tepeapulco 62
Texcoco 54, 71, 154
Tezcatlipoca 25, 32, 36, 37, 52, 85, 119, 198
Tezozómoc 56
Tikal 8, 13, 14, 37, 44, 51, 248
  architecture 45, 46, 47, 77, 142, 166–7
  decline 48–9
  growth 47, 51
time
  cycles 8, 9, 37, 94, 117, 120–1, 129, 163, 237
  event dating 234–5
  measuring 45, 94, 121
  world ages 19, 37, 215
Tlahiuzcalpantecuhtli 176
Tláloc 15, 25, 26, 33, 35, 36, 37, 43, 192
Tlálocan 37
Tlapacoya 43
Tlatecuhtli 36
Tlatelolco 56, 59, 70
  market 72–3, 180, 185
Tlatilco 43
Tlaxcala 7, 142
Tlazoltéotl 95, 102
tobacco 122
Tollán 6, 8, 13, 14–15, 26, 39, 52, 132
  architecture 148, 174
  sacking of 52, 54
Toltecs 6, 13, 14, 54, 74, 126, 204
  Chichén Itzá 52–3
  influence 8–9, 39, 53, 132, 133
Tonacacíhuatl 36

Tonacatecuhtli 36
tonalamatl 129
Tonatiuh 35, 90, 213
Toniná 51, 204
tools 40, 41, 42, 48, 87
Totonacs 6, 163
trade 44, 46, 49, 50
  Aztecs 64, 65, 68–9, 70–3, 77
  long-range 42, 64–7, 68–9
  Maya 29, 64–5, 66–7, 69, 71
  Olmec 59, 60–1
  Teotihuacán 63, 64
transport 65, 77, 180
trees 30–1
tribute 68, 74–5, 82, 85, 156, 178, 222, 228
Triple Alliance 56, 74, 156, 181
Tulum 13, 55, 57, 67, 71
turquoise 8, 65
Tutul Xiu 55, 56–7
Tzintzuntzan 55, 178

Uaxactún 14, 27, 45, 47, 120, 121
underworld 123
  ball game 76, 77, 119, 151
  caves 44
  cenotes 29
  kings 9, 31
  Mictlán 119
  Xibalba 91, 150, 188
Uxmal 11, 13, 55–7, 144–5

Valley of Mexico 24, 25, 26–7, 28, 44, 59
Valley of Oaxaca 24
Venus 37, 71, 97, 119, 120, 122, 176, 233, 237
Veracruz 6, 24, 34, 41, 42, 186, 187
volcanoes 23, 25, 26–7, 41

warfare 48, 50, 51, 63, 130
  Aztec 90–1
  Maya 91
  tribute 74, 75

water 28–9
weapons 40, 41, 84, 85, 87
weaving 86, 87, 178, 196
wheeled toys 65
woodcarving 214–15
writing 16–17, 88, 94, 234–5

Xipe Totec 61, 131, 194, 223
Xitle volcano 26, 44
Xiuhtecuhtli 117, 212
Xochicalco 50, 142, 176, 177
Xochipilli 114
Xochiquetzal 95, 100
Xocolatl 107
Xólotl 54

Yak Moch Xoc 46
Yax Kin, King 166, 228
Yax Kuk Mo' 47, 172
Yaxchilán 16, 29, 47, 150, 248
  architecture 170–1
Yucatán 24, 25, 29, 76, 144–5
  power shift 56–7

Zapotecs 6, 24, 33, 43, 44, 46, 48, 74–5, 162, 179, 204–5

This edition is published by Hermes House

Hermes House is an imprint of
Anness Publishing Ltd
Hermes House, 88–89 Blackfriars Road,
London SE1 8HA
tel. 020 7401 2077; fax 020 7633 9499;
info@anness.com

A CIP catalogue record for this book is
available from the British Library.

Publisher: Joanna Lorenz
Editorial Director: Helen Sudell
Editor: Joy Wotton
Designer: Nigel Partridge
Illustrator: Peter Bull Art Studio
Production Controller: Wendy Lawson

10 9 8 7 6 5 4 3 2 1

PICTURE ACKNOWLEDGEMENTS
Ancient Art and Architecture Collection Ltd:
4.5, 5bl, 6t, 9t, 15b, 32b, 34t, 36l, 37b, 42t, 49t,
52b, 53, 62b, 71b, 83b, 84t, 87, 91t, 93b, 94b,
96–7, 102b, 107tl, 108b, 109b, 115b, 123t, 126t,
127t&b, 129b, 130t, 132b, 133b, 135b, 150t, 152t,
206t, 207t&b, 212t, 215b, 222, 223b, 227t&b,
229t&b, 235b, 240t, 250t&b; /Dr S Coyne: 122b;
/Israel Museum: 123b, 128b; /J. Stevens: 62t.
Art Archive: 1, 98b, 124; /Antochiw Collection,
Mexico/Mireille Vautier: 85t, 99t, 199t&b;
/Archaeological Museum, Copan, Honduras/Dagli
Orti: 89b; /Archaeological Museum, Teotihuacan,
Mexico/Dagli Orti: 63, 242b; /Archaeological
Museum, Tikal, Guatemala/Dagli Orti: 192t;
/Archaeological and Ethnological Museum,
Guatemala City/Dagli Orti: 5.3, 93t, 112b, 182–3,
240b, 246b; /Biblioteca Nacional, Madrid/Dagli
Orti: 111t, 113t, 131, 181bl; /Biblioteca Nacional,
Mexico/ Dagli Orti: 10–11, 13t, 29t, 77t, 88b,
147t; /Biblioteca Nacional, Mexico/Mireille
Vautier: 29b, 114; /Bibliothèque de l'Assemblée
Nationale, Paris/Dagli Orti: 89t, 110b, 119b;
/Bodleian Library, Oxford: 56b, 64t, 69b, 75, 82,
101b, 104, 105t, 126b, 157t, 195t; /British
Museum, London/Eileen Tweedy: 109t, 231b,
256; /Joseph Martin: 100b, 108tr; /Museo de
America, Madrid/Dagli Orti: 106t, 238; /Museo
Ciudad, Mexico/Dagli Orti: 81, 181br, /Museo
Ethnografico Pigorini, Rome/Dagli Orti: 214b;
/Museo de Jiquilpan, Mexico/Dagli Orti: 221t;
/Museo de Michoacan, Morelia, Mexico/Dagli
Orti 64b; /Museo del Popol Vuh, Guatemala/
Dagli Orti: 92b; /Museo Regional de Antropologia,
Merida, Mexico/Dagli Orti: 120t, 209b; /Museo
Regional de Oaxaca, Mexico/Dagli Orti: 5.5, 74r,
196t, 216–17, 219tl, 228tr; /Museo Regional,
Puebla, Mexico/Dagli Orti: 140t, 192b, 209t;
/Museo del Templo Mayor, Mexico/Dagli Orti:
7b, 129t, 194l&r; /Museo de Teotenango, Mexico/
Dagli Orti: 112t, 214t; /Museum of Mankind,
London/Eileen Tweedy: 68; /Museum San Pedro
de Sula, Honduras/Dagli Orti: 9b, 190b, 191;
/Museum für Völkerkunde, Vienna/Dagli Orti:
221b, 226; /National Anthropological Museum,
Mexico/Dagli Orti: 3, 31t, 34b, 36r, 60t, 83t, 85b,
105b, 106b, 107r, 113b, 115t, 118t, 125t, 132t,
134t, 135t, 149b, 188bl, 189br, 193t, 196b, 198,
204b, 211b, 213, 219b, 220t&b, 223t, 224, 228b,
230t, 234t, 235t, 249t; /National Archives,
Mexico/Mireille Vautier: 110t, 130h; /National
Ethnological Museum, Mexico/Dagli Orti: 86t;
/Dagli Orti: 5.4, 28t, 31b, 37t, 60b, 71t, 73, 77b,
86b, 90b, 94t, 99b, 121b, 136–7, 141t&b, 142t,
143t, 145t&b, 147b, 149t, 151t, 154t&b, 155t,
160t, 163t, 167b, 172t, 173t&b, 174t&b, 178t,
179t, 200–1, 205, 208br, 234b, 242t; /Nicolas

Sapieha: 163b; /Mireille Vautier: 4.4, 4br, 18–19,
40t, 41b, 67t, 78–9, 80t, 84b, 125b, 230b, 239b,
248t&b, 249b; /Franceso Venturi: 69t, 215t;
/Xalapa Museum, Veracruz, Mexico/Dagli
Orti: 103, 118b, 161b, 187t.
The Bridgeman Picture Library: /Baluarete de
Santiago, Veracruz, Mexico, Banco Mexicano
de Imagenes, INAH 225t; /British Museum,
London 225b; /Museo Nacional de Antropologia,
Mexico City, Mexico/Giraudon: 231t; /Private
Collection: 12t, 236; /Private Collection, The
Stapleton Collection: 12b.
Corbis: 171; /Paul Almasy: 111b, 120b, 155b;
/Artephot/Corbis Sygma: 128t; /Yann Arthus
Bertrand: 30b; /Bettmann: 72b; /Bowers Museum
of Cultural Art: 184, 185b, 186b&t, 187b;
/Richard A Cooke: 165t; /Sergio Dorantes: 177t;
/Macduff Everton 21t, 66b, 152b, 169, 177b;
/Werner Forman: 92t, 101t, 157bl, 188r, 189t,
193b, 237t&b, 241b; /Arvind Garg: 27b; /Angelo
Hornak: 179b; /Jacqui Hurst: 197b; /Kimbell Art
Museum: 185t, 195b; /Robert Landau: 144b;
/Otto Lang: 160b; /Danny Lehman: 76t, 150b,
161t, 178b; /Charles and Josette Lenars: 8b, 133t,
146t, 156t, 162t, 170b, 204tr, 246t&t; /Craig
Lovell 170t; /North Carolina Museum of Art:
4.1, 22–3; /Gianni Dagli Orti: 14, 16t, 17b, 91b,
164b, 165b, 239t; /Della Zuana Pascal/Corbis
Sygma: 247b; /Reuters; 26b, 197t; /Kevin
Schafer: 121t; /Gian Berto Vanni: 153b, 204tl,
210b; /Vanni Archive: 153t; /Francesco Venturi:
144t; /Peter M Wilson; 5.1, 138–9.
South American Pictures: /Fabienne Fossez:
210t, 211t; /Robert Francis: 2, 20tl&tr, 24t,
30t, 47t&b, 54b, 151b, 166, 202bl, 208t;
/Tony Morrison: 4.2,4.6, 6b, 13b, 24b, 25t,
38–9, 40b, 41t, 43b, 52t, 95b, 116–17, 202br,
203; /Iain Pearson: 26t, 42b, 49b, 65b, 70t&b,
176t&b; /Chris Sharp: 4.3, 5.2, 5.6, 8t, 15t,
33b, 35t, 44t&b, 45t, 46, 48t&b, 50t, 51, 54t,
55t&b, 56t, 58–9, 61t&b, 66t, 67b, 72t, 74b,
76b, 80b, 90t, 95tr, 102t, 119t, 122t, 134b,
140b, 158–9, 175b, 190t, 202t, 206b, 212b,
218, 232–3, 243, 244t&b, 245, 251t&b;
/Kate Smith: 57t; /Karen Ward: 148t.

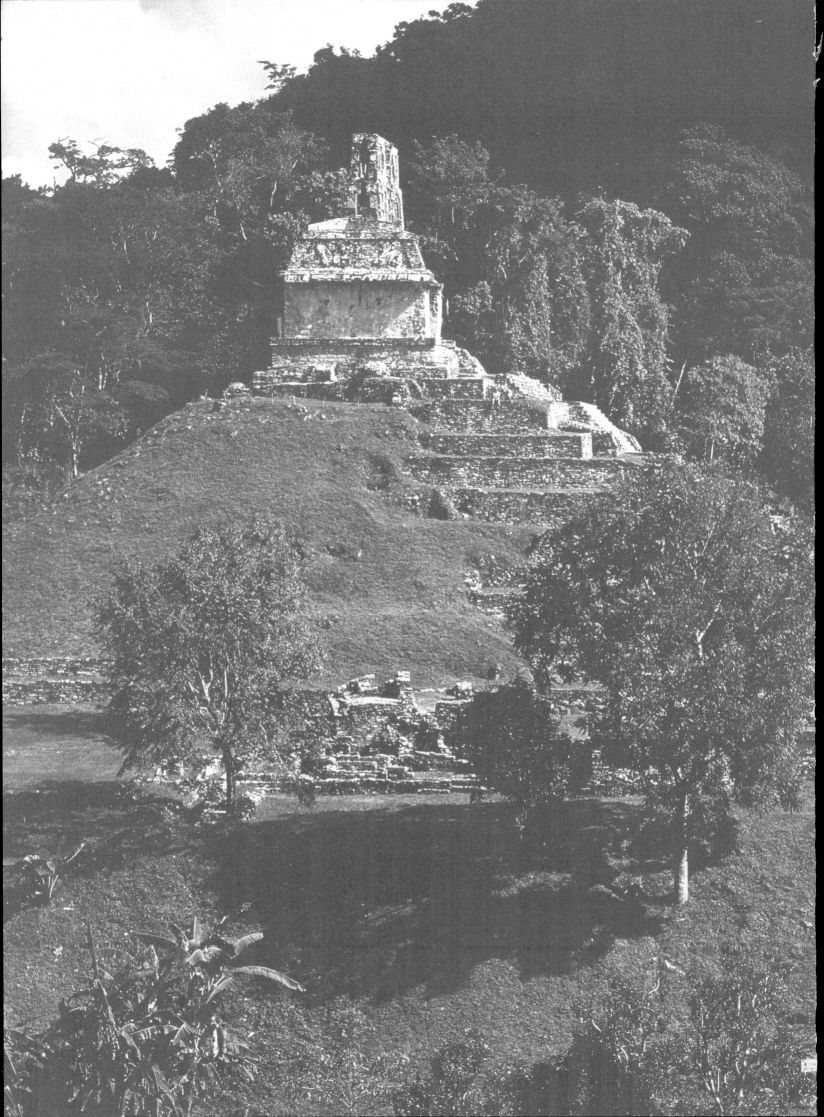